Explaining Social Life

Explaining Social Life

A Guide to Using Social Theory

By

John Parker

and

Hilary Stanworth

With Leonard Mars and Paul Ransome

 macmillan education   palgrave

First published 2015 by
PALGRAVE

Palgrave in the UK is an imprint of Macmillan Publishers Limited,
registered in England, company number 785998, of 4 Crinan Street,
London N1 9XW.

Palgrave Macmillan in the US is a division of St Martin's Press LLC,
175 Fifth Avenue, New York, NY 10010.

Palgrave is a global imprint of the above companies and is represented
throughout the world.

Palgrave® and Macmillan® are registered trademarks in the United States,
the United Kingdom, Europe and other countries.

ISBN: 978–1–137–48773–5   hardback
ISBN: 978–1–137–00764–3   paperback

This book is printed on paper suitable for recycling and made from fully
managed and sustained forest sources. Logging, pulping and manufacturing
processes are expected to conform to the environmental regulations of the
country of origin.

A catalogue record for this book is available from the British Library.

A catalog record for this book is available from the Library of Congress.

Typeset by MPS Limited, Chennai, India.

Printed and bound in the UK by The Lavenham Press Ltd, Suffolk.

MIX
Paper from
responsible sources
FSC® C010693
www.fsc.org

Contents

PART II: **The concept of nature**

PART III: **The concept of culture**

PART IV: **The concept of action**

PART V: **The concept of social structure**

PART VI: **Conclusion**

List of figures, boxes and biography boxes

Figures

Boxes

Biography boxes

List of key examples

Chapter 1

1. Personalities and skill in settling a land dispute in Pakistan (Barth, 1959)
2. Rational decision-making among Raika shepherds in north west India (Agrawal, 1998)

Chapter 2

1. Magical responses to uncertainty: financial traders (Crosthwaite, 2011), Melanesian fishermen (Malinowksi, 1922) and readers of astrology columns in 1950s America (Adorno, 2002)
2. Surviving poverty: making ends meet in a black American ghetto (Stack, 1997)

Chapter 3

1. Environmental conditions for the emergence of agriculture (Diamond, 1997) and the early state (Mann, 1986)

Chapter 4

1. The choice of hunting weapons, techniques and prey of two Amazonian forest peoples (Rival, 1996; Descola, 1997)
2. Aboriginal hunters' traditional way of life confronted by advanced industrialism in British Columbia (Brody, 1986)
3. Protecting Ecuador's Yasuní National Park (Gremillion, 2011)

Chapter 6

1. Recent Asian immigrants and Afro-Americans in the United States: comparative economic success and failure (Waldinger, 1996)

2. Religion and the differential treatment of 'mixed-race' people in different parts of the New World (Jordan, 1969; Degler, 1971)
3. Jewish dietary laws and the prohibition of pork (Douglas, 1970)
4. A homophobic ship's crew tolerate some gay men (Cunningham and Parker, 1978)
5. Elaborating culture to cope with change: dilemmas of Nuer cattle culture (Hutchinson, 1996) and Nigeria's 'culture of corruption' (Smith, 2008)
6. Cultural variety among the British middle classes in the 1990s (Savage et al., 1992)
7. Social mobility and responses to comedians (Friedman, 2011, 2012)

Chapter 7

1. Improvising jazz (Russell, 1972)
2. Resisting total institutions (Goffman, 1961; Elkins, 1976)
3. Walking home at night in Inner West Philadelphia (Anderson, 1990)

Chapter 8

1. How officials cope with routine crises in a welfare bureaucracy (Zimmerman, 1971)
2. How haematologists diagnose and treat blood disorders (Atkinson, 1995)
3. Performing the 'art crit' (Thornton, 2008; Elkins, 2012) and the architectural competition (Kreiner, 2009; Van Wezemael et al., 2011)

Chapter 9

1. The effects of birth order (Sulloway, 1996)
2. Properties of networks (Granovetter, 1983; Morris, 1992; Giuffre, 1999)
3. Structural contradictions:
    (i)   Deskilling and quality (Sennett, 2008; Ritzer, 2010)
    (ii) 'The computer boys': dependency on experts and maintenance of control in complex organisations (Ensmenger, 2010)
    (iii) Advantages and limits of bureaucracy (Weber, 1968)
    (iv) Maintaining social order and a flexible labour market: the role of rural-urban migration in China (Marx, 1858; Lee, 2007)
4. The American 'subprime' mortgage crisis: reproducing the black: white wealth gap (Oliver and Shapiro, 1997; Rugh and Massey, 2010; Shapiro et al., 2013)

Chapter 10

1. Supremely individual acts?:
    (i)   Who commits suicide? (Durkheim, 1952)
    (ii) Who falls in love with whom? (Parsons, 1954)
    (iii) Differences in fighting performance in the First World War trenches (Ashworth, 1980)
2. The origins of modern nationalism and the nation-state (Gellner, 1983, 1997)
3. Differential exposure to patriarchal risk: Bangladeshi women in London and Dhaka from the late 20th to the early 21st century (Kabeer, 2000; Kabeer and Ainsworth, 2011)

Chapter 12

1. The challenges of climate change (Shove, 2003; Soper, 2008; Hulme, 2009; Urry, 2011)

Coda

1. Why do artists put up with low economic reward? (Abbing, 2002)

Preface

This book is a thoroughly revised, extended and updated edition of *Social Theory: A Basic Toolkit* (2003). Since the first edition Paul Ransome has sadly and far too prematurely, died, and Leonard Mars, while encouraging us, has not contributed to the rewriting. Consequently this edition has been jointly authored by John Parker and Hilary Stanworth who are solely responsible for its current weaknesses. We have maintained our fundamental approach which is to treat basic social theory as a necessary resource to be used by those who are curious about the social world and want to understand why it is the way it is. We continue to insist that there is no great divide between what we all do, as ordinary people living social lives, to explain our social experience, and what social scientists do. The book is intended to encourage people to reflect on their existing explanatory practices, and help them to see social theory as an important set of tools for thinking about the substantive and practical problems that everyone faces and which social scientists specialise in. It presents social theory as fundamental for making sense of social life and as something relevant for everyone – a thoroughly practical business.

Approaching social theory from the point of view of identifying what is required to build explanations (the technical term is 'explanatory methodology') allows us to suggest that there is a minimum set of fundamental concepts, the equivalent of the DIYer's hammer, saw, screwdriver, pliers and drill, tools which, with a little luck, allow us to deal with most everyday problems because the functions they perform are universal and unavoidable. Thus we introduce five fundamental social theoretical concepts – Individuals, Nature, Culture, Action and Social Structure – and demonstrate their effectiveness by applying them to a wide range of everyday, and not so everyday, examples of puzzling social phenomena to reveal the strengths, but also the limits of each concept. Rather than focus on which particular theorists said what, we choose to engage the reader's theoretical imagination by referring to a wide range of interesting empirical examples.

By arguing that the most powerful social explanations take account of the interaction among all five concepts, we are taking a highly receptive attitude to contributions from across the often contested field of social theory. Finding value in often opposed positions means we have to be careful about maintaining the consistency of our own. Readers will have to judge how successful we have been in this respect.

Because the book introduces theoretical fundamentals in a straightforward way without unnecessary elaboration and without requiring readers to have any prior specialised knowledge, it can be used by students at any stage of their development and of any social science. Our examples are drawn widely from sociology and anthropology – but are intended to appeal to an interdisciplinary audience being relevant to those studying economics, human geography, development studies, politics, history and applied social studies of all types. Our mode of presenting the fundamentals makes them accessible to absolute beginners at undergraduate and post-graduate levels, but it can also provide a useful summarising, contextualising or reframing of existing knowledge for the non-beginner.

Acknowledgements

The most important stimulus for attempting a second edition has been the positive response from students and teachers to using the book. So we must thank again all of those involved in the *Introduction to Social Theory* module delivered until 2006 at Swansea University, mentioned in the acknowledgements of the first edition.

The authorial team has shrunk to two because of Leonard Mars' retirement and the tragically early death of Paul Ransome. However, we have insisted on consulting both Leonard and Paul's family as the project has progressed and are grateful for their support.

We thank Joseph Parker for the last minute technical revision of our discussion of the new genetics in Chapter 1. He reminded us that 60 per cent of our genes are common with fruit flies and managed not to mention his favourite Pselaphidae.

This second edition has had a rather long gestation. We were originally encouraged by Anna Reeve at Palgrave Macmillan and have more recently been given impetus by her successor, Lloyd Langman. His clever choice of anonymous reviewers provided a fertile spread of criticism, suggestions and enthusiasm, which has made the end result much better – so whoever you are, thank you.

Introduction: social theory as a 'tool kit' for social explanation

This book aims to make social theory accessible to and usable by our readers. This means developing an approach which works against several misconceptions about social theory which are deeply seated in general culture and often reinforced by the structure of academic curricula. Social theory is commonly thought to be abstract, expressed in esoteric language, intrinsically difficult and requiring highly specialised skills and scholarship to understand. To non-specialists the claims for theory may seem extravagant, serving the interests of academic **elites** in preserving intellectual exclusiveness. Social theory is too often treated as somehow separate from, perhaps superior to, the other more ordinary and less forbidding aspects of producing knowledge of the social world.

To challenge these misconceptions we will firstly make some general points about what we understand social theory to be. We use 'social theory' as a term to refer to a number of different kinds of ideas many of which are not particularly difficult, specialised, or linguistically esoteric, and which when abstract, are justifiably so. Rather than being the preserve of specialist elites, they are necessary elements in the ordinary business of producing **explanations** of social phenomena – which everybody does. We understand social theory to be a basic resource for responding to our curiosity about our social experiences, because it supplies ideas about the different kinds of **causation** to be taken into account when explaining social phenomena. Since we all have a practical interest in being able to explain such phenomena, elements of social theory are relevant for everyone.

The object of social theory: collective phenomena

Social theory has its origins in the ordinary common-sense recognition that firstly, interaction with others is an unavoidable condition of human life, and

1

secondly, that the events and changes in this social world and the behaviour of individuals, are powerfully affected by the ways individual people are **'collectivised'**. People, living together in space and time, do not just vary individual by individual. Rather than there being as many varieties of belief and behaviour as there are individuals, peoples' beliefs and behaviour are patterned and the conditions of their lives are shared because of the many collectivising processes working over time on populations of interacting individuals. What people do and think is powerfully conditioned by forces that have 'clumping' effects, making them share significant characteristics. Everyone understands that people are collectivised and are likely to share characteristics with others and that this makes a difference to how they are likely to act and what they are likely to think. Knowing these things helps us when we have to deal with them. Being able to give answers to questions such as, 'Why do these people typically or regularly do that?' or, 'Why did that event or kind of event happen when and where it did?' is a practical requirement of life for everyone.

Social science and everyday social knowledge

In everyday life we use our knowledge of how we and others are collectivised. But this knowledge varies in quality, is often partial, and formed through various processes about which we tend not to be methodologically critical. This is not just because we may be lazy. In the mix of causes shaping social life are processes encouraging us to accept as knowledge, accounts which facilitate participating in social life without adequately explaining it. For our approach, this *difference between the causally powerful knowledge which enables practical participation, and the knowledge which incorporates this kind of causation in its own menu of inter-related causes when producing explanations*, is very important. Social life requires us to use something passing for knowledge and to get enough of it right to be practical. But being practical does not necessarily depend on that knowledge being complete, nor able to withstand criticism from some other point of view, such as that of social science.

Social theory, critical practice and making complexity intelligible

The social sciences like sociology, anthropology and history take on this job of critically evaluating and supplementing the competing everyday **understandings** of collectivisation and of 'collective' phenomena – which are the aspects of people's lives that they share with at least some others and are not unique to any one of them. Though not all collective phenomena are products of social forces, many are, and it is these that the social sciences concentrate on. The critical potential of the social sciences is founded in the practice of basic social theory which tries to define and understand the general kinds of causes which must always be taken into account when explaining collective phenomena. The distinctive contribution of the social sciences to elaborating a more developed version of what we use all the time in our everyday lives, whenever we try to explain some social phenomenon, is an understanding of the relevant causation. Identifying this has stimulated a rich intellectual creativity as theorists have tried to imagine processes and mechanisms, and invent ways of representing them, sufficiently simple to be intelligible, yet complex enough to do justice to the multiplicity of forms and actual instances generated by reality. The creativity involved is disciplined by the demands placed by a complex reality on objective comprehension. This must start with imagining possibilities. Making complexity intelligible involves strategic choices about abstraction – the job of choosing to concentrate on some elements at the expense of others.

The important point is that scientific abstractions are means of engaging with reality rather than escaping from it. The invention of, and arguments about the value of, alternative theoretical abstractions are driven by the desire to get to grips with realities which are complex, changing and as a consequence difficult to get a handle on. Abstractions can make reality accessible and researchable. A simple example might be the abstract concept of 'pressure'. This is not itself a 'thing', a tangible entity, but can be formally defined relative to other variables (temperature and volume) allowing the empirical behaviour of a class of things, for example gases, to be predicted (by Robert Boyle). As we shall see in the context of social science, much theoretical debate is about the costs (in terms of reduction of complexity) and benefits (in terms of explanatory effect) of various alternative abstractions.

This book's approach to social theory involves our choosing abstractions which yield worthwhile benefits. It is built on the fact that everyone has an interest in knowing how social forces explain collective phenomena, and that most people are already able to develop many practically useful explanations. Effective human beings must have a practically sound grasp of some appropriate concepts needed to analyse social reality. Social theory develops and elaborates or refines such concepts and makes them explicit. It has ethical and political implications. Everyday social life is likely to change when guided by reference to rational arguments about the relevance of certain abstractions and causes. Since it has the potential to change everyone's awareness of what shapes social life, it is likely to be welcomed or resisted depending on what interests may be strengthened or weakened by embracing any 'new', more complete, knowledge.

Hypothesising and explaining

What follows is framed by two guiding principles, pragmatism and realism. The first, pragmatism, regards producing social explanations and knowledge as necessary to be effective in the practical world. In general, people's attempts to understand and explain social phenomena are motivated by their interests in solving practical problems. People have an interest in enhancing their knowledge of the circumstances in which they perceive problems and set about solving them in various ways. The knowledge brought to bear on problems is produced by us human beings as embodied and minded animals in a complicated process which inter-relates our bodily experiences to our ideas and symbol systems, such as language, used to represent these ideas. However, though knowledge depends on the properties of human beings who are able to experience and symbolise, to be practically effective, knowledge must be about something other than us. This is because, though knowledge is dependent on experience and symbolic representation, these are not reliable. Experience and accounts of it are variable. For example, a given room temperature (say 66 F) may be experienced in winter as comfortably warm but in summer is felt too chilly. Such feelings tell us about the relativity of temperature perception, that is something about the person's experiences, but clearly these cannot be relied upon to tell us about the objective matter of fact, what the temperature actually is. Hence the need for some objective concept of temperature, units for measuring it and instruments such as thermometers. Moreover, symbolic representations are not confined to reporting experience but also provide a realm for the creative imagining of fictional worlds. If we have any interest in maintaining the difference between subjective experience and matters of fact, and between fiction and non-fiction, we must be committed to the idea that there is a difference between experience and symbolic representations, on the one hand, and the reality these are experiences and representations of, on the other. Though both scientists and artists employ creative imagination to generate symbolic representations, only the former *have* to distinguish between representation and reality and be concerned with the adequacy of representations to capture the real world they are designed to represent (Nisbet, 1962).

Thus our second guiding principle to partner pragmatism, **realism**, is the idea that there is a real world existing independently of both our direct physical experience of it and what we can say about it. Our pragmatic interests are served by knowledge-building and attempts at explanation which accept that the ultimate test for explanations is what objective reality is, rather than their consistency with our experience or the logic of symbolic systems. When we try to explain our experience we must keep our talk open to being influenced by the way the world really is. This is not easy but is greatly helped by using appropriate scientific methods and by understanding reality to be a collection of objective mechanisms and **generative processes**, which pre-exist and cause what we at any point in time, subjectively, experience and describe.

The key point is that explanation of social phenomena involves discovering and understanding the mechanisms which cause them. It involves more than just making accurate predictions about their occurring and more than accounting for particular occurrences by noting them to be instances of a predictable pattern. To predict the sun will rise in the east and set in the west because it has always done so, and to account for today's sunrise by saying 'this is what always happens', is not the same as explaining why the sun rises in the east and sets where it does as the outcome of a mechanical process of daily rotation of the Earth on its axis and its orbit round the Sun. Realist explanations uncover the causal mechanisms which contribute to producing the social phenomena we are puzzled by (Figure 0.1).

As we have already said, theory's function is to distinguish, conceptually and by processes of discovery, the kinds of causation useful when framing our attempts at explaining particular phenomena. It allows us to invent relevant hypotheses, that is, speculations about the various processes and mechanisms, which in combinations and sequences might produce the phenomena we want to understand – hypotheses which we can then test against reality. Theory's discussions about kinds of causality help ensure that our hypothesising is relevant. We do not just suggest any old reasons for why things happen! Rather, we control our speculations by reference to what we take to be the

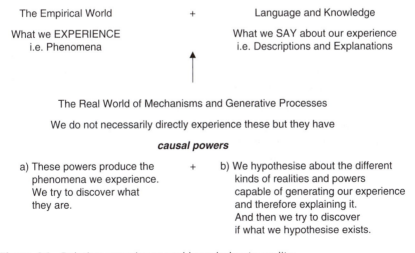

Figure 0.1 Relating experience and knowledge to reality

best general ideas about the kind of things we are trying to explain and the kinds of causes likely to have produced them.

So, for example, if I want to explain why my bicycle tyre punctured this morning, I would hypothesise about likely causes such as broken glass or drawing pins, rather than absurdly unlikely ones, such as what I had for breakfast or the colour of my socks. We would be surprised if someone thought that hypothesising about breakfast and socks was useful in solving this particular puzzle. Why? Surely it's because (nearly) everyone has a basic understanding or 'theory' about the general kind of processes involved in the problem being dealt with. Armed with a grasp of how pneumatic tyres work, their invulnerability to socks and breakfasts but general vulnerability to sharp objects, it is possible to focus quickly on the task of identifying the mechanisms causing this particular puncture. Hypothesising about this puncture will have been guided by a what we might call general 'pneumatic tyre theory' involving abstractions such as 'pressure' and 'sharp objects' (the fruit of many people's long experience and thought about such problems). This helps us look in the right places when attempting to explain this specific example of a 'tyre' problem.

It is exactly the same when we try to construct social explanations of collective, social, phenomena. Our hypotheses are governed by our ideas about the general characteristics of social phenomena and what sorts of factors are most likely to be at work in shaping any particular case we are dealing with. Social theory's job is to identify what might have the power to make things happen. In this way it contributes to *explaining* social phenomena.

The set of fundamental concepts: a tool kit

In this book we aim to provide readers with a small but powerful 'tool kit' comprising five fundamental social theoretical concepts – which we will argue are all necessary to conceptualise the kinds of causes whose interaction is relevant for social explanation. We claim that social reality being what it is, these concepts provide five interrelated abstractions. These though pitched at a level of simplicity enabling intelligibility and usability, are nevertheless sufficient to maintain a respect for the complexity of the reality. These concepts of the kinds of causal forces which together produce social phenomena are

Individuals
Nature
Culture
Action
Social Structure

While it is possible to argue about the 'levels' at which complex wholes are assembled and distinct types of causal power emerge, all the above can be broken down into constituent parts (as will be discussed in the first of each of the pairs of chapters devoted to the concepts). For example, it is when the components, bodies, brains and minds interact over time, that something important happens, namely the **emergence** of the complex entities, 'individuals', with their own distinctive causal powers. These emergent powers result from the combination of components but cannot be regarded as merely a sum of the causal powers of those components. Our five concepts thus refer to complex realities which interact to produce social phenomena. Anything which has its own way of exerting causal influence on phenomena does so as the emergent outcome of a process whereby its constituent elements have been related or assembled. We suggest that all the concepts in our set of tools have their own way of contributing to producing social phenomena by virtue of the character of their constituent elements and the way that these are related or assembled.

When producing explanations, social scientists have to consider not just the various causal powers, but the fact that their causal force is conditional upon how they *interact*. Explanatory adequacy demands we avoid assigning explanatory pre-eminence to any one kind of causation but show the interaction among a range of relevant causal powers as they inter-relate and work together, over time, to produce what is being explained. In the following chapters we will be showing that the way in which the particular causal powers of each of the concepts in our tool kit, produce effects, is conditional upon its relationships with the other causal powers. It is in this sense that the concepts are an interacting set, which means that each is best described as possessing only a ***relative* autonomy** (Figure 0.2).

Applying this approach in what follows, we argue for a basic strategy when creating social explanations of the variety of events and social forms arising

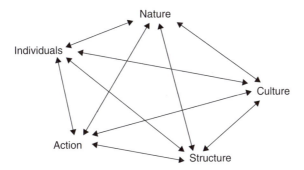

Figure 0.2 The five causal powers are mutually inter-related: each is only relatively autonomous of the others

in the spatio-temporal medium of human social interaction. We suggest that explanatory adequacy can be practically achieved by focussing attention on the clusters of causes associated with the five basic concepts of the tool kit. Strong claims can be made that each cluster possesses specific and forceful kinds of causal powers.

Trying the tool kit

To help convince you that these five concepts of clusters of causes really are important, let's take an example of a 'collective phenomenon', and invite you to begin explaining it.

Here's the question:

Why are children with working-class parents under-represented among the educationally successful? What do you think? Use your imagination to think of all the possible causes.

We guess, almost immediately, you identified relevant causes which you reckoned were likely to affect achievement, such as access to relevant material resources (books, quiet and transport), individual motivation (emotional rewards, encouragement from parents and teachers, and peer group support), cultural resources (language, world-view and moral values), school organisation (selection criteria, 'streaming', discipline regime and performance indicators) and the curriculum (traditional knowledge hierarchies, political initiatives and local emphases). But *why* would you think these were relevant? We suggest that it is because, just as when explaining the puncture example, you understand the general kind of problem being dealt with.

You already know the sorts of considerations which are relevant. You have general ideas about the kind of things 'educational achievement' and 'social classes' are. 'Achievement' (an example of a cultural idea) requires an environment providing relevant material resources to enable individuals to act effectively within educational contexts, and 'social classes' (an example of social **structure**) function to distribute material resources and hence opportunities to 'achieve' educationally. Similarly you have general ideas about what kind of thing 'individuals' are, that they are self-directed **persons** with **rationality** but who are collectivised by being socially and emotionally attached to members of their family, neighbourhood, peer group and respond to the encouragement or discouragement of others. Again, you have general ideas about the kinds of things '**institutions**', and 'education systems' are. Thus you know that 'achievement' involves one's performance at specific tasks being evaluated by people who have the power to judge you by virtue of the positions and **roles** they occupy in institutions. You know that institutions are organisations of social positions to which functions and powers attach – people in different positions have different powers of action.

Each of the five fundamental concepts denotes something with causal power which can make a difference to outcomes. Thus though you know that individual ability and effort can contribute to success or failure, they cannot make all the difference by themselves. You suspect that they have to be related to many other success-producing or inhibiting factors emergent from their social relations and institutional environments, of the kind we have just been discussing. Just as having natural ability cannot make all the difference, neither can going to a 'good school' or having rich parents. It is the *interaction* of these and other variables, which makes the difference. And you know this because you have an understanding of the interplay among mechanisms at work in social reality contributing to the formation and activity of individuals. You recognise that individuals are not self-created beings, but the products of socialisation and location within social worlds, which distribute access to resources and opportunities and which have consequences for what they are able to do and be. Hence the relevance of hypothesising that position in social classes (being 'clumped' into such collectivities) affects achievement.

In other words, non-specialist everyday thinking about this problem has been guided by an understanding of the relevance of considering the *interaction of different kinds of real causes* involved – that is by basic social theory. The social theory may not have been articulated before you started to think about this problem, but when you got going, your assumptions about the nature of individuals and collectivities, and how they are related, would have been brought into play, organising your hypothesising which would also structure any empirical enquiry you might subsequently make. If you don't believe that the brightest and most hard working inevitably do best, (if you doubt that we live in a 'meritocracy') ask yourself why not. Is it because you believe that the powers of individuals are to some degree, and in various ways, effects of their being located in positions in organisations and structures of material inequality? Social theorising involves thinking about how such social phenomena are produced and how they affect individuals.

Different levels and kinds of theory and creativity in social explanation

By now perhaps you are asking, 'If I already hypothesise about social phenomena using social theoretical ideas, why do I need this book? Isn't it all just common sense?' Well some may be but certainly not 'all'. As we suggested earlier, we need to be critically reflective about how we assemble and evaluate our explanations. Thus what we are offering, besides continual encouragement to be reflexive about your own social theorising, is an opportunity to learn a basic set of social theoretical concepts and why they are all necessary and unavoidable for social explanation. We will show you their logical properties and modes of relation using a wide range of concrete examples and puzzles. Armed with this small 'toolkit' of what we claim to be fundamental concepts, you should be much better placed to evaluate common-sense explanations, create valuable hypotheses – and understand what the major social theorists are up to. We are claiming that every social explanation must use these five concepts, (individuals, nature, culture, action and social structure) which are the sufficient set to give us access to social reality given the kind of reality it is.

However we also recognise that many other derived, subsidiary, concepts will also be required, problem by problem, as will become apparent when considering actual explanations in the following chapters. Thus we are suggesting that explanation can be launched by adopting a strategy of harnessing the respective powers of this set of five kinds of causes, but that though these are 'basic' that only means that they provide a sort of foundation upon which to invent other theoretical ideas (a glance now at the glossary will show you many of them). These are equally necessary for social explanation – the five concepts of our explanatory strategy function to initiate employing the elaborate edifice of social theory and do not, and cannot, do all the explanatory work by themselves. Thus, for example, it is necessary to have the concept of 'social structure' before one can have a particular concept of a type of social structure, say a '**stratification** system', and that concept is a precondition of being able to theorise different kinds of stratification systems, such as '**class**' and 'caste' systems, which may be further refined by distinguishing between 'relatively open' and 'relatively closed' class systems. Here we see four levels of theoretical refinement.

Similarly it is necessary to have the concept of **culture** before one can have a particular cultural concept, for example, 'gender' or 'religion' or '**social identity**'. Or again, the human individual can be theorised as having the potential to develop a personality and become, not just an individual, but a person. A person has a unique point of view and ability to think about themselves, that is a *personal* identity, which means there must be a complex relation between this and the way they are recognised by others (that is their various *social* identities). Logically the concepts 'individual', 'person', 'personality' must come before theorising different types of personality ('conformist', 'type A' or whatever). Similarly 'social identity' and 'personal identity' are two sub-types of the more general concept of 'individual identity' and each can be further subdivided in their turn – 'parent', 'driver', 'patient', are examples of social identities an individual can possess, while 'John' and 'Hilary' label specific personal identities (Figure 0.3).

Derived concepts, such as those of religion, gender and identity, are very important and indispensable for social theory. Nevertheless they are not

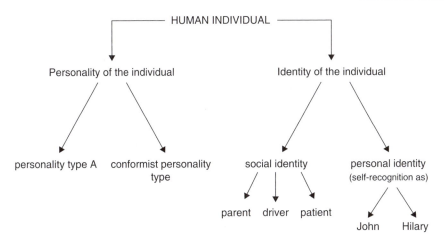

Figure 0.3 Relations between fundamental and subsidiary concepts: the concept of the individual

foundational in the way that the concepts of 'culture' and the 'individual' are. The way the foundational encourages the invention of other necessary, though subsidiary, concepts enables us to relate easily to the riches of social theory.

Theorising involves working out the mechanisms which are operating in what foundational and subsidiary concepts refer to. So, for example, the general theory of the foundational concept of social structure supports subsidiary theories of how different types of stratification structures, class, caste, slave and so on are formed, develop and change (Box 9.2). And these may be further refined. For example, there are theories of slavery (a type of social structure) in general, and of the particular varieties found in ancient Greece and Rome, in Asia, Africa, the Middle East and America (Westermann, 1955; Davis, 1966; Watson, 1980; Pipes, 1981; Patterson, 1982; Lewis, 1990; U.N., 1991). Likewise there are theories of revolution in general, and of its historical varieties, English, American, Russian, Chinese and so on (Moore, 1967; Skocpol, 1979). Such special and subsidiary theories vary in their abstractness, generality and empirical scope.

With their associated concepts, they may sometimes acquire their own momentum and autonomy. For example, Runciman (following Merton's theory of **reference groups**) developed the theory of relative deprivation to explain the willingness of some of the disadvantaged to accept their lot rather than struggle to change the class system (Merton, 1957; Runciman, 1966). The theory suggested that people only object to the inequalities they actually perceive. This helps explain Runciman's particular concern – which was why some working-class people can be easily mobilised against the system and others not. But the theory of relative deprivation can equally illuminate other problems such as the role of access to Western media in changing the aspirations of non-western populations and destabilising their societies.

Similarly there are theories of specific historical phenomena which have wide application. A famous example is Weber's analysis of the consequences of the rise in the West of a particular cultural form, Protestantism. He developed this to account for the dominance of **capitalism** in Western societies but it has also been used to begin explaining the rise of science (Merton, 1957), the character of American urban development (Sennett, 1990) and Swedish environmentalism (Stanworth, 2006).

Our claim that our five basic concepts are fundamental for social analysis is supported by the requirement to mobilise them to account for all of the wide-ranging empirical examples we deal with in the text. That they can provide the theoretical underpinning for deriving a further multitude of concepts, strengthens our claim that they provide the basis for social explanation, and that initially mobilising them is a good basis for elementary explanatory strategies. In the following chapters, we shall inevitably be considering the less basic, but equally necessary, concepts and levels of theorising to show how they depend on the basic concepts, but also to suggest that the social sciences are a huge resource of imaginative ideas and examples of effective explanation for us to follow. However we can only provide you with a taste of what is available.

Describing and justifying how the book is organised

The book is organised around the five concepts we claim are fundamental for social explanation. As already indicated, we will look at each in turn via a pair of chapters which make extensive use of examples. The range of examples has been chosen for three reasons. First, their great variety shows that the five concepts have *general* application. Second, by providing material from different places and different points in time we emphasise that the human social world is global and historical: social phenomena are always spatially distributed and emergent in a process of **conditioning** by preceding **history**. The case studies illustrate that the long history of mutual influence and inter-dependent relations between, for example, what have been called 'western' and 'non-western' societies, continues. Third, by drawing on studies from across various disciplines and the history of the social sciences, the examples establish that, to an important degree, social science is interdisciplinary and its knowledge is cumulative. The insights from earlier work continue to be valuable, and repay attention.

The first chapter of each pair examines the general properties of the concept in question, beginning to show its usefulness with reference to short examples. The second chapter of each pair uses fewer, more detailed, examples to reveal further the explanatory strength of the concept under consideration, but also to show its limits and that it must be supplemented by the other concepts. This mode of presentation derives from our belief that *all* of the concepts are necessary for social explanation and that each has its strengths but also its limits.

We have already implied that our position is multi-causal, in that we argue it is the interaction among all five kinds of causation which is important. Satisfactory explanations will show how phenomena are produced as a result of specific processes of interaction of the various causal forces in each case. The logical implication of this claim that *all are necessary* is that *no single one is* **sufficient** alone to do all the explanatory work. Thus though each of the paired chapters focuses on *one* of the basic concepts, all begin to examine how the different causal powers interact to generate the outcomes we are trying to explain.

Our mode of presentation resists theories which hold that any particular one or other of these concepts is more important than the others in all circumstances, or is capable of forming the basis of all social explanation. These one-sided biases, which we refer to for convenience's sake, as '**individual*ism***', 'natural*ism*', 'cultural*ism*', 'action*ism*', and '**structural*ism***' are, or have been, very influential in social theory. Our position, on the other hand, is pluralist or multi-causalist because, in contrast to, for example, individualism or structuralism (which claim that social phenomena can be explained by reference to, respectively, individuals or social structures alone), we hold that all five concepts are necessary for social explanation but that none alone is sufficient (Figure 0.4).

The distinction between what is *necessary* and what is *sufficient,* for explanation, is of fundamental importance. Which range of concepts is needed for any given explanation, and which concept(s) have most strength will vary between cases and may also relate to how far 'back' down the causal chain we want our explanation to go. (For example, the natural configuration of the human voice-box helps account for the ability of two people to engage in a noisy argument, but normally if we want to explain why they are shouting at each other, we are happy to take their vocal capacities for granted.) As we have noted, each of our key concepts has relative autonomy. It has 'autonomy' because it has its own irreducible, distinct capacity to exert a causal force. But it is a 'relative' autonomy because it always operates 'relative to', that is, in combination with, the other kinds of causal forces. Explanations achieve sufficiency only when, with the aid of specific subsidiary concepts, they specify the interaction among all the necessary causal mechanisms responsible for the phenomena being explained.

Multi-Causalism	Five Basic Concepts	Five types of Mono-causalism	
All five concepts are **necessary**. Each has relative causal autonomy. **None alone is sufficient.**	**Individuals**		Individual*ism*
	Nature	One kind of causal mechanism	Natural*ism*
	Action	alone has causal primacy	Action*ism*
	Culture	and is necessary and sufficient	Cultural*ism*
	Social Structure		Structural*ism*

Figure 0.4 Multi-causal pluralist and mono-causalist requirements for social explanation

In Chapter 11, we extend our discussion of the fundamental social theory underlying our approach to social explanation and we show why we think it is scientific, comparing our position with others'. Finally, in Chapter 12, we underline how using the tool kit can help us understand our own and others' predicaments, as well as be more technically and politically effective when we try to change things. Every chapter ends with a set of questions designed to help you think about the issues it has raised.

A framework for distinguishing different kinds of social theory

As an introduction to basic social theory, in the sense we have been outlining, this book is self-contained and can be read on its own. Although our selection of tools for the kit draws on the long history of social theory, we do not presume readers have any prior knowledge of social science theories and theorists. Our primary aim is to encourage our readers to begin quickly participating in the creative and critical practice of building explanations about collective phenomena without first having to become knowledgeable about *particular* social theorists and theories. We give priority to understanding and valuing social theory as a practical activity, over knowing about the lives and work of particular theorists. Students may benefit from becoming effective users of theoretical reason before they become scholars and some readers may be happy to end this chapter here.

However, acquiring scholarship is not unimportant, so we can note that to help the interested reader use our basic schema to develop an understanding of differences between a range of social theories and theorists they are likely to meet elsewhere, we have also provided various 'hooks' in the text itself, plus supplementary text boxes. In addition, the glossary offers definitions and further elaboration of some key terms (these are indicated in bold in the text).

To facilitate the understanding of readers who are curious about the relation between our fundamental schema and the wide variety of social theoretical possibilities, we can also expand on Figure 0.4. This showed how each concept can be used to identify a theoretical bias, and that together the five basic concepts can be mobilised to provide a classification of six broad varieties of social theory, each characterised by its understanding of the relative importance of the five fundamental kinds of causal powers we suggest are together responsible for social phenomena.

Figure 0.5 tentatively assigns a range of named theorists and social theoretical stances to positions within the broad sixfold classification (individualism, naturalism, actionalism, culturalism, structuralism and our own multi-causalism).

Individualism	utilitarianism, rational choice theory, Collins' 'interaction ritual chains', subjectivism, psychologism
Naturalism	positivism, Comte, social evolutionism, Spencer, biological determinism, environmental determinism, varieties of feminism, Levi-Strauss
Actionism	symbolic interactionism, Goffman, ethnomethodology, social constructionism, Giddens' structuration theory
Culturalism	idealism, cultural Marxism, Foucault, varieties of feminism, Douglas and cultural theory
Structuralism	Parsons' later systems functionalism, Bourdieu, Althusser, economistic Marxism, Marxist feminism, actor network theory
Pluralist Multi-causalism	Marx, Weber, Durkheim, pragmatism, Habermas, early Parsons, Elias, contemporary historical sociology, Mann's theory of social power, Archer's morphogenetic critical realism, DeLanda's assemblage theory

Figure 0.5 A crude, but useful, classification of common social theory labels, writers and schools

This kind of assigning is suggestive rather than definitive. This is because almost all writers and schools of social theory, as they develop, change their ideas, sometimes quite dramatically, and may also express them with an ingenuity and complexity which makes them difficult to classify. Theorists' own understandings of how positions should be defined may also lead them to disagree with the labels others give them (King, 1999, 2007; Archer, 2000b). As pluralists indebted to those whose ideas, however classified, we try to combine, we benefit from continuing to pay attention to as much of the field as possible.

Questions related to themes in this chapter

This chapter has begun to explain what we mean by social theory, and introduced the five key concepts which comprise our basic social theory 'tool kit'.

1) In what sense are we all social theorists, regardless of whether or not this is our academic specialism?
2) Social theory is concerned with explaining collective phenomena. Offer some examples of collective phenomena.
3) Give an example of how your experience of social life has stimulated a desire to try to explain a collective phenomenon.
4) How have you tried to explain the above example? What kinds of cause did you use in your explanation? Did you use any of the five concepts?
5) Here is an example which stimulated our desire for explanation: in the Netherlands and Denmark there are no significant differences in rates of bicycle use between the genders and social classes and there is only a small decline with age. This contrasts with Britain, where cycling is strongly differentiated by gender, social class and age (most cyclists are young or middle aged, middle class, males). Why do you think this difference exists? Try to use the five concepts in your explanation(s).

PART I

The concept of the individual

CHAPTER 1

What do individuals explain?

When people in their everyday lives try to explain social phenomena – social events and patterns, they often think whether the phenomena can be plausibly accounted for by the characteristics of the physically distinct *individuals* involved in them. There are two very strong pressures to make this move.

First, all social collectivities such as classes, families, teams, groups, tribes, clubs, nations, queues are composed of, among other things, embodied human individuals. The terms classes, families and so on, but also ranks, roles and statuses, refer to ways in which such physically distinguishable individuals can share characteristics and thus be described as being the same as one another. These concepts refer to orderings of existence that overarch physical separation between individuals. There could be no ranks or roles, or tribes and clubs without people to fill or join them. A queue is a way of arranging human bodies in a line to satisfy certain values about turn-taking. To the extent that there are no social phenomena without the individuals who participate in them, they must be regarded as necessary for social phenomena to exist. However, the question remains whether one can explain social phenomena by referring only to the properties of this necessary human material.

The second pressure encouraging attempts to explain collective phenomena by reference to the individuals who are collectivised, is the fact that particularly in industrialised, relatively wealthy, parts of the world, a very high value is placed on each human individual. Enabling individuals to flourish has become a powerful value-commitment shaping contemporary political, educational and economic debate, aspiration, and struggle. In this context the term 'individual' is used unreflectively as though everyone knows what is being referred to and supports its well-being. Given this preoccupation with what happens to 'individuals' and what they may be capable of, it is unsurprising if the powers attributed to them have been inflated so that it seems reasonable to regard them as, in the last instance, entirely responsible for social phenomena.

This positive valuation of the individual has a long history and has been encouraged by, for example, the freedom of rural producers to trade in local markets, the development of cities and citizenship and the invention of the religious idea of equality of the fate of the soul. Its global spread during the last three centuries was helped by **industrialism** and 'de-traditionalisation'. Major changes in techniques of material **production**, such as the development of inanimate power sources to run machinery, tended to de-stabilise ancient ways of life, belief, knowledge, work, social roles, hierarchies and distributions of **social power**. This was not just a once-and-for-all change from the old ways to the new, but made the pursuit of endless change a way of life in its own right. Faced with this condition of **modernity**, individuals became more self-reliant for solutions to their problems, as the traditional answers offered by authority figures such as fathers, priests, grandmothers and rural landlords appeared outmoded. Every sphere of life was affected. Typical are the growth of Protestantism and anti-clericalism in religion, the application of science to technical innovation in production, the democratisation of politics, and the support for **'creative individualism'** in art.

The example of 'creative individualism'

Take this development in art for example. In pre-industrial traditional **contexts**, art conformed to established patterns. Art makers such as the medieval masons responsible for the decoration of religious buildings, were trained in families and in quarries specialising in different kinds of stone. Their work was closely prescribed and disciplined by technical criteria. The rules, techniques and standards were relatively clear, and typically only a few individuals are known today from contracts with their religious patrons (Knoop and Jones, 1933). Contrast non-traditional contexts; artists increasingly work for themselves making what they like, struggle for recognition, and sell their 'signature works' in an open market relatively free of dictation from patrons. Prominent examples are Hogarth in 18th century England and Picasso in early 20th century Spain and France. What counts as art is increasingly strongly contested and there tends to be a proliferation of alternatives. The emphasis shifts from being exemplary to being original. More or less anybody can present themselves as an artist and what should be taught as art education becomes problematic (Roberts, 2007). In other words, the 'creative individual' steps into the space opened up by the de-stabilisation of traditional patterns of art-making, art education and consumption.

In response to industrialisation, the cultural movement known as romanticism regarded making art as a defence of human creativity against the supposedly dehumanising effects of mechanisation and urbanisation. Artistic creativity, demonstrated by a few heroic individuals, was regarded as the residual symptom of the truly human, capable of resisting the negative effects of an industrialising society. The artist, rather than exemplifying socially approved patterns, came to stand against society.

However, this attractive heroic vision, originated over two hundred years ago, has gradually been generalised into a contemporary banal version. Claiming that all **practices**, artistic or not, are creative, it suggests that 'everyone is an artist', thereby removing the romantic opposition between art and society. Society is thought of as populated by more or less powerfully creative individuals (a.k.a. artists) who are the primary determiners of social phenomena. With the de-traditionalising of art, artists defined by their 'creativity' no longer have to practise anything in particular. The traditional idea of the creativity of individual artists is elided with all the other kinds of social creativity such as those of entrepreneurs and politicians (Joas, 1996).

The necessity and sufficiency of individuals in social explanation

'Creative individualism' has become a common-sense, taken-for-granted principle informing how people understand themselves, as well as much policy-making. This tenet of popular culture may seem intuitively plausible. However, though social theory may begin from such intuitions it must judge their worth using a critical method. For us that method involves assessing the *necessity* and *sufficiency* of the causes featured in causal stories. With regard to creative individualism we can accept that individuals are necessary for the production of social phenomena, have some creative potential and are responsible for some elements of what happens. Note the 'some' in the previous sentence! We may think that had certain individuals chosen and acted differently, things would have turned out differently. But the business of deciding which individuals are responsible for what in particular cases, is usually complicated because their powers to make a difference must be set in a field of other causes with various degrees of power to shape outcomes. Thus it is rather unlikely that everything in society is explicable simply in terms of the physical individuals who belong to it.

Despite this, there is a kind of social theorist, often called methodological individualist, who believes in **methodological individualism** (MI), saying that individuals are the only kind of reality with the necessary and sufficient causal powers capable of generating social phenomena. However, being complex entities, individuals provide plenty of scope for theorising what their socially productive causal powers might be. This means that meth-odological individualists do not automatically agree about which particular causal powers of individuals are necessary or sufficient, or about their relative importance. So, in this chapter we will start by taking seriously the claim that some of the attributes of individuals have explanatory potential and are therefore necessary for explanation. What are these attributes and how might they shape social phenomena? But we will also begin considering whether any, or some combination of them, can really provide us with all that we need, that is, whether they are sufficient for social explanation, as methodo-logical individualists claim. Referring again to the case of artists, we need to question if what they do can be explained by pointing only to the power of their individual creativity.

Before we get going, it will help to point out, firstly, that *if* we are to agree with MI, we will have to be convinced that the causally effective attributes of individuals are not themselves produced by social factors. Individuals must possess these attributes independently of society, not as socially derived, since MI demands that the social is derived from them. Usually such prop-erties are referred to as *innate*, that is, as biologically given at birth. For example, we would have to be sure that what artists call their 'creativity' was innate and not the product of a cultural, economic, political and edu-cational context, what Howard Becker (1982) calls an 'art world'. Secondly, if the pre-social and causally important attributes of individuals are alone to explain different patternings of phenomena, we will have to agree that indi-viduals are differently endowed with these attributes in the first place. For, if individuals alone produce outcomes, how could people who were quite the same, generate a variety of effects? Ultimately if we support methodological individualism we must believe that families, tribes, classes, clubs, queues, even societies, are ultimately nothing more than, are reducible without remainder to, the sum of the properties of the concrete individuals who belong to them.

In the rest of this chapter we will, firstly, begin to think about what kinds of natural and innate attributes of individuals, flowing from their physical properties, might be considered sufficient for explaining social phenomena, such as the course of events and patterned regularities. Secondly we will consider individuals as (more or less) rational and knowledgeable actors and the extent to which their **decision-making** can account for social pat-terning. Methodological individualism treats individuals as natural beings, endowed with objective, pre-social, socially productive properties (such as the capacity for rational choice) discoverable by natural science. This is a specific understanding of nature and science which we will return to in Chapter 3.

Individuals as embodied objects with natural, innate properties

The first possibility is to take seriously the immediately perceptible physical and mechanical properties of the individual's body. Are any of the natural bodily properties of human individuals productive of social phenomena and thus relevant for social explanation? We can start answering this question by considering whether the course of history and the shape of the social world would be the same if, for example, women, generally, were very much bigger and stronger than men, both sexes could get pregnant, babies were born able to walk and feed themselves, humans lacked tongues and the ability to speak, and had dog-like paws instead of hands. The social arrangements we have, for example, for bearing and bringing up children, the shape and scale of social products like tools and the houses, furniture, clothes we make with them, are all the way they are, in part, because individuals, as members of the human species, have the physical and biological form they do. What humans need to survive and act is constrained by their biology and that will condition their collective lives. Already it's clear we can't ignore the significance of individual's human biology. But can we say more and is the necessity of considering the properties of human bodies sufficient for social explanation?

Recently the 'new genetics' has been increasing our knowledge of human biology and some have seen this as meaning we will be able to explain more of social life in terms of it. The basic hope of late 20th century genetics was that it would illuminate causal biological mechanisms (cellular, developmental and physiological) producing all sorts of significant conditions, particularly illnesses and pathologies, but also, possibly, behavioural traits. For political reasons there has been particular interest in research focusing on the genetic sources of what are defined as social problems or pathologies. There was some hope that many physical and, some believed, assorted social ills would be found to have their origins in particular individual inherited genes or genetic variants which were differentially distributed throughout the population.

For a variety of reasons the early hopes that the new genetics would reduce explanations exclusively to genetic factors were misplaced. In part this is because of what the new genetics has itself revealed about the complexity of genes and how they work (Rose, 1997; Nuffield Council on Bioethics, 2002; Henderson, 2008; Parry and Dupré, 2010). Thus this fast-changing and technically complex area of knowledge has seen the early optimism that many conditions and **dispositions** would each be found to stem from the specific action of a particular individual gene or comprehensible set of genes, generally give way to more modest and realistic appreciation of the typical complexity of the processes through which genes contribute to biological phenomena. The question for us is – how far do recent developments show that the mechanisms producing socially-significant phenomena derive from the genetic make-up of individuals?

Mapping the human genome has established that there is a collection of genes (estimated at approximately 21,000) that together provide the genetic contribution to specifying the human species. Some genes occur in the human genome and not elsewhere, but many are shared with other life-forms. This is because humans, like all biological organisms, descend from an evolutionary tree and thus share common ancestry with all other creatures further back in evolutionary time (it's estimated we have about 95% of our genetic inheritance in common with our close primate relative the chimpanzee, while our more distant relative the fruit fly shares about 60% of its genes with us). Many aspects of our biology, in particular various sub-cellular biochemical processes, are highly conserved across organisms, having arisen far back in evolutionary time. It is no surprise to find a huge range of life forms sharing the genes that govern these fundamental biological functions. Other aspects of our biology, such as binocular vision, arose in more recent ancestors, and hence the genetic instructions for these are distributed across only a small branch of the evolutionary tree containing us and other primates.

Equally important is that individuals, as parents, transmit variants of the genes making up the human genome to their children. What children inherit is a unique combination of genes, or more precisely, of gene variants called alleles (Box 1.1). These are stored on the 23 sets of paired chromosomes they receive when egg and sperm fuse at the moment of conception, one part of each pair from each parent. Only monozygotic (identical) twins start genetically the same as each other. But like everyone else, during their lives their genetic inheritance can undergo change. This is because when cells divide during our development and adult life, some genes are replicated imperfectly (mutate), and because each individual's genetic inheritance undergoes a unique series of interactions with environmental factors originating outside the body. For example, recent research is showing that early life exposure to certain dietary and emotional experiences can have biochemical effects which strongly condition whether or not, or the way in which, certain genes come into play later in life. Viruses and bacteria can have similar gene-influencing effects. These interactions can sometimes alter the DNA of a gene. Or they may lead to it becoming 'epigenetically modified' – altering where in the body and when during life the physical, functional product (usually a protein) encoded by the gene's DNA is produced (or 'expressed'). How a gene is expressed depends on many positive and negative conditions, including not only external factors, but also the particular characteristics of the other genes with which it interacts. In some cases, possession of a single gene variant is

Box 1.1 Genes and alleles

Individuals generally inherit two alleles (that is two variants) of each type of gene, one from each parent. The alleles differ from each other by way of mutations in their DNA sequences. However, although each *individual* will only possess two alleles of any given kind of gene, across populations of individuals, some *genes* come in more than two variants. If the two alleles of a given gene an individual possesses are the same, the individual is *homozygous* for that gene; if the alleles are different, they are said to be *heterozygous*. For many genes, if the two alleles are heterozygous then one allele may be dominant over the other (recessive) allele. In such cases, the function of the gene is provided by the dominant allele, while the recessive allele does not, typically, produce any determinable biological effect. Where such a gene has more than two alleles, which one is dominant in any individual person's case may depend on which other allele it is paired with. An allele dominant in relation to one particular other allele might be recessive in relation to a third allele of the same gene. But it can be passed on to the next generation where it may be paired with a new allele to which it is dominant, or it may pair with an identical partner, with both homozygous alleles now contributing to the gene's biological function. There are also some genes whose alleles can be co-dominant. Here in heterozygous cases, both alleles contribute to gene function. Thus, in general, the effects any allele can produce will be conditioned by the character of the other allele with which it is paired.

Henderson, M. (2008) *50 Genetic Ideas You Really Need to Know*, London, Quercus.

sufficient to determine an outcome regardless of other circumstances. The gene variant for Huntington's chorea is a frequently cited example of such genetic ultimacy. Its possessors will inevitably succumb to this disease. But for a great many human traits, including many diseases and behavioural characteristics, what individual gene variants do is best understood as providing *possibilities* rather than *inevitabilities,* making some outcomes more probable – and in some cases much more probable, than others.

This understanding of the genome gives us a picture of each individual at any given moment possessing a uniquely realised version of the human genome, made up of the various genes operating, not in isolation, but with their functioning potential (expression) realised or inhibited by the enabling or constraining effects of their relations with other genetic and non-genetic conditions. In other words *the power of any gene is typically mediated* rather than being direct. Their operation is conditioned rather than autonomous, and their effect is to condition rather than determine outcomes.

Understanding how genes produce effects contributes to our grasping the mechanisms of individual human biology, but it strengthens the view that this biology is always in interaction with its environment. It offers a more detailed way of understanding the permeability of the divide between the human body and its environment and how the latter can affect (and be incorporated into) the former.

Implications for social theory

If we turn to look at the implications of genetics for the understanding of social phenomena there are various ways it may be helpful. For example, it's possible that genetics will help identify the necessary biological *mechanisms* contributing to the potential of individuals to behave *as* social beings, complementing recent developments in neuroscience. The latter developments are also underlining the importance of the interrelations between biological matter and the environment with which it interacts, revealing the extent to which individuals shape the architecture and functioning of their brains by the ways they use them, particularly in childhood, but also throughout their lives (Johnson, 2001; Hyde et al., 2009; Kays et al., 2012). There is undoubtedly a complex biology underlying all the capabilities individuals bring to bear in social existence – the ability to use language, to empathise with others, to interpret faces, to value approval for example.

We don't want to rule out the possibility of there being a degree of hereditability of various socially significant abilities, conditions and pathologies, and genetics may be able to help us untangle the relative importance of genetic and environmental factors and how they work together. For example, if we suspect that the ability to judge musical pitch perfectly might have an innate element but could also be affected by early musical training, we could compare groups who had and had not experienced the latter. If perfect pitch were found in the early educated alone we would doubt any biological cause. But if it was distributed between both those who had and had not experienced training, and if we were able to find some gene or gene variant occurring much more frequently in the perfect pitchers than the others, we might be willing to suggest a strong biological input. If we understood how this gene worked (more precisely, how it is expressed, and what biological function is served by the gene product it encodes) we might also be able to understand the mechanisms which enabled some to judge pitch better than others (Theusch et al., 2009).

However, whether or not possessing perfect pitch has any social significance, is not given by genetics. That entirely depends on whether the individual in question lives in a society or belongs to a culture whose social practices make it relevant. This very important point can be made more generally. We have already seen that the new genetics suggests that few genes work in isolation. Firstly, external factors in the social and the natural world may affect if genetic potentialities are expressed and realised. Then secondly whether these genetically-related outcomes have any social significance will depend on social circumstance. For example, following research (Alia-Klein et al., 2008) which suggested there may be some connection between propensity to 'violence' and particular alleles of the MAO-A gene which encodes the enzyme Monoamine Oxidase, there have been popular claims that 'scientists have found a gene for violence'. Such simplistic claims are problematic. Firstly they take what is to count as violence as self-evident, but this needs careful consideration given that identical physical actions are often perceived as violent in some contexts but not in others. Secondly, it is most unlikely that there is just one gene relevant to violence however that is defined. But even were that to be the case, it wouldn't produce effects in isolation. Two major environmental influences are the availability of roles which require violence and control it with rules and sanctions (e.g. disciplinary, defensive and sporting functions) and the situationally specific absence of effective alternative non-violent means of achieving ends (e.g. through persuasion – moral and/or economic). Thus, on the one hand, most people are capable of violence in some circumstances. On the other, there may be centuries-long social structural processes such as Elias's 'civilization process', which work against individuals, whatever their specific genetic inclination towards this kind of behaviour, resorting to it (Elias, (orig.1939), 2000).

Norbert Elias (1897–1990, German)

(1939) *The Civilizing Process: Sociogenetic and Psychogenetic Investigations,* (edition trans. Jephcott, E., ed. Dunning, E. et al.) Oxford, Blackwell (2000). *The Court Society: Collected Works of Norbert E. Elias* (ed. Mennell, S.) Dublin, University of Dublin Press (2005).

We could almost infinitely expand the list of examples of where social context shapes the significance of the biological characteristics of human individuals, whether we explain the latter genetically or not. In some cases we might argue that the social significance of the features in question more or less entirely depended on the fact that importance was assigned to them – skin colour or hair type would be examples. Some features only have an intrinsic relevance in particular kinds of society. Inability to focus close-up in old age is a real difficulty in societies with tasks that demand close working, but lack spectacles. Lower limb paralysis is more disabling in societies without wheelchairs or proper facilities for wheelchair access. Importantly there are also some species-wide biological features that are intrinsically significant in all societies. We have already noted that human biology entails that individuals are highly dependent when young. If they reproduce they must do so sexually, they are very likely to become frail in old age and are certain to die. All societies have to deal with the resulting problems. The biology may set some limits to the available solutions but they don't determine them entirely – as evidenced by the *range* of ways they have been responded to.

Lastly we might note that societies often use biological attributes to classify human individuals and to put them into collectivities to which a range of further social significances may be assigned. 'Sexes' and 'races' are the two key cases here. But once again, biology itself is not totally determining of the classifications that result. Although people may believe this is the case, classifications can't just be automatically 'read off' from the reality which is being classified. This is a generic feature of any classificatory system – which means that there is always a social/cultural element in classification. For example, decisions always have to be made as to how many potentially relevant variables are mobilised to make the classification. The more you choose, the more complex the classification will be. Moreover, once you have your classificatory principles, decisions must be made about the anomalous cases they will almost inevitably throw up. Do you pretend they don't exist and push the anomalous into one of the non-anomalous categories, or do you create one or more separate, additional categories for them?

Thus 19th century theorists of 'racial' classification quarrelled among themselves as to whether they should put people into 'racial' groups on the basis of their skin colour, their hair type, the shape of their eyes or their noses. The number of categories arrived at and who was 'racially' separated from whom depended on the choices made. Today we would further question whether limiting attention to such externally observable biologically related physical features was appropriate. What about gene variants that code for something less visible, blood group for example – and which cross-cut 'external' features like skin colour? Today natural scientists prefer not to talk in terms of discrete races, or even to use the term to categorise human populations at all. They think in terms of fluid gene pools, with fuzzy boundaries distinguishable from each other only in terms of the relative proportion, not absence or presence, in their members of a vast range of genetic variables (Lewontin et al., 1990; Lorusso, 2011).

'Sexual' classification is perhaps a bit less problematic but also not entirely determined by biology. The classification of individuals into sexes typically makes some kind of reference to the differences in role that individuals play in the reproductive process. The objective fact that humans constitute a species which reproduces itself sexually, potentially generates a dimorphic, two-fold, 'sexual' classification. But equally objectively, other variables relate to, but don't always neatly line up with, possession of particular types of reproductive apparatus and capacities. For example, genitalia can be ambiguous, or can 'mismatch' with chromosomes (either naturally or as the result of surgical or other intervention). Further, the character of individuals' erotic drives (which probably contain strong naturally given elements) may or may not line up with what is reproductively effective. Most societies collectivise people with some reference to their reproductive capacities. But there are historical and cross-cultural differences in how they deal with the other related variables and thus whether they operate in terms of a two, three or even more sexed system (Herdt, 1996). To complicate things still further, we can find societies which, under certain circumstances, at least symbolically, allocate some individuals to sexual categories on the basis of behaviour rather than biology – we provide one example in Chapter 6 (Littlewood, 2002; Trexler, 2002; Young and Twigg, 2009).

Moreover, the members of a society may contest what classificatory principles should be used. Human sexual biology has evolved to combine reproductive and non-reproductive potentials. Relating to these potentials is done from various positions under changing conditions and is the basis for political **strategies** and the development of disciplinary techniques and regimes for regulating and supervising bodies (Foucault, 1963, 1976–84). These ideas about potentials and dispositions, and their mutability in principle and practice, both *express* relations of social power and have *implications for positioning* individuals in occupations and power structures (Herdt, 1993; MacKinnon, 2006).

Michel Foucault (1926–84, French)

(1961) *History of Madness* (ed. Khalfa, J. trans. Murphy, J. and Khalfa, J.) London, Routledge (2006).

(1963) *The Birth of the Clinic,* London, Routledge (2003).

(1966) *The Order of Things,* London, Routledge (2001).

(1975) *Discipline and Punish: The Birth of the Prison,* Harmondsworth, Penguin (1991).

(1976–84) *The History of Sexuality: 1 The Will to Knowledge*, Harmondsworth, Penguin (1989).

The History of Sexuality: 11 The Use of Pleasure, Harmondsworth, Penguin (1998).

The History of Sexuality: 111 The Care of the Self, Harmondsworth, Penguin (1990).

We have been showing that 'human material' presents a constant challenge to the understanding, which has to be responded to. We have also seen that cultural resources have to be used to make sense of the human material and that the terms in which cultures do this sense-making are not determined by what they are making sense of. In general we have seen that we must acknowledge the significance of the naturally given components of human individuals, but take care not to over-estimate them and always bear in mind that social context will mediate the impact of naturally given features. Misjudging the importance of biology can have politically pernicious consequences. Particularly in cultures which propose that what is biologically caused is impossible or very difficult to change, over-estimating the extent that biology determines the attributes of people as individuals, or as members of socially defined collectivities such as 'sexes' or 'races', can lead to a shutting down of possibilities and a legitimation of inequalities.

Individuals as (non-rational and rational) personal subjects

Are there other attributes of individuals, besides their physical embodiment and genes that we might think were relevant for social explanation? Though all the properties of human individuals depend upon their being embodied this need not mean that we only consider human beings as reactive objects. As we suggested in the Introduction there is a strong case that the specific character of their objectivity enables them to become subjects. While not claiming that **subjectivity** is a property only of human animals, it is true that each human individual goes through a development process in which they gain the capacity for self-recognition as being a unique personal identity with their own point of view which is able to use learned cultural resources and communicative interaction with others to assign meaning to their experience. The details of how one becomes a self-reflexive user of languages and producer of subjective meaning need not detain us now – suffice it to say that self-recognition (the core of subjectivity) involves being able to treat oneself as an object in one's imagination and consider alternative lines of conduct in advance (Box 3.5). This capability results from the interaction between the individual's biologically endowed, emotional and cognitive potential for self-formation, and an environment of other people who enable the individual to learn about itself and achieve self-reference. (We will return to this in Chapter 3 on human nature but can underline now that the fact that individuals are formed in a social process is fatal for MI.)

Studies of the higher, long-lived animals like elephants and dolphins suggest some capacity for self-recognition, but it is difficult to determine the extent of any capacity for imaginative anticipation. In humans this capacity is highly developed. Having a point of view from which to engage in self-monitoring and direct one's own behaviour in response to imagining the possible effects that behaviour might have, is the mark of being a fully functioning person and not just a body. Human bodies are vehicles for persons; persons are dependent on being embodied, but being one means having some capacity to mediate that dependency. For example, bodies require food, but eating is done by persons, firstly as members of collectivities using their beliefs, habits, tastes, values and emotions, and secondly on the basis of accumulated personal experience and likes and dislikes relating to eating. There is interaction between the biological imperative to eat, and personal and social sources of preferences. Though it is likely that there is some biological hard-wiring involved in distinguishing what counts as food, that mechanism does not explain the great variety of ways food has been defined in human history and across cultures. We will return to this topic in Chapter 5 on culture.

Human individuals, as self-directing persons, have emotional and cognitive powers which can qualify how their bodily conditioning impacts on behaviour. To be dependent on bodies is not to be determined by them. And the same point can be made about the relation between human individuals and the social forces which impinge on them. Personhood means that, though human individuals are conditioned by all sorts of physical and social circumstances, they have some capacity to influence the force and manner of their impact. Thus there is a good scientific reason for taking seriously the possibility that human individuals have some power to shape social life. Though we may want to reject MI, we do not want to throw the baby out with the bath-water, because without the self-recognising, meaning-producing, socially interacting person at the heart of our social theory we will be left with forms of biological and sociological determinism which are no better!

Historically significant individuals

However we don't want to assign too much significance to individual persons. One common-sense way of looking at history, which over-emphasises the powers of individuals, sees it as a series of events caused principally by the crucially influential actions of exceptional individuals who are viewed as the 'creators' of history. Sometimes referred to as 'the great man – or woman – theory of history', it suggests that the unique 'power of mind', 'clarity of vision', 'genius,' 'determination', 'strength of feeling' of key, political, economic, religious and cultural figures (Elizabeth Tudor, Fry, Picasso, Einstein, Curie, Hitler, Gandhi, Mandela or Thatcher for example) leads them to make decisions and to act in ways which are historically highly influential. Certainly we can agree that in some contexts, the actions of exceptional individuals in the right (or wrong) place at the right (or wrong) time have been crucial for how events actually turned out. When we are trying to explain what happened, it is always worth considering whether and how outcomes were influenced by the decisions and actions of some key responsible individuals.

But the question here is 'what makes them key?' Can we ultimately explain all social phenomena in terms only of an understanding of individuals as thinking or feeling beings? And, moreover, as individuals whose capacities for and modes of thought or emotion are innate, that is, capacities that only cause social phenomena and are not originally generated by them (the basic premise of MI)? Can leadership for example, be explained as a function of personal uniqueness and without reference to position in the organisations which are being led? Some theorists think it can. They have tended to derive the social creativity claimed for individuals from models of the individual as either innately rational, or as the opposite, that is as a non-rational creature fuelled by biologically given drives for sexual gratification, or power and the domination of others. Thus, for example, in the non-rational camp, Freud's famous psychoanalytic theory explains the action of individuals by reference to a universal process of personality formation in which biological instincts for sexual gratification motivate behaviour. Desire is held to be so strong that its self-destructive implications must be disciplined by mechanisms of repression and civilisation. Social orders are thus 'explained' as emerging to fulfil the function of organising and channelling sexually-motivated behaviour into productive rather than destructive activities.

There are interesting insights here. We might, for example, usefully consider various arts, drama, sports, popular entertainment, elements of religious practice, rites of passage and so on as means of providing psychological gratification in controlled forms. But there are problems with this kind of perspective. Not least in resolving how there is such variation in forms of social life if they are all motivated originally by desires for sex (or power). Individual variations in the extent to which people manifest universal drives might help us understand some differences in behaviour between members of the same society. But such individual variety does not easily account for differences in social institutions and practices between whole societies, even if we believe that all these institutions and practices are ultimately linked to the need to control potentially destructive universal desires and dispositions. Even if we could show that the members of some societies were more strongly endowed with the drive for sex or the will to power than those of some others, this could scarcely account for all the inter-societal variations of social institutions and culture that we find. Moreover, we would have to be careful how we established that the strength of drives was in fact differentially distributed. This would have to be done without reference to the differences in social outcomes which are being explained by differences in innate non-rational properties of the individuals involved. A more productive approach would be to analyse an interaction over time in particular settings between the pressures to satisfy individuals' drives, and pressures arising from changes in the organisation and scale of political and economic practices such as states and markets (Elias, (orig. 1939) 2000).

Rational choice theory

Rather than treating social phenomena as caused by what drives individuals, an alternative form of MI focuses on what enables individuals to make effective choices. Making choices involves evaluating alternatives. The capability for defining alternatives, deciding criteria for evaluating them, and choosing between them is rationality supported by commitments to various sorts of values. Theorising social phenomena as the outcomes of individuals exercising their rationality is the work of rational choice theory (RCT) which is worth examining in some detail. It is a sophisticated updating of a longstanding theory which has tried to derive moral rules for action from scientific knowledge about what makes people happy. This theory, (called 'utilitarianism'), thought of individuals as essentially the same, all motivated to want happiness, rationally seeking their own interests, as they typically do in economic markets (Box 1.2). Social phenomena are seen as the product of individuals trying to achieve their own happiness. Good actions and sound social institutions are those which give the greatest happiness to the greatest number.

Rational choice theorists, with utilitarians, hold that interests (ends, goals, desires, purposes, call them what you will) can be shared, but are more usually selfish. Individuals seek to satisfy their interests through strategic action, that is, action designed to get what is wanted by manipulating the

---

Box 1.2   Utilitarianism

John Stuart Mill (1806–1873) offered the most sophisticated version of utilitarianism in *Utilitarianism* (1861). This school of moral and political philosophy thought that it could identify universally-valid moral principles for organising society by referring to natural science. Natural science was thought to be an unbiased and objective guide to morality because it based its statements only on what could be observed. This **empiricism** was thought to provide a way of escaping the influence of competing religions and traditional cultural prejudices about how human beings should live together. The good society could be based on the relevant universal natural laws. Given that society was thought of as made up of human individuals, the relevant scientific laws were ones about human nature. The simplest, most general, law about human nature which could provide an empirical and objective foundation for the values used when designing society was the 'principle of utility', that all human beings desire happiness. Thus empirical information about what makes the majority of individuals happy should be used to test the moral justifiability of acts. This 'principle of utility' was individualist and empiricist. Talcott Parsons criticised the whole mode of thought from the perspective of classical social theory in his major early work *The Structure of Social Action* (1937).

Mill, J. S. (1861) *Utilitarianism*, Create Space Independent Publishing Platform (2013).
Parsons, T. (1937) *The Structure of Social Action*, New York, Free Press (1967).

circumstances and controlling the means to achieve the desired result. This is where rationality comes into play. Decisions about what means to use to get what is wanted are rational to the extent that they involve objective evaluation of the different costs of alternative methods. From this perspective, for example, money can be thought of as a tool for rationalising economic exchange by making it possible to price everything. It is functional for the sort of rationality required to find the cheapest way to solve problems. RCT refers to rationality as 'instrumental', 'technical' or 'calculative'. The crucial resources to calculate rationally the best available means are *logic* (for conceptual consistency), *measurement* (for descriptive precision), *technical knowledge* (for understanding how things work) and *information* (about the specific circumstances of the problem being dealt with). In sum, RCT sees individuals as naturally disposed to seek their self-interests and as using their innate capacity for rationality to decide how to get what they want. Rational individuals acquire the relevant information and know what to do with it to construct their strategies to achieve their goals (Elster, 1986; Becker 1976, 1996).

Differences between individuals: personalities and skill in settling a land dispute

So, under what conditions might this approach to social explanation be useful? What kind of phenomena might it explain? It might be helpful for understanding the differences in the success with which given individuals pursue their interests. Variations in individual's logicality, knowledge, skill, imagination, practical experience and so on are all potentially relevant to whether or not they achieve their ends.

Barth's classic study of *Political Leadership among Swat Pathans* (1959) provides an example. These Pathans, though Muslims, are divided into castes, and live in the Swat valley in Pakistan. Barth describes one of their village assemblies, which met to decide a land dispute between two leading members of the Pakhtoun, land-owning caste, Rashid Khan and Abdul Khan. From time to time each rival would disappear behind a haystack and have secret conversations with one or other of the assembly members to try and ensure they did not ally with their opponent. However, at one point in the general meeting a minor supporter of Rashid began to speak, and Abdul interrupted him, telling him to be quiet and not to contradict his betters. This high-handedness violated the Pakhtoun ethic that all men are equal and have a right to speak, and the meeting broke up in uproar, with Rashid's party eventually bringing a case against Abdul for contempt of the assembly.

Fredrik Barth (1928–, Norwegian)

(1993) *Balinese Worlds*, Chicago, University of Chicago Press.

(1969) *Ethnic Groups and Boundaries: The Social Organization of Culture Difference*. Oslo, Universitetsforlaget.

(1959) *Political Leadership among Swat Pathans*, London, The Athlone Press.

Barth claims Abdul knew this would happen, and strategically sabotaged the meeting having calculated that the price of doing so was worth the gain of ending the assembly, which his secret conversations suggested was not going his way. In the end his dependants continued to use the land and he retained his position as an effective political operator and patron. We could say Abdul won because he was more skilled than Rashid in sizing up the situation and quicker off the mark to implement the best means in the circumstances to achieve the outcome he wanted. Had Rashid been smart enough he might have been able to insist that the land issue was resolved before moving on to the case for contempt.

End-seeking 'games' as framing rational choice

Pointing to the skill in strategic action and the calculative rationality of individuals like Abdul and Rashid, can help explain events, outcomes and patterns in contexts where the ends being sought and the 'games' being played to get them, are given and can be taken for granted. The focus is *on the calculating* and not on the creation of the situation in which it is being done. *Given* a chess game, we can analyse how it is well or badly played, and explain who won in terms of the different skills, or the degree of concentration of the players. RCT is a promising approach when the problem to be explained is differential outcomes for individuals participating in the limited interaction of end-seeking 'games'.

The primary aim of the social scientist using this approach must be to clearly identify that there really is a game-like system framing the exercise of rationality by actors. An impressive depiction of such a system is Agrawal's *Greener Pastures* (1999), a study focused on Raika shepherds from the village of Patawal near Jodhpur in northwest India, many of whom also farm small plots of land. Most years, some of the Patawal households combine with others from neighbouring villages to form migratory camps which roam, sometimes for thousands of miles, and for many months, with their flocks on routes which vary from year to year. Why do they do this? And why are the range of decisions involved in initiating, organising and ending each migration differentially distributed between the camp leader (Nambardar), the camp council of elders and the owners of the individual flocks?

Agrawal shows migration is an economically rational response to the region's generally semi-arid climate when, between the monsoon rains, there is insufficient food for large flocks on the small village commons. By travelling they can find where, that particular year, forage is available for their animals – usually the stubble remaining on farmers' fields after harvest, to which the Nambardar negotiates access in return for the fertilizing droppings the sheep leave behind. Travelling through already populated environments collectively, rather than as individual households, reduces the risks of attack, increases the pool of information and skills available for a successful migration and provides potential economies of scale, and of effort-saving through delegation – although also potentially creating possibilities of free-riding or fraud. The Raikas' rational attempts to maximise the potential gains and minimise the potential downsides of their collective migration help us understand the decisions that they take. So for example, Agrawal shows how monitoring of other's actions tends to be proportionate to the risk of collective resources being illegitimately used for individual ends. He explains how the sale of sheep is undertaken by flock owners because it is a high risk decision for them and one with no economies of scale. They decide timing of the sale of individual animals which vary in quality and negotiate prices with the traders who regularly visit the camps. By contrast, the quality of fleeces and of droppings is not differentiated, and the returns on them (and therefore risks) are relatively low. Thus negotiation for the camp as a whole, including arranging for sheerers to come and sheer all the flocks together is advantageous, and is typically left to the knowledgeable and skilled negotiation of the Nambardar. He also uses his authority to delegate some shepherds to herd the camels which accompany the flocks, an economy of scale given two individuals can manage the camels of all the migrating households. He may also make the potentially tricky decision of when to end the migration, although the council of elders sometimes does this. Selected to represent different interests and from different villages, they may possess local information and be best able to deal with potential conflicts between those Raika who own sufficient land to favour an early return to plough before the monsoon arrives, and others who have large flocks and prefer delaying until the rains have produced new grazing on their village's common. Overall, Agrawal presents the modes in which the Raika 'cultivate community' and organise their lives together in the migrating camps as an outcome of 'rational calculation of self-interest ... a rational calculus over what would be in [their] material interest' (130).

Agrawal's is an exemplary analysis of the Raika shepherds' 'game'. Earlier we had a glimpse of what is involved in securing land tenure in a Swat village. But many kinds of activities can be treated as games, from actual games like playing chess, to maintaining one's position in a queue. These are all situations where the ends are pretty clear, what counts as success is relatively easy to determine, and the relevant variables which actors need information about can be defined. Each is a setting in which the self-interest of, and knowledge available to, the individual can be identified in theory – and possibly in fact, if you can ask them.

For bounded situations such as games, markets, courts, ghettos or seasonal migrations, where a special sphere of conflict has been separated out and relatively insulated from external influence, one can attempt to create abstract models of possible lines of strategic action open to individuals. One can define the logic of the actor's situation – that is the possible strategic alternatives open to them under the specific conditions, with given ends and access to certain information and resources. When one has asked oneself, 'What else could Abdul have done to get what he wanted in the circumstances, assuming he was not misinformed about the level of support for his case and about the rules governing the conduct of assemblies?' then one may feel that one has a reasonable basis for retrospectively accounting for why he acted as he did as a product of his being rational.

Explaining the social patterning of action and differences between collectivities

Conceptualising individuals as (more or less) rational and knowledgeable decision-makers may help us grasp, in particular situations, why this or that person acted as they did, and why they succeeded or failed in getting what they wanted. But can we explain broader patterns and similarities and differences between collectivities in this way? There are three main possibilities.

Firstly, just as we might explain why one individual does better than another by revealing how they more rationally pursued their goal, so in principle, we might be able to account for the success and failure of whole categories of individuals, in terms of all the members of one group having a greater capacity for rational action than all the members of another. But, just as we warned earlier, when considering the possibilities of explaining societal differences in terms of variations in the strength of their members' non-rational drives, so in this case we must not deduce differential degrees of rationality on the basis of a differential outcome, which might actually be due to quite other factors. As the next chapter will show, it is unwise, for example, to assume that lack of economic success is necessarily the result of insufficient rationality.

Secondly, without presuming any differential distribution of rationality, we might be able to explain some recurring patterns as common solutions to common problems. Thus, if we all have an interest in solving technical problems using rational techniques, patterning may sometimes result from a convergence on the relatively few effective solutions to any given problem by many different individuals and cultures throughout history. Why do so many societies develop or use written languages, bureaucracies and scientific medicine for example? Isn't this because these are all extremely powerful technical or organisational solutions? People will keep on using, or reinventing the wheel if it really is the most technically rational way of moving heavy objects along the ground (roundness is one property of wheels which is not optional or culturally relative).

Thirdly, 'game theory', a development of RCT, offers a possibility. Rather than suggesting that patterns are the outcome of different people arriving at the same solution in isolation, it tries to show how new collective patterns, including patterns of cooperation, emerge as often unintended consequences of interaction between self-seeking rational individuals. Here 'game' is as in 'game plan', the strategy an individual devises to achieve their goal. This has application in situations where an individual's ends can only be achieved at the expense of someone else. Where an individual defines others' ends as their own, altruistically, there is no incompatibility and nothing for game theory to rationalise. For example, giving up the chance to survive say, a mining disaster, to enable fellow victims to live, is best explained as caused by the particular moral commitment of the altruistic rather than as an unintended effect of a self-seeking strategy. The strength of that commitment is the problem to be explained – and here RCT is silent.

However students of the non-altruistic behaviour of markets, political selection processes like voting, and of the global balance of military power have all embraced game theory. We will start with a very simple example taken from Baert (1998: 161–2). He gets us to think about what happens when two people simultaneously want to get into a lift, whose door is only wide enough for one. If they both step forward together, blocking the door, or if they both stand back, neither gets what they want. We know the kind of thing that often happens. Each senses the problem, suggests 'You go', 'No, after you', until someone feels that enough has been done to allow them to enter first. The other quickly follows and the lift gets under way. A measure of cooperation has been achieved which benefits both self-interested individuals – without recourse to altruism. Subsequently the problem might be solved for the same individuals by taking turns and acquire a high level of predictability – and there is our social regularity.

In seeking to identify the potential for continuous, more or less orderly interaction in a social world held to be populated by self-seeking, rational individualists, rational choice/game theory typically analyses hypothetical situations and works out how individuals devoted to their own best interests, and calculating what they should do on the basis of available information, could choose to coordinate and cooperate. Where, as in the lift example, everyone can get what they want by cooperating (there need be no losers), and the individuals involved are few, it is relatively easy to understand how actions can be coordinated. Relevant information can easily be shared; everyone increases their capacity to get what they want and nobody has to sacrifice anything.

Explaining cooperation between many individuals with mutually conflicting interests is more problematic. To reach their goals each rational individual must act against the interests of some others, since there must be some losers. What then stops people relentlessly, rationally, trying any tactic to optimise their self-interest at others' expense? If most people in fact set limits to their 'nastiness', can rational choice game theorists explain why this is so? Their answer is that 'going it alone' is a high-risk strategy, especially where, because of the numbers involved, information about others' actions is imperfect. Thus most of us eventually learn that nastiness is a luxury available only to those who can rely on the future cooperation of others (by making them dependent, threatening them and so on) or who are able and willing to forgo it. For most of us selfishness is modified by dependence on others and the desire to be successful in the future. Rational choice analysis shows that in the long run it is more productive, to be 'nice', cooperate, compromise and accept less than optimum outcomes. Being altruistic in this mundane or weak sense is in fact self-interested. Being 'nice' and cultivating trustworthiness lowers risk and increases certainty about the future. Rational self-seeking involves pursuing one's interests partly by investing in the willingness of others to cooperate in the future. That means that each has an interest in making sure that their potential partners in future action will be sufficiently rewarded for their cooperation. The upshot is that we all have an interest in investing in the formation and maintenance of collectivities such as partnerships, teams, networks, unions, families, organisations and migrationary camps.

Despite its artificiality, RCT's explorations of the social consequences of rational self-interest have resulted in an intuitively plausible account of why and how rational self-seekers achieve long term cooperation. Most people, most of the time, need to enter alliances to secure the power to be gained through cooperation. But some people, sometimes, see opportunities to go it alone and maximise gains just for themselves, and are tempted to defect from alliances. Stories about members of lottery syndicates decamping with the winnings come to mind! So the problem we all have is to stop our partners defecting when they are tempted, and to keep the costs of our own contribution to alliances as low as we can get away with. We must look after our own interest but not so enthusiastically (by defecting) that our partners punish us. Usually the advantages we seek by being selfish are not so great as to allow us to make a clean break from being dependent on those we betray. Similarly, defectors are usually still valuable as future partners. So the RCT formula for social life is as follows: (1) cooperation is the original condition; (2) defection is punished by refusing to continue cooperation; (3) the first offer of cooperation from the defector is accepted and cooperation resumes. The basic rule is 'respond to nice action with nice action and nasty action with nasty action'. This is called 'tit for tat' reciprocity. It shows that it is rational for individuals to cooperate, be intolerant of defection, but to forgive returning defectors.

Conclusion

This chapter has provided various examples of the ways we might gain from considering the attributes of individuals, when seeking to account for social events and regularities. But we have already begun to point to difficulties with the methodological individualists' claim that looking at individuals alone, offers sufficient explanatory power. And we have already briefly referred to a yet more fundamental issue, that is, the validity of their claim that individuals' powers of action rest on pre-social, innate characteristics. All forms of MI assume that these powers are given. Thus even a sophisticated analysis of the context-dependence of decision-making, such as Agrawal's, nevertheless assumes the Raikas' powers of rationality to be naturally given. There is no interest in wondering whether these powers are socially formed, and might vary, not by individuals but by collectivities – as our later chapters on nature, culture and social structure will suggest.

Moreover there are further problems. Any methodological individualist reduction of the individual to one key kind of attribute loses sight of the explanatory role that other aspects of individuals might play. We have spent most time looking at RCT, which abstracts the contribution of rationality to individuals' action, ignoring other factors. This is certainly tempting, since situations of rational problem solving are ones where the analyst can easily suggest what the actor is thinking and understand their **reasons** for acting. However, not all action which can be analysed as the conduct of rational, self-seeking individuals is necessarily action of this sort. We previously presented Abdul's disruption of the Pathan village assembly as a rational move following his careful calculation of various possibilities on the basis of available information. This seems plausible. But couldn't one equally interpret the break-up of the meeting as an unintended consequence of the insult to Rashid's supporter, occasioned by Abdul's emotionally motivated, unpremeditated, anger and frustration mounting as he lost support? The whole episode can be modelled as rational, but perhaps that is not the whole story.

Rationality does not and cannot operate in isolation from the emotions. What makes something worth seeking as an end depends on its being able to attract a sufficient strength of positive feeling. Even where an end, such as making money, can be objectively quantified, the numbers do not in themselves define the worth of trying to increase them. Money has to be thought important and that involves giving it a positive emotional charge.

Rational choice theorists sometimes suggest we consider any action which achieves a desired end as 'rational', and retrospectively analyse it as though everything which led to that outcome was rationally chosen. Thus they would deem Abdul's actions rational simply because they produced the end he wanted. But this kind of move is unsatisfactory. It illegitimately protects RCT from refutation, while simultaneously avoiding the necessary but difficult task of trying to understand the spontaneous or habitual emotionally fuelled reasons that may be contributing to how people act. Conversely, of course, abstracting and focusing only on the non-rational elements of the individual is similarly restrictive, if we agree that individuals are, at least in part, rational actors.

We could say that the above difficulties for RCT connect to the fundamental problem of what rationality is. RCT requires rationality to be a universal capacity of individuals, sufficient to enable them to act. As a property originating in individuals it cannot be socially, or culturally, or historically relative. Basically, this amounts to saying that, short of ignorance and lack of skill, everyone interprets the world in the same way. We might be willing to grant that tools of rational thought, such as logic and measurement, are universal. But rationality implies more than these. It involves using ideas about what is in the world and how it hangs together. Not only does rationality operate on fields of conflicting and incomplete theories; it is profoundly dependent on actors making judgements about what is to count as 'sufficient evidence', relevance and consistency. These judgements are fuelled by emotions and cultural commitments. The formal tools of rational calculation must be supplemented by judgements about their applicability and what their results signify. How, for example, do you choose between two equally technically feasible and cheap ways of getting what you want? Do you use non-rational methods for deciding? How rational is it to choose a bicycle because of its colour? In other words, rationality itself is not entirely clear-cut and is only part of what is involved in making up our minds and choosing. Rationality is a powerful capacity of humans, but it cannot be used without something else to fill the judgemental gaps. The question for rational choice theorists is 'how do individuals fill the gaps without recourse to non-rational elements of individuals, or to existing collectivities?' We explore these themes further, especially in Chapters 7 and 8.

This also relates to another important problem hinted at earlier, when we suggested that RCT was well suited to situations (the chess game, the Swat land dispute, the Raika migration, for example) where the external parameters were already clearly set. It is suited because RCT simply assumes the social context within which individuals are located and from which their interests are derived, taking the ends they seek for granted. Once what are likely to be socially conditioned ends are given, it looks at the outcomes of individuals' rational attempts to reach them. But it does not offer a rational explanation for the choice of ultimate ends themselves, which therefore remain mysterious. Those who see the individual as fundamentally motivated by non-rational drives offer one possible way out of this dilemma, since the goal of satisfying the drives is seen as built into people. The other (non-MI) possibility again, is to look at the role played by existing collectivities. Subsequent chapters suggest plausible, alternative non-individualist solutions to the problem of where goals and interests come from.

Thus confining social explanation to the effects produced by the innate properties of individuals soon runs into a range of difficulties and also closes off a range of useful possibilities. Methodological individualism claims that there are no non-individual forces or processes which contribute to the **determination** of social reality and could feature in our explanations. This amounts to denying that what individual actors produce, intentionally or unintentionally, becomes autonomous and has some causal force in its own right, conditioning the future action of individuals. It is these products of action which are referred to as 'culture' and 'social structure'. MI sees actors as constrained only by their innate dispositions in the present, by their 'human nature', however that is conceived. But is this true? Are there other forms of constraint? Do the consequences of action *now*, acquire constraining power in the *future* independently of the individuals and their activity, which generated these consequences? Later chapters will begin answering these questions by considering the range of 'non-individual' forces constraining the actions of individuals, which, we argue, must play some role in social explanation. Before we do this however, we will use the next chapter to further elaborate on the strengths and weaknesses of RCT by applying it in more detail to some particular puzzling situations. This will reinforce this chapter's claim that individual persons play an important role in social explanation but that they are not sufficient, and must be supplemented by other, non-individual concepts.

Questions related to themes in this chapter

This chapter has considered the role that individuals as embodied objects and as rational actors can play in social explanation.

1) Provide an example of a named individual who you think played a causally important role in an historically significant event. How do you think they affected the outcome and were there any other, non-individual, factors which also contributed to the event?
2) Doctor, teacher, waiter, landlord, parent are all 'roles' that people play. To what extent do people's individual attributes affect how they play these roles?
3) List some of the problems that are posed for all societies by the fact that human individuals reproduce sexually and that human infants are unable to fend for themselves for a considerable period after their birth. Do some research and find two societies that have solved these problems in significantly different ways.
4) The unemployment rate for individuals with no hearing is considerably higher than that for people with normal hearing. If a gene for deafness were to be discovered, would this make any contribution to explaining these differences in employment rates?
5) What role does rationality play when we decide what and when to eat? What else might we need to enable us make these choices?

CHAPTER 2

Testing the explanatory value of individuals

The last chapter ended by outlining some of the generic difficulties of trying to explain social phenomena entirely as the outcome of the properties and actions of individuals. However, this book claims that while none of the key concepts examined is sufficient to explain social phenomena, all are necessary. So in this chapter we will further explore the potential of the properties of individuals who participate in them for explaining social phenomena.

For simplicity's sake we will confine ourselves to the utilitarian/rational choice account of the socially productive capacity of individuals. We have just seen that this pictures (or 'models') individuals as producing collective phenomena by using their rationality when choosing means to further their interests. It is an approach inspired by the desire to understand the behaviour of participants in markets, trying to make a profit through economic exchange. High (and/or continuous) profits are regarded as the desired and intended reward for being as rational as possible about one's choice of means – the deals one agrees to, the investments one makes, the decisions to cut one's losses and so on. Rationality is the property of individuals which enables them to assess risks, that is (for a given economic project intended to achieve an end) the potential for losses relative to the potential for gains. Rational strategic action assesses these potentials using the best information and making as precise calculations as possible. This approach assumes that what counts as 'success' can be objectively determined for each such project, although it allows that individuals are likely to balance their interest in making an immediate gain against their long-term interest in maintaining the willingness of economic partners to co-operate in the future. Short-term losses may have long-term benefits and enterprises may be pursued in interconnected collections with various time frames. The implication is that the success of the successful is sufficiently explained by their expertise as rational choice makers.

Testing for the 'sufficiency' of the rational individual

One approach to testing the strengths of a theory and method of explanation is to examine it on ground of its own choosing where its relevance and necessity is unlikely to be questioned. But the issue then becomes one of its sufficiency. If it is shown to be insufficient to provide a complete explanation, even for phenomena to which it is best suited, we can be fairly confident that it will be insufficient elsewhere. We might call this a 'sufficiency' test. Since RCT is a theory of risk-assessment based in economic action it should feel most comfortable explaining social phenomena where the risk-taking involved has an economic character. Because the theory holds that rationality is the cause of success, it predicts that successfully managing risks indicates being rational and failing to do so indicates being irrational. So to test the sufficiency of the theory we can use cases of either successful or unsuccessful economic risk management.

Financial traders

We can begin our testing of the sufficiency of rationality for risk management by briefly considering studies of contemporary finance culture and the recent activity of financial traders (Crosthwaite, 2010, 2011). Though the latter do assemble relevant information before making choices about which stocks, shares, or bonds to buy and sell, their problem is that uncertainty cannot be eliminated. Rational risk assessments can usually only go as far as producing accounts of the relative likelihood of potential losses and gains, not say what actually will happen. Thus a given rational risk assessment could equally support the range of choices between risking big losses in the hope of making big gains or risking limiting chances of big gains to minimise the likelihood of sustaining large losses. It is not the risk assessment itself which can tell you which way to go. That will depend on an additional property of individuals, namely their *attitudes* towards the potential losses and gains in question. Attitudes towards something (here, gains and losses) place it in a position of relative importance.

In the case of financial traders, they have sometimes been affected by payment systems which shifted the costs of failures from them personally and onto the institutions that employed them. But they were also conditioned by an occupational culture which not only favoured seeking gains over avoiding losses, but which discouraged caution and encouraged continuing to trade in situations where information was inadequate to make rational risk assessments. In the wake of the 2008 financial crisis, Crosthwaite discusses some of the paradoxical effects of contemporary financial markets. He shows how information inadequacy could be a perverse consequence of the development of complex hedging and derivative schemes and the intensive mechanisation and automation of much market activity aimed at reducing uncertainty by using advanced, complex forms of knowledge, administration and technology. This extreme attempt at **rationalisation**, however, actually resulted in a degree of complexity and opacity which often made it impossible for human decision-makers to engage in risk assessment as modelled by RCT.

Faced with such circumstances, Crosthwaite (2010) depicts traders who recognised their lack of control but were disinclined by their occupational culture to stop chasing big gains and to proceed instead with caution. Rather, they coped with their consequent anxiety by resorting to irrational, supernatural and magical thinking. He presents the financial trading system as inhabited by superstitious traders invoking the powers attributed to brooding supernatural beings presiding over esoteric, phantasmagorical, other-worlds. Though there is nothing automatic about overcoming fear by resorting to magical thinking, it is often resorted to when levels of anxiety are high and the desire for control and certainty is frustrated. The traders behaved in the same kind of way as the Melanesian Islanders described in *The Argonauts of the Western Pacific* (Malinowski, 1922) who refrained from magic when sailing in placid coastal waters but not when preparing for the high risk, high uncertainty of sailing into the dangerous deep ocean. They acted similarly to German citizens facing the post-First World War hyper-inflation and Israeli citizens at the highest risk of Iraqi Scud missile attack during the First Gulf War (Markle, 2010).

Bronislaw Malinowski (1884–1942, Polish)

(1922) *Argonauts of the Western Pacific*, London: Routledge (2014).
(1926) *Crime and Culture in Savage Society*, London: Routledge (1985).
(1927) *Sex and Repression in Savage Society*, London: Routledge (2003).
(1944) *Scientific Theory and Culture and Other Essays*, Chapel Hill: University of North Carolina Press (1990).

Magical thinking is not rational, but it is psychologically understandable and, Markle suggests, may actually be functional for its practitioners. Once people assume that the areas beyond their control are being taken care of by the supernatural, they are freed up to focus on those aspects of their situation where they can themselves make a difference. However, this may not always be the case. For example, Adorno (2002) saw people's use of newspaper astrology columns in 1950s America, as an attempt to reduce their anxiety in the face of a lack of confidence in their ability to understand and control their lives in a complex, late capitalist society. But he felt that, even if anxiety was reduced, this was ultimately *dys*functional. Readers should have sought ways to change the problematic social order, rather than become dependent on the astrologer's comforting advice.

Theodore Adorno (1903–1969, German)

(1941) 'On Popular Music', *Studies in Philosophy and Social Science*, New York: Institute of Social Research, IX.

(1944) with Horkheimer, M., *Dialectic of Enlightenment*, trans. by Jephcott, E., Stanford: Stanford University Press, (2002).

(1950) with Frenkel-Brunswik, E., Levinson, D. J., Nevitt Sanford, R., *The Authoritarian Personality*, New York: Harper & Brothers.

(1953) *The Stars Down to Earth: and Other Essays on the Irrational in Culture*, London: Routledge Classics, (2001).

(1964) *The Jargon of Authenticity*, trans. by Tarnowski, K. and. Will, F., London: Routledge & Kegan Paul (1973).

(2001) (ed. Bernstein J. M.) *The Culture Industry: Selected Essays on Mass Culture*, London: Routledge Classics.

Methodological individualists might see the resort to magic in high-stress situations as a property of individuals, one with explanatory power and which works alongside the property of rationality. Expanding the list of such properties is what methodological individualism has to do to preserve its method for explanations.

However, there may also be a cultural, non-individual encouragement to a magical and/or authoritarian response to stress. What definitely undermines the methodological individualist approach is analysis of *what produces the situations of stress* and consideration of the *origins of the values* in terms of which individuals arrive at their choices when taking risks. Given that individuals use values but do not originate them, MI is incomplete. We have seen that traders' high valuation of the possibilities of making big gains, led them to choose risking big losses – and even to do so when there was no means of rationally evaluating the relative probabilities of different outcomes. Israeli citizens may also have been making value choices. Those who stayed in high risk areas when there was a possibility of moving beyond range of missile attack need not have been irrational. They may rather have been making the different, but equally rational decision to risk personal harm for the gain of refusing to be intimidated and of showing their loyalty to the integrity of the

Israeli state. So it is as rational to protect oneself by avoiding Scud missiles as it is rational to support the state by not avoiding them.

Making ends meet in the ghetto

We now turn to consider in greater detail the role of rationality in a rather different structural and cultural context of economic risk-management – that of the long-term poor in contemporary capitalist societies. How might rational choice theorists explain the macroscopic fact that people are born into poverty, rear children in poverty and die in poverty, seeming unable to lift themselves out of it with the resources available to them? Surely here, if anywhere, we will find the failures of rationality which the theory predicts lead to economic weakness.

What we need, to decide if the poor are rational or not – a precondition of considering if this explains their poverty – is a description of how they really think and behave. A frustrating aspect of much rational choice theorists' theorising is its remoteness from real flesh and blood people in actual circumstances. We need concrete evidence to test the predictions based on abstract theorising, and that requires detailed ethnographic observation. Such research into ways of life offers invaluable opportunities to follow actors through the whole process of making choices. It makes it possible to identify meanings, reasoning, symbolisation, patterns, repetitions and socially reproductive effects. It provides the descriptive richness that forces development of more sophisticated explanations and more careful generalisations. Detailed ethnographic studies take a long time to produce and are relatively rare. They tend to undermine facile generalisations, making it impossible to say what all the poor do. But for our purposes, since it claims universal applicability, rational choice theory need only to be shown to be insufficient when tested against one reliable ethnographic description of those suffering long-term economic failure, to be rejected as a general basis for explaining phenomena such as poverty.

Fortunately Carol Stack's *All Our Kin* (1974), a study of the poor in 'The Flats', a black ghetto in a small affluent mid-west US city, is a gift to anybody testing the RCT of poverty. Hers is the kind of clearly expressed, politically

Carol B. Stack (1940–, American)

(1974) *All Our Kin: strategies for Survival in a Black Community*, New York: Basic Books (1997).

(1996) *Call to Home: Afro-Americans Recall the Rural South*, New York: Basic Books.

engaged and influential analysis, which our approach to practical social theorising intends to encourage. Read it to learn what constitutes good social research, theorising and writing (Duneier, 2007).

Stack began her fieldwork in the 1960s as a single, expecting mother and it continued during her son's early years. This is unusual, but was crucial in securing acceptance as an educated white woman into the domestic world of poor blacks, and particularly poor black women struggling to raise their children. She was in the same predicament, potentially dependent, needing help to make it with her child on her own (Stack, 1974: 14). Sharing this predicament over-rode differences of colour to a sufficient degree to enable her to build trust. She was thus well placed to discover the '**rules** of routine behaviour' which individuals followed to cope with poverty. Because the ghetto dwellers were descendants of black migrants from the rural South, their parents and grandparents had also been poor. This meant that little of economic value was transmitted from the past. Nobody inherited significant material resources. Everyone was very dependent on what they could get in the immediate present. Although the American economy was generally buoyant in the 1960s, the black ghetto's unemployment rate was over 20% for a variety of reasons, which included racist restrictions by the city's biggest employer (the hospital) and certain labour unions. What work was available to them was poorly paid and insecure. Social welfare (in the form of Aid to Families with Dependent Children) was ungenerous, and only available to women without a co-resident, male partner. This meant that it was impossible to accumulate surpluses of money and material goods to tide people over crises. Stack's respondents were 'forced to use most of their resources for major monthly bills, rent, utilities and food. After a family pays its bills they are penniless' (Stack, 1974: 29). In short, saving was not an option. Poverty was 'perpetual' (Stack, 1974: 22). Everyday life was lived on the edge of sustainability. Racial segregation in access to jobs, housing and services, were the external conditions setting up the economic game of survival unfavourably for blacks. Thus poor blacks, unlike better-off whites, could not use the resources distributed through a relatively impersonal market and accumulate personal private property to gain their economic ends. They had to play the game by different rules.

Stack, with expectations conditioned by mainstream white society, first realised there were rules to be discovered, when she observed ghetto-dwellers making what seemed absurdly generous gifts and loans to others. It initially appeared RTC expectations were confirmed; the poor, apparently, were not behaving rationally. At first sight it seemed irrational that people who had so little should give it away so enthusiastically. Prized furniture, new clothes, food, ornaments, tools, cars and so on, were not defended with the sort of possessiveness typical in Stack's own background. The poor were doing the opposite of what most better-off people would think sensible. They were not maintaining the exclusive access to their possessions, and on the few occasions when they had some surplus, they were not saving this for their own predicted future expenditure – Christmas, possible ill health and children's school requirements. Instead they typically gave it away to others who were facing an immediate crisis. Long-term individual economic prudence seemed alien to these poor blacks. But was this in fact evidence of their pathological economic irrationality? Are they responsible for perpetuating their own economic failure?

The way to think about the **situational logic** involved is to ask what you, as a rational individual seeking the survival of yourself and those you care about, would do in similar circumstances. What would you do in a situation where you required money to get what you need but don't have it, because the only income comes from AFDC welfare cheques or wages from the low-paid, seasonal and temporary jobs left open to you by economic racism?

There are several options. You can 'cut your coat according to your cloth' and reduce your costs of living. Right-wing politicians suggest this. But costs of living have already been pared to the bone. Stack describes certain modest expenditures, such as routine use of a laundry, which could be economised on perhaps. Though maybe they are practically required by, for example, lack of heating and drying space. Also, while Stack does not discuss this, resistance to menial tasks like hand washing clothes might be a reaction against the symbolic degradation inflicted by slavery, or motivated by a desire to ensure that, though poor, one can at least keep up appearances. However sympathetic we may be to the strategies used by socially degraded poor people for maintaining personal identities, costs of defending status and dignity could, in principle, be saved, and not to do so may seem economically irrational. Such tactics would make little difference though, because the ghetto dwellers' only major variable cost (besides those of feeding, clothing and housing) is rearing their children. Short of ceasing to reproduce themselves, the best they could do is have fewer children. But though costs might be reduced by this, the problem remains, because their poverty is so great that even a single child per adult is not easily supported. Moreover, AFDC payments were a major source of money income for the ghetto community, reducing the incentive to limit births. Even the most frugal, disciplined, individual, without dependants, is likely to fail to support themselves unaided.

Thus the second major option is to get help from inside the ghetto. What individuals cannot manage independently might be achieved through co-operation by making informal, dyadic contracts. This can potentially be done in either a hierarchical or egalitarian way (Stack, 1974: 156). If there are a few well-off individuals with surpluses, they may be willing to act as patrons to the very poor, doing them economic and political favours in return for services, deference, gratitude and moral indebtedness. Thus one possibility for poor people is to subordinate themselves to a patron. White immigrants to the US often did this through local political 'machines' run by city politicians and union elites, an opportunity barred to blacks and anyway largely removed by the 1960s, through reforming legislation. Unfortunately, even the most ambitious ghetto dwellers find it difficult to accumulate legitimately sufficient surpluses to offer patronage to inferiors. Thus, where this sort of relationship does develop, it typically involves organised criminality. Here the surpluses needed to break out of poverty are only accumulated at very high risk – as shown, for example, in Bourgois's devastating study of the mid-1980s crack trade in East Harlem (Bourgois, 1995).

So without decent incomes from legitimate earning opportunities, without much scope to reduce costs of everyday living and child rearing, without local patrons or low risk, legal opportunities to accumulate surpluses, strategic options are reduced. If we discount gambling and petty crime, tactics which however popular, are extremely unreliable for securing long-term advantages, two main life strategies, which *are* rational in the circumstances, remain: egalitarian co-operation, and individual escape (Stack's 'social mobility'). These tactics are in contradictory tension with each other. This is exactly what rational choice theory suggests; long-run egalitarian co-operation depends on punishing defectors, which is what those who attempt to escape poverty by achieving upward social mobility, are.

Stack's work shows ghetto dwellers prefer egalitarian co-operation and that this is a valid, rational choice. Everyone recognises that they need help and that the pressure is most intense when they acquire dependent children. 'You have to have help from everybody and anybody' is the common wisdom. You cannot be too proud or fussy. Since women are the prime child carers, they have the strongest interest in building a network of helpers and becoming experts in keeping these networks going. That means they tend to discipline participants, recruit new members, testing their reliability, and punishing deviants and would-be defectors. Through dyadic network building, each woman assembles a 'multi-household kin network', sometimes more than a hundred strong (Stack, 1974: 24). Biological relatives and friends are potential members, but their rights to participate have to be proved by deeds, not mere theoretical or legal claims. The idiom of kinship is used to identify individuals who actually deliver, especially fathers (Stack, 1974: 50–3). They must be self-sacrificing when necessary, giving or loaning their goods on demand, and show their commitment to caring for one another and especially for each other's children.

Stack's **ethnography** illustrates an intensity of domestic life in response to frequent crises, as individuals and households resort to the resources which, at any given moment, may be located in other households containing network members. Households themselves are fluid, with people (especially men and children) moving between them, as personal relationships falter and economic circumstances change. What are largely stable are the functioning 'alliances of individuals trading and exchanging goods, resources and the care of children' from which the constantly reconfiguring households are constructed. (Stack, 1974: 28) It is the 'informal circulation of children' between households, which facilitates the distribution and exchange of the limited resources.

People with immediately pressing needs follow the resources as they flow intermittently through the households of the ghetto. Network dependence means participants have a strong interest in gathering information about who has what, through visiting and gossip. They must also maintain their good standing, which is continually tested by requests for the giving or loaning of non-essentials, such as clothes. They typically say, 'The poorer you are the more likely you are to pay back' (Stack, 1974: 28). Ensuring one's reliability, as not being a free rider, is paramount. The most honoured service was 'child-keeping', temporary fostering of other's children. The most trusted were those with whom you could safely leave your children. As Stack says, 'Temporary child-keeping is a symbol of mutual trust ... People began to accept my trust and respect for them when I trusted my son with them' (Stack, 1974: 28–9). The closest personal relationships were between women who reciprocated 'child-keeping'. This was the powerful charge that flowed through the strongest dyadic relationships between friends and which made possible Stack's own friendship with her black contemporary, Ruby Banks (Stack, 1974: 11–21).

The final option is individual escape, or defection, the pre-condition for which is self-sufficiency. How can people get enough for themselves, avoid the costs of contributing to the care of others and deal with crises out of their own private resources without the help of their kin networks? There are potentially two ways. They can get a secure job with a wage sufficient to enable them to buy what they need in the market. This is only a remote possibility and it favours those without dependants or the likelihood of acquiring them – in practice, men. But as Stack says '... those who attempt social mobility must carefully evaluate their job security, even at poverty level, before they risk removing themselves from the collective help of kinsmen' (Stack, 1974: 24). Having broken free of one's network obligations, unemployment will be disastrous unless one can repair the old relationships or make new ones. Help may depend on those one left behind and refused to share with. They must be willing to forgive you. One can easily imagine this position of great weakness will motivate considerable caution about trying to escape.

The other way to seek independence from kin networks is through a stable marriage, that is, a long-term alliance with one other individual who is highly trusted and can supply all the necessary resources to supplement one's own in times of crisis. This is a possibility open to women, but requires finding a man with a secure job and a wage large enough to support his wife and provide for the care of any children – substituting AFDC payments and all the help supplied by the kin network. This is not an easy task given black men's weak position in the labour market.

Not only must a woman make a careful calculation about the viability of marriage as a method of escape, she must also resist the attempts of the other members of her network to prevent her defection. That networks 'fear the loss of a central, resourceful member' (Stack, 1974: 114) is shown by Stack's friend Ruby who provides a typical case of social control working against marriage because of the strong conflict between kin-based domestic units and lasting ties between husbands and wives (Stack, 1974: 115).

> Me and Otis could be married, but they all ruined that. Aunt Augusta told Magnolia [Ruby's mother] that he was no good. Magnolia was the fault of it too. They don't want to see me married! Magnolia knows that it be money getting away from her. I couldn't spend the time with her and the kids and be giving her the money that I do now. I'd have my husband to look after ... I couldn't come every time she calls me, like if Calvin [Magnolia's husband] took sick or the kids took sick, or if she took sick. That's all the running I do now ... You think a man would let Aunt Augusta come into the house and take food out of the icebox from his kids? ... They broke me and Otis up. They kept telling me that he didn't want me and that he didn't want the responsibility ... they kept fussing and arguing, so I went and quit him. (Stack, 1974: 114)

Ruby's commitment to Otis was undermined by the tactical negative gossip of senior female kin out to maximise their potential resources including the money and services which could flow to them through their daughters who themselves have children. They inhibit defection by ensuring that anybody considering marriage knows all the risks. When Ruby did eventually pluck up courage to break with the security and stability of her kin group and marry, she immediately left the area, to prevent them sabotaging her escape attempt (Stack, 1974:115).

Enough has been said to justify claiming that in this case the poor are not irrational. They think hard about their options and calculate how best to serve their own interests. The favoured method of maintaining 'multi-household kin networks' involves 'tit for tat' reciprocity including forgiving contrite failed defectors. Thus when Ruby's marriage failed she returned to her mother's house 'embarrassed, disappointed and depressed', admitting her mistake and accepting readmission to her network as a potential contributor (Stack, 1974:126). The rules of the game are learned by children as they 'observe their mothers, fathers, and other men and women in the Flats manage one another. They observe goal-oriented behaviours and try them out on each other, on their fathers when they come around, and on their mother's boyfriends' (Stack, 1974:120).

Stack's study is an ambiguous one for RCT, revealing both its usefulness and its insufficiency. On the one hand we have seen that analysing the pattern of ghetto dwellers' social behaviour as the outcome of individuals rationally pursuing their interests, clearly helps us explain why it exists as the preferred option. All the elements are there which RCT predicts on the assumption individuals are rational self-interested actors. Under conditions of severe deprivation you would expect individuals to energetically gather information about who has what, to build large networks of reciprocating 'kin' and to constantly test their reliability, as well as make calculations about how best to draw on the network without compromising their own reputation. You would expect people to give to others who are in difficulty as a kind of insurance that others will give to them in turn – particularly if they should have the kind of major crisis which cannot be solved with a small saved surplus, but which can be coped with by mobilising a multiplicity of contributions from a large number of network members.

RCT is relevant and useful in this kind of situation. The poor can be shown to be rational actors and their rationality contributes to making their actions intelligible to us. But in revealing the rationality of the ghetto dwellers Stack undercuts RCT's suggestion that economic failure is the outcome of irrational action. Here are people who are both poor and rational. To explain this we need first to identify the 'game' being played. The economic situation of the ghetto poor is tightly bounded by external conditions. These are capitalism (an economic system), and racism (a culture), in the US (a territory and state), at a certain point in history (conditioned by a past). Imagine how differently the game might look without racism restricting black access to job opportunities. How different would it have been if there had been more demand for the relatively low-skilled labour poorly educated blacks could supply? The difference between being rational or irrational pales in significance when set against the difference between being black and being white, being skilled and unskilled or being well or poorly educated. However rational ghetto blacks were in the 1960s, they had virtually no chance of breaking out of poverty through their individual efforts to better themselves. Thus RCT, though helpful in understanding how ghetto dwellers respond to their poverty, does not explain this long-term impoverishment itself.

Conclusion

RCT helps us explain what people do, as being the consequence of their choices. Choice is important. However, RCT thinks of choices as being made only by individuals making rational calculations of the best ways to get what they want. But we must remember that what can be analysed as the outcome of rational choice may actually, in some cases, be the outcome of irrational belief (as with the financial traders), emotion, habit or accident. Also people are often cross-pressured by contradictory interests. Economic interests may conflict with status ones, or with interests in pursuing satisfying personal and sexual relations for their own sakes. What is rational for achieving one goal may be irrational for achieving another. One cannot account for the choice between ends in terms of rationality.

But where interests can be taken as given, because the 'game' being played can be safely assumed, rational choice analysis can be fruitful. It helps us see, not just that people make choices but that they make them on the basis of a hand that has already been dealt them, in technical language, an **opportunity structure**. (Given that reliable employment and individualised saving were not options, Stack's people had at least five opportunities – gambling, becoming a criminal patron or accepting their patronage, cost cutting, escape and long-term sharing). This sets up what is possible at what cost, which is what has to be understood by rational actors. However, RCT does not explain how these opportunity structures are set up. Poor blacks routinely make pretty accurate 'opportunity cost' calculations. But explaining these involves resorting to social theoretical concepts such as 'racism', 'capitalism', 'labour markets', 'wage labour', 'social welfare programs' and so on, which are not properties of individuals, rational or otherwise! They are cultural and social structural concepts, which define the 'game' rather than the rationality of the players. Rationality is only one mode of relating to an environment of action. It is not the environment itself. Though the concept of the choosing individual has been shown to be relevant and necessary for social explanation, it is clearly not sufficient on its own as methodological individualists claim. At the very least it must be supplemented by the concepts of culture and social structure: which is why we also give these concepts their own chapters.

Questions related to themes in this chapter

This chapter has tested the explanatory value of individuals by considering how they make choices.

1) What do the examples in the first part of this chapter suggest about the possible causes of non-rational, magical thinking?
2) How does Stack show that the very poor inhabitants of 'The Flats' were not being irrational when they lent or gave away their valuable possessions?
3) Think of another example of a situation where people's behaviour, which might, at first sight seem irrational, can be shown to be rational when understood in context. Try to use the concepts of **'opportunity structure'** and **'situational logic'** in your explanation of the behaviour.
4) What do you routinely share, and whom do you share with? Do you follow any explicit or implicit rules about what and with whom you share?
5) Take an important decision you have made in your life and analyse the factors that made you decide to make the choice you did. How far can Rational Choice Theory explain the decision that you made?

PART II

The concept of nature

CHAPTER 3

What does nature explain?

So far we have suggested that to explain social phenomena we can begin by considering the causal powers flowing from the properties of the people who are the contemporary participants in these phenomena. We started with the basic concept of individuals because it is intuitively plausible that social phenomena are made up of people. However, we have begun to see that this basic intuition has to be refined so, more carefully stated, we should say that pluralities of individual people are *among* the basic components of social phenomena. This is a central principle of social theory. But it has already become clear that we will need to look beyond the contemporary participants to find the full array of causes which shape particular social events or patterns. The forces at work may be longstanding and relatively resistant to the activity of actors in the present. In the case of the ghetto poor such causal forces were capitalism and racism – not people and not easily changed. From here on in the book we will consider the variety of factors shaping the circumstances within which participating persons act, namely nature, culture and social structure. Another way to put it, used by Giddens, is to say that we will be discussing the different kinds of forces capable of *enabling* and *constraining* human existence which must feature in any attempt to explain social phenomena (Box 3.1).

Anthony Giddens (1938–, British)

(1971) *Capitalism and Modern Social Theory: An Analysis of the Writings of Marx, Durkheim and Max Weber,* Cambridge, Cambridge University Press.

(1973) *The Class Structure of the Advanced Societies,* London, Hutchinson.

(1976) *New Rules of Sociological Method: A Positive Critique of Interpretative Sociologies,* London, Hutchinson.

(1979) *Central Problems in Social Theory: Action, Structure and Contradiction in Social Analysis,* London, Macmillan.

(1986) *The Constitution of Society: Outline of the Theory of Structuration,* Berkeley, University of California Press.

Box 3.1   The interdependence of 'structure' and action

Social theory in the 1970s seemed polarised between 'objectivism' (which sees behaviour as determined by the causal forces of nature, culture and social structure) and '**subjectivism**' (which sees behaviour as voluntarily chosen by self-determining actors). Anthony Giddens thought both these positions were wrong because there was a bit of truth on each side. Giddens calls all the forces emphasised by objectivism, 'structure'. Accepting that these forces *constrain* action, Giddens insists that they also *enable* action, and that though actors cannot just do as they like, 'structures' are reproduced or transformed by action. 'Structure' (in Giddens's very general sense) and action are interdependent. Each is *defined* as the condition of the existence of the other, leaving it to substantive social theory to show the various and possible ways in which they have conditioned each other over time, in specific historical settings. Kalberg shows how Weber set about this task in the early 20th century. Giddens, Archer and DeLanda provide important landmarks in the discussion.

Kalberg, S. (1994) *Max Weber's Comparative Historical Sociology*, Cambridge, Polity.
Giddens, A. (1986) *The Constitution of Society*, Cambridge, Polity.
Archer, M. (1995) **Realist Social Theory**, Cambridge, Cambridge University Press.
DeLanda, M. (2006) *A New Philosophy of Society*, London, Continuum.

In this chapter we will look at our second concept, 'nature', and again consider whether it provides not only *necessary* but also *sufficient* explanation of social phenomena. As the chapter progresses we will see that the terms 'nature' and 'natural' often carry considerable moral, political and emotional weight and that they have been used in a range of ways. Different definitions will have different implications for *how* nature may be held to contribute to the explanation of social phenomena and for whether it can be held to be *sufficient* for this task. We will conclude that though extremely important, nature is insufficient unless its very broadest possible definition is adopted – and that narrower definitions are generally more useful for our aim of separating out different types of causal factors. Most broadly defined, nature means everything that exists and isn't supernatural. If we define nature in this way by placing it in binary, mutually exclusive, opposition to the supernatural then *all* the kinds of explanation we think have any value are natural ones. (In this sense we are 'scientific naturalists'.) Such broad **naturalism** can recognise that some people believe, and can act in relation to their belief in the supernatural and that this can affect outcomes. But it sees such beliefs and actions as requiring explanation in terms of non-supernatural factors. Sociologists of religion, for example, try to explain why such beliefs are held, and how they are used, but without being committed to their truth.

'Nature' as the natural environment: a conditioning factor

To begin our consideration of more restricted concepts of 'nature' we suggest that another possible common-sense understanding of why social phenomena are as they are, is that they are the outcome of nature understood as the 'natural' *environment* in which humans live. This typically refers to the plants and animals examined by botany and biology, together with the Earth's features and forces studied in geography, geology, astronomy and climatology which are understood as determined by a range of natural laws including those of chemistry and physics. In everyday thinking the natural environment and 'the laws of nature' that help explain it are often thought of as substantially unchanging. And, at least in our modern, western world, the natural environment is often spoken of as in some sense 'opposed to' or qualitatively different from the people who inhabit and are shaped by it. From such a perspective it might initially seem plausible to account for the specific characteristics, and differences between the ways of life, of peoples living in, for example, the Amazon basin, and those in the Arctic in terms of the radically different natural environments they live in. Another example might be to explain a perceived difference in the speed of technological development between temperate and tropical regions as an effect of climate on the inventiveness of the respective populations. (Perhaps heat makes people lethargic?) But how far is this kind of common-sense understanding of the role of nature as environment sustainable?

It's easy to think of examples where the natural environment has played a very important role in the outcome of socially significant events. The erupting volcano, the earthquake, the tidal wave, can have major social consequences. Pompeii was totally destroyed by Vesuvius's eruption AD 79. Lisbon's destruction by an earthquake on the morning of All Saints Day 1755, not only massively weakened the Portuguese state, but encouraged a bout of religious theorising about the doctrine of providence (notable contributors were Voltaire and Rousseau) to try to understand how a supposedly just God could allow such a disaster. Consider the importance of wind direction for the use of poisonous gas during the First World War or the 1980's Iraq–Iran conflict or for naval warfare in the age of sail. The severe winter climate helped defeat both Napoleon's and Hitler's armies when they invaded Russia (in 1812 and 1941). We might say that in these cases as well as those of various harvest failures and famines, had the weather been different so would the outcomes.

At first glance environmental *determinism* might seem legitimate in these cases. On the one side we have the forces of nature making things happen, and on the other the things and people affected. But we should remember, firstly that cataclysmic events are relatively uncommon and so offer weak support for more generalised claims. Secondly, even where events would have turned out differently if a particular factor hadn't happened, this still allows for the possibility that had other elements of the situation also been different, another set of outcomes might have resulted. There were more pre-conditions for a successful march on Moscow than just mild weather. Equally importantly, the impacts of even very dramatic environmental events are often mediated by other factors. Probably nothing could have saved the inhabitants of Pompeii, but retrospective analyses of natural disasters often show that damage might have been reduced. An earthquake might have killed fewer people, for example, if officials had enforced building regula-tions more strictly (comparing the quakes in Haiti, 2010 and Japan, 2011 might be instructive here). Or a volcano's eruption might have been less devastating if peasants had not been living on its slopes because large land-holders had taken over their farms in the valley. And once the earthquake has happened, or the tidal wave has hit, factors such as the efficiency with which people are mustered for rescue-work will affect how many survive. Many elderly French people died 'because of' an exceptional summer heat wave in 2003. But the mortality rate would have been much lower had long French summer holidays not significantly reduced staffing levels in old peo-ple's homes. More staff would have enabled better attention to be paid to the inmates' hydration.

In this kind of case we can say that the natural environment is highly significant, but not determining, because human actions and institutions which could have been other than they were, have affected the impact of those natural events which occur independently of human **agency**. In other instances the natural environment can *condition* outcomes in the sense that it makes some forms of life or some courses of action more likely than oth-ers, or easier to achieve in one place than another, but doesn't make them inevitable. Relations between nature as environment and what it conditions are those of complex interaction and mutual influence.

The way the potential resources of the world are laid out, for example the regional climatic variations, the differential distribution of native plants and animals, of raw materials, the barriers to or facilitators of easy movement or defensibility provided by mountain ranges, deserts and rivers all constitute a collection of **constraints** and opportunities (or **enablements**) among which humans have made their way since they first evolved. Though it is true that the character of the environment creates strong **tendencies** for humans to act in certain ways (avoiding harsh environments, preferring easy ones perhaps), it is also true that its characteristics only set the scene. It is up to human beings to play it out. In the case of harsh environments, short of cataclysms, negative conditions may be overcome by combinations of human ingenuity, determination and courage transforming the conditions. The Raika discussed in Chapter 1 show that migration is also a possible response to difficult circumstances. As do mercenaries who come from mountain regions where poor agricultural opportunities have inclined men to look for work elsewhere – think of the British army's recruitment of Nepalese Ghurkha troops or the 14th century Italian city states' employment of Swiss pike and cross-bow experts (McNeill, 1983: 118). Alternatively, in the case of relatively favourable conditions, which make certain beneficial activities easy, it is always possible people will fail to take advantage of the opportunities the environment provides.

But whilst people can always to some degree 'go against the grain' of what the natural environment offers or threatens them with, that it makes certain lines of action easier than others helps us understand some significant human developments. So for example, if we are interested in the origins of agriculture, we have to be interested in how plants and animals which can be eaten and used by human-beings are domesticated (Diamond, 1997). Only certain plants can be digested by humans. One reason grain cultivation began in the 'Fertile Crescent' (the eastern Mediterranean through Turkey, and south-east into Iran) rather than elsewhere, was because that region had by far the greatest concentration in the world of large-seeded grass species as potential candidates for domestication. These species developed there because its climate alternates between wet and very dry and plants had to evolve large seeds to survive the dry periods. Because these seeds can be both digested by humans and stored for long periods, cereal farming was more likely to start there. Ancient Egyptian civilisation was one memorable outcome of this grain cultivation, with the fertile alluvial soils of the Nile's flood plains providing good opportunities for agriculture and a reliable food supply. Further, the fact that these plains were surrounded by inhospitable deserts effectively 'caged' the peasantry making it easy for landlords to exploit and tax them. Exceptional geographical circumstances provided the basis for an exceptional accumulation of power as Mann's historical sociology shows (Mann, 1986) (Box 3.2).

Just as some grasses were intrinsically more suited to cultivation than others so only a few species of animals are suitable for domesticating. Those

Michael Mann (1942–, British)

(1981) *Consciousness and Action among the Western Working Class*, Basingstoke, Palgrave.

(1986) *The Sources of Social Power: Volume 1, A History of Power from the Beginning to AD 1760*, Cambridge, Cambridge University Press.

(1993) *The Sources of Social Power: Volume 2, The Rise of Classes and Nation States 1760–1914*, Cambridge, Cambridge University Press.

(2003) *Incoherent Empire*, London, Verso.

(2004) *Fascists*, Cambridge, Cambridge University Press.

(2005) *The Dark Side of Democracy: Explaining Ethnic Cleansing*, Cambridge, Cambridge University Press.

(2012) *The Sources of Social Power: Volume 3, Global Empires and Revolution, 1890–1945,* Cambridge, Cambridge University Press.

(2012) *Sources of Social Power: Volume 4, Globalizations 1945–2011*, Cambridge, Cambridge University Press.

Box 3.2   Mann: 'social caging' and the emergence of nation states

Mann uses the idea of 'caging' to help understand how nearly all humans today live in nation states. Caging implies the constraint of human activity by natural geographical boundaries or by social institutions (including nation states). Strong *social* caging is a very recent (less than 1%) part of human existence and was facilitated by the exceptional vulnerability of a very few populations to geographical caging. This spatially concentrated them as a basic resource for forming much larger organisations. The geographically caged could not move away from domination attempts, which, if successful, could result in larger and more hierarchical forms of social organisation.

Phase 1. The beginning of human existence (evidence for the earlier parts of this period are limited).

99% of human experience to date.

Hunter-gatherers moving relatively unconfined by space; un-caged.

Family groups and bands; 20–70 persons.

Loose confederations of bands: 175–475 persons, tendency to split above about 400–500 persons.

Unacceptable domination resisted by splitting and moving.

Very difficult to make power advantages long-lasting.

Phase 2. Begins around 10,000 BC.
0.6% of human experience to date.
Transition to agriculture, domesticated animals, permanent settlements.
'Delayed return investments' create an interest in not moving.
The beginnings of long-lasting differences of 'social power'.
Division of labour, social inequality.
Some increase in the amount of 'social caging'.
No literacy or cities – yet.

Phase 3. 3000 BC onwards.
0.4% of human experience to date.
Beginnings of emergence of 'Civilisations' (few at first).
E.g. Ancient Egyptian kingdoms exploit caging effect of harsh environment surrounding the fertile Nile flood plain.
'Civilisations' are characterised by:
  Centralised States and permanent power structures,
  Consolidation of elites, inheritance of dominance and privileges,
  Stratification and Patriarchy,
  Literacy and Administrative expertise.
Capacity to integrate populations greater than 500 overcomes earlier tendency to split above this size. Nation states emerge.
Strong 'social caging'.

Mann, M. (1986) *The Sources of Social Power, Vol. 1 A History of Power from the Beginning to AD 1760*, Cambridge, Cambridge University Press.

which pay off well are large, relatively docile, fast growing, mammalian herbivores, living in herds, with a dominance hierarchy in non-exclusive territories. Sheep, goats, pigs, cattle, horses (all Eurasian in origin) and dogs are the ones providing a good return on the effort to domesticate them (providing meat, milk, manure, propulsion for ploughs, transport and military assault, hunting assistants, and materials such as bone, wool and leather). Their suitability is proved by their adoption all over the world. Whereas, despite their potential as meat there are no grizzly bear farms and no rhinoceros mounted cavalry! These species just cannot be domesticated.

The domestication of large-seed grasses and of relatively docile animals is an example of people taking advantage of favourable conditions. There was nothing inevitable about the development of farming. But given the human interest in and devotion of effort and thought to securing reliable food, it is not surprising that effort should have first succeeded where the conditions made it relatively easy. The early farmers of the Fertile Crescent simply exploited the naturally available, easily grown, stored and digested grains. They were luckier, we might think, than the inhabitants of the Amazonian basin where manioc was available. To make it edible they had first to perfect the technique of squeezing out poisonous prussic acid from its roots. Surely a tribute to their ingenuity, not to say courage, this case shows that people may begin cultivation despite discouraging environmental conditions.

Hence it is reasonable to see chains of causation between climate, potentially domestic plants and animals, and farming. We can also extend these causal chains further into human social organisation. Thus if we wonder why cities and early forms of extended power networks (such as the ancient Egyptian kingdoms) emerged when and where they did, part of the reason is that they depend on settlement, which in turn depends on the reliable food production of farming. So the environment (climate, plant and animal evolution) makes farming possible, which then permits large-scale sedentary organisation (Box 3.2). It can also create the possibility of destroying nomadic peoples, hunters and gatherers with whom the farmers and city dwellers come into contact, thus helping us understand why, throughout history, these earliest forms of life have tended to loose out to agriculturalists (Brody, 2001). This is because settled societies with large storable food surpluses can support non-agricultural specialists in, for example, organisational technique (bureaucracy), the control of information (literacy), military technique (metallurgy and guns) which make them powerful enemies. They may also have another, devastating if unintended 'weapon' up their sleeve, in the immunity they have acquired to the diseases of their domestic animals, diseases which can be fatal to those conquered by settled societies (Diamond, 1997).

Before we proceed it is important to reiterate that we have discussed environmental effects as creating possibilities, potentialities and tendencies. Environmental conditions constrain and enable human action, favouring certain lines of development and disfavouring others. But it is always possible that people may choose not to take advantage of favourable circumstances or that they may struggle to overcome unfavourable ones. There is nothing automatic about responses to the environment.

Nature and the natural environment as subject to change

When we began the previous section by noting the elements which are generally thought of as comprising the natural environment, we suggested the latter is sometimes assumed to be unchanging. There is one sense in which this is the case. That is, it is subject to natural 'laws' which science currently sees as universal and immutable – though there are still uncertainties about what some of these laws might be. So, for example, masses of sufficient size will always exercise some degree of gravitational force on each other, holding air pressure constant water will always boil at a specific temperature and aluminium expand more than tungsten when heated. Moreover, in these cases scientists can now *explain why* these correlations occur by referencing the *processes* which produce them, rather than merely predict what will happen in the future by generalising from what has happened in the past.

However, if we can talk of the unchanging laws of nature, in all other respects the natural environment is subject to continual processes of transformation – although at a very wide range of rates and in some spheres so slowly that we can afford to ignore their changes as relevant for social explanation. The planet Earth and the solar system of which it is a part have a millennia-long history. The gravitational pull the Earth exerts has changed as its mass and density have altered in the course of its formation. The seasons with their relatively autonomous causal powers are not fixed for all eternity and may be influenced by other developments in the solar system. Land masses change their position by virtue of plate tectonics and continental drift. Plant and animal species have evolved through natural selection, influenced in part by interaction with other, also evolving, species. They don't have a static or pre-determined essence (Box 3.3). Processes of change in the natural environment have their own dynamics. They have been going on long before humans were around and will continue if and when we are no longer here.

Though the world would get along very well without us (Weisman, 2007) humans are here, and as natural beings are capable of contributing to environmental change – as our earlier discussion of the development of agriculture and animals' domestication begins to show. Sometimes to a comparatively insignificant degree, sometimes with enormous effect, sometimes

---

Box 3.3   Distinctions between essentialist and modern scientific understandings of nature

The word 'nature' is often used to refer to the essential character of something. An example of a loose and everyday version of this sort of usage is to claim that 'it's in the nature of cats to catch mice' – meaning that mice-catching is a core or essential aspect of 'catness'. The essentialist understanding of nature conceptualises reality as populated by different kinds of things each formed by its unique, internal, self-forming potential, or 'nature'. These natures may involve some typical internal developmental process such as a life-course, but these processes are not themselves the product of any process (unless a supernatural creator is introduced). On this view, natural things can be characterised by their specific internal process, (sometimes referred to as essence, potential or telos) which determines what they are and can become – a thing's nature defines its potential. Individuals have often been thought of in this way.

Early natural science (inspired by Aristotle) aimed to describe the timeless 'natures' or unique changeless 'essences' of different things. Essentialist knowledge understands a thing by identifying it with an appropriate essence which is then seen as permitting prediction of what is possible for it. 'Knowledge' involves revealing how the world conforms to a pre-existing collection of candidate essences, showing how particular bits of it fit into the predetermined pattern. There is a strong link between this form of science and religious thought, the idea that everything is preordained fitting belief in an original creator.

The achievement of modern science (Galileo, Newton, Darwin, Marx and Einstein) was to abandon the search for timeless essences. Breaking with religious thought, it regards reality as radically under-determined, chaotic, with only occasional moments of orderliness and predictability. Koyré speaks of moving from a 'closed world to the infinite universe', that is from demonstrating an order of essences, to finding only statistical patterns among external and contingent relations shaping everything. Seeing everything as in a constant process of change with outcomes uncertain, modern scientists look for the sources of ordering, such as gravity, energy and mass, which might be at work among these relations. Phenomena, instead of becoming, predictably, what was dictated by their essential natures, are now recognised as emerging, each as the outcome of their unique history of external relations – subject to very general laws of nature. Armed with this sort of understanding no modern concept of nature or science, including social science, can employ the idea of timeless 'essences'.

Koyré, A. (1957) *From the Closed World to the Infinite Universe,* Baltimore, John Hopkins University Press.

with deliberate intention, sometimes as an unintended outcome, humans have always had an impact on the natural environments they inhabit.

However, because both humans and the non-human elements of the natural world have their own properties and dynamics, there are limits to the changes humans can bring about. How humans are able to change the natural world is dependent on their own capacities and the qualities of what they are dealing with, both of which change. People can breed new types of plants and animals, tunnel through mountains, alter the course of rivers, create new, synthetic materials. But they can only do so within the parameters of their own historically changing capacities and of what nature itself permits. How easy it is to blast through a mountain depends on the geological and physical properties of rock and the chemical properties of available explosives. What new materials and which new animals can be created is ultimately limited by physical, chemical and biological natural processes with their own logics, our understanding of which may change over time. Thus recent advances in humans' understanding of genetics and genetic engineering have enabled them, for example, to create new life forms with characteristics previously thought to be impossible, such as cows that produce spiders' silk in their milk. Some want to call such creatures 'artificial' or 'unnatural' – and may judge them as morally undesirable on these grounds (Box 3.4). But they can also be considered 'natural' in so far as though not spontaneously occurring in 'nature', 'nature' allows them to happen. They are biologically possible, although they are potentialities which may be judged unlikely to have happened without human intervention.

Should a given human intervention cease, the processes of the natural environment will reassert their autonomy, interacting with whatever is left from the episode of human intervention. Stop gardening and non-cultivated weeds will soon return; neglect the flood defences and dry land may revert to marsh. But simple reversion to a pre-intervention condition is rare. The legacy from the human activity is usually detectable, and even short-lived human actions can switch nature to another path of development. Many

---

Box 3.4   Nature as religious and moral value

Social science uses the concept of nature in social explanations differently from two historically related and very influential ways of referring to nature in modern western culture.

First is the religious idea of nature as eternally given conditions of existence which set limits to human ambitions. Here nature becomes an ultimate authority – a kind of 'god' concept. This understanding of nature is deeply embedded in contemporary romantic culture which sees it as an alternative, perhaps 'purer', realm which can heal the damage of human foolishness and moral failure.

Ethical naturalism links to this, distinguishing right from wrong by the extent actions conform to 'nature's rules'. Defining what ought to happen in terms of what happened in the past is empirical conservatism. However, choosing our ideals can benefit from a sound understanding of the objective realities of the natural processes at work in the context of their application. Whether an ideal can or cannot be realised in principle, ought to make a difference when deciding what to value.

From the point of view of social theory, the romantic legacy must be qualified. We do need to refer to the powerful forces and processes which condition social phenomena and our efforts to realise moral values. However, respect for things 'natural' does not mean that we view nature as if it were a religious power, a separate order of being from that which it is used to criticise, namely human activities and social arrangements thought of as 'artificial', 'against nature' or 'un-natural'. Unsentimentally recognising that nature and human activity exist inseparably on the same ontological plane makes them accessible to scientific causal analysis.

contemporary deserts result from agricultural and other practices which 'ruin' the land. But once ruined, a challenging environment has been created with its own relatively durable, self-subsisting properties. Though the desert may have taken centuries to produce, once established, it is set on its own developmental course which may no longer depend on human intervention to remain in being. Much of what we refer to as 'the natural environment' is the product of human activity which has subsequently acquired autonomy from the processes which originated it and now functions to contribute to setting the scene for contemporary action.

Humans as part of nature: moving away from binary thinking

In the preceding sections we have shown that nature, in the form of the natural environment, conditions human life but that human activity also contributes to shaping aspects of that environment. Our use of the concept is thus *relational, interactional* and *historical,* not essentialist and timeless. Thinking of humans and nature as separate, even opposed, entities is wrong. Another reason why this is the case is that humans must be thought of as *part of nature,* as *one species among others living on Earth,* with their own particular natural and potentially developing species characteristics. They have their own biological, physical and chemical properties as we began to show when considering individuals in Chapter 1. There we discussed the implications of thinking of individuals as biological bodies with certain physical properties at least partly linked to their genetic endowment. We also considered the consequences of conceptualising them as innately endowed with either, or both, non-rational drives and natural capacities for reason. The methodological individualists saw key causal powers as located in individuals, and believed these were 'already there' prior to any interaction individuals had with each other – an assumption we suggested was problematic.

However, there is an alternative tradition of recognising the natural character of humans which, rather than attempting to derive species characteristics by generalising from the prior properties of individuals, *begins* by focusing on species characteristics, deriving the attributes of individuals from this. In particular it stresses the human species is a *social* species. Theorists in this tradition variously recognise that humans can't in general survive or even initially become fully human without co-existing and interacting with others of their kind. A correlate is that the human species naturally develops culture and is dependent on it.

Marx takes for granted the human ability to interact and focuses on the higher level of collectivisation, that is, why there is an organised social world of roles to occupy and kinds of people to become. He suggests that this happens because humans must produce what they need to survive. To produce they have to cooperate. Lone individuals cannot do this producing, except for short periods, and then only with the benefit of knowledge gained from other people. Marx contrasts humans with other species. The latter are typically confined to their own specific ecological niches, while the nature of humans is both consciously and collectively to transform the natural world into things they can use, enabling them to make large parts of the globe habitable for themselves. Homo sapiens does not just adapt to its environment, but as already seen, deliberately adapts environments to meet its needs – developing its own capacities in the process. This is not to say that every anthropogenic change to the environment is intended – for example humans' developing capacity for industrialised production may produce unwanted effects on the climate. It's also true that some other species modify their habitats. Beavers as well as civil engineers can alter the course of rivers and thus wider environments when they build their dams. But beavers don't consciously aim for these broader consequences nor calculate the costs and benefits for those who live downstream. Moreover, it seems likely that, while they may improve with practice, their basic dam-building capacity is innate. By contrast, civil engineers are highly dependent on their ability to learn from their predecessors, although they may also develop and add to the stock of civil engineering knowledge. This distinction between ways of behaving that have to be learned, including learned from others, and those which are innate and immediately hard-wired into a species, is important and clearly recognised by Marx.

However, he doesn't say much about how humans develop this capacity for meaningful interaction with others – how babies become adults. To understand how an additional process of **primary socialisation** works to generate a human person out of the genetic endowment of the neonate, we can initially turn to the equally seminal work of Mead. This provides a complementary way of showing that there is no contradiction between thinking naturalistically about human beings and thinking non-individualistically. For both Marx and Mead, 'being social' is built into the very foundations of the human species (Goff, 1980).

Karl Marx (1818–1883, German)

(1844) *Economic and Philosophical Manuscripts*, Moscow, Progress Publishers (1959).

(1845) *The German Ideology: Introduction to a Critique of Political Economy*, (includes *The Theses on Feuerbach*) London, Lawrence and Wishart (student edition) (1974).

(1848) *The Poverty of Philosophy*, San Francisco, Elibron Books (2005).

(1848) *The Communist Manifesto*, Harmondsworth, Penguin (2004).

(1852) *Eighteenth Brumaire of Louis Bonaparte*, New York, International Publishers (1994).

(1857) *Grundrisse*, Harmondsworth, Penguin (1993).

(1867–1894) *Capital, Vols 1, 2, 3* Harmondsworth, Penguin (1992).

George Herbert Mead (1863–1931, American)

(1934) *Mind, Self and Society*, Chicago, University of Chicago Press (1967).

De Silva, F. C. ed., *G. H. Mead: A Reader*, London, Routledge (2012).

Mead tackles one of the fundamental social theoretical problems; how are the raw materials of human babies transformed into socially competent people? He suggests it is a process of successive stages during which children acquire the necessary language skills to symbolically represent themselves and others, play social roles, and respond to others' expectations. Basic for social interaction is the ability to imagine how others, in various social positions, are likely to respond to one's behaviour. Social cooperation requires this sort of imaginative anticipation – a skill which cannot be developed in isolation (Box 3.5).

Mead tries to specify a universal process of socialisation undergone by all young of the human species, given genetic endowment alone is insufficient to produce adult human beings. However, while everyone must undergo the broad processes he depicts – the specific ways primary socialisation is effected (and understood), is culturally variable. 'Childhood' is not a given (Ariès, 1996).

Box 3.5   Mead: on mind, self and society

Traditional religious thought regarded a person's unique personality as 'a fixed substance.... given at birth to be carried eternally'. By contrast, Mead's rigorous naturalistic approach treats the self as 'an achievement rather than a given fact'. He derives personal consciousness and the self from participation in social interaction. Human life depends on social interaction using language. Communication is less to express a private meaning than to secure a response from others. Meaning is thus logically and functionally tied to interaction – meaning is defined in terms of the 'response' of the other. Imaginatively anticipating others' responses Mead calls 'role-taking'. This is a precondition for individuals to 'know their own minds' and form intentions.

Born as objects, individuals over time become subjects/self-conscious. They are always objects but acquire a selfhood. New-born children begin unintentionally communicating – that is, carers treat the child's behaviour as if it were meaningful and act accordingly. Children learn that their behaviour elicits specific responses from others and is therefore meaningful. They learn to anticipate these responses and treat their own behaviour as an object which can be used to produce the desired interaction and response.

Playing develops 'role-taking' skills, particularly in multi-role games which require players to imagine and anticipate the reactions of various others to their own activity. As it grows older the child becomes able to handle social abstractions, distinguishing roles from actual persons playing them. At the most sophisticated level of role-taking, the child learns how to relate its actions to impersonal, highly 'generalised others' such as communities, states and traditions – social objects which may not be persons at all. At this stage we are a long way beyond the person-specific intimacies of early childhood where no distinction can be made between person and role. We have here an explanation of the beginnings of self-consciousness and 'mind'.

The structure of the self has two parts, the 'I', the pre-social unique bodily responses to experience, and the 'Me' which reflectively interprets what experiences might mean from the different view-points of relevant other people, and tries to anticipate such responses when deciding what to do. The 'I' is associated with uncontrolled spontaneity and the 'Me' with self-control. A person is a self-recognising object who has learned how to represent itself, using the symbols used by others. Thus Mead defines the self as 'an organisation of social attitudes'.

Mead believes persons are in an unending process of self-development, learning how others might regard them or respond to different kinds of behaviour or communication. Persons and society are not fixed but in a condition of continual change. Mead is against the reification of society, arguing it is a condition rather than a thing.

Mead, G. H. (1934) *Mind, Self and Society*, Chicago, University of Chicago Press (1967).

The way the boundaries between childhood and adulthood are drawn, the degree of difference between counting as a child or as an adult, the kinds of skills the former must acquire to qualify as the latter, and how they acquire them, all vary. As does the time taken to develop from one status to the other.

One key variant is the degree of importance attached to children learning self-control of bodily functions and drives, and sexual, violent and emotional responses. The extent to which individuals, particularly as infants, have their psycho-somatic systems conditioned or 'attuned' (Elias, 2000) to control themselves automatically, has profound implications for the kind of human persons they become and whether their modes of interacting are typically spontaneous or more considered. The socially conditioned degree of ability to inhibit spontaneous drives and reactions comes to work below the level of rational deliberation and choice. It penetrates so deeply into the individual that what is in fact a product of specific historical, social and cultural contexts is subjectively experienced and often explained as being universal, inevitable and natural (Bourdieu, 1985). A range of theorists have suggested there are significant differences between the deep character structure of individuals in the West in different historical periods. They have investigated historical changes in the broad context of interaction – especially in the character of stratification systems and the economy, in the range of social relations and the extent of monopolisation of violence by the state. They argue that the long-term historical shift from traditional, relatively local to late modern, relatively extensive forms of social life, particularly through their implications for child-rearing, has produced significant changes in individuals' 'second natures' built on the basis of what is genetically given (Sennett, 1986; Simmel, 1997; Elias, 2000; Weber, 2005; Archer, 2012). Mead shows that the ability to become a human being with a sense of self and a capacity to interact with others, is itself dependent on the experience of social interaction. The authors just listed suggest that the specifics of that interaction affect the particular kind of human beings we become.

The important difference between behaviour which is innate and that which is learned is sometimes referred to as one between nature and culture. But it is clear that what we have just referred to as 'second nature' is itself a product of that entirely natural process which is culture. The cultural elements of nature interact with the non-cultural elements. The nature:culture binary (which thinks of culture as unnatural) is very common in various societies and we may want to explain why this is so, or investigate particular cases, but it is not useful for building social scientific explanations. For this task we need an historical and interactional understanding of 'nature' and to recognise humans' capacity for and resort to culture as one of their natural, species characteristics. When moles make mole hills these are natural products which do not require the concept of culture to be understood. But when humans build cathedrals or office blocks these are cultural products, made possible by human's natural capacity for cultural production.

In this section we have shown that we can recognise humans as part of nature by focusing on their species rather than their individual characteristics and that it is the social nature of homo sapiens that forms the core of both Marx's and Mead's understanding of humanity. We should now note, however, this does not mean that conflict is ruled out. Humans' intrinsic sociability makes coordination possible, but the models we have been discussing allow plenty of scope for non-harmonious interaction and antagonism between the coordinating social units. Though we are necessarily interdependent, cooperation is not automatic or free of tension, as we saw in the last chapter, where the poor try to control those they depend on. One major implication of cooperation is a degree of organisation and that requires the use of social power, which is generally unequally distributed. Indeed the necessity of production is one very powerful incentive for some sets of people to act together to try to dominate others and force them to cooperate in the productive process on terms unfavourable to themselves. This is a major insight of the political and economic thought of Marx and later, Weber (Box 3.6). Cooperation can involve the threat or use of various kinds of power including physical force. Generally the dominated and exploited are weak because they have few alternatives open to them and are compelled to cooperate on disadvantageous terms just in order to survive. So, these non-individualistic

Max Weber (1864–1920, German)

(1895) *Weber: Political Writings*, (ed. Lassman, P. and Speirs, R.) Cambridge, Cambridge University Press (1994).

(1904) *The Methodology of the Social Sciences*, (ed. Shils, E.A. and Finch, H. A.) New Brunswick, Transaction Publishers (2011).

(1904–05) *The Protestant Ethic and the Spirit of Capitalism*, (trans. Kalberg, S.) Oxford, Blackwell (2002).

(1917–19) *Ancient Judaism*, New York, Free Press (1952).

(1921–22). *Economy and Society*, Vols 1 and 2, (ed. Roth, G. and Wittich, C.) Berkeley, University of California Press (1978).

From Max Weber: Essays in Sociology, (ed. Gerth, H.H., and Mills C. W.) Oxford, Oxford University Press (1958).

Max Weber: Readings and Commentary on Modernity, (ed. Kalberg, S.) Oxford, Blackwell (2005).

social theories are not the least bit 'innocent' about the character of 'society'. They recognise that social organisation involves the exercise of social power and that social reality is therefore not necessarily the 'solution' to the problem of antagonism and conflicts of interest, as individualists suggest. Not just individuals, but society composed of various kinds of interest groups can be a source of 'nastiness'.

So, we can say that when we are trying to explain social phenomena, these kinds of non-individualist understandings of human nature immediately direct us to the social level. However, as we have variously shown in Chapter 2,

---

Box 3.6   Conceptualising the fundamental sources of domination: Marx and Weber

People are vulnerable to being dominated when they lack the power to ensure control over the means of satisfying their fundamental needs without being subordinated to others.

	Fundamental needs which constitute the basis of interests	Bases of domination
Marx	Transformation of natural resources into utilities by human labour	Ownership of the means of production enables owners to dominate labour in relations of production via threat of removing access to the means of production. E.g., landlords control access of peasants to land (feudalism); capitalists control access of workers to the means of industrial production (capitalism)
Weber	Transformation of natural resources into utilities by human labour	Similar to Marx above
	Security: protection from physical violence	Specialism in threatening violence and/ or offering protection (as exercised by warlords, mercenaries, police etc.)
	Access to sources of meaning	Specialism in supplying meaning (as exercised by prophets, priests, religious orders, scientific specialists, intellectuals, etc.)

we cannot account for differences in outcomes entirely in terms of a universal attribute (such as rationality), and this applies whether the attribute is seen as based in the individual or the species. Thus pointing to humans' naturally given and necessary capacity for sociability in general, will only get us so far. It is an answer to why we always find people 'collectivised', grouped together, but not to why the boundaries between collectivities lie here rather than there. It helps us understand why all people cooperate to produce, and have language and are able to interact, but does not explain why they organise production in one way or another, nor why we find the particular range of languages that we do. However, later chapters will show that the concepts of 'culture', 'action' and 'social structure' can all be usefully developed with reference to an understanding of human nature as primarily social. As we shall see, these three concepts provide powerful resources for helping us get to grips with the problem of what makes collectivities different from one another – the problem of 'difference'.

Nature and the role of technical rationality and technology in social evolution

In this chapter we have now presented humans as constituting a species among others, one characterised by its intrinsically social nature and which is both affected by, but also to a degree shapes, the natural environment in which it lives. As Marx made clear, one element of nature, the human, has the capacity to mediate the other, the environment. However, this then poses a major problem of social explanation – how to analyse the process of **mediation**. Since mediation involves human actors making choices and decisions, the issue is how they make choices about relating to the natural conditions of their existence.

In seeking to answer this question we are again faced with a divide between those who place the attributes of individuals at the centre of their analysis and those, including Marx, Weber, Durkheim and Parsons, who suggest this is insufficient to account for how humans deal with their environment. All four insist on the importance of the structural conditioning of individuals to which Weber and Durkheim add an equal emphasis on the relatively autonomous effects of culture (Parsons, 1937) (Box 3.7). Aspects of their legacy will be considered in Parts III and IV after we have completed the present discussion of naturalistic social theory which tries to do without reference to structure or culture. One very influential strand of such theorising, historically and in contemporary culture, is associated with social evolutionism and is closely related to the individualistic rational choice theory (RCT) examined in Chapters 1 and 2. It holds that the really significant choices people make in responding to the environment are essentially *technical choices* informed by empirical knowledge and logical reasoning. These choices matter most because they are motivated by the requirements for survival set by the environment. Being efficient means achieving survival in the prevailing environmental conditions with the least effort.

Emile Durkheim (1858–1917, French)

(1893) *The Division of Labour in Society,* New York, Free Press (2014).

(1895) *The Rules of Sociological Method,* New York, Free Press (2014).

(1896) *Socialism and Saint Simon,* London, Routledge (2009).

(1897) *Suicide,* Harmondsworth, Penguin (2006).

(1900) *Professional Ethics and Civic Morals,* Oxford, Taylor and Francis (2002).

(1903) *Moral Education,* Currier, Dover (2002).

(1912) *The Elementary Forms of the Religious Life,* New York, Free Press (1995).

Talcott Parsons (1902–1979, American)

(1937) *The Structure of Social Action, Vols. 1 and 2,* New York, Free Press (1968).

(1951) *The Social System,* New York, Free Press (1964).

(1954) *Essays in Sociological Theory,* New York, Free Press (1964).

Box 3.7   Talcott Parsons and the 'action frame of reference'

In *The Structure of Social Action* (1937) Parsons argues it is possible and desirable for scientific sociology to treat human beings as *subjects* capable of voluntary *action*. He aims to show the 'scientific relevance' of subjectivity is that behaviour is the product of actors. There is a tension between treating people as free and as objects of analysis by a determinist science. However if actors make choices using criteria of value, or 'legitimacy norms' and this choosing makes a difference to outcomes, then it becomes scientifically relevant as a sort of 'causation' in its own right.

Parsons presents early theories of action such as utilitarianism (Box 1.2), as seeing human actors choosing the ends of action 'randomly' and the means to achieve their chosen ends according to the 'norm of rationality' (empirical knowledge and logic) typical of technical problem solving. Parsons claims Durkheim and Weber, by contrast, adopt a complex model of action and actors, which shows that actors use both norms of rationality or technical adequacy and of *legitimacy.* Legitimacy norms help explain ('de-randomise') the choice of ends and choices between equally efficient means. *Action is therefore 'doubly normative'.*

For Parsons, classical sociology (from which he excludes Marx) sees all forms of social collectivities (families, status groups, religions, occupational categories and so on) and their related cultures, as sources of legitimacy norms. From this perspective the individual is an actor by virtue of being a member of various collectivities which reproduce cultural traditions and value systems.

Though closely related to it, social evolutionism differs from RCT in that it does not leave open the question of the ends people seek. RTC holds peoples' goal is 'happiness', a highly variable and subjective concept, while social evolutionism argues that all human activity has the same functional and objective end – survival. RTC, we suggested, needs supplementing with a consideration of the character and origins of the values which might guide the use of rationality when making choices. Social evolutionism on the other hand, explains the ends of action by suggesting that they are driven by a biological imperative to survive and so are not really chosen at all. Given survival is a universal imperative, the scope for choice is reduced to selecting between alternative means for ensuring it. Choice is thus essentially technical and is the way people mediate the impact of the environment. Technical reason (grounded in the rationality of individuals) is the basis of the various technologies and forms of social organisation with which humans respond to the problems set by the environment. Though there is scope for choice in the sphere of technology, the constraints set by the environment and the criterion of efficiency, on what can function as an effective solution, are seen as pretty tight.

We need to recognise that, though an element of choice is allowed, this approach to explaining social life is nevertheless a form of naturalism. Though nature is seen as acted on by human beings this fact does not weaken the claim that everything is being caused by a natural environment, understood as having its own independent characteristics and internal processes. This is because the capacity of humans to influence outcomes involves yet one more set of these natural processes. Using their naturally given capacity for technical rationality they develop technical, objectively effective, solutions to the problems set by the natural environment. There is no escaping the circle of nature – the natural environment determines humans who in turn shape it. From this perspective technical rationality is only a sort of halfway house on the road from natural determinism to recognising the relative autonomy of 'culture' (to be discussed in Chapter 5); it is 'culture' reduced to the knowledge involved in technically solving environmental problems which humans naturally undertake. It is the one element of culture which theorists committed to explanation in terms of environmental forces feel able to accept, since it is thought of as the cultural element most directly influenced by such natural forces. Granted the superior technical power of the human species (which eventually equips itself with the forces of industrialism), it is still nature which calls the shots, setting the agenda for human action. The limited freedom to make technical choices is no escape from being ultimately determined by the two components of nature, the natural rationality of humans, and the natural environment.

We might suppose that the environment will most clearly 'spell out' the strategies people need to follow when at its most extreme – in regions of great cold, or heat and drought for example. In such unforgiving conditions it might be thought that what counts as an efficient solution to the problems are obvious. Knowledge and rationality should be enough to decide what needs to be done. For here the dangers of making a technically inappropriate choice will be greatest. People will be forced to live in a way that ensures their immediate survival. Their choices ought to be highly predictable. But they are not – as the following chapter's discussion of technical choice in examples of extreme environments will show. We will see that even in these extreme cases, people can live in the same environment, at the same time, in some-what different ways. Harsh environments powerfully constrain how people act, but they do not appear 'automatically' to compel the use of particular technologies nor the development of particular ways of life.

When enthusiasts for explaining social life as shaped primarily by technology try to explain technological variation in similar environments, they typically point to the fact that technology changes over time. Using technical rationality and its criterion of efficiency, to invent technologies, implies a constant search for ways to improve efficiency. So here we have a sort of 'motor' for historical change; technology is constantly being 'upgraded', which explains why there is also change in the institutions and culture associated with particular technologies. Given that what counts as an improvement in efficiency is thought of as decided by applying objective tests (such as energy and costs savings for example), the history of technical development can be interpreted as a story of 'progress'. It is held that over time technology will get better and better, and all peoples will eventually converge on the relatively limited number of highly efficient technologies which have emerged.

The least effective techniques and organisational forms fall by the way-side, the most effective ones are maintained and developed. The course of change is therefore directional, not merely random.

The social evolutionists who see history as a story of technically driven progress are impressed particularly by the development of scientifically based industrialism. Industrial technique appears so much more powerful than others that its claim to superiority seems irresistible. Its status as the cutting edge of human development is based on the promise that it offers the greatest power to deal with whatever the environment might have in store for us. Sometimes making an analogy with Darwinian theories of natural evolution, social evolutionists believe there is a 'progressive' trend for all societies to 'converge' towards industrialism. This is understood broadly to encompass material techniques and related institutional and cultural elements, such as capitalist markets, nation states, rational law, bureaucracy, individualism, secularism and egalitarianism.

Evaluating naturalistic explanations of technical choice and technical development

We can accept that industrialisation has been a very important and continuing development in history. But explaining why it has happened is difficult. A fundamental problem is the co-existence of technologies of different levels of sophistication, and the fact that societies have become industrialised at different rates.

Attempts to explain this from the naturalistic perspective, argue *either* that there are natural variations between different peoples (often characterised as 'races') in their capacity for technical reason, *or* that it results from the different potentials offered by the particular environments they are adapting to. In the first case those making slowest 'progress' are seen as intrinsically less well endowed with technical capacities. If technical reason is a property of human nature, but some humans are defined as having more or less of it, then we have to find some additional principle of nature to explain this difference. Doctrines about intellectual differences between, for example, 'races' try to do that job, though we would argue, fail.

In the second case, some environments are seen as offering more resources for development than others, better raw materials, easier communication routes for example. Or it may be argued that harsher locations, ones with less easily available food supplies perhaps, or more demanding climates, spur people to invention, to overcome these difficulties. We have already provided some instances where the different global distribution of natural resources can help us understand large-scale historical developments and contribute to explaining why particular techniques (for example grain cultivation) first emerged in one place rather than another. Clearly, technical rationality and the potentialities and demands provided by environments are major inputs into the process of technical development. But they are not themselves sufficient to explain it. The human mediation of the environment certainly involves making technical choices, but these choices are not only informed by environmental pressures and technical reason.

Firstly, those who argue people develop their technologies in response to the natural environment alone, fail to recognise the impact the political relations between sets of people can have on the development and uptake of techniques. Economic and political competition between the states of Europe helped hasten industrialisation. Europe's first place, and quick pace, on the road to industrial development was also influenced by the (largely exploitative) relations it had with peoples in other parts of the world who made slower 'progress'. For example, the forced removal of Africans to work on slave cotton plantations in Britain's New World colonies (from the mid- 17th century), and the forced transformation of India from textile exporter to that of raw cotton only (during the 18th century), both contributed to the great 'success' of Lancashire cotton manufacture. Moreover, convergence on particular technologies may have as much to do with a desire to keep up with, or deal with competitors, as with any original dissatisfaction with the way existing techniques coped with external nature. Native North Americans were not necessarily dissatisfied with their bows and arrows and did not feel a lack of guns and horses, until Europeans invaded them. When that happened they quickly became expert horsemen and equipped themselves with guns to defend themselves. It was the new element in their social surroundings, not the natural environment that produced this change in their technology. Similarly, nuclear technology was pushed forward in the context of world war and super-power confrontation. Technological choices are usually framed by the circumstances of intra-human competition (Runciman, 1983).

Walter Garrison Runciman (1934–, British)

(1966) *Relative Deprivation and Social Justice: A Study of Attitudes to Social Inequality in Twentieth-Century Britain*, Harmondsworth, Penguin (1972).

(1972) *A Critique of Max Weber's Philosophy of Social Science*, Cambridge, Cambridge University Press.

(1983) *A Treatise on Social Theory: Vol. 1 The Methodology of Social Theory*, Cambridge, Cambridge University Press.

(1989) *A Treatise on Social Theory: Vol. 2 Substantive Social Theory*, Cambridge, Cambridge University Press.

(1997) *A Treatise on Social Theory: Vol. 3 Applied Social Theory*, Cambridge, Cambridge University Press.

(1998) *The Social Animal*, Ann Arbor, University of Michigan (2000).

(2004) ed. *Hutton and Butler: Lifting the Lid on the Workings of Power*, OUP/British Academy Occasional Paper.

Second, technological change (including 'development') can be influenced by '**autocatalytic**' or 'feedback' processes which technologies may set in train. Technologies have positive or negative long-term consequences for what can be done in the future. Farming was one such autocatalytic process, multiplying food supply, reducing birth intervals, expanding populations which made everyone more dependent on the success of farming and so on. But it was also vulnerable to soil exhaustion so was not necessarily sustainable, which is why today the 'Fertile Crescent' is no longer fertile. The wetter Western Europe has been less prone to soil exhaustion but having chosen to expand agricultural productivity using agricultural chemicals and manufactured animal feed, it similarly faces a crisis of sustainability.

The same point can be made about industrialism. It was developed to raise production and place life on a securer footing. But its inherent tendency to exhaust raw materials and pollute, makes it itself a threat to sustainable existence. It becomes a problem rather than simply the solution to scarcity. We should not just focus on the dramatic cases such as the Chernobyl (1986) and Fukushima (2011) disasters and think of the downsides of technologies as exceptional. The point is rather that the experience and consequences of past technologies set the scene and present us with choices, for future technical development. The way people have solved technical problems in the past, with the successes and the negative consequences, becomes a condition of how they must now solve them. This leads us to recognise that technical choices must use non-technical values to guide which benefits we want and which prices we are prepared to pay and these are not decided by natural imperatives. They are decided by the way risks are assessed.

This point has implications for the meaning of 'progress'. Awareness of the downsides of so-called advanced technologies forces us to ask: 'are we entirely better adapted to our environment than our predecessors?' Is driving a car using ozone-depleting, non-renewable fossil fuels, unequivocally an advance on earlier forms of transport? This kind of question also suggests that what counts as 'progress' is always relative to some goal and that 'survival efficiency' is as variable a concept as the 'happiness' of the utilitarian. If what we want is quicker, easier movement for us in the present, the car may well be progressive. But if we want to maintain a useable environment for future generations then maybe it's not. There is similarly no value-free answer to whether ways of producing which increase products but reduce leisure, are advances or not. Hunter-gatherers in well-endowed environments can find enough to live on with a few hours activity each day. Are they necessarily less well environmentally adapted than farmers or industrial workers, who own more goods, but have to work much harder? Problems of the insufficiency of technical criteria on their own, to account for why people react to their environment as they do, also arise when there are different, but equally effective means available to reach the same goal. You may need to paint your house's exterior woodwork to protect it from rot, but does this explain why you chose a green rather than shocking pink for the window frames?

Conclusion

In the various sections of this chapter we have shown how both the natural environment and human nature should be thought of as only relatively fixed. While the environment is subject to its own autonomous dynamics of change, its actual development can also be affected by human action, and human action can mediate the effects produced by any given environment at any particular point in time. Conditioning is the concept we need to combine (a) recognition of the force of the environment in shaping human life, with (b) recognition of the capacity of humans to intervene to modify the way the environment impacts on them. In the final two sections we focused on theorists who saw humans' natural capacity for technical reason as the key explanation for the way they respond to the natural environment, but began to suggest some limitations of this kind of account.

The relation between environment and technology is obviously an important dimension of human existence, but to explain why people deal with their environmental problems in the ways that they do, requires that we refer to more than simply the environment and their technical knowledge. The idea that members of the human species have the capacity to transform nature positively, implies that they can impose their will on it to some degree, and that implies that they use more than technical knowledge to assign meaning to their worlds. This is the lesson of Weber's and Durkheim's critiques of utilitarianism (Box 1.1). Humans have much more than the essentially reactive capacity for technical problem solving claimed by environmental determinists or social evolutionists. In the chapters on culture we will consider this issue of 'meaning' and what a full-blown concept of culture has to offer social explanation.

However, to give the idea that social behaviour is driven by the objective forces of the physical environment the best chance to impress us, we should look at cases where the force of the environment seems extremely strong. The next chapter will therefore consider in some detail studies of how the behaviour of people living in some very harsh environments is shaped.

Questions related to themes in this chapter

This chapter has looked at various understandings of how nature conditions social phenomena.

1) Was the devastation caused by Hurricane Katrina in New Orleans in 2005 a 'natural event'?
2) Both humans and other animals can affect the environments they live in. What are the most significant differences between the ways in which beavers and civil engineers build dams?
3) The conditions of human action have two implications: they make it possible to do certain things (enable them to happen) but at the same time they limit what can be done (constrain them). Think of examples of *natural* conditions of action which clearly show this two-sidedness.
4) Think of some examples of cases where the way in which humans have treated the natural environment at one point in time has later affected the options open to them or their descendents.
5) Why do you think that the moral and the natural have often been connected? Are there any difficulties in deciding what is natural and what is not? Should naturalness be the definer of the good?

CHAPTER 4

Testing the explanatory value of nature

In this chapter we will follow the same tactic as we did in Chapter 2. The limits of the concept of 'individuals' were shown by considering cases of social phenomena which seemed most likely to be explained by it. This easily demonstrated the necessity of using the concept. But the concept was also shown to be insufficient on its own to explain the sort of cases preferred by enthusiasts, thereby establishing its insufficiency in general. In Chapter 2 we called this strategy a 'sufficiency' test. In the case of 'nature', we will focus the discussion on arguments about the influence of the natural environment.

Before examining cases chosen to test the sufficiency of natural causation, we will briefly reaffirm its necessity. First of all, there are the obvious cases; for example there can be no doubting the destructive potential of cataclysmic events. At least at the moment of initial impact of sudden and unexpected events such as floods, volcanic eruptions, tsunamis, the environment is clearly necessary and approaches being sufficient to do all the explanatory work. But these sorts of cases do not prove the universal necessity of referring to natural causation – for this we need examples of collective phenomena where, on the face of it, natural conditioning appears to be absent. But remembering the discussion of the limits of binary thinking in Chapter 3, it is not surprising that it seems impossible to find cases where nature is absent: you might like to try. Collective phenomena are embodied by human animals, with all their natural properties, inhabiting a material world with all its properties – there seems to be no escaping natural conditioning. We might, for the sake of argument, suggest that the cultural practices of the creative arts, with their variety and freedom to change, avoid natural conditioning. But given the duality of enablement and constraint it is better to assume that cultural freedoms are made possible by natural conditioning as well as limited by them. As we will see when we discuss the concepts of culture and social structure, even cases which seem independent from natural conditioning and highly autonomous nevertheless interact with, and are conditioned by, whatever human or environmental circumstances they occur within.

Returning to the testing of sufficiency, enthusiasts for environmental determinism should accept a tougher case than those of environmental disasters. Though still favourable, enthusiasts ought to test 'sufficiency' against cases with some historical depth. Such cases are ones where human beings have been subjected for substantial periods of time to the constraints of severe or 'extreme', environments. Since patterning takes time, we need non-cataclysmic cases where people have time to respond to the environment. These cases give us the opportunity to see if environments most likely to pattern behaviour actually do so (thereby supporting an argument for sufficiency), and if any other factors are at work.

If we accept, with most environmental determinists, that the effects of the environment are mediated by the technology which humans develop to cope with it, then studies of technological development provide good cases for testing such determinism. Is the technology which people use entirely dictated by the nature of the environment, and do they respond to the environment only with technical rationality? Enthusiasts for the powers of the environment and technical reason say 'Yes'. They argue that technological choice is tightly constrained by what is technically functional for survival in a given environment. That is the basis for their arguments about the tendency for societies to converge on increasingly 'efficient' technologies. In 'extreme' environments these pressures are at their greatest and technological choice seems most limited.

Technological determinists suggest that history is a story of 'progress' from 'primitive' to modern, as people discover the most efficient methods for dealing with nature. We can test this theory by making two kinds of comparisons. First we can compare the technological choices of different peoples in the same 'extreme' environment, who the theory would claim to be at the same level of development. Do they have the same technology? If not, what else, besides the environment and technical reason, influences their technological choices? Second, we can compare the technological choices of peoples the theory defines as more and less advanced in terms of their respective technical development when relating to a given 'extreme' environment. Is it the case that the so-called advanced cope best? How is technical competence to be judged? European colonisation provides cases of confrontation between technologies with very different principles and powers, where we can examine the possibility of technological alternatives and what influences technological choice. How do we explain the abandoning of established technologies for new ones, or the persistence of so-called primitive technologies and the failure of the more recent, 'more efficient' technologies to eliminate them? Is history really a story of technological 'progress'?

Before considering actual cases, what do we understand by an 'extreme' environment? We use this term to refer to environments which we would find difficult to inhabit, as typical people used to living in industrialised societies. This kind of understanding informs, for example, the use of the word 'extreme' in the advertising rhetoric of the leisure industry trying to sell excitement and opportunities to 'test oneself' against elemental forces which many feel have been excluded from our normal everyday life. The cases we choose in this chapter are intended to excite this sort of response.

However this is not to say that these environments are actually easy to live in even by people who have done so successfully for generations without the benefits of industrialism. The dangers are real because these places demand specialist knowledge and techniques and are relatively intolerant of mistakes. Survival requires a level of concentration and attention to detail, which a more forgiving environment does not. But although environments vary in the degree of difficulty and specialisation they impose, it remains true that the perception of an environment as extreme depends partly on what one is used to. Amazonian visitors to modern cities might be as frightened by the 'extreme' traffic menace, as the inhabitants of those cities would be by peccaries, jaguars, piranhas and even monkeys.

The divergent technological choice of two Amazonian forest peoples

Our first case is the upper Amazon forest environment, the region of the border of Peru and Ecuador between the Maranon and Napo rivers, which flow east into the Amazon basin, an area which has probably been inhabited for thousands of years by many tribal groups. We discuss the technical hunting choices of only two tribes, the Achuar and the Huaorani, studied by Philippe Descola (1997) and Laura Rival (1996, 2002) respectively. Here are societies whose hunting practices are constrained by the same 'extreme' environment and which allow us to see the extent of any technological convergence. If there are differences, in order to explain them, we shall have to find factors additional to environmental constraints. Moreover Rival's accounts also discuss recent changes in Huaorani hunting technology, providing an opportunity to see if these are motivated by considerations of improved 'efficiency'.

First, both peoples are subject to an environment with a specific range of potentially edible plant and animal species living either on the forest floor or in the canopy. Their economy as a whole has always been diverse including cultivating manioc, gathering fruits, and ensuring the continuity of forest growth, as well as hunting, and today includes manufactured goods donated from such outsiders as missionaries, teachers and oil companies, or bought with money from the likes of eco tourists in towns and villages made accessible by new roads, outboard motors and airstrips (Rival, 2002: 177). But for the moment we will focus only on traditional hunting practices, concentrating on the techniques for taking the major prey species. These are herds of peccaries (tusked pigs foraging in vegetation on the swampy forest floor), and various monkeys in the canopy (spider, howler, but mostly the abundant and highly territorial, woolly). However birds and monkeys can only be killed with projectile weapons (traps being too difficult to set at great heights). So it is no surprise to learn that Amazonian peoples have developed sophisticated bows and blowpipe technology to fire arrows made deadly with curare poison. Large and tree-living species can be efficiently taken. The basic fact that the Amazon forest environment contains abundant tree-living prey strongly disposes people to develop these, particular, hunting technologies. Similar technology has been independently developed by other forest peoples, for example in South-East Asia.

Descola tells of a hunting trip with an Achuar couple, Pinchu and his wife, Santamik. Pinchu uses his blowpipe to kill a woolly monkey and two peccaries from a foraging herd, which they have tracked, aided by his wife's pack of dogs. The Achuar use their indigenous technology for both types of prey but are enthusiasts for the scarce rifles and shotguns they get by trading, and which have been available in the region for a century. As a note for later, they keep orphaned baby peccaries as pets.

Contrast this with the traditional behaviour of the Huaorani ('real people'). Their preferred prey is woolly monkeys killed using blowpipes. They do not use bows and arrows, though the technology is available among their immediate neighbours. They never kill tapirs or giant river otters despite this being technically feasible. They do not deliberately track peccaries in the way Pinchu did, however, they do kill them with spears to defend their settlements from any occasionally encroaching herds. Many peccaries are killed as the herd is driven off and the abundant meat is eaten to excess, making people ill. So here is the problem. Why do these people refuse to kill certain species such as tapirs, prefer to hunt woolly monkeys (and other tree-living prey) and confine their use of blowpipes to these, and do not routinely hunt peccaries, killing them only with spears when forced to drive off a herd?

Here is a case where clearly the technology chosen has to be effective enough to provide sufficient meat from the available prey. Consider meat supply. By routinely only killing birds and monkeys and not peccaries, the Huaorani do not suffer any shortage of meat (enjoying around 200 grams per person per day). By the same token, the Achuar need not routinely kill peccaries. Neither people can be said to be more or less technologically efficient on that count. Next, consider hunting technique. Both use blowpipes to kill monkeys because projectile weapons are necessary. Both could use bows and arrows but these are not more efficient and may be less. Shotguns (available to the Huaorani since the 1970s) are useful but scarce, expensive, noisy and not more efficient at bringing down monkeys and birds. The major difference lies in the refusal by the Huaorani to use blowpipes to kill peccaries. But their use of spears for this purpose is not less efficient; it is just a close-quarters killing technique as opposed to the distanced one of the blowpipe. Huaorani insist on closing with peccaries to spear them, while Achuar are happy to keep their distance.

It is not possible to explain this kind of patterned difference in technological choice in terms of differences in availability of technical alternatives or in terms of differences in technical rationality. Both peoples are technically competent when responding to the environmental pressures. They act sustainably by not over-killing monkeys and, for example, by leaving fruit on trees in monkey territories for them to eat. So what else is influencing this difference? Rival suggests that Huaorani preferences about prey, and rules governing the use of weapons, are not dictated by the environment or considerations of technical efficiency. What they do is certainly technically efficient but could be done differently without loss or gain in efficiency. So what explains their strictness about the choice of prey and weapons?

Rival points to a 'striking homology' between the way Huaorani traditionally treat animals and one another. Until recently they have always lived away from the main communications routes provided by rivers, in upland nomadic enclaves in extreme isolation between powerful neighbours. This is important: their response to external threats (associated with cannibalism in the past) has been to move away. They defended their independence by strongly emphasising their boundary, closing themselves off from outside influences and relying entirely on their own resources. They refused to trade with, or marry, outsiders. In this tightly closed social world cross-cousin marriage is typical, and strong, life-long, brother-sister alliances are encouraged. For people constructing a social world in this way, territorial monkeys are 'sociologically interesting' (Rival, 1996: 150). With other Amazonian tribes – including the Achuar (Descola, 2005) – the Huaorani do not sharply contrast the human and the animal world. Huaorani hold humans and animals belong to a single world – one structured into predators and prey. Thus tapirs and giant otters are not prey because they 'are like brothers' with bodies similar in size to human beings (Rival, 2002: 76). Woolly monkeys are recognised as individuals and as members of unthreatening groups with which reciprocal relations can be established. Monkeys and Huaorani look after each other. Monkeys are admitted within the Huaorani social order. However peccaries are not. There are no pet peccaries here, but monkey babies orphaned by the hunt are taken care of – they may even be breast fed. As members of parasite-infected, destructive, uncontrolled, anonymous crowds, peccaries symbolically represent distrusted outsiders, enemies to be fought off. Huaorani contrast the corrupting soft, bland flesh of peccaries with the tough, chewy virtue of monkey meat.

But the closeness of relations within this introspective world, between individual people living in the longhouse, and generally between animals and humans, which preserves control and independence against outside threats, itself presents dangers. First, sufficient distance must be maintained to preserve a necessary minimum of internal **differentiation**. The most obvious danger is that of incest. Secondly, and more routinely, cooperation is undermined by jealousy between same-sex siblings who compete for the affections of siblings of the other sex. Brothers tend not to get on well with brothers or sisters with sisters. Also outbreaks of often homicidal violence may follow any community member's death, since only death in old age is held to be natural and unintended and not requiring a response. Those who kill community members become outsiders.

It is more complex than this, but enough has been said to follow the logic of Huaorani technological choice. Take first the relation between peccaries and spears. Peccaries are actually destructive but Rival's analysis suggests that they also symbolically represent human enemies (outsiders) who over thousands of years have been construed as cannibal predators. They are therefore killed with the weapons used to wage war, namely hardwood spears used by armies of men in a high state of aggression. The group fights off the herd. That the spear is associated with killing enemies is suggested by the fact that shotguns, though available, are not used to kill human enemies. Enemies have to be ferociously speared to death, close up. In Rival's words the spear is 'a technology of exclusion' (Rival, 1996: 157).

Now consider blowpipes and monkeys. This is a 'technology of inclusion' because it is a technology of deliberation and self-control. Blowpipes are products of a long, skilful production process resulting in objects representing beauty, maturity and 'a sense of balance'. All children grow up playing at 'blowing' and both men and women learn the posture and breath control to become competent. Blowpipes are given to kin but not traded, and good ones become precious, inherited items. Blowpipe hunting is a quiet, measured process, lacking in forcefulness or aggression (Rival, 1996: 154–5). Its effectiveness depends on judging the right distance, not too close to alarm prey, but not too far (beyond 30–40 metres) to be out of range.

The distance and time which blowpipes introduce in relations between hunter and prey provide a model of how relations between all insiders should be conducted. Using a blowpipe depends on relations of distanced intimacy with the target prey. It is possible for a targeted monkey to 'speak with its eyes' and be spared (Rival, 1996: 150). Among a strongly endogamous, isolated people, where internally generated emotional tensions can become explosive, the habits associated with blow hunting, of stopping to judge the distance, of being close but not too close, are highly functional for the social order. Giving way to anger disqualifies membership – it is no surprise that 'it is much easier to cease to be Huaorani than to become one!' (Rival, 2002: 185). It is this requirement to consider carefully how to deal with those who are close to you, to inhibit spontaneity, which makes blowpipe technology potent as a symbol regulating Huaorani social relations.

As Rival puts it, 'The blowpipe, which can either bring closer (if too far), or remove (if too close), is a powerful instrument for monitoring social closeness. It puts men in [....] control, as defenders of endogamous relationships [threatened by] both incest and open exchange' (Rival, 1996: 157). As such its use cannot simply be a matter of its technical effectiveness. Considerations of effectiveness are not irrelevant, meat is needed and weapons have to kill prey, but such criteria do not help decide between equally effective technologies. The two examples show that in a situation of alternatives, technical rationality is insufficient to explain choices even in response to a harsh environment, and we have to find other reasons such as the social relations symbolically represented by weapons.

Descola doesn't offer a comparable analysis of why the Achuar chose their specific hunting methods, though he does show that there are parallels

TARGET	Peccaries = Outsiders/Enemies	Monkeys = Members/Insiders
LOCATION	Forest floor (realm of corruption)	Forest canopy (realm of purity)
VALUE OF MEAT	Low: Soft, bland, fatty	High: Tough, chewy, muscular
MODE OF KILLING	Occasional, communal, aggressive	Routine, individual, non-aggressive hunting
WEAPON (technical choice)	Spears – used by Men: Technology of exclusion	Blowpipes – used by everyone: Technology of inclusion
MODE OF RELATION	Emphatic, physical rejection	DISTANCE KEPT

Figure 4.1 Huaorani technical choice

between the key divisions they draw in the natural and in their social world. Nature is split into plants and animals and Achuar society into consanguines and affines. Women nurture plants referred to as their children, while the men perceive themselves to be 'in a complex relationship of competition, negotiation and complexity' (Descola, 2005: 23) with the animals they hunt, just as they are with their brothers-in-law. Perhaps they do not need to use different hunting techniques to symbolise key differences in social relations since the plant/animal divide does this for them. Horticulture seems to have been important for the Achuar, whereas Huaorani were reluctant gardeners (Rival, 2002: 100).

Technical choice and change depends on more than simple functionality. It is no surprise to learn therefore that as a result of forming relations with trusted outsiders (American missionaries, first contacted in 1956), the Huaorani have started using shotguns to kill all kinds of animals. This is not simply because missionaries bring the guns or that guns are more efficient than blowpipes (which they are not). It is because the traditional weapons no longer have to do so much symbolic work. The commitment to fierce separateness has been undermined, opposition to open exchange and the need for careful management of interpersonal relations, relaxed. The young travel the rivers to experience the ways of the towns and develop new tastes in dancing, music and industrially produced foods. Given a more favourable attitude to outsiders, the rules about prey and weapons have become less strict and a matter of inter-generational argument. Brothers may get on better, brothers and sisters may not need to be so close, or marriage partners chosen from among one's cousins, and the special relationship with woolly monkeys and the rest of the forest has changed though it is unlikely to be abandoned. Spending more time in semi-permanent river-side settlements, more dependent on agriculture, river traffic and manufactured goods, means a new way of life less dependent on the meanings and meat of monkeys. Perhaps some other animal will become as 'sociologically interesting' to represent the newer social choices. However, Rival ends her major monograph by noting that Huaorani retain a sense of their and the forest's vulnerability to outside influences, which now include major oil companies. They sometimes say, 'What does not grow decays. The times of war and destruction will not be long in coming' (Rival, 2002: 188).

The Dunne-za: aboriginal hunters versus advanced industrialism in British Columbia

We have seen that environmental pressures underdetermine technological choices. Projectile weapons are necessary to hunt in the forest but where there are alternative, equally efficient weapons, which ones are used to kill which kinds of prey is decided by non-technical criteria. We now move to consider the claim that technical change is a linear development where later technologies, better able to cope with the environment, displace earlier less efficient ones. If blowpipes give way to shotguns, this ought to be because they are more efficient, but as we have just seen, the more recent technology of the Huaorani is not more efficient and is adopted as part of a whole 'package' of transformed social relationships, particularly with outsiders. Technological choice clearly has political and symbolic dimensions.

The political framing of technological choice can be further explored by considering another, and a longstanding, confrontation between exponents of the oldest and new technologies. Hugh Brody's *Maps and Dreams* (1986) gives a moving account of the confrontation in the Canadian sub-arctic region of British Columbia, between the Dunne-za people (long referred to as the Beaver) living in reserves along the Alaska Highway between Fort Nelson and Dawson Creek, and an advancing frontier of oil and natural gas exploration, commercial logging, farming, roads, tourism and sport hunting. As such the Dunne-za have long experience of the same forces of change that are now accelerating in the Huaorani's Amazon forest.

The Dunne-za developed an efficient hunter-gatherer way of life in this region following the end of the last ice age 12,000 years ago. The sub-arctic is an extreme environment, not just because of the winters, but because it forces hunter-gatherers to be more hunters than gatherers. Hunter-gatherers who live in generalised ecosystems (like the Amazon forest) benefit from substantial opportunities to collect food (the Huaorani eat a lot of fruit for example). For them hunting is a secondary source of food. Such environments are relatively tolerant of hunting failures. However the sub-arctic is a specialised ecosystem with large numbers of a few species and little edible vegetation (mainly summer berries). Dunne-za are therefore primarily hunters, their traditional diet coming from large, dispersed, land mammals (moose and caribou), supplemented by smaller prey (beaver, rabbits, grouse and fish) (Paine, 1971: 162–3). Brody estimates Dunne-za people harvest between 450 and 900 grams of meat per person per day, much more than the Huaorani. The cold and dependence on meat mean that Dunne-za hunting has to be highly energy efficient. Mistakes are costly.

Despite this, until recently (1970s), the Dunne-za shared the hunter-gatherer tendency to be confident they can feed themselves. This confidence depends on three principles of practice – movement, open access and flexibility, which the Huaorani (who see their forest as a 'giving environment') also recognise. Expert knowledge of animals, the environment and development of efficient hunting techniques yield reliable supplies of meat for everyone in a long-term, sustainable way. The taking of prey is limited by the principle of least effort, (hunters giving up an area or species long before their predation affects the capacity of the prey to reproduce (Paine: 159)) but also by restraint, by not killing more than is needed. Where there are only a few species, sustainability depends on being able to move between areas. So the critical issue for the Dunne-za is being able to move freely within their very extensive hunting grounds. Brody gets them to draw the boundaries of their hunting grounds on maps. These show huge areas, including places which may have only been visited once in a lifetime. The whole of these areas are thought of as stores, or 'banks', of food which may be taken when needed. On this basis, hunter-gatherers appear unconcerned about shortage and enthusiastically share food, behaving 'as if they had it made' (Sahlins, 1968: 86).

Central to successful living by hunting for thousands of years, is this method of responding to difficulty by flexibly changing species and/or hunting area. Brody tells of hunting trips conducted in a spirit of improvisation and willingness to follow any favourable circumstances which crops up (Brody, 1986: 35–48). A 'state of attentive waiting' is typical (Brody, 1986: 43). So although there may be an intention to kill, say a cow moose, (the largest, but relatively uncommon, prey) other smaller animals (rabbits, trout) will be taken on the way, if the opportunity presents itself. Initial searching for tracks is apparently random. Failure to pick up clues to the whereabouts of large prey simply prompts moving to another area. The basic assumptions are that alternative areas are accessible and that the prey they contain has not been taken already.

However, for five centuries the aboriginal population of North America has confronted the successive frontiers of European colonisation. This has imposed powerful competition for the resources of the land from people operating a different economic system. Europeans cleared forested land for farming and hastened the near extinction of the bison whose northern range once extended into Dunne-za territory. Dunne-za responded to competitive pressure by withdrawing westwards further and further into their 'reserve' hunting grounds, the eastern foothills of the Rocky Mountains. Provided there has been animal-rich territory available to retreat into, the Dunne-za have moved away.

They have always known how to change. Willingness to move is only one of their ways of flexibly responding to difficulties. They have survived by developing an economy and technology based on traditional values and skills, but accommodated to the Europeans' world of money, markets and the modern state. The fur trade, well established by 1800, is now thought of by the Dunne-za as essential to their economy. It partly explains their English name, the Beaver (they supplied the furs to make the hats so fashionable among the British elite in the late 18th century). The trade reinforced their traditional skills (Brody, 1986: 56–7; 2001). Over centuries they have adopted guns, horses, metal traps, snare wire, plastic sheeting, pickup trucks, chainsaws, electricity, store-bought groceries, and now take radios with them when hunting. But none of this has displaced skills such as tracking, or making snow shoes and walking long distances in them.

A series of 'white man' frontiers have whittled away at the land, the animals and the Dunne-za's opportunities to continue moving away. The 19th century saw farming and railways extended ever westwards, bringing homesteaders and several gold rushes. The indigenous peoples were confined to living and hunting on reservations. Essentially this amounted to conquest. During the 20th century the whole region has been rapidly opened up. White farms expanded rapidly between 1900–1920 followed by the growth of white trappers during the 1920s and 30s. Prospecting for coal, minerals, oil and gas has gone on for a century or more. Today the whole area of the traditional hunting grounds is riddled with roads, the roughest of which can be travelled by four-wheel drive pickups. The current incursion results from a synergy between the temporary access roads cut deep into the forest for oil and gas prospectors, and the weekend leisure activity of sports hunting by urban Canadians with pickups, high-powered rifles, and poor navigation and tracking skills. (Sports hunters kill four times as many moose in two months as the Dunne-za kill for food in a year (Brody, 1986: 231–7).)

In the face of these incursions, Dunne-za confidence has faltered. A central figure in Brody's story, the elder, Joseph Patsah, encounters a seismic drilling camp with its air strip, and a 'hippie' squatters' cabin in Quarry, his most remote and precious trapping lands, and is over-taken with pessimism (Brody, 1986: 9–13, 181, 224–5). There is no more time, no more room for the white man's intrusion. When asked by a white hunter for advice about where to hunt, he jokes ruefully, 'Deer, moose, chickens, cattle, pigs, everything gone to the west. Pretty soon everything will be gone. All the meat' (Brody, 1986: 271–2).

Confrontation between renewable meat and fossil fuels

Here we have an example of a hunter-gatherer way of life being virtually destroyed by an industrial society whose emergence was possible, as explained in the last chapter, because of agriculture. Arguably the Dunne-za have endured what is now beginning to face the Huaorani, particularly as oil interests seek to expand in Ecuador. Rationally calculating opportunity costs, and assessing risks, the Dunne-za people skilfully invest in renewably harvesting the abundant animals. Their energy comes from meat. In a sub-arctic environment farming was not an attractive or necessary option. Though the Dunne-za are rational, energy efficient, and do no irreparable damage to the land or its animals, their method has limit conditions. The most important for this discussion, is maintaining a balance between the rate of killing animals and sufficient territory to allow them to reproduce. The higher the rate, the bigger the territory required. Joseph's pessimism flows from realising that due to the activity of whites the rate is going up while the territory is effectively getting smaller.

The incursions of Europeans, in both Amazonia and British Columbia, show that the sustainability of hunting has depended on a political condition of low inter-societal competition between people of similar, low social power. Europeans could colonise America because they had a huge power advantage, in weapons, organisation and numbers, derived ultimately from a long history of agriculture. Their technology was superior as a technology of conquest. But the ability relatively quickly to dominate and dispossess non-industrial people is only one criterion of technical superiority! Their power techniques were honed in the long history of intense territorial competition within Europe itself. Expansion into the Americas was partly motivated by attempts to gain advantages over rivals, exemplified by the late 18th century struggle between France and Britain for Canada and between Spain and Portugal for Latin America. As mentioned in the previous chapter, European technical development has been driven substantially by the strategic and military implications of competition between states. This competitiveness created pressure on all parties to expand their resources, and immediately convert any technical advantage into dominance over rivals. This short-term value trumps thought of long-term sustainability. The end result is dependence on inanimate power and energy from non-renewable fuels.

The 'energy frontiers' in Ecuador and British Columbia are a manifestation of this dynamic. The Alaska Highway was built during the Second World War. Following the discovery of gas fields in Prudhoe Bay during the 1960s, the Alaska Gas Pipeline project was mooted to help increase energy self-sufficiency in the United States (Mair, 1980). Canadian business and government wanted to be made rich by selling fossil fuels to the United States. It is therefore unsurprising that the 1978 proposal to lay 400 miles of pipe straight across their lands galvanised the Dunne-za into realising that withdrawal is no longer possible. When Brody was researching his book this project was a lightening conductor for the accumulated frustrations of repeated incursions from forestry, farming, hydroelectric flooding, oil and gas drilling, road building and sports hunting. The still uncompleted Alaska Gas Pipeline is still contested, as are other symptoms of incursion such as the proposed Site C hydroelectric project on the Peace River (Treaty 8 First Nations Community Assessment Team, 2012) and Northwest Transmission

Line (NTL) which became operational in 2014. Both schemes are designed to supply electricity to massively expand the extractive industries throughout the region, including the mining of minerals such as gold and lithium vital for contemporary micro electronics.

Here two approaches to the human predicament of anticipating future needs confront one another, shaping maps and dreams. Small bands of aboriginal hunters, in situations of low inter-societal competition, learned to deal with the future by limiting needs and by renewable resource harvesting, seeing themselves as *part of* a natural world which they respect. They are confident that the resources will be there if the land is left untouched. That is what they dream and record on land-use maps. On the other hand, Americans and Europeans face the future anxiously, imagining resources will not be there in the future unless they take steps to accumulate, store and defend them. They try to secure the future by expanding and developing their resource base and establishing exclusive access to it. Their dreams are of self-sufficiency based on economic growth and monopolies. Theirs are the fears and dreams of the elites of settled societies with long histories of agriculture and then industrialisation, political apparatuses, stratification systems and high levels of inter-societal competition. Maps are maps of political frontiers and territorial prizes.

However, like all methods, the success of the European way of securing the future has limit conditions, natural, political and economic. Long struggles reduce fields of competitors to those capable of defending their independence. At this point further efforts at elimination become so costly, that cooperation seems more likely to pay. The creation of the European Union following a period of world wars (1914–1945) is a clear example. Expansion by colonisation becomes less attractive once the valuable territories have been mopped up. The military contribution to domination is expensive and tends to be replaced by economic and cultural techniques. An example is white fur-traders supplying alcohol to force addicted native trappers to visit trading posts to sell their furs. Finally, renewal and growth of access to natural resources by geographical extension, and intensified extraction, must stop when those resources are exhausted, or when the consequences of their use become massively and obviously counterproductive. All technologies have to adjust to the consequences of the way they have been used in the past. Even technologies which have been very successful as technologies of conquest become unsustainable and have to change their tune.

Both the Dunne-za and the Huaorani might take some encouragement from the happy coincidence that just as they are experiencing the limit conditions of their way, created by land pressure from industrialism, industrialism itself is hitting its own limit conditions. Both are at a threshold of sustainability. None of the respective strategies of 'mobility and flight' (Huaorani), 'flexible movement' (Dunne-za), or expansionism and new techniques of resource exploitation (industrial capitalism), can rely on the 'comforting vastness' of the Amazonian forest or Canadian wilderness. Just like agriculture (discussed in Chapter 3), industrialism has negative feedback consequences, as it encourages demands which cannot be met without depleting or despoiling the resource base. Even if new technologies to extract gas and oil from shale and tar sand deposits have recently increased potential reserves of fossil fuels, the negative consequences for climate equilibrium become more apparent. Picture the sport hunter's pickup travelling the access roads of the oil prospectors, burning the petrol they work so hard to extract. Burn more means extract and pollute more. Sustainability by resource renewal, which the Dunne-za have done for thousands of years, has become vital for securing the future of industrialism. The possibility exists, therefore that if whites can see that it is in their interests to conserve resources, limit wants (like sport hunting), reduce demand for non-renewable and environmentally damaging fuels, slowing the rate of use, and develop the use of renewables, the pressure on Dunne-za and Huaorani lands might reduce.

Joseph's sense that soon it will be too late, nevertheless acknowledges that there is some time left to turn the forces of environmental destruction. However recent developments do not give much grounds for optimism. As the first edition was being written (early in 2001), the centre of contemporary high technology, California's 'Silicon Valley' was suffering power failures and responded by importing electricity from British Columbia whose energy companies consequently viewed the future demand for natural gas-fired electricity generation as likely to grow over the next 20 years. However, in the face of increased competition for energy from rapidly expanding industries in India, China, South-East Asia and Latin America, the United States has tried to increase its energy self-sufficiency quickly by developing the new techniques for extracting gas and oil from its hitherto unworkable or 'uneconomic' deposits. Despite some large investments in renewables, it has sought self-sufficiency via hydrocarbons for 'the foreseeable future' until reliance on renewable energy becomes technically and economically practical.

Meanwhile, Canadian energy companies have responded to the threat of declining American markets by targeting those elsewhere, and particularly in Asia, for example securing a $20 billion investment from the Malaysian state oil company Petronas, to develop Port Edward into a deep water terminal able to handle liquid natural gas tankers. At our present time of writing, the British Columbian Premier, Christy Clark's ambition is for BC to be the second largest LNG exporter in the world. So the 'energy frontier' is as vibrant as it was when Brody lived with the Dunne-za in the late 1970s. But since then the **postmodern** sense that industrial energy consumption may have caused irreversible environmental damage, and be ultimately self-defeating, has grown. Time is very short for preserving the Dunne-za's hunting environment, but it is becoming clearer that it could also be ominously short for industrialism too.

This realisation lies behind the recent (though now compromised) attempts in Ecuador to limit industrialism's demands on the environment in a country that gains about 70 per cent of its revenue from oil exports. Generous land rights have been granted to First Peoples including the Huaorani and an innovative initiative was launched by President Rafael Correa in 2007 (Rival, 2010; Gremillion, 2011). The latter was designed to prevent damage to the enormous biological diversity of the forests of the Yasuní National Park adjacent to Huaorani territory and to reduce carbon emissions, by means of an agreement to forgo exploitation of the Ishpingo-Tambococha-Tiputini (ITT) oil field within the park. The initiative proposed leaving the oil underground indefinitely in return for the international community raising half the value ($3.6 billion by 2023) of the estimated oil reserves (850 million barrels) to pay for Ecuadorian social development. Correa argued before the UN Assembly that everyone has an interest in preserving bio-diversity, indigenous ways of life, and environmental security which are all beyond ordinary market pricing mechanisms. Combining preserving the forest and raising money for housing, health and education was politically popular at home and abroad. However, in August 2013, Correa, blaming overseas interests for not providing the money promised with the speed or in the quantity originally agreed (only $13 million of the $3.6 billion envisaged had been secured) scrapped the ITT scheme and declared oil extraction would be allowed in '1 per cent' of the Yasuní National Park. Some critics queried Correa's original commitment to the scheme and environmental protection noting, for example, the government's attempts to sell extraction rights in other parts of Ecuador's rainforest (including in Achuar territory where some companies had been put off by local resistance). However, whatever the original strength of Correa's commitment to ITT, it seems that by 2013 he was feeling under short-term pressures to find money to repay loans to China and for the domestic spending promised the electorate. Opening up what was argued to be only a small area of Yasuní was a tempting means to try and do this. In 2014 various environmental groups failed to institute a referendum to overturn the president's decision. At our time of writing, the building of new roads into the forest has started and it is very likely to be polluted to some extent if extraction goes ahead.

We may regard this as a sad story and a failure, but it was not inevitable. Whether industrialism can be made environmentally sustainable will depend on the choices and action of many peoples. The history of the ITT scheme is just one story of people making choices from positions in structures of differences of social power about how to use their resources, to satisfy their own and other's conflicting interests, in this case in particular the conflict between the long-term interest in preserving the forest and the shorter-term interest in providing a better life for Ecuador's voters. Correa seems to have judged that he had only limited time to put off raising the money to begin improving schools and health care and to pay back loans. Potential donors from the industrialised states have not given environmental sustainability high enough priority to pay promptly (though some query Correa's good faith). This all shows that change involves assessing the threats and opportunities, the risks, presented by new circumstances. It applies at the point of taking new initiatives as well as while monitoring their implementation. What to do when a course of action does not seem to be working as hoped? Carry on or pull the plug? Assessments are done by combining rationality with commitments to cultural frames of reference which guide choices about how to rank the relative importance of conflicting interests. Put starkly, Correa is steering a political course through very high possible negative stakes, for example future collapse of biodiversity and climate, the impossibility of raising development loans, and the continued unavailability of schools and health care for contemporary Ecuadorians and their children.

We will return to the question of how social change happens and its implications for responding to environmental sustainability in Chapter 12. The Ecuadorian example suggests it is a problem involving relations within fields of potentially cooperating and competing interests articulated by a range of elements – *persons* with their personalities and temperaments (creative imagination and patience for example), in *social roles* deploying *institutional resources* (e.g. being President of Ecuador), making *judgements and choices* about *orders of priority* guided by *rationality* and by *values* (e.g. poverty and pollution are both bad), using *powers* subject to *time constraints* (e.g. the next election) and *material* ones (e.g. the near impossibility of avoiding oil pollution).

Conclusion

We end by noting two lessons from the Huaorani and Dunne-za. The first is that they are witness to the practical possibility of practices and values which combine satisfying short-term and long-term interests (though this possibility had certain structural conditions of low inter-societal competition). The second is that change is always undertaken conditioned by what has been given priority and attracted the investment of resources in the past. Generally the legacy of having pursued earlier priorities is in part enabling and in part constraining. In this chapter we have focused on two hunter-gatherer socie-ties and a third social type – call it global industrial capitalism. All three have been changing and in choosing or being forced to do so have applied their well-established concepts of identity, core values and orders of priorities. Thus both the Dunna-ze and the Huaorani have responded to the unasked for pressures from expansionist outsiders, by looking for ways to continue to be themselves under the new conditions, seeking compromises they are able to live with for the time being. Marketing their services to sport hunters and eco tourists are contemporary examples. As are the Huaorani's treating the mate-rial goods supplied by outsiders via the roads, towns, rivers and airstrips, as equivalents to either the gifts they traditionally gave each other on demand or as extensions of the forest's bounty. In the adjustment to new circum-stances, access to modern medicines might be judged to be worth taking big risks for in terms of relaxing the boundary between insiders and outsiders.

In the case of our third society, that of the industrialised outsiders, the same process of assessing risks, threats and opportunities posed by new circumstances, is under way. A change to sustainability is required by a combination of industrial expansion, intensified competition for scarce resources, and environmental damage to biodiversity and the climate. People need to move from focusing on their own medium-term sufficiency and framing this as a competition of their interests with those of others, to recognising the need for long-term cooperative interdependence. The process of transition will involve inventing mechanisms which might allow pursuing sufficient existing commitments to enable necessary medium-term continu-ity while adjusting to the new priority of a long-term interest in preserving the environment. Ecuador's contribution to inventing these mechanisms has been to present an area of oil-deposits covered by mega-diverse species as hav-ing two mutually exclusive values – conserved forest and reduced emissions, or working oil field, and then to suggest a way of pricing the former, asking the world to make a choice.

Like the Huaorani and the Dunne-za, we are all involved in making assess-ments of the costs and benefits of sticking with established, proven technolog-ical practices, or experimenting with new ones which might be better in some way. Articulating the old with the new goes on all the time. The economic argument which might persuade industrial interests to refrain from the utter destruction of hunter-gatherer lands and ways of life, is that the resources of species, materials and culture are more valuable as potential for the future than squandered on short-term economic growth. Of course there is a moral argument about the injustice of destroying a people which is persuasive to many, but the economic argument appeals to the self-interest of the powerful and morally unresponsive, and is therefore strategically very important! Even they might understand that rather than pursue impossible dreams of exclusiveness and self-sufficiency, the future might be better secured by policies encouraging technological pluralism, the maintaining of alternatives, within relations of inclusiveness and mutual dependency – typically post-modern dreams. There are choices to be made, motives to make them and sufficient time for them to have positive effects. It is because this is so that the natural environment and technology only condition how we live and are not sufficient to explain what we do or how events turn out.

Questions related to themes in this chapter

This chapter has considered whether the natural environment determines technical choices.

1) How far does technological necessity explain why the Huaorani use blowpipes to hunt monkeys and spears to kill peccaries?
2) Decide who you think is better adapted to the environment they live in – you or the Dunne-za – and provide reasons for your answer.
3) Give examples of how your life is conditioned by the weather and changes of the seasons.
4) Imagine that you and your neighbour are of similar age, have similar incomes and the same number of children, but own very different kinds of car. Hypothesise why this might be the case.
5) Do you think that technological considerations determine the relative emphasis governments give to renewables and non-renewables in their energy policies? What other considerations might they take into account?

PART III

The concept of culture

CHAPTER 5

What does culture explain?

We have now reached a major turning point in this book as we begin to consider the concepts of 'culture', 'action' and 'social structure', which are the primary concerns of anthropologists and sociologists. We are moving to our own turf so to speak, and can explore the specific contributions of the social scientist to the explanation of human life. Though we do not want to draw too sharp a distinction, it is fair to say that anthropology (particularly in America) has concentrated attention on culture and sociology has focused on social structure, while both have had to reckon with action. This chapter begins to show you why all students of social phenomena, be they anthropologists, sociologists, social and cultural geographers, political scientists or historians, with their respective emphases, are nevertheless, dealing with a common realm defined by the interaction between culture, action and social structure. The easiest way to begin characterising this realm is to discuss the role of culture in social explanation (Figure 5.1). For the moment we can say that culture comprises all that humans believe and do that isn't an unmediated outcome of natural instinct. However before proceeding we can recap our progress.

The story so far

We have considered the place of two concepts in social explanation – 'individuals' and 'nature' (Figure 5.2). We have explored what is involved in referring to these as causal forces in shaping social regularities and patterns of behaviour. In each case we have argued that the concept refers to

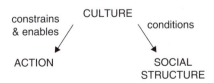

Figure 5.1 What the social sciences contribute to social explanation: culture

Relatively autonomous causal forces	Properties
Individuals (who are part of nature)	biology, body, instincts, species characteristics, psychology, dispositions, personality, emotions, knowledge, rationality, technical creativity and so on
Natural environment	physical, chemical, biological, ecological, geographical, mechanical, and so on

Figure 5.2 Individuals and nature: necessary but not sufficient for explaining collective phenomena

a fundamentally important factor in social explanation. On the one hand, individuals, with their bodies, minds, innate dispositions and unique differences from one another, are always playing their part. Likewise the natural environment is always at least conditioning, social interaction. Individuals and the natural environment are irreducible and have a degree of autonomy, that is, a capacity to exercise a particular kind of influence on social life. Each is consequential, or matters, in social explanation.

On the other hand we have argued that there are real difficulties in trying to explain social life by referring to any one of these concepts as though it was the only thing that mattered for social explanation. They are *necessary* elements in social explanations and must figure in our hypotheses. But they are not *sufficient* elements; that is they cannot do the job on their own. Thus a very important implication of what we have been saying is that social explanation must always involve showing how the various kinds of causes *interact*. Moreover, these factors will have varying degrees of importance in different cases. We ought, in principle, to be interested not just in the different kinds of factor influencing what we want to explain, but also in the relative strength of each factor. This implies the value of being able to measure differences between the powers of different contributing causes. Here we will only raise this issue of the role and possibility of measurement in the social sciences, leaving to one side the technically difficult discussion it requires. However, we think that where it is possible to make measurements of the power of causes, such measures are extremely valuable for explanation.

So far we have considered explanatory methods which analyse the interaction between individuals and their natural and social environment by treating people as either determined by forces which they do not control, or as exercising control by using their naturally given rationality, technical creativity and empirical knowledge. This latter form of explanation involves a mode of thinking about how actors interpret their situations and give them meaning. But though it recognises the importance of meaning for human action, its theory of meaning is universal and acultural. It implies all people interpret the material world in the same way, as they make the calculations and use the information to manipulate it to get what they want. It explains differences in what people do as the result of the variable quality of the information available, and their relative success in being rational and avoiding technical errors. But when trying to explain social behaviour individualistically or naturalistically, we found that it was virtually impossible to explain what people do by simply conceptualising them as rational problem solvers.

So we can approach the idea of culture by asking if the differences between the ways various individuals and collectivities interpret the world are no more than differences between the well informed and ill informed, the rational and the irrational, those who know the truth and the mistaken? Our discussion of technological choice and the idea of 'progress' in Chapter 4 suggests the answer 'no'. This is because mediating the forces of nature is not simply a matter of technical calculation and coming to the one correct conclusion (Figure 5.3). There are different kinds of knowledge besides technical

HUMAN MEDIATION OF NATURE INVOLVES:

BIOLOGICAL ENDOWMENT: INSTINCTS
    (insufficient in human species)
     +
RATIONALITY
     +
TECHNICAL KNOWLEDGE
    Are these sufficient?
    Methodological individualists answer 'yes' but we say 'no'
     +
CULTURE: FRAMES OF REFERENCE
    enabling
    INTERPRETATION (MEANING)
     +
VALUES supported by
emotional commitment
+ rational argument
        enabling
        EVALUATION (JUDGEMENT)

Cultures are created by collectivities, not individuals.

Figure 5.3 What enables humans to mediate the forces of the natural environment?

know-how. Moreover interpretation involves the use of particular frames of reference and making judgements involves using values. Meaning does not just involve the cold reason of logic but also the hot influence of emotion. Think of the depth of feeling underlying Huaorani technical choices for example (discussed in Chapter 4).

If one answers 'no' to the question of whether differences in people's interpretation of the world are due only to a differential distribution of irrationality, ignorance and error, it is because one recognises that variations between interpretations can be evidence of the existence of cultures. Every culture makes those subjected to its influence share certain socially important characteristics. Culture collectivises individuals and in the same process makes them different from others.

What does 'culture' mean?

A proper understanding of cultural conditioning must guard against some mistaken habits of thinking. Firstly it must avoid conceptualising culture as breaking down into a plurality of distinct and more or less easily identifiable and clearly bounded cultures. This idea of cultures as separable bounded entities corresponding to particular societies (for example, 'French culture', 'Italian culture') or to bounded sets of individuals, only applies as a simplifying approximation from time to time. Even though the members of collectivities, such as states, religious sects or specialist professions may sometimes believe they are distinguished by sets of practices, beliefs and values unique to them and perhaps incompatible to those of others, this is seldom entirely the case. Generally people are exposed to a range of cultural influences which may not be systematically ordered and do not have just one source, history or location. Culture is best approached as a changing mass of possible resources which have potential to be found useful by those who have access to them. Cultural elements are constantly being added to and lost while at the same time being made use of to interpret the circumstances people face.

This links to a second mistake which is to think of cultural influence as necessarily a matter of positive identification and conviction. Culture is a messy realm of creativity and struggle, which results in histories made up of moments of invention, elaboration, affirmation, renunciation, criticism, fragmentation, hybridisation and so on. Culture conditions in complicated ways. We may be aware of some of these and be able to make choices about some of our cultural commitments. Indeed strong identification and emphatic conviction is one way of coping with the messiness, but it is the messiness which motivates it. Humans have to find ways of making their cultural resources work well enough for them and that means managing culture's inadequacies.

At one extreme one can deny these inadequacies, insist on cultural purity, the one 'true' or 'real' or 'original' version; one can be a traditionalist and face down the need for change. Or one can place the emphasis on maintaining the relevance of a cultural tradition by adapting it and be a critical moderniser, perhaps seeking inspiration from outside it.

However taking a conscious reflective stance towards one's cultural resources and traditions is only one possibility. Generally cultural conditioning has a powerful unreflective dimension. Usually sharing cultural elements puts a population of individuals in the same boat, in some respects, not because they have consciously come to some agreement but because they have been influenced to approach their experience of the world in certain ways which they take for granted. This shared approach, which they may think of as 'common sense', provides the parameters within which debate can take place. If you want to explain why certain things are done and said repeatedly by a certain population, for example when responding to environmental problems in a certain way, it makes sense to consider if these social regularities are due to some shared cultural conditioning. It would be foolish not to include in our explanation of social phenomena anything which has collectivising effects. Culture certainly has such effects, though we must always query if it provides the total explanation. Not least we need to ask what generates the cultural features we decide are causally powerful. We cannot simply take their existence for granted.

So far we have talked about properties of cultures in order to bring out their collectivising effects and ways they contribute to differences between populations. But now we must return to the issue of how to define culture in general, elaborating on our earlier definition which contrasted the cultural with the instinctual. A good guide to how the term has been used is Raymond Williams' *Keywords* (1983). In ordinary language, the term 'culture' is often loaded with evaluative connotations to do with **social status**. It can be associated with claims to social respectability by persons with a certain education, who believe they possess rare powers of critical judgement about the 'finer' or 'higher' spheres of achievement. 'Culture' in this sense is associated with the arts, refinement, cultivation (reminding us of very early horticultural uses of the term). Or it may be used to claim respectability for subordinated or threatened traditions, communities and practices, to improve their position in the competition for resources. Here the term is used to refer to whole ways of life (such as that of the Dunne-za or the Huaorani) felt to be at risk. In the contemporary world, being 'cultured' or having 'a culture' is politically important, and we ourselves might want to challenge the snobberies implied in the first usage, or defend the possessors of a culture in the second sense, from having it incorporated into homogenising modernity. But for our purposes here, we need a general concept of culture which will explain why the term can be used in these evaluative, socially competitive ways and what these have in common. What is at stake in such struggles?

Transmission and learning

The stakes are high because of the way humans relate to their various and changing environments. As we have already suggested in Chapters 1 and 3, they have a few, highly generalised instincts, which are no match for the complex sophistication of the instincts of other species. But this sophistication is a function of evolutionary specialisation in the problems of a few specific environments which carries the weakness of dependency on such environments continuing to exist. Specialists tend to be endangered by rapid change. Humans, as non-specialists, are less dependent on specific environments, more adaptable and better able to survive rapid change. Their weakness is that when they are born they are utterly dependent on others for a long time. The few automatic responses they do have (crying, smiling, grasping, sucking and so on) are designed to get others to take care of them. There then follows an extraordinarily long period of learning about how to relate to environments, particular ones, and in general. What is learnt is language and culture. Basic to culture is that it is transmitted non-biologically, and has to be learned.

Speaking biologically, the human species has invested in developing its capacity to learn culture rather than in the specialised instincts typical of other species. Though this has paid off in evolutionary terms, culture does not make humans independent of their environments, and cultural practices are still conditioned (though not determined) by relations with particular environments – as seen in Chapter 4. Culture is an accumulation of what has been learned from past experience of problems and ways to cope with them so that those who come after can benefit from it and do not forever have to reinvent the wheel. Birds instinctively know how to build their nests, but architects can rely on much inter-generationally transmitted knowledge to help them devise their buildings. Architects can also improvise with new materials if a traditional supply disappears, but the bird that instinctively makes its nest from mud, when faced with a drought, cannot shift quickly to using material quite unlike mud, such as leaves, which could be functional for nest building. Lacking culture, the bird must move to an area where mud is available or fail to nest. Culture, by contrast, offers humans both *history* and an open future. Disciplines such as sociology and anthropology dealing with culture (and with social structure) are always involved with situations whose explanation must reveal how the past influences the present and the present the future. In the social sciences, non-biological, historical processes (some but not all of which are cultural) are mechanisms of change to be considered alongside the biological processes of evolutionary change.

Thus one way of characterising culture is to say that it consists of processes and mechanisms which enable the past to be carried into the present and on to the future. These processes enable people to live practically in a changing world by always having some way to begin relating meaningfully to whatever they experience. A major feature of culture is the use of ways of formulating the lessons from the past in transmittable, teachable and practical form.

At the heart of cultural methods for giving us the past, lies the use of signs to represent experience and the world, and the development of rules, general principles, formulae and 'recipes'. That is why language is so highly developed in humans, but in addition, why special representational systems like mathematics are invented. Memory techniques, writing systems, libraries, encyclopaedias, information storage and retrieval systems, the Internet, are symptomatic of our being culture-dependent. But culture would not work if it were just some enormous shed, electronic or not, filled with the lessons of the past. We need some way of deciding the relevance of these lessons for the present. Given past and present are not identical, there is a universal cultural problem of matching up the present case to some past cases and generalising from them. Generalisation is valuable, but also perilous and much cultural energy has been devoted to trying to improve its reliability. 'When is it safe to generalise?' and 'When ought the rule to be broken?' are culturally generic questions.

Cultural production and elaboration

Implicit in this is that cultures are collective products, typically produced over long periods of time by large numbers of individuals, most of them now dead (Archer, 1995: 72–3). Culture enables their influence to continue after they have gone. But their influence is *only* influence. Cultural products provide the wherewithal for shaping our activity but they do not actually shape it. Cultural resources have to be applied; they do not apply themselves. Cultural production is the by-product of this application. It is a process of applying, and thereby modifying or elaborating what has been learned, to ever-changing conditions. Applying what has been learnt enables yet more learning and cultural change.

When we learn cultural lessons, especially as children, we are given a way of representing the world as a world of a particular kind, classified and organised in a particular way, one which is recommended by those who teach us. Adults exercise power when they transmit a preferred version, one they would like to see continued in the future. Such versions provide starting points for our own cultural elaboration as we try to use them to conduct our lives. More than that, our early learning provides some basic, enduring, mental furniture which we will share with others with similar upbringing. As Pierre Bourdieu insists, it creates a deeply ingrained, general disposition ('habitus') to interpret our later experience in particular ways. People with a common upbringing tend to share, not just particular ideas and images, but styles and methods of thinking and imagining (Box 5.1).

Pierre Bourdieu (1930–2002, French)

(1979) *Distinction: A Social Critique of the Judgment of Taste*, Oxford, Routledge Kegan Paul (1984).
(1966) *The Love of Art: European Art Museums and Their Public*, Redwood City, CA, Stanford University Press (1991).
(1992) *Rules of Art: Genesis and Structure of the Literary Field*, Redwood City, CA, Stanford University Press (1996).
(1999) *Weight of the World: Social Suffering in Contemporary Society*, Cambridge, Polity (1999).

Box 5.1 Bourdieu: 'symbolic violence', 'habitus' and 'distinction'

Bourdieu synthesises elements of Marx and Weber to explain findings from his empirical research. The core of this synthesis is the logic of practical action and the way social power is exercised culturally through 'symbolic violence' in the form of 'habitus' (elaborating Marx on 'ideology') and/or through competition for 'distinction' (elaborating Weber on status competition).

A 'habitus' is an historically emergent culture produced by a **collectivity** (typically a social class) in response to being positioned, long term, in structures of power. These enduring patterns of response are transmitted across generations, becoming deeply engrained in the make-up of members as their most general orientations or dispositions, guiding their practice. Habitus conditions the ordering of priorities and what people believe it is realistic to expect. It forms an unquestioned background, what is taken for granted, limiting the alternatives which can be imagined. It frames what is felt to be natural, normal, trustworthy and morally and aesthetically acceptable.

'Distinction' (i.e. representing what is socially valued) is the ambition of people who participate in cultural practices as competitors for social status or 'esteem'. What is valuable has to be 'deemed' to be so. The 'distinguished' at the top of status hierarchies are able to strongly influence how status competitions are conducted. Cultural practices are ranked, as are individual performances in any one of them. Ranking cultural practices involves 'symbolic violence' because privileging some cultural practices (the 'high') over others involves social control. Methods include demanding special education, using cost to maintain exclusiveness, and wealth to cultivate an expensive life-style and demeanour. Disparagement, condescension and ridiculing of aspirants, can protect the 'high' from challenges from 'lower' down a cultural **hierarchy**. These practices are typical of the 'habitus' of aristocratic or quasi-aristocratic strata. They might explain, for example, the sense of dislocation felt by the working class high achiever at an elite university.

Bourdieu has been criticised for generalising from cases where consciousness is strongly conditioned by positions in relatively enduring and simple stratification systems. Where social structuring is complicated, pluralised and de-stabilised, then competing forces, not least the education system and media environment, condition consciousness. Here 'distinction' becomes less easy to determine. People may be exposed to a mix of contradictory and changing suggestions about how to act, think, make choices, take risks and so on. 'Habitus' does not fit well where people are relatively unconstrained and a high level of reflexivity may be needed.

Bourdieu, P. (1990a) *In Other Words: Essays towards a Reflexive Sociology,* Redwood City CA, Stanford University Press.
Bourdieu, P. (1984) *Distinction: A Social Critique of the Judgement of Taste,* Cambridge MA, Harvard University Press.

It is in this sense that humans are caught up not only in the natural world, but also in a cultural 'second nature' as discussed in Chapter 3. They cannot avoid being involved. Moreover, all this effort put into teaching and learning represents an investment (even if the young do not volunteer for it) in a way of defining and dealing with the world which may make people rather defensive (or assertive), when confronted with other ways of relating to reality. This claim is reinforced when we remember that among the things we learn are our identities (who we are) and what we really value. Cultural learning can bring in train commitment and a deep conditioning of the emotions.

But we must realise that culture cannot exercise its influence without being used and when it is used it has to be applied, interpreted, elaborated and thus changed. Although we do not have any choice about having to use culture to live, culture cannot do our living for us and we cannot but use our creative and discretionary powers. Culture is a bitter-sweet realm of human self-determination.

How culture binds: (a) socialisation

In general, culture cannot be taken as a fixed force which makes us do things. It is not that sort of mechanism. But it can have compulsory effects, particularly on individuals during their **primary socialisation,** and over social phenomena of relatively short duration, where the cultural framework is set and can, for purposes of analysis, be taken as given. In such circumstances individuals may certainly be very strongly constrained by it. This is clear if one focuses on the role of culture in the formation of individuals. Obviously, culture contributes greatly in the process of forming individuals, but this truism has provided the basis for some theorists to make a much stronger claim that it is culture which integrates individuals into society. **Functionalist theories** as different as those of Talcott Parsons (inspired by Durkheim) and Louis Althusser (building on Marx), have held that social organisation itself is only possible because individuals are socialised to be committed to a culture (Parsons, 1951; Althusser, 1971). This shapes their aspirations, identity and values, patterning their activity into socially productive forms. However, this sort of theory tends to treat culture as a 'given', overlooking what shapes the cultural menu to which individuals might be exposed. This might involve, for example, struggles by different economic or religious categories to promote orientations, or (in Marx's term) 'ideologies' favourable to their interests (Box 5.2). Functionalist theory moves directly to emphasise the strength of the mechanisms whereby individuals are hooked up to culture, to explain its constraining force. Focussing on these mechanisms tends to ignore the histories during which individuals and collectivities have used their political, creative and discretionary powers in cultural struggles (Box 5.3). Instead actors are imagined to simply relay culture rather than apply, develop or contest it. On this basis, it is tempting to try to explain why people behave in patterned ways by saying that they are programmed by their socialisation and neglect the process during which the powers and content of the programming were formed and distributed. This is a popular and relevant tactic when trying to explain, for example, the differences in behaviour between those classified as

Louis Althusser (1918–1990, French (born Algeria))

(1965) *For Marx,* London, Verso (2005).
(1968) *Lenin and Philosophy and Other Essays,* New York, Monthly Review Press, US (2001).
(1968) (with Balibar, E. et al.) *Reading Capital,* London, Verso (2009).
(1964–73) *On Ideology,* London, Verso, (2008).

Box 5.2 Marx: social structure and ideology

Marx assumes that human beings, by virtue of their nature, have a con-sciousness capable of understanding their experiences and that everyone is, in principle, united by a common identity grounded in their universal inter-ests in productive labour. Marx suggests that differences in social power explain why for most of human history this unity has not existed. Dominant classes have prioritised their own particular over general interests, resulting in various kinds of long-term class inequality. Marx's political purpose was to find the social and economic mechanisms, such as those depicted in his theories of value, profit and ideology which enabled class dominance. In suggesting that the mechanism of 'ideology' institutionalised (false) ideas and supported class systems, he recognised that social structure was a cause of thought. Ideology 'naturalises' and justifies unnatural and unjust social arrangements. It falsely represents the interest of the dominant class as the universal interest. For example, the feudal aristocracy promoted a knightly ethic of personal virtue and service, grounded in Christianity, to win acceptance of its privileges which depended on the domination of rural workers by military force. Similarly, under capitalist conditions, ideology makes individual self-interest, meritocracy, consumerism, economic 'growth' and **nationalism**, for example, appear natural and self-evident. Class divi-sions are falsely represented as necessary and inevitable.

Marx, K. (orig. 1845, 1974) *The German Ideology,* London, Lawrence and Wishart.

Box 5.3 Durkheim: society and the social structuring of thought

Durkheim argues 'society' can influence thought but he makes no reference to Marx's differences of social power, or ideological deceptive functions, and conceptualises 'society' differently. For Durkheim 'society' is the reality of universal collectivising mechanisms which differentiate individuals into groups and positions within groups (e.g. families and roles within families). Human nature is 'dual', i.e. both individual and collective. As entities existing within social structures, individuals must necessarily know how to identify and relate to differences between and within groups. The formal properties of social classification frame social relations and interaction. Differences of social identities are produced by a natural process which is not an optional technique of domination. Social identities potentially cross-cut loyalties to universal interests defined by rational theories like Marxism.

Durkheim suggests each culture develops its substantive classification scheme expressed as 'collective representations'. These use categorical differences of space (inside/outside, left/right, above/below etc.), time (beginning/end, before/after etc.), causation (creator/created etc.) to generate symbol systems enabling implicit structural relations to be physically perceived, for example in religion and ritual performances. Socialisation in any culture involves learning its particular version of the universal requirement for structure. Durkheim suggests that the 'truth' of religions is that what they worship as 'sacred' is actually a symbolic proxy for 'society'. And how any society structures the sacred mirrors how it itself is structured.

Durkheim's intuition is that the age-old philosophical question of how human understanding is possible, is answered by reference to the natural requirement to comprehend the structuring entailed by social existence which uses the basic categories of human reason. Rather than being a precondition for comprehending social experience, the categories originate in that process, and are subsequently used to make sense of all kinds of experience. This highly controversial, cautiously argued, claim has nevertheless inspired influential theories of cultural difference, such as attitudes to environmental risk. (See Chapters 6 and 12.)

Durkheim, E. (orig. 1912, 1995), *The Elementary Forms of Religious Life,* New York, Free Press.

Fournier, M. (2007; trans. 2013) *Emile Durkheim: A Biography,* Cambridge, Polity Press.

men and women within a particular society in a particular period. But it does depend on taking the cultural forms as somehow just there as a 'given', rather than as changing and contested, as well as ignoring the scope for individuals and groups to act against type.

How culture binds: (b) the autonomy of culture

The second broad view of how culture binds focuses on the materials and processes of cultural forms and practices themselves. An important feature of culture is that its media, methods, formulations, and representations, its ideas and images, just by virtue of being given cultural form, acquire a large measure of autonomy. That is they acquire properties of their own which are not the properties of the people who first produced them, or later, try to use them. These things have objective properties, which then feed back to condition the action of those who try to use them. In what follows we want to focus on these properties because they are fundamental to explanation in terms of culture where we might hypothesise that it is culture which makes people behave in certain ways. Explanation in terms of culture does not consist only in seeing it as a kind of environment, rather like the natural environment, which imposes itself on individuals. Culture consists of practices; these have to be actively pursued by actors who use them for their purposes. So culture should be viewed as providing actors with ways of doing things, as facilitating and enabling action. But though such practices enable, they also constrain.

The logic of cultural systems, practices and objects

In general terms what we have to consider is the constraining force of the systematic logic of cultural practices, traditions, cultural objects and ideas. By 'logic', we mean any internally generated properties, which both set limits on what can be done and provide opportunities for elaboration of particular kinds. By 'internal' we mean that the various kinds of cultural 'stuff' are made up of elements which fit together in certain ways. Take a very simple example: $2 + 2 = 4$. This describes relations between numbers which are governed by the rules of addition and the meaning of the concepts 'two', 'four', 'addition' and 'equals', as well as the meaning of the visual, writable symbols '2', '4', '+' and '=' , taught to young children round the world. There are right and wrong ways of using these concepts and symbols. What do you make of $4 + 2 = 2$, or $= 4 + 2 \ 2$? Elementary arithmetic is a cultural system with objective features, which are stated as rules of the practice. So you can be examined in it for example, and can do it well or badly.

The rules of arithmetic seem pretty universal, though there is a debate about how culturally relative mathematics is; perhaps there are several mathematics, not just one (Bloor, 1976). But even if most cultural systems are relative, not universal, that does not weaken the claim that they have objective internal properties and exercise a relatively autonomous power over action. Take languages for example; each language demands those who learn and speak it to conform to its way of fitting the parts of speech together, its vocabulary and its pronunciation. It has to sound right, and if written, look right. But what counts as 'correct' depends on how the system has been elaborated and what the people who use it reinforce in each other's practice. There is a large element of 'cultural arbitrariness' about this, meaning what is reinforced could as easily have been something else without loss of linguistic functionality. But despite this arbitrariness, once a way of doing things has become conventionalised and institutionalised, nobody seriously doubts the objective constraining force of languages, nor that there are many different ones. And the arbitrariness is not such as to prevent worthwhile if imperfect translations based on acceptable equivalences between elements of different systems.

But all cultural practices are like this; they are many, internally complex, may be mutually incompatible with one another, include a large measure of arbitrariness, and are subject to conventionalisation and institutionalisation. Everybody is engaged in cultural practices and all of them have internal properties which constrain the people doing them. It is not just the important-sounding practices of mathematics and languages. For example, think what constrains you when you have a meal or throw a party. You will be using ideas that you have picked up about how these things should be done. You will be aware of certain rules, or general principles, which guide you in the choices you make about, for instance, what times of day are appropriate, or what qualifies as appropriate food. Such rules describe a preferred way of doing such things, and given that we do not make up our activity from scratch, these rules constrain and enable us, conditioning what we do. Cultural rules offer templates shaping our action. They simplify life with their ready-made formulas, but at the same time these formulas have internal complexities which can make life difficult. For example, is it possible to have a party without any form of drink? And if not, can any drink become the basis of a social occasion? The Huaorani offer manioc beer to manage diplomatic encounters with outsiders; the Dunne-za mark autumn with alcoholic binges (but never drink when hunting). Tea party, coffee morning, sherry party, 'wine and cheese' – but what about a 'water party'? Perhaps not.

The deeper reaches of culture

The 'party' example suggests that, though cultural practices vary enormously there may be general properties of 'parties' which unite people across their different conventions and traditions. So if you are going to have a party, you need something for people to share to help symbolise their participation and interest in one another's well-being. Contributing drink ('Bring a bottle!', the manioc beer), holding a glass with something in it ('Do you need a refill?'), exchanging rounds, officiating in the distribution of the drink (pouring the tea) and so on, have their equivalents in many cultures, because drink is what it is, and the problems of achieving sociable occasions, are what they are.

There seems to be a set of basic conditions which have to be met if you want to throw a party. Similarly if you want to communicate using any language, or use clay to make pots, or make maps, you cannot just do as you like. What you do will be constrained by the objective possibilities for relating things to each other, available to anybody attempting these, or any other, kinds of task. To make pots you have to follow the properties of clay – workable while damp, but unworkable when too wet or too dry. Similarly, any language must offer sufficient parts of speech to allow objects and actions to be described and evaluated. Making maps must use some system for projecting three-dimensional space onto a two-dimensional surface. Just as parties do not work well without something doing the function of drink, so potting needs something to control the dampness of clay, language will not work without something doing the work of nouns and verbs, and maps need something to represent gradients, mountains and valleys.

At this level we find universal cultural problems setting tasks which have been solved culturally in different ways. So there are many languages and traditions of potting and mapping, but each must satisfy the minimum requirements of any functioning language, potting technique or projection scheme. The way culture constrains action, flows from how the material and symbolic elements of cultural practices fit together: vocabulary and grammar, pots and clay, maps and projection, parties and drink; in each case these are *internally related* elements of cultural practices.

This has several implications for explaining patterns of social behaviour. When trying to explain some bit of behaviour it is often helpful to be able to relate it to other bits of behaviour by knowing the relevant cultural context. We can go some way by identifying the cultural practices or games being pursued, and finding out what their rules are. We can benefit from finding out how people fit different games together. Participants are often consciously aware of how they go about this and can describe it to us. Much anthropology is devoted to identifying these kinds of cultural contexts and using them to make sense of patterned behaviour. But we also have to consider the nature of the games being played, why the games are the way they are and why people play them in the ways that they do. These questions are about the deeper levels at which practices, dispositions and orientations of people, operate. Since these act as the 'spectacles' through which they look at the world, people tend to be less informed and informative about them. They may not themselves 'see' the underlying frameworks which structure how they view the world. Some analysis is required.

Ideas and beliefs: consistency and contradictions, rationalisation

When we turn from considering cultural practices and objects to the other major slice of culture, ideas and beliefs, the same principle that you cannot do just anything you like, applies. Now we are faced by culture in the form of theories, sets of propositions, and arguments. The **internal relations** involved here are those of logic rather than the requirements of practices such as organising a party. These internal relations are themselves the object of reflection and elaboration. Much culture is devoted to reflecting on and developing culture itself as a semi-autonomous realm.

This cultural reflexiveness and elaboration produces various 'traditions', ways of doing cultural work of thinking and imagining, centring on particular origins, exemplars, institutions and leaders. For example, ideas and objects may be produced within, and ascribed to, an entity such as a 'school', 'workshop', 'imprint', 'region', or 'manner', which suggest that they are representative of some tradition of thought and/or practice. Traditions are formed when cultural practices and ideas come to have themselves as their point of reference and leads to the formulation of rules and criteria of conformity. These define what doing it correctly amounts to and what sorts of innovation are acceptable. This tends to happen to any practice or set of beliefs which seems to pay off well enough for long enough.

For example, the early centuries of Christianity saw a struggle to come to terms with two contradictory propositions about Jesus: 'He was a man who was once living and was killed' and 'He is God and is alive'. Given the concepts of 'man' and 'God', 'killed' and 'alive' are mutually exclusive, how could Jesus simultaneously be both man and God, alive and dead? Many argued that if he was a man he could only be a dead man, and not living God. However they lost the argument, because at the first Nicene Council in 325 AD, the bishops decreed that Jesus was indeed both, and that what looked like a contradiction, was in fact the 'divine mystery'. If both propositions were true, logic demanded that they come to this conclusion. The Nicene Creed became the most influential formal statement of Christian belief. The point here is that the bishops were forced into action by the logic of their beliefs about Jesus and the need to finally resolve the scandal of a contradiction, which they did by declaring it a 'mystery'.

In this case the contradiction was between two sets of concepts. But equally people may find inconsistencies between ideas about the world and their experience of it. As examples in the next chapter show, this is particularly likely in periods of rapid change and/or when people encounter different cultures. This 'gap' between existing ideas and experience is fundamental to the process of revising our beliefs about the world. This is not just a matter of improving empirical knowledge through experience. It also applies to our ideas about the extent that the reality of our lives matches up to our ideals. But in all cases formulation of beliefs into sets of logically related propositions makes them available for inspection, and has a tendency to reveal contradictions or gaps in supporting arguments. It also facilitates separating the quality of beliefs from that of the people who subscribe to them. We can disapprove of the Nazis because of their appalling and murderous racial policies, but, perhaps uncomfortably, recognise as sound, the anti-smoking policy they advocated, on health grounds, in the 1930s. Questions of truth can be separated from questions of loyalty or identity. We can acknowledge that even really bad people can have (some) good ideas.

The most systematic kind of cultural self-reflection is the process of rationalisation. **Rationalisation** is what happens when people try to make their ideas more consistent, accurate, relevant and comprehensive. Rationalisation is essentially objective and unending – it tends therefore to push at the limits set by traditions usually to the dismay of traditionalists! Rationalisation can be moderate or ruthless. Notice how, in the example of early Christianity the bishops did not question the truth of either of the two contradictory propositions. They applied rational criticism to remove a contradiction between two fundamental beliefs but did not go as far as to criticise these fundamental beliefs themselves. It was precisely because these beliefs were exempted from criticism that there was a contradiction to resolve in the first place. Aspects of their belief were protected from rationalisation by their sacred status.

However rationalisation does not limit itself automatically. Thus the practice of formulating ideas and beliefs in propositional form, reveals objective properties, and exposes them to logical analysis and the tests of consistency and sufficient evidence. Such analysis explores how the elements of belief fit together, and where the fit is poor, tends to galvanise people into elaboration, revision and research. Similarly, we have already found it useful to separate analytically the question of the moral status of a believer, from the question of the truth of their belief. Others have found the precision of measurement invaluable. These are just two examples of rationalising techniques for enhancing the effectiveness of culture as a resource. Nothing is necessarily sacrosanct and immune from the reconstructive force of rationalisation.

Whenever we think hypothetically, ask 'what if ...?' questions, speculate about future possibilities, try to imagine how things could be different, playfully juxtapose unusual combinations, invent metaphors and jokes, we are exploring the logic of our repertoire of ideas and representations and, at least informally and sometimes humorously, rationalising them. This is not to say that all people are embroiled in the finer points of critical methods. Nor that rationalisation is inevitable. It is often resisted. But it is to say that questions of the fit between ideas, other ideas, experience, practice, and the social and moral status of the people involved, are always there to be coped with in one way or another. There are two major alternatives to the logic of rationalisation as ways of deciding about the acceptability of ideas favoured by supporters of traditions; these are tests of collective identity ('this is what *we* believe'), or tests of authority ('this is what the parent, leader, priest, expert, or teacher, says').

Conclusion

The properties of culture are summarised in Figure 5.4. As we initially suggested, discussing culture reveals something fundamental about the subject matter of the social sciences. We said that along with nature and structure, culture was the product of social and historical processes. It has to be explained by reference to these processes. It does not originate itself but is produced by actors under natural and social structural conditions. Being itself a kind of social phenomenon it is explained like any other, as the product of interaction between all five relatively autonomous causal powers. By the same token, when contributing to any social explanation it works in relation to the four other kinds of causation, its causal powers being only relatively autonomous. Thus it cannot by itself be sufficient for explanation (Figure 5.5).

Culture shows us that social reality is historical. As social scientists we have to get to grips with such historical processes if we are to explain social life.

CULTURE supplies necessary lessons from the past

PROPERTIES OF CULTURE

Is Learned and Compulsory
Socialisation shapes basic dispositions, emotions and commitments.
+
Has Communicable Form
Non-biological mechanisms for transmission between generations.
+
Has Media of Transmission
Signs and sign systems, languages and information storage & retrieval technologies.
+
Cultural Practices and Systems
(e.g. pottery, arithmetic, theories)
have Internal Relations
+
Propositions have Objective Logical Properties
(*e.g. consistency and/or contradiction*).
+
Has Traditions and may be subject to
Rationalisation
+
Has Rules and General Principles
which facilitate orientation to new situations and application.
+
Cultural Products 'escape'
from control by their creators.

RELATIVELY AUTONOMOUS POWERS CONDITIONING ACTION & SOCIAL STRUCTURE

CULTURE is **necessary**
for social explanation

Figure 5.4 Summary: the properties of culture

1) Culture is insufficient because it is only *relatively* autonomous. This is because
      a) culture is *caused* – and not only by other cultural factors
      b) culture has to be *applied* in order to generate effects.

Causes of culture

↓

CULTURE

↓

Application of culture to *contribute* to producing the
phenomenon to be explained

2) Culture is insufficient because all social phenomena are caused by an interaction between 'nature', 'individuals', 'action' and 'structure' as well as 'culture'. Each one of these has a relatively autonomous role to play.

nature   individuals   culture   action   structure

phenomenon to be explained

Figure 5.5 Two reasons why culture is insufficient in explanation

This means that social scientists are always dealing with problems where the social behaviour to be explained is conditioned by the results, or outcomes, of previous social behaviour. Culture is one set of processes where this takes place. The social sciences are therefore faced by a reality where the object to be explained, also plays a part in doing the explaining.

Emile Durkheim recommended as a rule for social explanation, that we explain the social by reference to the social (Durkheim, 1895). This is because social behaviour has effects which condition social behaviour. It feeds back into itself. But this does not mean that our explanations in terms of culture (or social structure) are circular. Circularity is avoided for two reasons. First, the culture that does the conditioning and the cultural practice to be explained, are distinguished by a difference of *time*. So the behaviour which does the explaining is not the same behaviour as is being explained. And second, as Margaret Archer makes clear, the mode in which the past impacts on the present is that of influence, filtered by the creative elaboration of actors responding to their experience and circumstances (Archer, 1995). Marx captured this situation by suggesting that though men make history they do not do so under conditions of their own choosing, and that they cannot evade the influence of the past (Marx, 1852).

Margaret Archer (1943–, British)

(1984) *Social Origins of Educational Systems*, London, Sage.
(1988) *Culture and Agency*, Cambridge, Cambridge University Press.
(1995) *Realist Social Theory: The Morphogenetic Approach*, Cambridge, Cambridge University Press.
(2000a) *Being Human: The Problem of Agency*, Cambridge, Cambridge University Press.
(2012) *The Reflexive Imperative in Late Modernity*, Cambridge, Cambridge University Press.

Questions related to themes in this chapter

This chapter has begun to explore the concept of culture and the implications of culture for explaining patterns of social behaviour.

1) Discuss the evolutionary advantages and disadvantages for the survival of the human species of becoming dependent on learning and applying culture.
2) Provide some examples of the way in which culture can be both enabling and constraining.
3) How does culture help shape people's identity? Can you have more than one cultural identity?
4) What kinds of factors might make people try to change a set of cultural beliefs or practices without abandoning them entirely? Can you provide some examples of changes *within* a culture?
5) Have you ever held any beliefs or engaged in any practices which were inconsistent with each other? If so, how did you deal with the inconsistencies between these beliefs or between these practices?

CHAPTER 6

Testing the explanatory value of culture

By now readers will be familiar with the general form of our discussions of the necessity and insufficiency for social explanation of each of the concepts with which this book deals. We are choosing empirical cases which offer favourable opportunities to show that each concept is necessary, yet cannot do all the explanatory work by itself. It is particularly important to make the latter point in relation to the concepts central to, and most enthusiastically supported by, the social sciences. Indicating the insufficiency of individuals and nature to explain social phenomena involved showing, among other things, that culture is a sort of historically emergent collective environment, working alongside the natural environment, to condition the thoughts and actions of individuals. The previous chapter argued in effect that culture was itself a social and collective phenomenon with very powerful collectivising force and a high level of autonomy.

As with 'action' and 'social structure', 'culture' is a social theoretical concept. It specifies a kind of collective phenomenon, examples of which may themselves need to be explained, and also a kind of cause, examples of which can contribute, in combinations with other kinds of causation, to explanation. Any cultural entity is both the outcome of a social causal story and able to play its part in one. Though cultural causation may sometimes be very powerful, such causes work in relations with other kinds – natural, social structural and so on. However where the thing to be explained is itself cultural, and the role of culture in causing it is powerful, it might seem reasonable to neglect the contribution of the other kinds of cause and lapse into what might be called 'methodological culturalism'. So while it is relatively easy to resist methodological individualism and environmental determinism, the temptation to explain collective phenomena solely in terms of cultural causation may be seductive.

Certainly there have been many attempts to give culture an ultimate status when explaining social phenomena. It has even been argued, most famously by the German philosopher, Hegel, that human history as a whole can be understood as a process of realising a logically necessary sequence of ideas. He claimed first, that ideas drive the development of ideas, so sophisticated ideas are only thinkable if preceded by earlier unsophisticated ones. So unlike biological evolution this logical evolution is not an open-ended process but one leading towards increasing sophistication. For example, the advanced idea of democracy is said to depend on earlier more primitive concepts of tyranny and slavery. Second, he claimed that it is ideas (such as democracy) which enable change in the way people live (the actual development of democracies). In this way culture is said to be responsible for actual, concrete historical developments (Hegel, orig. 1824, 1956). Or, as mentioned in the last chapter, culture (usually typified by religion and 'ultimate values') is said (by Talcott Parsons among others) to explain the existence of social order in society. These theories treat the objective logic of ideas as having compelling force which imposes itself, rather like a force of nature.

Georg Wilhelm Friedrich Hegel (1770–1831, German)

(1807) *Phenomenology of Spirit*, Oxford, Oxford University Press (1977).
(1812) *Science of Logic*, London, Allen and Unwin (1969).
(1821) *Elements of the Philosophy of Right*, Cambridge, Cambridge University Press (1991).
(1824) *Philosophy of History*, New York, Dover (1956).
Houlgate, S ed. (1998) *The Hegel Reader*, Oxford, Blackwell.

Another prominent, if less grand, form of 'culturalism' argues that social relations are best understood as relations between ideas; that is, as Peter Winch insisted, that social relations are actually logical relations (Winch, 1958). From the truism that people use ideas of social relations expressed in language to conduct their interaction, the argument moves to claim that the logic of those ideas is sufficient to explain what people do. So social scientists need do no more than find out what people say are the ideas animating their activity. There are two problems here – firstly, as Marx pointed out, even shop keepers can tell the difference between what people say about themselves and what they are (Marx, 1845). Secondly, social phenomena do not easily reduce to the logic of the ideas in the heads of people who are caught up in them, even if they will correctly tell you what these ideas are.

Peter Winch (1926–1997, British)

(1964) 'Understanding a Primitive Society', *American Philosophical Quarterly I*.
(1958) *The Idea of a Social Science and Its Relation to Philosophy*, London, Routledge (1990).

(1972) *Ethics and Action*, London, Routledge and Kegan Paul.
(1987) *Trying to Make Sense*, Oxford, Blackwell.

Moreover, if you accept that explanations employing cultural factors have to deal with the central question of how cultural resources are applied, that is related to cultural and non-cultural circumstances which already exist, then 'culturalism' must be ruled out (Figure 5.5). Finding out what people say are the ideas guiding their activity is only a starting point for explanation. In fact one of social science's major problems is to find languages and concepts, such as may be found in theories of culture and ideology, which can help explain why people being studied describe their doings in the ways they do (Benton and Craib, 2010, 184–195).

However, though we argue culture is insufficient, we must not understate its importance for social explanation. Indeed the case for its insufficiency is strengthened by showing culture at its most powerful in explanation. We will start with a couple of examples from the field of 'race' and ethnic relations where ideas which people might *consciously hold* could contribute to explaining one specific phenomenon (and might initially be thought sufficient). Then we will consider instances where a range of apparently disparate phenomena can be connected, and partly accounted for, with reference to a complex of beliefs which people may be *unaware they hold* (and which are thereby shown to be necessary for explanation).

What can consciously held ideas explain? Examples of differential ethnic economic success, and differential treatment of 'mixed-race' categories

Waldinger showed that towards the end of the 20th century, many recent Asian immigrants to the United States had already 'overtaken' substantial numbers of long-established Afro-Americans, on a number of indices of economic success (Waldinger, 1996). Why was this? Some commentators plausibly suggested cultural causes for the Asian ethnics' economic achievements. They argued that Asians value marital stability and extended family obligation, which means that large kin groups could assemble greater amounts of capital for business investment than individuals on their own. Asians are seen as prepared to sacrifice their own good for that of their kin group (providing cheap and compliant labour, facilitating successful, family-run enterprises). They value hard work and accept deferred rather than immediate gratification. Waldinger shows commentators, by contrast, holding Afro-Americans' ghetto culture to be the obverse of this, which might seem to explain their economic failure.

Our second related puzzle concerns differences in the treatment of 'mixed-race' persons resulting from miscegenation between white European colonisers and their African slaves in different parts of the New World. These differences are partly outcomes of responding to the generic problem (discussed in Chapter 1) of how classification schemes create anomalies which then have to be accommodated. In the North American English colonies, persons of mixed 'race', regardless of the relative proportion of 'black' and 'white' in their ancestry, were classed as 'black'. Whereas in the Spanish and Portuguese colonies of Latin America, those of mixed 'race' were allocated a separate category or categories of their own. (New Orleans, French-held for a time, also had a distinct mulatto category.)

How can we explain this pattern? One possibility is to look at differences in the religious ideas (part of the culture) of the colonists. The Latin Americans were Catholic, and committed to the belief that the world was ordered hier-archically. This allowed them to recognise degrees of difference in people they wished to assert were inferior to themselves. In particular they could claim that others were inferior to themselves without having to assert that they were sub-human. In North America however, the dominant religion was Protestantism, which stressed the equality of all human beings. To be consist-ent, North American Protestants had to choose between seeing non-whites as equal to themselves (ruled out if they were to be enslaved), or as not 'humans' at all. There was no possibility of seeing them as some degree of lesser, but still human, beings, as Catholics could. Some commentators suggest this was one of the reasons why miscegenation was felt to be so much more of a sin by the North American Protestants than by the Catholic Latin Americans, for whom it had no connotations of bestiality. The extra sinfulness of mixed 'race' sex in the Protestant case may then have then led to the categorisation of all those of mixed 'race' as 'black' – effectively denying their mixed 'race' status and thus that sinful sexual relations had taken place (Tannenbaum, 1946; Diggs, 1953; Harris, 1970; Degler, 1971).

In both these examples, differences between ideas correlate with dif-ferences in behaviour and/or other ideas, which suggests a possible causal connection. But though these explanations may seem plausible they have limits. Even if their assumptions about the nature of the ideas in play are right, we have to question their sufficiency. In the first case, we still have to ask what causes the relatively weak commitment of Afro-Americans to marital stability and extended family obligation, deferred gratification and hard work, which such explanations allege. Possibly, the historical experi-ence of forced family separations under slavery weakened the kinship and particularly marital commitments – although we have also seen in Chapter 2 how poor economic circumstances themselves contribute to a looseness of the ties between husbands and wives in the black underclass. Probably the experience of slavery means that working long hours, for white bosses, for low wages is less tolerable to blacks than to newly arrived Asians. Blacks may refuse, as a form of resistance and statement of self-worth, jobs which Asians, with their different history perceive as a foot on the economic ladder. However, regardless of how they originated, differences in Asians' and Afro-Americans' cultural forms are not the only significant causal factor when accounting for their economic success and failure. We also need to consider, as Waldinger underlines, differences in levels of racial discrimination against the two categories, the capital some Asian migrants were able to bring with them, and their differential geographical distribution between the declining North Eastern states (Afro-Americans) and the economically expanding South West (Asians).

The completeness ('sufficiency') of an explanation in terms of (religious) beliefs alone is similarly limited in the second case. Firstly, we have already touched on the exploitation of the black slaves by the white colonisers in explaining why Protestant whites choose not to see slaves as equal to themselves. However, explanation in terms of religious beliefs alone are problematic because mixed 'race' categories are actually recognised in all the Caribbean islands, only some of which are Catholic. If there are cases, like the Caribbean slave societies, where Protestants, as well as Catholics, recognise mixed race categories (i.e. the correlation between type of religion and type of 'racial' classification is not perfect) then the explanation, though generally promising, needs buttressing by some other kinds of cause.

Culture is used, often intentionally, to motivate, mobilise, organise and justify taking positions in social competitions and struggles over distributions of resources. So when trying to explain the content or change of either beliefs or classification systems, it pays to consider how these are conditioned by, and condition, power relations. Thus when trying to explain the difference between Protestants who do (Caribbean) and do not (North America) adopt 'mixed-race' classification systems, a potentially significant factor is the impact on power relations of varying white to non-white population ratios in the different places.

Where whites were in a very small minority, their dominance in critical situations often depended on securing allies from outside their own ranks. These could be found by splitting the non-white population to produce one or more intermediate 'mixed-race' categories whom whites could, when needed, encourage to ally with them against the ('pure') black majority. This was the case in the Caribbean and Latin America, where we do find mixed 'race' categories, irrespective of religious differences. Strategic interests can plausibly be suggested to have motivated elaborating the logic of classification.

However in the United States, whites far outnumbered blacks and had much less need to establish alliances with non-whites and thus little interest in overcoming their religiously induced propensity to think in terms of black and white alone. Strategic interests motivated maintaining the dualist logic of classification and the absence of mixed-'race' categories we find there (Jordan, 1969).

In general, ideas/belief systems have 'causal powers' and as such explanatory relevance. The specific effects produced by the causal power of any given set of ideas/beliefs will depend on the characteristics of the particular circumstances in which they are mobilised, which will include more than merely 'other ideas and belief systems'. Ideas will have to be linked to non-ideational factors and the interaction between them specified. Even where the causal powers of ideas and belief systems are significant contributors to generating a particular phenomenon, they will not be the sole causal factors, and hence will be insufficient to explain the phenomenon.

Moreover, if we use a set of ideas/belief system as part of the explanation, we must recognise that these ideas which do the explaining ought themselves to be explained. Otherwise we will simply be taking them as 'given', which they are not. Further, as the discussion of implications for power relations suggests, it is not usually possible to explain ideas *entirely* by reference to other sets of overtly held ideas alone. However, so far we have only discussed the causal force of ideas which are consciously held. Now we have to consider the fact (already touched on in Box 5.1) that beliefs people can consciously articulate may well be linked to underlying systems of thought of which they are *unaware* and which are *not chosen*.

Culture at full power! What can 'unconscious' ideas explain?

We might talk of cultural explanation as at its most powerful when we can use it to make systematic causal links between a range of apparently unconnected spheres of behaviour and thought. To demonstrate culture operating at full power means going below the level at which people consciously make judgements and choices and can give reasons for what they do. It involves going deeper than was necessary when explaining why Protestants, given their beliefs in the equality of 'man' were led to see and treat slaves as less than human, since they could not hold them to be both human and inferior. There we used actors' desire for logical consistency to explain their actions. But to demonstrate the conditioning force of culture at its strongest, we need cases where it is necessary to resort to its deeper reaches (which are most resistant to choice) to explain the phenomena (the patterns of thought and behaviour) we want to understand. This is the level of methods, paradigms, habits, biases, dispositions and generative principles, which powerfully pattern the workings of preference, imagination and reasoning. Here, where the very lenses through which people view the world are installed, the autonomy of culture, and hence its necessity for explanation, is at its most impressive.

The cases we need to show culture at its strongest must allow us to demonstrate that there can be deep, underlying cultural relations capable of working very generally (though often unrecognised by those who use them) to organise a wide range of behaviour, preferences and beliefs. Useful cases for this 'necessity' testing, might be ones where there are contradictions between two or more ideas held by particular people, where what people do contradicts the ideas they consciously hold, or where ideas or behaviour seem to be completely arbitrary. Cases of apparent arbitrariness, or contradiction between ideas, or ideas and behaviour, make us ask what might be sustaining the ideas or behaviour in question. We will have provided some examples of culture at full power where we can show that in fact there *is* some other kind of cultural logic operating at a more fundamental, barely conscious, level of thought, which holds the contradictions together and explains what seems arbitrary.

Explaining 'arbitrary' ideas and practices: Jewish dietary laws and the prohibition of pork

Everyone knows that Jews, despite not being vegetarians, are forbidden by their religion to eat pork. Many, especially those who routinely eat this meat, see no harm in doing so and find it difficult to understand why anyone should find it objectionable. So why do Jews, among others (e.g. Moslems, Coptic and Ethiopian Orthodox Christians) place so much emphasis on avoiding pork? This is the same sort of question we asked (in Chapter 4) about the Huaorani insistence on only using spears to kill peccaries. The anthropologist Mary Douglas rejects explanations of Jewish dietary laws in terms of the intrinsic characteristics of the pig itself, such as its meat being particularly likely to go 'off' in hot climates. Instead she argues that the prohibition can only be understood in relation to fundamental Jewish belief that what is anomalous is polluting, and a subscription to a complex classification of animal species in terms of which the pig (as a cloven hoofed animal which does not chew the cud) is *category-crossing*. Other category crossing-creatures, such as shell-fish (which live in water but lacks fins and scales) are also taboo (Douglas, 1970, 1975, 1996).

Mary Douglas (1921–2007, British)

(1966) *Purity and Danger: An Analysis of Concepts of Pollution*, London, Routledge Classics (2002).

(1970) *Natural Symbols: Explorations in Cosmology*, London, Routledge (2003).

(1979) (with Isherwood, B.) *The World of Goods*, London, Routledge (1996).

(1983) (with Wildavsky, A.) *Risk and Culture: An Essay on the Selection of Environmental Dangers*, Berkeley, University of California Press.

(1992) *Risk and Blame: Essays in Cultural Theory*, London, Routledge, (1994).

In fact, uncovering that Judaism places considerable emphasis on classification as such, and that it generally rejects what is anomalous in terms of its classificatory schema (that is, which cross the boundaries of its classificatory 'boxes') facilitates understanding a wide range of apparently disparate features in the culture. In other words there is something about the way orthodox Jewish culture is put together at a very basic level, which has implications for its characteristic beliefs and rules. This example shows that culture is multi-layered or stratified; on the surface we find propositions which members of the culture can articulate, for example, about what is permitted to be eaten, or what one is

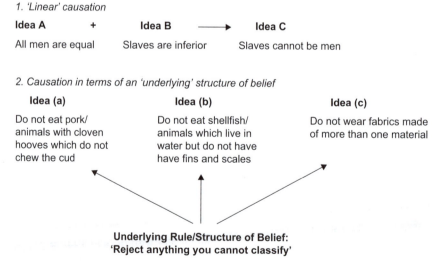

1. 'Linear' causation

Idea A   **+**   **Idea B** ⟶ **Idea C**

All men are equal   Slaves are inferior   Slaves cannot be men

2. Causation in terms of an 'underlying' structure of belief

Idea (a)   **Idea (b)**   **Idea (c)**

Do not eat pork/ animals with cloven hooves which do not chew the cud   Do not eat shellfish/ animals which live in water but do not have have fins and scales   Do not wear fabrics made of more than one material

Underlying Rule/Structure of Belief:
'Reject anything you cannot classify'

Figure 6.1 Two ways in which ideas cause other ideas

allowed to wear. But these are generated by a cultural 'method', (a kind of causal mechanism) of which participants may be unaware, which makes a virtue of removing ambiguity. Douglas's analysis points to the possibility that 'ideas' may generate other ideas, not just in terms of 'linear' causation (holding idea 'A' leads to holding idea 'B'), but also in the sense that 'underlying' structures of belief or 'cultural methods', can generate a potential multiplicity of 'surface' forms. The rules 'Do not eat pork' or 'Do not wear clothes containing more than one kind of material' are but particular instances of a more fundamental rule 'Reject anything you cannot classify.' Figure 6.1 summarises the difference between these two types of causation.

Explaining 'contradictions' between belief and behaviour: the case of homophobic acceptance of gays

Cunningham carried out research on a passenger ship in the 1960s, which found that whilst the male, heterosexual deck and engine-room crew were deeply hostile to the idea of homosexuality, they nevertheless tolerated and had positive relations with the openly gay men they interacted with onboard (Cunningham and Parker, 1978). Though generally regarding gays as deviants, they accepted them subject to very specific conditions. They had to be in certain occupations (waiters or hairdressers, not engine-room or deck crew), not be in positions of authority and command (there must be no openly gay officers), conform to the stereotype of gay camp style, take the role of surrogate women (e.g. as dancing partners) during male-only leisure in the crew's quarters, and avoid interaction with crew in the presence of real women or ashore.

Part of the explanation of the apparent contradiction of homophobic crew tolerating members of the category they hated, is to be found in the deeper logic underlining the system of rules which they imposed on gays on the ship. At its simplest, the crew used a dyadic model for conceptualising the social world. Things were either one thing or its opposite. Thus social relations of work, power and sex were defined in terms of 'us' and 'them'. Occupations were coded into 'hard' (deck and engine-room work) and 'soft' (waiter, hairdresser or musician). The ship was worked by those who gave orders (officers), and those who obeyed them (crew). Men (who are 'hard' and give orders) were starkly contrasted with women (who are 'soft' and obey orders). So for the crew, women were at the bottom of their imaginary hierarchy. As for gays, they were dangerous men who do not define themselves as dominating women, and were imagined to want to treat other men as women. They were 'witches', normally needing to be banned.

Given this method for imagining the social world, but faced with the fact that gay men on the ship could not actually be got rid of or even avoided, this 'intolerable' situation was dealt with by enforcing the symbolic transformation of the gays on the ship into 'women'. Forcing gays to fit into the dyadic scheme as 'soft' and subordinated symbolic women, removed the need to recognise them as a third distinct category or sex (as discussed in Chapter 1). Crew actually tolerated 'women', not gay men. This maintained the consistency of the crew's social world. Just as with Douglas's explanation of Jewish dietary laws, the explanation of the crew's pattern of tolerance posits a deeper level of culture constraining belief and action. They are both cases of strong classification and low tolerance of ambiguity which infect every interpretative act, by Jews and crew alike.

However though these examples do demonstrate the necessity for culture, we still have to ask what causes the factors we have used in our explanation – in these cases what causes the disposition to avoid ambiguity? We saw when discussing response to mixed 'race' people that social power relations may help explain why cultures vary in the extent to which they stress keeping things neatly classified and bounded. Why should Jewish culture classify so strictly? One possibility is to look for interconnections between the realm of ideas and the ancient Israelites' geopolitical situation – discussed by Weber in his *Ancient Judaism* (Weber, 1952). Surrounded by other tribes and lacking a clearly defined territory of their own, constantly bullied and displaced, and experiencing a very high level of insecurity, it is plausible to suggest that the biblical Jews invested heavily in cultural control by claiming a special relationship with God and developing a rigorous classification system. Anxious about geopolitical boundaries they could not fully control, they created and maintained symbolic boundaries which they could. Maintaining symbolic boundaries has remained important throughout their history as a marginalised people.

Similarly, compensation for subordination at the bottom of the formal organisational hierarchy of the ship might have led to the ship's crew placing so high and uncompromisable value on what they felt they *did* possess, that is pure masculine power. Perhaps this stance was also reinforced by their background in the traditional working class whose social and often geographical segregation from other classes has been similarly seen as fostering a general and deep propensity to classify dichotomously in terms of 'us' and 'them' with no intermediary categories (Lockwood, 1966; Bernstein, 1971; Martin, 1981).

Basil Bernstein (1924–2000, British)

(1971) *Class, Codes and Control 1: Theoretical Studies towards a Sociology of Language*, London, Routledge (2003).

(1973) *Class, Codes and Control 2: Applied Studies towards a Sociology of Language*, Hove, Psychology Press (2003).

(1975) *Class, Codes and Control 3: Towards a Theory of Educational Transmissions*, London, Routledge and Kegan Paul (1977).

(1990) *Class, Codes and Control 4: The Structuring of Pedagogic Discourse*, Routledge (2003).

Cultural change: change of and/or by culture

These examples show that the content of the culture people produce and the methods they use to produce it may be strongly conditioned by experience of positions in structures of power. But though the positions may seem permanent, they are outcomes of and subject to, processes of historical change. So too is cultural production. Though cultural systems, practices and objects constrain what may be potentially felt, said and done, this autonomy is not by itself sufficient to explain what elaboration/ development/change actually occurs. Talk of cultural 'systems', as though they were bits of machinery with their own internal logics, is useful, but it is more important to think of culture as historical media. The elements of autonomy that cultural practices enjoy do not just arise from their specific materiality and logics. They also connect to their being open and transformable, meaning they give people resources for expressing their responses to and interpretations of experience. Culture is continuously changed as it is used, as are the users by using it. This requires us to consider, case by case, the way people make use of possibilities offered by their cultural resources when responding to their changing experiences of, for example, the natural environment or positioning in power structures. When people need to make sense of new or changed experiences, they have motives, interests and opportunities to exploit the potential of cultural resources by creatively applying, modifying and varying their emphases.

Making creative use of cultural resources involves interaction between the users and the constraining yet enabling properties of cultural resources. Cultural resources may be more or less 'elastic' and users may be more or less imaginative and willing, for example, to accept novelty or tolerate contradictions. Where there is relatively easy access to cultural alternatives, and the possibility of putting them into practice, we must attend to users' modes of choosing and relating to any specific cultural practice or taste, as a component in a set of other practices which form a profile and to how these modes may change over time. Cultural consumption may be more or less habitual, reflexive, experimental, ironic, critical, enthusiastic, knowledgeable, deferential and so on. Generally, explaining the way cultural resources themselves are changed involves analysing contextualised episodes of interaction between, on the one hand, the potential for elaboration offered by the resources – their rigour or fuzziness for example and, on the other, the array of interests possessed by those engaged in transforming the old cultural forms into something different.

These points can be illustrated using two African cases. The Nuer, a tribal cattle people from Southern Sudan, have always symbolically equated cattle with people (Evans-Pritchard, 1940). They are given in exchange for brides, and as reparation for offences – as when the kin of the victim of a killing demand cattle from the perpetrator and his family. Traditionally they have been a primary medium of social life. Hutchinson in *Nuer Dilemmas* (1996) shows what happens when it becomes possible for the Nuer to buy and sell cattle for money (a recent medium of social life) in a market. Taking advantage of the market opportunities does not displace the traditional meanings and uses of cattle. The Nuer avoid having to choose between traditional and modern meanings by distinguishing special categories of cattle and of money. Thus the 'cattle of money' which have been bought with money are less special than 'cattle of girls' obtained as bride wealth on daughters' marriage. Similarly the special 'money of cattle' gained selling cattle is distinguished from 'money of work' gained from other sources. Obligations to kin operate differently in respect of these different types of cattle and money. Elaborating traditional culture to make these modern distinctions allows the Nuer to preserve much of the traditional importance assigned to cattle, as well as their social uses, while also permitting pursuit of their new interest in entering the market economy and making money from cattle sales. Their simultaneous desire to preserve tradition and to gain wealth, has stimulated cultural invention.

Edward Evan Evans-Pritchard (1902–1973, British)

(1940) *The Nuer: A Description of the Modes of Livelihood and Political Institutions of a Nilotic People*, USA, Oxford University Press (1987).

(1937) *Witchcraft, Oracles and Magic Among the Azande*, Oxford, Oxford University Press. (1976 abridged edition).

Our second African case also shows how culture is used and changed to cope with new circumstances. Daniel Smith's *A Culture of Corruption: Everyday Deception and Popular Discontent in Nigeria* (2008) draws on long-term field work to analyse why Nigerian society has a reputation for dishonesty and how Nigerians accommodate to low levels of everyday trust. Different kinds and degrees of corruption are discussed, from the everyday bribery of low-level officials, demands for favouritism and the notorious e-mail scams (favoured by unemployed but educated young men), through to larger-scale misappropriations by politicians of government funds and development aid. Most Nigerians are complicit in corrupt practices at some level, and may admire particularly skilful, complex or audacious deceptions, especially where victims (as with email scams) are foreigners. But they nonetheless typically condemn corruption in principle. Smith presents contemporary enthusiasms for vigilantism, witchcraft accusations, Pentecostalism (in the Christian south) and Islamic fundamentalism (in the north) as anti-corruption responses to this situation.

Corruption is common around the world, but why is it so pervasive in Nigeria that Smith can talk of 'a culture of corruption', despite a complex ambivalence towards it? How did it get to be like this? The emergence of this pattern is too complicated to deal with properly here. But we can note that Nigerian society has been transformed by the colonial imposition of a single state over several tribally distinct regions, by independence, and then by increasing participation in the global economy, especially as a major oil producer but also as recipient of international development aid. It is a particular case of the 'modernising' and globalising of a traditional society.

In their traditional world 'Nigerians' shared a morality based on the particularistic values and loyalties associated with tribal identities, kinship and local patron-clientism, balancing inequality with reciprocity. People had a duty to favour their own. But the 'modernising' process brought with it a different ethos, demanding that **universalistic** rather than **particularistic** criteria apply in the public realm where no one should be treated differently because, for example, of their religion, tribe, kin group or regional identity. These two sets of values tend to cross-pressure individuals, while the post-colonial state and globalising economy provide new opportunities for private appropriation. Thus we can suppose that people initially tested out post-colonial officials to whom they had no special ties, to see if they would be treated impartially. If officials continued to show favouritism to others or demanded bribes, citizens would withhold trust. The same goes for the early experience of voting for anti-corruption politicians (many of whom failed to live up to their promises, taking advantage of new possibilities for personal gain and patronage). Corruption and mistrust don't have to be routinised over time, but if after initial experience they are, this tends to become very difficult to change. There is a self-reinforcing effect once people have to participate in corruption in order to carry on their everyday lives. Thus Nigerians are not just cross-pressured between traditional and modern values but between the latter and the everyday practicalities of getting by in a society where corruption has become endemic. They understand that they perpetuate it by, for example, paying bribes at police road blocks (and also recognise that low and intermittent police pay is often both a cause and a consequence of corruption). But if they refused to pay, people couldn't travel. Moreover, once officials are found to be routinely open to 'persuasion', then the pressure to ask for favours for those one has immediate or traditional obligations to is strong. There are many ways of invoking practical excuses and of describing doing the 'right' thing for others by doing the 'wrong' thing (an idea we will return to in Chapter 12 when considering how people justify their carbon use.)

Cultural variety and change among the British middle classes

We can pursue the issue of cultural change in a quite different context by discussing important research into the cultural characteristics of the British middle classes towards the end of the 20th century. This sort of research, which seeks to characterise durable underlying organising principles of the cultures of such large collectivities as classes, or sections of classes, offers further examples of cultural explanation at its most powerful. Many interesting attempts have been made to characterise fundamental differences between the cultures of the working and the middle class (Bernstein, 1971; Martin, 1981; Bennett et al., 2009). With the latter's relentless expansion, and stimulated by the parallel growth of 'post-modern' cultural practices and sensibilities, late 20th century showed the emergence of significant differences within a British middle class which had often previously been thought to be rather culturally homogenous. This development suggests that the experiences of members of the middle class, and the ways they pursue their interests have changed and continue to do so. Cultural change may have been motivated by changes in the social structural environment in which interests are followed.

We will begin by focusing on the account offered by Mike Savage and his fellow authors, of the developing variety of middle class cultural forms – an analysis based on data from the 1987–8 British Market Research Bureau survey of spending patterns (Savage et al., 1992).

Savage identified three major types of middle class culture, the 'undistinctive', the 'ascetic' and the 'post-modern' (Figure 6.2).

	Hierarchist	Professional
Public sector	**Undistinctive** cultural preferences (two different varieties of)	**Ascetic** cultural preferences
Private sector		**Post-modern** (omnivore) cultural preferences

Figure 6.2 Varieties of middle-class culture (by structural location)

The 'undistinctive' is the British version of the cultural pattern of what Americans dub 'organisation men' – for example, civil servants and traditional managers, whose lives are governed by their experience of stable organisational hierarchies (Whyte, 1957). Until recently, British companies have tended to emphasise loyalty and context-specific knowledge and recruit managers from their own employees rather than drafting in external recruits with professional educational qualifications. The employment advantages of the British internally appointed managers and the civil servants tend to be dependent on remaining within and moving up in their organisations which recognise their specific, but not always transferable, skills (Figure 6.3). Savage reports the managers showed strong preferences for modified versions of traditional country pursuits (kinds of shooting and fishing), squash and golf clubs, and most sorts of drinking, but an aversion to all types of 'high' culture (classical concerts, galleries, plays, opera). They avoided camping, holidays in France, and 'keep fit'. The data for civil servants, on the other hand, showed them lacking strong dispositions either for or against any specific form of consumption, though they are 60 per cent more likely to play bowls than the general population (Savage et al., 1992: 110). Otherwise they showed a slight disinclination to take foreign holidays, go camping or play tennis or keep fit, and they avoided squash. 'High' cultural forms, as manifested in biases in consumption, do not seem particularly important to them (Savage et al., 1992: 108, 114). However, despite these differences, there are good grounds for putting managers and civil servants together as 'hierarchists' since both are dependent on their positions in formal organisational hierarchies and deeming their cultural preferences undistinctive because neither considers high cultural forms as a way of achieving 'distinction' (Bourdieu, 1984) (Box 5.1).

We now turn to look at two categories of the professional middle class. Distinguished from each other in terms of their location in the public and in the private sector, they both have more independent accreditation than the traditional managers and civil servants. The cultural biases they exhibited can be labelled respectively 'ascetic' and 'post-modern'. The BMRB data summarised by Savage et al. (1992: 108, 114) show considerable differences between

	Hierarchist	Professional
Public sector	e.g. (routine) civil servant/bureaucrat	e.g. education, health, welfare workers
Private sector	e.g. traditional manager	e.g. non-traditional managers, legal and financial sector workers, public relations and marketing workers

Figure 6.3 Varieties of middle-class structural location elaborated

the two categories. Professionals in the public sector have strong interests in the consumption of 'high' culture largely lacking for their counterparts in the private sector. But probably their opposing styles are most starkly represented by the ascetics' enthusiasm for climbing, rambling and yoga (absent from post-modernists' preferences) and their rejection of the clubs, champagne and golf (which the post-modernists favoured). These differences act as social barriers, including some, and excluding others. That such barriers exist suggests that relations among these sectors of the middle classes have a potential for conflict. When interpreting survey data such as these it is helpful to keep in mind one's own experience of the practical realities of interaction between those with the different tastes and practices referred to. By inspecting the data can we find any deep cultural principles organising the biases of these two professional categories?

Take the 'ascetics', so-called by Savage et al. because of their commitment to a lifestyle based on mental and bodily health and exercise, and modest overall consumption (represented by below average alcoholic drinking). What do their enthusiasms for the county-side, climbing, hiking, yoga, camping, museums, 'high' culture and self-drive foreign holidays have in common? All involve effort, making use of education, and manifesting a certain sort of virtue. Ascetics seem to need to work to demonstrate their competence, sensibility, healthiness and independence. Their resistance to commercialism and to insufficiently health-promoting activities such as snooker and fishing, suggests a commitment to upholding a moral ideal, an idea about what is right. This ideal is held in common with others like themselves. The statistical patterns in consumption indicate the existence of a large group of like-minded individuals prepared to uphold a way of life by the ways they use their time and bodies.

It is plausible to suggest that the 'ascetic' pattern is actually formed by a commitment to upholding a collective identity. Can we say anything about the kind of group it is? The rejection of clubs and luxuries, and the enthusiasm for energetic and self-organised activities of a largely non-competitive kind, suggests that ascetics do not acknowledge established social structures and hierarchies, but prefer each individual to equally represent the group. It is a collectivity of moral equals who are not insulated from one another by positions in established structures. They share responsibility equally and can be called 'egalitarians'. Cultural preferences are therefore very important for marking the external boundary of this group. That a boundary is being marked is suggested by the fact that so much is rejected or excluded. Preferences are motivated by the desire to experience and demonstrate moral authority as worthy group representatives and be accepted as legitimate members of the cultural community.

Sometimes described as a desire for 'authenticity', this means using tests for distinguishing the genuine from the sham (often associated with commercialism) (Urry, 1990; Bagguley et al., 1990). Effort and education and willingness to acquire real experience for oneself (the long walk to the historic site, detailed guide book in hand) are the defences against inauthenticity or outsiders. 'Ascetics' tend to be suspicious of others, testing their moral quality before allowing them to join in, and are defensive of what they consider matters of principle. They know what to condemn (e.g. 'ignorant' audiences, snooker, fishing, the golf club, champagne drinking, commercial culture generally). They insist that things be done 'properly'.

The 'post-moderns', though also individualised, are quite different. They condemn virtually nothing, suggesting that they are not committed to upholding a group identity or cultural hierarchies. They are not self-appointed guardians of cultural and moral values and do not seem to be distinguishing between 'us' and other categories. With no boundary to defend they are in some ways more relaxed than the ascetics. Commercial culture, which has not been academically authorised by education and state institutions such as museums and galleries, is not criticised as 'inauthentic'; in fact they do not use criteria of 'authenticity' at all (Savage et al: 128–9). All forms of culture can be used for whatever short-term advantage they might bring. Consumption seems guided only by individual self-interest, opportunity, pleasure and requirements of flexible networking. Each person is at the centre of their instrumental networks. As 'individualist' cultural 'omnivores' they can participate in anything on an experimental basis (Peterson, 1992). Joining clubs as a means of doing things and making contacts carries no moral obligation. Weak commitment and frequently changing preferences are typical. Symptomatic of the apparently contradictory and disorganised character of post-modern cultural consumption is their propensity both to consume rich food and especially alcohol, but also to favour sports and exercise – often of a competitive and high-energy kind. They may want to get fit and train themselves, not as a matter of principle, but rather for any benefits this gives them when marketing themselves inside and outside work (Savage et al.: 115–16). Their basic commitment is to self-promotion rather than any group.

The 'deep' organising principles of each of the types of professionals (to uphold an internally somewhat egalitarian collective identity, or unbounded, competitive individualism), makes each collection of cultural preferences into a set with a high degree of predictability. Even though survey data paints with the crudest brush-strokes, we can recognise the portraits. We begin to see why ascetics and postmodernists place high value on the things they do. We are not very surprised that postmodernists seem to cast their net wider than ascetics when it comes to choosing holiday destinations. If we know the deeper principle governing their selections, we can make shrewd guesses about how they are likely to make other kinds of choices. So we might hypothesise that when gardening, ascetics will tend to take the time to learn about plants and the history of garden design, do the planning and planting themselves and wait for their efforts to mature, whereas postmodernists will tend to go for the quick 'make-over' following whatever model has caught their eye.

Different attitudes to time and nature are also suggested by this example. We can predict that, for post-modernists, nature is a robust resource available for competitive exploitation, which can be used with only short-term consideration. They are likely to play down talk of environmental crisis. For more anxious ascetics, on the other hand, nature, often conceptualised as the most authentic thing of all, is likely to be viewed as needing long-term conservation for the general good (Box 3.4). They will tend to play up talk of environmental crisis. If we bring the non-professional managers and civil servants type back into the picture, we might hypothesise first, that as hierarchists, they are likely to devote their gardening to keeping things tidy and acceptable to their neighbours. Second, they will probably concede that nature is vulnerable to irresponsible action, but believe that the appropriate policies will be forthcoming from the scientists and state authorities. They will not play up or talk down environmental crisis (Douglas, 1970, 1982; Thompson et al., 1990: 25–38).

This brief discussion is sufficient to suggest that knowing how to operate the deep organising principles of cultures makes it possible to predict how people using them will respond to all sorts of dilemmas. Attitudes to squash can be linked to attitudes to environmental politics, for example. But, as with the earlier examples in this chapter, we still need to explain why a whole category of people adopt a particular 'deep' cultural principle in the first place. The beauty of Savage's discussion is that it clearly links each type of cultural preference or taste profile, to a particular occupational condition with its associated economic and political interests. Thus the reason why the culture of the British middle classes has divided towards the end of the 20th century is that the growth of the service sector of the economy has multiplied types of professional expertise. By the late 1980s middle classes formed two broad categories, those that relied on state employment and those that did not. 'Post-modernists' explored ways of enhancing their individual market attractiveness in the private sector where competition and instability reigns. Hence their being weakly committed cultural omnivores.

Against this, 'ascetics' still had cultural assets which could not easily be sold on the market and were therefore reliant on state employment, where job security (if not pay) has been higher and norms of service rather than competition have predominated. They needed to maintain the collective legitimacy of their expertise, to justify taxpayers continuing to fund the public sector. Finally those managers and bureaucrats still dependant on maintaining and improving their positions in organisations, continue to draw on their length of service and organisation-specific, non-credentialised knowledge. This contributes to their tendency to despise, rather than invest in, intellectualising 'high' culture. (Figure 6.4 summarises the argument.)

Some later studies, including those with which Savage has been involved, suggest the post-modern, omnivorous cultural orientation has become much more prevalent (Peterson and Kern, 1996; Warde, 2007; Bennett et al., 2009). They suggest that very many of the middle class are now happy to enjoy a multiplicity of cultural forms, including 'popular' ones traditionally seen as typically working-class. Some argue this shows class/occupational experience no longer influences cultural preferences (either within the middle class or between it and the working-class). But our previous discussion allows an alternative interpretation. That is that the growth of omnivorousness connects to changes in class structuring and the growth of the kinds of work and market situation which Savage's original work suggested supported this post-modern outlook. Today the public/private sector divide is weakening. Much public sector work has been directly privatised or is outsourced. That which remains offers reduced security, less routine promotion and requires a greater worker focus on personal development and 'marketing'. That class remains significant is suggested by evidence that the middle class omnivore's appropriation

OCCUPATION & EMPLOYMENT	MANAGERS & GOVERNMENT BUREAUCRATS	PUBLIC SECTOR PROFESSIONALS IN EDUCATION, HEALTH AND WELFARE	PRIVATE SECTOR PROFESSIONALS IN LAW, FINANCE, MARKETING, PERSONNEL, ETC.
MAJOR INTERESTS	Preserve organisational positions, rewards and opportunities.	Preserve the legitimacy value of cultural assets against degradation by the market.	Exploit market opportunities to convert cultural assets into economic rewards.
CULTURAL TYPE	'UNDISTINCTIVE'	'ASCETIC'	'POST-MODERN'
'DEEP' CULTURAL PRINCIPLE	Each member fulfils their social functions in complex social hierarchies.	Each individual is committed to maintaining and embodying the social whole.	Each individual is committed to their self-interest and competitive advantage.
	'HIERARCHISTS'	'EGALITARIANS'	'INDIVIDUALISTS'

Figure 6.4 Occupational interests underpinning the three types of middle-class culture

of popular culture is often more intellectualised and disinterested than that of the working-class (Lizardo and Skiles, 2012). Also, the working-class have not expanded their cultural horizons 'upwards' to the same extent as the middle class have 'downwards'.

Social interests and the relative autonomy of culture

We have been arguing that occupational and class interests can influence a person's cultural profile – a set of classifying and evaluating practices which they may use to strengthen their competitive position. Cultural behaviour (manifested in leisure, aesthetic taste, self stylisation, language or sense of humour for example) is used to claim or test claims to be recognised as belonging to some social category with implications for future partnerships of all kinds. Status ambitions motivate either cultural deference, imitation, and simulation, or transgression, while status defence and monopolisation motivates conservatism, secrecy, condescension and ridicule (Box 5.1).

A telling example is given by Friedman (2011, 2012) who shows how upwardly mobile individuals from working-class families encounter a subtle mode of middle class cultural 'distinction' in their experience of comedians. He distinguishes between the down-to-earth, often obscene style of comics whose appeal is immediate and unreflexive for their working-class audiences, and the 'alternative comedy' the middle class favour and consume in a more intellectualised and 'disinterested' manner. If the previously working-class person now wants to 'perform' as middle class, they may have to inhibit the wrong kind of laughter at the wrong kinds of jokes in middle class company. And also discover how to laugh in the controlled middle class style at what they may think isn't really funny. This may cause anxiety because laughter is often involuntary, difficult to inhibit or simulate, and is therefore a powerful medium for expressing and detecting social identities (See Box 7.1).

This example of the social structural conditioning of responses to comedians is a good one for reasserting the relative *autonomy* of culture. Though cultural phenomena may be explained to some extent by social competition, this is not sufficient. People consume comedy not just to make status claims, but because it is a form of cultural practice operating within cultural frameworks which has the capacity to be enjoyable, pleasurable, relaxing, stimulating or whatever. If comedy didn't have its own specific properties devoted to provoking laughter, it would not be an effective medium for expressing and judging claims to social status or identities. Reflexivity is an intrinsic feature/property of much comedy, so it is unsurprising that the ambiguities and troubles arising from the status order provide comedians with much of their material.

Conclusion

We have seen how culture plays its part in social explanations. We have shown that the internal relations of culture are complex and multilayered and that the **generative (causal) mechanisms** involved may be very powerful; more powerful than we might have first thought, and therefore necessary for explanation. The mechanisms at work are often not obvious and can only be brought to light by forms of cultural analysis which may be technically difficult. But as our examples suggest, such mechanisms both explain and allow powerful predictions to be made allowing us to test if we have got the mechanism right. So for example, if our predictions about differences between private and public sector employees' attitudes to environmental risk do not square with the facts, then we would have to rethink the generative mechanism. However though culture can be shown to have strong constraining effects, the effects are conditioning not determining, just as was the case when we considered the effects of nature. So despite having underlined the necessity of culture we have also had to insist that it is insufficient.

In the Introduction we spoke of social theory (a particular kind of cultural product) as offering a set of tools for understanding social life. Now we can suggest that culture, in general, can be thought of as a toolkit which people use all the time and which becomes significant as it is mobilised to sort out particular problems as we live our lives. Some tools operate near automatically, priming actors to respond to problems in routine ways. But often we lack the perfect tool in the kit, and then we make do by elaborating, modifying, stretching those tools we can consciously reflect on. Moreover cultural elements interact with the psychology of individuals, the competitive interests and power of collectivities and groups, and the material and social circumstances of interaction.

It is always important to identify the principles ordering the reasoning and preferences of the people whose behaviour and belief we might want to explain (whether or not they consciously recognise them). Knowing the rules of the game being played and the 'logic' of actors' orientations to the playing is important, just as it was in the case of explaining action in terms of rational choice, as we saw in Chapter 1. Given the 'frame' of some culture and its internal relations, explanation can proceed.

But there are two major limits to cultural explanation, which we will be dealing with in the remaining chapters (see Figure 5.5). The first, as we have already seen, is the problem of explaining the cultural elements themselves. As in the examples of the Huaorani (in Chapter 4), Jews, ship's crew, contemporary Nuer, Nigerian citizens, and British middle classes, this can involve reference to their social structural location in relation to surrounding societies and position in structures of power. So the first limit of cultural explanations is the need to supplement them with social structural considerations.

The second limit is that though culture may involve complex and 'deep' generative mechanisms, and have a strong claim to be relatively autonomous from individuals who operate it, as well as from nature and social structure, it nevertheless depends on the agency of human actors for its impact. Even the most enthusiastic 'culturalist' does not imagine that culture can bypass the mediation of human actors, even if only as relays, or as Harold Garfinkel puts it, 'cultural dopes' (Box 7.3). If you do not think that people are 'dopes', merely using their cultural resources automatically, then you must be interested in understanding what is involved in 'using', 'applying', 'interpreting' and 'creating'. In the next chapter we will look at the nature of human action, at what is involved in 'doing'. 'Doing', being practical, is the process in which the constraining legacies of the past, both cultural and structural, are resisted and exploited.

Questions related to themes in this chapter

This chapter has considered how we might explain differences in cultural forms and the relationships between culture and social structure.

1) How does Mary Douglas explain why Jewish dietary law prohibits pork? Think about your own eating practices – what non-religiously derived rules are you following when deciding what to eat and when?
2) You and your partner often have big arguments about household expenditure, which surprises you both, as you are not particularly short of money and don't want to quarrel. Might the suggestion that there are differences in the fundamental structure of the deep culture you each subscribe to, help explain your arguments? And if so, how could it help resolve them?
3) What criteria do you use when deciding if an item of clothing is clean enough to put on again the next day? Why might some people make different decisions to the ones that you make?
4) Make two lists, one of the kinds of leisure activities you enjoy, the other of the kinds you dislike. Are there any underlying patterns in your preferences?
5) What practices do you use to make claims to social status? Do you make different kinds of claims to different audiences?

PART IV

The concept of action

CHAPTER 7

What does action explain?

The discussions of nature and culture and their place in social explanations suggested that they are conditions of action. Conditioning is a relatively 'open' concept of constraint which helps to explain regularity, patterning and typicality, but leaves room for the possibility of novelty, innovation and variation from the typical. As used here, 'conditioning' does not mean 'determining'. The force of the relative autonomy of natural and cultural conditions is mediated by how people interact with them. The potential of any particular kind of condition to have some effect, itself depends upon its relations, under specific circumstances, with the other kinds of conditions.

In the case of social reality, we are interested in the potential causal powers of conditions to constrain and enable when set in complexes of relations constituted by the action projects of people trying to do things. 'Action' makes a particular kind of contribution to the causal mix, not more or less important than the others, but necessary. So we now have to think about the properties of the action involved in this mediation. This chapter discusses why action is a central concept in social theory and why the way action is related to culture and structure is said to be its fundamental problem. We have already argued that it is necessary to think of these three concepts as a subset of our set of five; it is not really possible to do social explanation without using all three (Figure 7.1).

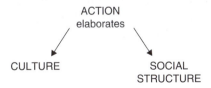

Figure 7.1 What the social sciences contribute to social explanation: action

To appreciate the distinctive contribution of 'action' to enabling the conditioning potential of culture and social structure to be actualised, it is important to remember that in the social sciences we are always dealing with problems which are the outcomes of historical processes. (In the last chapter we described cultural forms as historical media.) These processes result in events (with their own durations) which start, modify and/or stop collective practices and patterns. Though the outcomes of these historical processes may be, and often are, quite extensive in time, we are just as interested in those which are short-lived and what brings them to an end. If we are trying to explain some regularity or pattern which, by definition, must exist for some period of time, however short, and accept that the origination and sustaining of such a phenomenon involved various kinds of actions, all of which have been constrained by certain changing conditions (natural, cultural and structural), then we must be interested in the moment by moment process of action. To repeat; it is not that action alone is responsible for social phenomena ('action*ism*') but that it is a necessary condition of much of the causal potential of culture and social structure.

Social phenomena are the products of processes which operate at two levels of time; the long durations of emergent patterns and regularities, and the shorter time of the unfolding situations of practical action when people actually do whatever is involved in mediating the force of conditions. As we saw when considering culture, what people do in the present, not only mediates the impact of pre-existing conditions, but contributes to whether or not those conditions continue (i.e. are reproduced) or are changed (i.e. are transformed). What people do has constitutive effects; action is involved in bringing things into existence and action is required to keep things going. Both the impact and reproduction of enduring conditions depends on how people interact with them in the present. Using ancient philosophical language, the actions of people are 'efficient causes', that is they 'make thing happen' in the sense that, by trying to produce outcomes, actors put in train context-specific interactions among the various relatively autonomous 'non-efficient' causal powers of the cultural and structural conditions. By providing occasions which energise and contextualise relations among conditions, action brings their causal potential into play. But that is certainly not to say that action controls the causal powers it unleashes or that actors intend all the outcomes (Lewis, 2000; Parker, 2006: 133).

These relations between action and its cultural and social structural conditions are clearly central to the historical character of social reality (discussed in Chapter 5). They are fundamental to the way in which, at every moment, social reality feeds back into itself, absorbing the legacy of the past, and at the same time generating the sometimes intended, but generally unintended, outcomes which will become its legacy to the future. We can picture the process as in Figure 7.2.

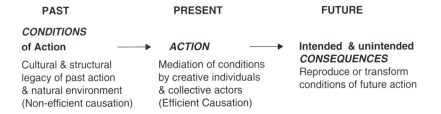

PAST	PRESENT	FUTURE
CONDITIONS **of Action** →	*ACTION* →	**Intended & unintended** ***CONSEQUENCES***
Cultural & structural legacy of past action & natural environment (Non-efficient causation)	Mediation of conditions by creative individuals & collective actors (Efficient Causation)	Reproduce or transform conditions of future action

Figure 7.2   The historical process

What are the processes at work in the moment by moment advance into the future? Clearly, what goes on in the present of action is very important. If we want to explain cases of repetition leading to social regularities, patterning and continuities, or the opposite, that is cases of novelty which might lead to discontinuities and transformation of patterns, then we have to be interested in the unique conduct of each action situation and what makes such conduct possible.

First, we will be interested in any general characteristics of action and interaction which structure the way people conduct themselves. What is it to 'interact' socially? What is involved in 'interpreting' the action situation? What is involved in 'being practical'? What 'methods' do people use? How is the relevance of rules and information decided so that they can be applied? What are the necessary conditions of orderly everyday routines? Second, we will be interested in the precise 'micro-histories' of interaction in specific situations. We will want to get close to 'where the action is' (to use Goffman's phrase), in order to account for the productive process resulting in both regularities and exceptions (Goffman, 1969) (Box 7.1).

Erving Goffman (1922–1982, Canadian)

(1959) *The Presentation of Self in Every day Life,* Harmondsworth, Penguin (1990).

(1961) *Asylums, Essays on the Social Situation of Mental Patients,* Harmondsworth, Penguin (1991).

(1963) *Stigma: Notes on the Management of a Spoiled Identity,* Harmondsworth, Penguin (1990).

(1969) *Where the Action Is,* Harmondsworth, Allen Lane.

(1971) *Relations in Public: Microstudies of the Public Order,* New York, Basic Books.

(1974) *Frame Analysis: An Essay on the Organization of Experience,* Boston, Northeastern University Press (1986).

Box 7.1 Goffman and the interaction order

Goffman suggests that producing the 'interaction order' of normal and pre-dictable everyday face-to-face interaction is a complex business. His detailed observations of interaction situations show the basic mechanisms and methods which produce reliable, routine interaction. He draws on observations of conduct from novelists, diarists, etiquette manuals, diplomats, military training schemes etc. – any source offering advice about what is required to produce reliable interaction. The effort to avoid embarrassment, suggests that a lot is at stake in every interaction. If it goes wrong feelings of anger, confusion, embarrassment, shame, loneliness, hope are triggered.

Face-to-face interaction takes place between embodied selves

To interact we communicate using bodily demeanour, gesture and verbal language. Communication involves providing external, physically perceptible signals for others to interpret – constituting a performance in space and time which Goffman initially thought of as a sort of dramatic staging. However, because we are not in complete control of our behaviour and give off invol-untary signals, there is a problem of maintaining consistency between our voluntary and involuntary behaviour.

Each of us exists in a condition of selfhood

As 'selves' we symbolically represent ourselves to ourselves, treating our-selves as 'objects', which can be defined in all sorts of ways. Goffman defines a self as a 'stance-taking entity' capable of self-constructing projects.

Self presentation and its 'impression management' is a process of try-ing to get others to confirm our ideal selves – our preferred moral status. We control distribution of information, depending on what we know about the prejudices and knowledge of those with whom we are interacting. We 'give' information which will put us in a good light, and try to conceal poten-tially discrediting information. Self-presentation, in nearly all cases, involves selective exposure, and tactical revelation about ourselves, depending on the circumstances.

When interpreting attempts to secure morally favourable recognition, we generally focus on the most easily controlled channels of communica-tion such as speech, while simultaneously looking for contradictory signals 'given off', usually involuntarily, by less easily controlled channels such as facial expression. Goffman describes how a crofter serving a meal to a visi-tor pays more attention to how fast the latter eats than to their polite claims to be enjoying the food!

Embarrassment is felt when we realise that others have got hold of discrediting information which compromises our ideal self. Impression management has broken down. The interaction cannot go on until some sort of explanation, usually an excuse, brings the ideal and the reality more into alignment. What to do about embarrassment is central to Goffman's thinking.

Interaction makes us vulnerable to confidence tricksters, one of Goffman's favourite topics. Interaction is not simply a cynical game of self-projection and suspicion of others. We all have an interest in maintaining the smooth flow of interaction at least as much as we have in unmasking the fraudulent and deceivers. Sincerity is important but it is not all important. Playing one's parts in organised interaction is so important that most of the time we do not go very deep into checking out whether others really are what they say they are. This tendency to trust first impressions is the basis of the confidence trickster's art.

Tact is necessary. Everyone makes mistakes, reaches beyond their grasp, is naïve, deceived, weak, cross-pressured between conflicting commitments. We are all vulnerable to our self-presentations being found wanting. Goffman's great insight is that social interaction involves participants in what he calls 'civil inattention', that is the tactful overlooking of discrediting information. We help one another recover dignity when impression management breaks down. Since we may all benefit from this, Goffman shows tact to be thoroughly practical for maintaining the flow of interaction.

His method is to focus on settings where the risk of embarrassment or 'havoc' is high. His work has close affinities with ethnomethodolgy's interest in methods for maintaining social order in the face of contingencies (see Box 7.3). But Goffman's more sympathetic interest is in the work of being a self.

Goffman, E. (1959) *The Presentation of Self in Every day Life,* Harmondsworth, Penguin (1990).
Goffman, E. (1961) *Asylums,* Harmondsworth, Penguin (1991).
Goffman, E. (1963) *Stigma*, Harmondsworth, Penguin (1990).
Goffman, E. (1969) *Where the Action Is.* Harmondsworth, Allen Lane.
Manning, P (1992) *Erving Goffman and Modern Sociology*, Cambridge, Polity.

Action, actors, subjects and objects

We have already used the concept of action in earlier chapters because it is impossible to avoid it. But now we must make its meaning clear. In ordinary language we speak of the action of all sorts of things – for example the action of acids, light, temperature. Used like this almost anything can be said to act in the sense of having some kind of effect. But we do not think of say a fire as being an actor just because it burns a house down. Although we showed in our discussion of nature, that we are interested in everything that can 'act' to condition social phenomena, we also have to be interested in the actions of actors, that is, of voluntary agents with intentions, motives and purposes. They can initiate action rather than being compelled to behave in some way. Actors, unlike acids or fires, can do other than they do, and what they do has to be explained, in part, by reference to the *choices* they make. It is this ability to make choices about conduct, which qualifies actors as 'subjects' (i.e. as having subjectivity) and not just 'objects'. Subjects have the ability to initiate action which may (but only may) have consequences for objects. The distinction between subjects and objects is very important in social theory because human beings are generally thought to have the status of subjects and to be capable of voluntary action. It is this capacity which qualifies them to be considered as 'efficient' causes in social reality.

If the problem we want to explain is a specific action or pattern of action done by a specific actor or actors, part of our explanation must refer to their intentions and reasons for doing it. As the subjective agents of the action(s) in question, their motives for choosing to do what they do have some explanatory power. However, motive explanations can only be partial, firstly because statements of motives are limited by the actor's consciousness of, and attitude towards, the real reasons for why they do something. Secondly, both the statement of motives, as well as the real motives themselves must be explained. The fact that actors can give reasons does not mean that their accounts of their reasons for acting are sufficient to understand those actions. Often it is valuable to pay attention to the individual and psychological mechanisms relating an actor to their action and how they account for it. And as we saw in the last chapter, it helps to know the cultural mechanisms and economic and political **interests** generating their reasoning. Knowing actors' reasons is only the beginning of explaining their actions and social explanation more generally, not its end.

Individual and collective actors

At this point it is important to limit the tendency to think of action as something only humans do. We ought not to deny powers of action to other animals whose behaviour may only be intelligible if we attribute **intentionality** to them. Nor ought we to think that action is only done by individuals. Methodological individualists make this mistake of deriving powers of action solely from the properties individual human beings. But there are two things to consider here. First, simply being human, at best only means one has a potential for action which has to be developed and socially acknowledged.

Babies are human, but are the newly born actors *yet*? Adults may also be deemed incompetent to act in particular situations. If you receive a form for jury service, it will ask if you are receiving treatment for mental illness and you may be ineligible to act as a juror if you answer 'yes'. Second, the capacity or power for action may depend on the formation of organised collectivities which can decide what they want to do, choose a course of action and mobilise the necessary resources to get what they want. It makes good sense to talk of the intentions and actions of collectivities, provided that one can specify the decision-making roles and positions of power within the organisation or movement, whose occupants contribute to defining how the collectivity will act. It is appropriate to say, for example, that the National Farmers' Union decided to try and change government policy on agricultural subsidies, and that the government acted to counter its demand.

Collective action depends on the capability of individuals to act in organised roles, often making decisions as representatives of collectivities. But conversely, contributing to the action of collectivities is a power multiplier, enabling individuals to do things on a scale and with a significance which would be impossible if they were simply acting on their own. Think what powers to act, and make some impact on the world, depend on your occupying roles within collectivities and organisations. Imagine you were not a citizen of a state, a member of a family, lacked access to financial institutions or markets, were not signed up to medical and dental practices, were completely unaffiliated to any specialised clubs or associations, shared nothing domestically. Would your powers of action be massively reduced? In general the capacity to act depends not just on one's 'humanity', but on the powers one has by virtue of one's relation to collectivities and institutions. No one would deny one's position in hierarchies of power affects what one can do. (We will return to these considerations in Chapter 9 when discussing the concept of social structure.)

Social action and interaction

Not all action is social. When one acts on some technical decision, say to remove a punctured bicycle tyre by 'beginning at the valve', one is acting, but not socially. One is just being technically correct! (Ask your local bike shop). All action is relevant for social explanation. But, as Max Weber's path-breaking analysis of these concepts has it, action is social when it involves the actor in relating to others and taking them into account in deciding what to do (Weber, orig. 1921, 1968) (Box 7.2). Orientation to others is crucial, and what flows from it obviously plays a very large part in social explanation. As we saw when discussing the role of culture in the

Box 7.2 Weber's ideal types of action

Multi-causal explanation

Weber holds that each event, structure, individual and action is historically unique – and that unique cases can be explained as the outcome of a specific interaction among many kinds of causation. *Social theoretical concepts give general definitions of these kinds of causation.*

Ideal types

Weber creates general concepts – ideal types – which define intelligible possibilities.

Ideal types can be used to produce descriptions. They can be compared, like 'bench-marks', with unique real cases which can then be described in terms of their similarities and differences relative to the idealisation. Ideal types offer suggestions about what is worth looking out for or likely to be the case, and also about features which might be expected to be associated with each other.

Ideal types of motivational orientations of actors

Motives for action are one kind of cause, because actors pursue interests on the basis of subjective meaning.

Weber defines four ideal types of action-orientation – i.e. kinds of meaning given to (explaining and justifying) action.

1. **Mean-ends rational (zweckrational) action;** '.... the end, means, and secondary results are all rationally taken into account and weighed.'
2. **Value-rational (wertrational) action;** '.... social action is determined by a conscious belief in the value for its own sake ... independently of its prospects of success.'
3. **Affectual action;** action is determined by specific affects and feeling-states 'which lack the consistent planned orientation' associated with mean-ends rationality or value rationality.
4. **Traditional action;** action is determined by 'ingrained habituation often lacking a highly self-conscious aspect.'

Real actions differ in the ways they are outcomes of various emphases and combinations of these four: rationality, value commitments, emotions, and habit.

Weber, M. (1921–22). *Economy and Society*, Vols 1 and 2, (ed. Roth, G. and Wittich, C.) Berkeley, University of California Press (1978).

competition for social status, social life and the formation of collective phenomena depend to a large degree on how actors regard and take account
of each other. These orientations help explain how actors interact and any
patterns in that interaction.

Interaction between actors can take place wherever there are means
of communication and need not be 'face to face'. It can occur between
soldiers shouting across No Man's Land (for interaction in trench warfare
see Ashworth, 1980), between presidents of nuclear superpowers through
coded messages, and between financial traders using stock-market computer
networks. Interaction through email, texting and various rapidly developing forms of personal digital media has become common over the last
20 years. However, these newer forms with their developing rules of usage
(Donner, 2007; Baron and Segerstad, 2010; Shuter and Chattopadhyay,
2010; Skierkowski and Wood, 2012) overlie the pre-digital face-to face-
variety which students of social interaction have tended to concentrate on
and treat as in some sense fundamental (Giddens, 1984: 64–73) (Box 7.1).
They have shown that face-to-face interaction is a universal dimension of
social life, possessing certain relatively autonomous properties, irrespective
of cultural differences and communications technology. This is because
only in the physical presence of those with whom we interact can we access
the density of fully embodied communicative action. Interaction without
the emotional information about sincerity, trustworthiness and tact we
can display and glean from interpreting face-work, body language, gesture
and tone of voice is generally less morally reliable. Current debates about
whether participants in court cases can give evidence via video-links, from
behind screens, or with their faces fully veiled, are relevant here. As perhaps
is the development of a whole range of 'emoticons' and 'emoji' – icons to
accompany email and other text-based messages to convey additional information about the feelings, mood, facial expression (such as sad, confused,
laughing) of the sender.

Rules, strategies and practice: what's involved in 'doing'?

What do we do when we act? This is a central question for social theory
since it is here that action's relative autonomy will be revealed. It is not easy
to answer because there are really two queries involved, one about actors,
another about action. Let's start with types of action defined by reference
to the actor's state of mind. Actions can be distinguished by the extent to
which actors are aware of why they do them. At one extreme lie those which
actors do deliberately – self-conscious action which is carefully considered in
advance, the kind of action rational choice theory (RCT) takes as its model.

RCT analysis (considered in Chapters 1 and 2) supposes actors carefully calculate the advantage in using some particular means to a desired end. But though this sort of rational planning does often happen, we have already queried whether it is universal. Indeed there are grounds for thinking that rational deliberation as a precondition of acting, is the exception rather than the rule.

There are a variety of reasons why actors may have imperfect knowledge of why they act. One is because rational deliberation takes time and is a bit of a luxury. Most actions are done under pressure of immediate circumstances, 'spontaneously', 'without a second thought'. Knowing what to do and making choices has to be based on something other than deliberate rational appraisal. Put slightly differently, only occasionally does action involve following some predetermined plan or ideal rule. Practical social life is not a matter of *first* deciding what to do, and *then* putting the plan into operation or conforming to a rule for ideal conduct. Rather than being governed by the logic of rationality and systems of rules, action is often better thought of as governed by the 'logic of practice' – Bourdieu's phrase captures the sense that to be practical we cannot base our action on deliberate rational anticipation (Bourdieu, 1990b) (Box 5.1). We are too caught up in the ongoing flow of life to sacrifice taking advantage of opportunities for the sake of sticking rigidly to a plan.

Routines, habits, dispositions, practical consciousness

Social phenomenologists, interested in the basic forms of pre-reflective consciousness of the social world (Schutz, 1962–1966, 1967), and ethnomethodologists, concerned with how actors maintain a sense of social order (Garfinkel, 1967) together with **structuration theorists** (Giddens, 1984; Parker, 2000: 55–7) all share an interest in how it is possible for actors to deal with the situations they face, in spite of lacking the time to deliberate and make carefully considered choices (Box 7.3).

Alfred Schutz (1899–1959, Austrian)

(1932) *The Phenomenology of the Social World*, Evanston, Northwestern University Press (1967).

Collected Papers I: The Problem of Social Reality: II. Studies in Social Theory: III. Studies in Phenomenological Philosophy, Dordrecht, Martinus Nijhoff Publishers (1962–66).

Collected Papers IV: Phaenomenologica, No. 136, Dordrecht, Kluwer Academic Publishers (1996).

(with Luckman, T.) *The Structures of the Life-World. Vol. 1 (Studies in Phenomenology and Existential Philosophy) and Vol. 2 (Structures of the Life-World)*, Evanston, Northwestern University Press (1975).

Harold Garfinkel (1917–2011, American)

(1967) *Studies in Ethnomethodology,* Oxford, Polity (1984).
(2002) *Ethnomethodology's Program: Working Out Durkheim's Aphorism,* Lanham, Rowman and Littlefield.

Box 7.3   Phenomenological sociology and ethnomethodology

As a theory of knowledge, phenomenology is characterised by what it understands the foundation or starting point of the knowledge process to be. This is a condition of being 'presuppositionless'. Phenomenologists such as Husserl and Merleau-Ponty try to specify a 'natural-attitude' of pre-reflective, pre-conceptualised direct experience of phenomena by individuals, prior to any mediation by culture, education, language etc. Schutz adopts the language of this frame of reference to consider what consciousness of 'social reality' in the 'natural attitude' involves.

Garfinkel develops Schutz's phenomenology of social experience for a different purpose, to solve Talcott Parsons' 'problem of social order'. In *The Structure of Social Action* (1937) Parsons asked why individual actors do not act randomly, but produce patterns of behaviour – showing that they are collectivised in various ways. Rather than seeing social order as an objective state of affairs Garfinkel approached the problem as one of how actors work to *represent* and *experience society as orderly*. He conceptualises social order as something people 'sense' as the result of a precarious 'practical accomplishment'. Ethnomethodology investigates the methods actors use to interpret their experience and establish meaning sufficiently plausible, for the time being, to provide a basis for continuing to act.

Practical action involves finding ways and means of responding to whatever the context of action presents. It is largely a matter of dealing with contingencies. Garfinkel presents meaning and the sense of social order as always teetering on the edge of being upset as actors try to use rules to make sense of contexts characterised as 'indexical' that is as unique, immediate and concrete. 'Ethnomethods' are used to wrest a sense of order from indexical conditions of action and bridge the difference between ideals about what should happen and what really happens in particular instances.

Ethnomethods are easily exemplified in the conduct of conversation; this would be impossible if we did not tolerate uncertainty about what was being talked about, and maintain the useful fiction that even if we don't understand we will eventually. We have to be willing to allow time for meaning to emerge. Ethnomethods generally work to limit uncertainty's power to derail our sense that we live in an orderly world as an intelligible and actionable reality. For ethnomethodologists the rationality of common sense lies in the skilled use of techniques for inhibiting doubt and uncertainty.

Berger, P. and Luckmann, T. (1967) *The Social Construction of Reality*, Harmondsworth, Allen Lane.

Garfinkel, H. (1967) *Studies in Ethnomethodology,* New York, Wiley.

Husserl, E. (orig. 1913, 1982) *Ideas Pertaining to a Pure Phenomenology and to a Phenomenological Philosophy,* Dordrecht, Kluwer Academic Publishers.

Merleau-Ponty, M (1945) *The Phenomenology of Perception*, London, Routledge Classics (2003).

Schutz, A. (1962–6) *Collected Papers,* Dordrecht, Nijhoff.

Schutz, A. (1967) *The Phenomenology of the Social World,* Evanston, Northwestern University Press.

Rogers, M.F. (1983) *Sociology, Ethnomethodology and Experience.* Cambridge, Cambridge University Press.

They point to a basic process of routinisation as a reason why much activity falls below the horizon of conscious decision-making. We not only don't choose to, but don't even notice that we are doing something in a particular way. As we grow up, we establish various personal routines (having corn-flakes for breakfast, brushing our teeth and putting our clothes on in a particular way each morning). These habits which we can change if it occurs to us are geared into the routines of everyday life, such as the 'working day', the 'weekend', driving on the left (in the U.K. and Australia), which we cannot do much about. But whether we could in principle change things, there are masses of apparently trivial details of our lives which we do not actually choose to do each time we enact them – something we acknowledge when we say that we are on 'automatic pilot'. The suggestion is that this is just as well. Imagine what life would be like if you had to decide about everything you do all the time. Routines and habits are very useful because they free us up to pay attention to relatively few issues which require us to make choices.

A second idea, already encountered when discussing culture, is that we can cope with the pressure of circumstances because we learn general dispositions (of which we may be unaware) which condition our expectations and strategies when dealing with any situation. A disposition is a generalising tendency to place a particular sort of interpretation on circumstances, which makes it actionable. We considered examples when discussing the varieties of middle class culture in the previous chapter and the relation to the environment of the Dunne-za in Chapter 4. Acting on the basis of disposition – what we might call a general-purpose method for living – results in regularities in our actions and the way we typically deal with problems. Bourdieu, among others, has suggested that there are long-term historical processes in which dispositions are formed for collectivities such as classes. For example, in response to their experience of subordination or domination, they learn about what it is practical to expect, what is achievable, what they can take for granted or presume. He calls this their 'habitus'. Such dispositions are thus clearly the product of cultural and structural conditioning (Box 5.1).

Giddens, influenced by the philosopher Wittgenstein (Wittgenstein, 1963; Giddens, 1984), also suggests that the consciousness of people is first and foremost a 'practical consciousness' rather than a theoretically reflective and rationally deliberating one. People know what to do and how to carry on, but they do not need to be able to give reasons for what they are doing. Once one has learned say specific motor skills like riding a bike, or the deep cultural bias of a culture, doing something such as leaning appropriately when cornering, or disdaining country and western music, no longer depend on explicit reasoning and making choices. But the fact that we may know what it is to do things wrongly, suggests that our action is being directed by some kind of conscious awareness and implicit knowledge of relevant rules. Typically it is when we experience mistakes that we find ourselves trying to make the rules we know and live by, explicit. This is usually possible but also difficult and often involves some sort of methodological research. What rules guide riding a bike? And just why do we feel aggrieved for example, to be offered water to drink at a party, or sense that it is better to say 'she did' rather than 'she done her shopping' when we can't immediately be sure why this is the case? The knowledge involved in most action provides a 'tacit', mutually understood basis for interaction, which actors may not be able to explain and does not need to be expressed. It is the kind of thing visiting social scientists such as anthropological field workers want to learn about and have difficulty getting anybody to tell them. But where they do, then, as Bourdieu puts it, the native informants often talk to them in the way they do to young children. Though children can of course ask questions which adults find unexpected, and maybe, impossible to answer.

Contingency (accidents) in social life and the uniqueness of circumstances

The above suggestions are intended to help explain how actors deal with the demands of practical situations where the priority is on 'doing' rather than reflection about what to do. The reason why time is normally too short for reflection, and what makes routines, habits and dispositions so useful, is that we are frequently required to respond to unexpected events and new things we have not previously experienced. Practice has a certain urgency. The routine stuff can be taken for granted, allowing us to concentrate on the urgent problems that always arise. However hard we try to anticipate and control events it is normal for these attempts to fail in some way. The old military adage, 'No plan survives first contact', applies to all kinds of planning. The really important question is how you cope when events do not go according to plan. Good plans may retrospectively be shown to have survived the test of emerging events relatively well, but good or bad, plans have to be supported by improvisation, 'making it up as one goes along'. This involves responding creatively to the opportunities presented by ever-changing situations, being sufficiently flexible about one's goals, and what one allows as acceptable means.

This is where we must return to consider the second question entailed in asking 'what do we do when we act'? This is the question about 'action' as such, rather than about actors and their states of mind. Being practical in the face of the unexpected, the new and the uncertain, requires that actors do the right kinds of things. Sustaining interaction in ongoing situations, despite not being sure about what they are doing, demands that appropriate skills are used. Improvisation is not just a matter of actors having the right 'attitude', but of using the right methods. Viewed in this light, social life is an ongoing process of discovery. The meaning of our conscious actions is likely to change as we undertake them. Being practical requires that we have second thoughts about what we are doing in the light of emerging consequences and changes in the context of action which become apparent. To the extent that we can reflexively monitor the effects of our actions, this helps to stop doing what may be turning out to be negative and to reinforce what seems to be positive for achieving our goals. To keep track of emerging consequences and changes of context is a practical necessity which requires actors to use the appropriate interpretative skills. It is after the event – retrospectively – that it is possible to begin to arrive at a conclusion about what some action meant. Actors must know how to manage before such conclusions become possible. Not even the relative stability of hindsight ends the possibility of reinterpretation, because the past is interpreted within an ever-changing context of present action, interests and knowledge.

Following Schutz's lead, Garfinkel and the ethnomethodologists have tried to specify the techniques of interpretation and action people use in the face of uncertainty about what is going on (Box 7.3). Irrespective of the specific content of one's disposition, which derives from membership of cultural and structural collectivities, actors must also rely on the universal techniques of 'common sense'. This is the practical form of rationality which allows for vagueness and mistakes, tolerates delays, accepts that there are many details and values which do not need to be made explicit, and can refer to a 'background' of 'what everybody knows' when making excuses. This is the rationality of doing the best one can in the circumstances, recognising that each circumstance may constrain action in its unique way.

The place of practical action in social explanation

If social life involves action which is highly responsive to the unique circumstances in which it is done, we must be interested in how conduct in these unique situations unfolds. It is here we see moment by moment, action by action, movement towards the eventual outcomes which we may want to explain. Every moment and act is a potential turning point in the emergence of outcomes, which could, retrospectively, be revealed to be important. *When* and w*hat* people improvise and create, and *how* they do it, in the face of unique circumstances are important elements in any explanation. And it is true that all actors have to act creatively just to cope with the most humdrum aspects of everyday life.

Unless one believes that nature, culture and social structure determine rather than condition behaviour there should be little reason to deny the creativity of actors and the productivity of action situations. Even performers in a play, following a text, make choices about how to say their lines. In real life, actors also adjust and rewrite the 'lines' they are given as they go along.

Jazz and total institutions

There certainly are examples where creative emergence from a unique situation appears very strong. Think of the improvisation of jazz. The music may not be written at all, and the musicians have an open mind about what they are going to do. They start, and what happens emerges as they play, in a complex, extended process of interaction. The performance is unique, unpredictable and may be literally unrepeatable; if not recorded, something of great musical importance may be lost forever. But even here, the players do not, and could not, start from scratch. They play around with standard songs, chord sequences or phrases which they all know inside out, and are likely to accept a minimum of musical conventions such as key and time signature for their performance. The speed with which improvisation can occur typically depends on having a deep grounding in a wide range of musical 'building blocks' that can be combined, stretched and mutated in many different ways. Actors never entirely escape their 'cultural heritage' – in the case of jazz, African-American culture, slavery, the 'blues', and so on. The freedom of jazz depends on having some relationship with traditions, even if only to contradict them. This dependence on some cultural starting point does not in any way prevent us from allowing that new sounds can be produced in the freedom and spontaneity of performance. The only problem is trying to unpick how the performance happened in the heat of the moment, by, for example, discussing memories, and analysing recordings. But however difficult this is, jazz, like any human social enterprise, establishes traditions in which past performances provide the reference points, model, and inspiration for current ones. It has been said that, 'If you want to play jazz and you're against thieving, you're in the wrong business'. Culture thus constrains and enables action, and traditions are reproduced and at the same time, developed and changed (Sudnow, 1978).

Thus it appears that what people do is not explicable by reference only to the actors and what they do in any given situation. This is true of all situations including those where people appear to act with the greatest possible freedom and spontaneity. Of course many situations are at the opposite pole, where actors have virtually no room for manoeuvre. Think of what Erving Goffman called 'total institutions'. Examples are prisons, monasteries, asylums, boarding schools, concentration camps and slave plantations. All specialise in intensifying control of action by means of tightly specified rules and powerful sanctions for breaking them. The amazing thing is that though, at the extreme, such harsh regimes can destroy the autonomy of actors, in practice there is usually a lot of effective improvisation and resistance by both staff and inmates. Inmates may exert some independence by 'internally' distancing themselves from the roles they are forced to play. But often they can engage in more overt forms of resistance. This is because even total institutions are vulnerable to contingencies and have to leave space for people to 'make it up as they go along' from time to time (Goffman, 1968; Elkins, 1976) (Box 7.4).

Box 7.4 Total institutions

Goffman developed the concept of 'total institution' in the context of an ethnographic study (begun in 1955) of the predicament of those defined as mentally ill, located at the bottom of the power structure of a mental hospital (*Asylums*, 1961). He suggests mental hospitals exist to discipline behaviour perceived threatening to the interaction order; '... mental symptoms are acts by an individual that openly proclaim to others that he must have assumptions about himself which the relevant bit of social organisation can neither allow him nor do much about' (1971: 356).

Total institutions, of which asylums are just one example (others being prisons, military training camps, boarding schools and monasteries), act as **'forcing house(s) for changing persons'** by imposing a **'discipline of being'** on inmates' self-expression. Goffman analyses becoming a mental patient into four stages.

1. **The pre-patient stage,** following rejection by family and friends, involves 'disintegrative re-evaluation' of self as 'insane'.
2. **The inpatient stage** is the core of the concept of a **'total institution'.** In a closed environment, patients are cut off from their previous contexts and contacts, and subjected to intensive supervision. The regime is **bureaucratically formalised** and **impersonal**. Inmates suffer **'civil death'** and **'mortification of the self'** by being stripped of everything they can use to symbolise their pre-patient person identity. Their clothes, hair, personal possessions, and privacy are removed; discrediting information is aired publicly so everyone starts stigmatised. Goffman says they must be 'disinfected of identifications', lose their 'identity kits' and have their sense of self-importance, crushed, to make way for the therapeutic efforts of the medical staff.
3. **Withdrawal and 'looking for angles'.** Initially patients 'withdraw', curbing their impulse to self-presentation. Total surveillance makes even temporary escape impossible. Patients learn what is required of them and a power struggle takes place. Staff try to control the behaviour of the patient by offering and withdrawing 'privileges' such as mail, cigarettes, television, toilet paper, coffee, sweets, etc. Patients try to assert themselves, looking for 'angles' so that they can get more of the valuable stuff without antagonising the staff.
4. **'Secondary adjustments'** involves four adaptive strategies for making the best of a bad situation. (i) **Situational Withdrawal** by daydreaming and fantasising; (ii) where attacks on self identity are too strong, **developing an intransigent line** by retaliating and non-compliance, such as hunger strikes; (iii) **Colonisation,** by re-defining the inside as preferable to the outside and inverting the formal aims of the hospital (i.e. to cure the patient); (iv) **Conversion**, by appearing to accept the staff definition of reality in order to be thought fit to be rehabilitated.

Mental hospitals expect their patients to identify their 'selves' with their institutional status. The **'underlife'** of secondary adjustments exists because human beings are self-defining entities who use institutional definitions of statuses and roles but are not reducible to them. 'Total institutions' exist because those who build them recognise the difficulty of controlling the way someone thinks about themselves and others. Mental patients' 'secondary adjustments' are the evidence of a fundamental human quality, the freedom of the personal self. The unintended consequence of attacking the self are defensive responses which will be treated as the symptoms the attack is designed to treat. Goffman thinks patients recover in spite of this kind of treatment, not because of it.

Goffman, E. (1961) *Asylums: Essays on the Social Situation of Mental Patients and Other Inmates'*, Harmondsworth, Penguin (1991).
Goffman, E. (1971) *Relations in Public: Microstudies of the Public Order*, New York Basic Books.

Conclusion: conditioning and action

Given so much goes on in the present, it is tempting to treat action situations as providing all we need, to understand the phenomena we are interested in. We can just look at the detailed process in which they emerged. Who needs history and the past? We have the immediacy of 'flesh and blood' actors in the full flood of ongoing interaction. The jazz session (Russell, 1972), the court-room drama (Atkinson and Drew, 1979), the intimate conversation (Goodwin, 1984), the recruitment interview (Button, 1987), walking home at night in the 'Village', inner west Philadelphia (Anderson, 1990) and so on are all unique complex events in which who does what matters. A new talent emerges, the innocent go free, a life's partner is chosen, a job is gained, a mugging avoided and mutual respect maintained – or not. But the present of each action situation cannot be abstracted out of historical time and treated as an autonomous, self-producing entity. Just as individuals cannot be understood without reference to non-individual social concepts (such as roles and statuses), so particular action-situations cannot be understood without reference to the wider and more enduring historical contexts of traditions and institutions in which they take place. Thus, for example, night walks in the 'Village' are risky because it's a boundary location where the paths of different 'racial' categories and of richer gentrifiers and poorer inhabitants can cross. The conventions and resources put into play by participants – such as the 'street wisdom' gradually built up by the old established Villagers – have to come from somewhere.

The creativity of action, the uniqueness of situations and situational emergence, are very important but they are not everything (see Fig. 7.3). The dynamic of historical change is not reducible to the creativity of actors, though there would be no history without them. It is actors, more or less skilfully, who put the conditions into play and in doing so transform them. But they do not make history just as they please.

ACTION is what actors do to make a difference to the outcomes of situations. It involves trying to influence the workings of various conditioning forces.

PROPERTIES OF ACTION

1. Voluntary Intentional Agents
+
2. Action situations
Actors respond to uncertainty, time pressures, imperfect information and
uniqueness of changing contexts.
They interpret, evaluate, judge to
give meaning to action-situations,
a) *less*, and/or b) *more*, reflexively.

a) Less reflexively
Practical sense of what's required:
'common sense','habitus', intuition
skill, 'flow', present emphasis.
Non-discursive; implicit rule-following.
Retrospective accountability
in terms of cultural frameworks and biases.

b) More reflexively
Prospective deliberation and planning.
Gather information and relevant theories
to define possibilities. Future emphasis.
Weigh relative merits of alternatives.
Means-ends rationality.
Costs and feasibility evaluated in relation to
value commitments, cultural frameworks
and biases.

**RELATIVELY AUTONOMOUS
POWERS of *Action*
elaborate the properties of**
INDIVIDUALS, CULTURE, NATURE,
and SOCIAL STRUCTURE.

Figure 7.3 Summary – the relative autonomy of action: how action works

So far we have considered this relation between conditioning and action by thinking about how culture conditions action, and action produces cultural changes (such as the elaboration of jazz) which become conditions of future action. However there are two sorts of conditions *of* action, which are substantially produced *by* action. Culture is one. The other is social structure. But before considering the similarities and differences between culture and social structure, the next chapter discusses more detailed examples designed to show just how important action is for social explanation, but which also show its limits.

Questions related to themes in this chapter

This chapter discusses 'action' as what is involved in guiding behaviour according to its subjective meaningfulness. It looks at the practical, creative and provisional ways actors determine sufficient meaning in often uncertain action situations, and how they determine the changing relevance of resources, such as knowledge, rules, models, and values, as courses of action unfold.

1) What are the important differences between the way in which foundations 'act' to stabilise a building and an architect 'acts' to ensure she designs a building which won't fall down?

2) Are individual human beings always actors?

3) Think of some area of your life which is governed by habit. What are the advantages of this and are there any disadvantages?

4) Find two areas of your life which you think would be very hard to routinise. Why is this the case?

5) What do we mean by 'collective actors'? Imagine some circumstances in which the following might become a collective actor: a random collection of commuters on the top deck of a bus; a queue of individuals waiting for a shop selling a new electronic product to open; the new intake of a university hall of residence.

CHAPTER 8

Testing the explanatory value of action

So far we have argued that social life is shaped by the interaction of the different kinds of force, each having only relative autonomy. This also applies to the force of action. Whereas nature, culture (and social structure) condition action, we have described action as *mediating* these conditions. This mediation is itself a special ever-present condition of social life. It must therefore figure in our explanations of what people do and what happens. However, though it can influence how conditions affect things, nevertheless it cannot escape being related to its conditioning context. There is no free-floating action as it were. Action is always done by specific, socially-related actors, (individual and/or collective) using specific cultural resources, to engage specific circumstances.

Action, intentionality and 'activity' in social life

Generally, ordinary action explanations tend to refer to these three elements: actors, culture and circumstances, focused round the conscious intentions of actors. We often try to explain the specific actions of specific actors by finding out what their intentions were, what they wanted to achieve by the acts in question. This kind of action explanation is best called intentional explanation and is really to be associated with individualism. It plays only a minor role in the task of explaining collective phenomena, if only because such explanations leave us with the problem of explaining the intentions themselves; they are not final causes.

Though action as a social theoretical concept has human intentionality (the actor's sense of purpose) built in to its definition, this is not what makes action a relatively autonomous force shaping social life. The properties of human actors (such as intentionality, consciousness, capacity for language) are conditions of action but not the properties of action as such. Intentionality may motivate participation in some project or field of action but does not govern what is required to pursue the project. Actors may want things but they must go about getting them in appropriate ways. Action as a relatively autonomous force is best thought of as a social process of activity, which makes its own demands of actors. They must have certain kinds of knowledge and competence to take part.

Satisfying the demands of action is not just necessary for actors to get what they want. A profound implication of the previous chapters for social explanation is that the existence of collective phenomena, such as economic, technical and cultural practices, depends on them being used and enacted. There is near unanimous agreement among social theorists about this point. Social reality is stuffed with human beings acting out the conditions of their collectivisation. So, for example, the informal economy of the ghetto (Chapter 2), the cultures of hunter-gatherers (Chapter 4) or the consumption patterns of middle class professionals (Chapter 6), exist because they are more or less continuously enacted practices; child-care and clothes are exchanged, moose tracked and monkeys darted, and consumer preferences for golf or 'alternative comedy', indulged. If those involved stopped being active, using their skills and making their choices, applying their sense of priorities, what we can identify as their respective collective conditions, would disappear. This is not to say that action alone is sufficient to keep a way of life in being, only that it is necessary.

When we select our examples of the role of activity in social explanation, we will concentrate on precisely how the social process of action contributes to the production and maintenance of collective phenomena. This means that we will ignore the impact of the unique creativity of the action of specific individuals, because we take it as given that individuals are ordinarily capable of creativity, and that it is very often necessary to refer to the actions of specific individuals in social explanation. The creativity of individuals is a given.

Best cases for testing the explanatory power of action

The force of action, and the necessity of including it in explanation, is immediately apparent in cases where actors seem to be free agents, able to shape the course of events more or less as they like. As we suggested in Chapter 1, creative artists are typically thought of as free agents and we evoked one such example in the previous chapter when discussing jazz improvisation – though we proceeded to show that the creative capacities of musicians were insufficient to explain the performance which was always also shaped by cultural factors, such as various musical traditions. Similarly, the requirements to take action into account can scarcely be disputed where especially powerful actors, in key decision-making positions, clearly shape the outcomes that occur. But once again, these actors are not entirely autonomous, since their individual or collective power flows from resources attaching to their institutions, or gained in a history of competitive struggle. While the directors of major corporations can make or break the economies of whole regions with their decisions about plant locations, they can only do so because of their positions in their firm and their firm's place in the structure of global capitalism. The forcefulness of the action of the powerful is (as we will elaborate in Chapter 9) closely tied to the effects of social structure.

Thus, even where action is self-evidently important for explanation, we can show that it is not, on its own, sufficient. But can we also provide cases where it is a necessary component for explanation even though this initially seems unlikely? A 'necessity' test of this sort would be possible where actors may not be especially powerful and appear to be very tightly controlled. If we can show that even in such circumstances the action of actors is of fundamental significance for explaining what is going on, then we will have made a strong argument for its necessity. Moreover if we can also show that their action makes a fundamental contribution to the long-term durability of collective phenomena such as institutions and practices, we will have made a very strong case for its importance for understanding social reality in general.

To follow this test strategy we need studies of the action of people operating within long lasting and highly disciplined settings. By 'highly disciplined' we mean that actors are required, subject to various sanctions, to account for their actions. Actors must justify themselves, either when challenged, or as a matter of routine. This is typical of contemporary occupational environments with complex divisions of labour, where getting work done depends on coordinating many different tasks and decisions by specialists. The need to incorporate action in any social explanation can be demonstrated by considering how specialised contributors to complex divisions of labour are disciplined and justify themselves. We will therefore discuss in detail, some examples from different kinds of highly controlled occupational environments.

Practicalities of bureaucratic action: coping with routine crises in a welfare office

We can begin with a classic type of a modern occupational environment, that of bureaucratic administration. Bureaucracy, as Weber made clear, is a technique to make performance predictable and reliable, creating routines by formulating what is expected of actors as precisely as possible in objective, impersonal (non-particularistic) rules (Weber, 1968: 956–8). These rules specify what must be done and the reasons for doing it, to deal properly with the whole range of cases that the organisation has been set up to cater for.

Personal discretion is reduced as much as possible. The bureaucracy's workers have tight scripts to follow. The cases they treat are processed by being fitted into a classification scheme, which enables them to be dealt with according to a general formula. The job of the bureaucrat is routinely to apply these formulae of general rules to actual, particular cases. The question is 'what is involved in trying to process real cases to conform to the abstract rules?'

Don Zimmerman (1971) explored this issue in his classic analysis of the conduct of day-to-day business in the Lakeside Office of the Californian Bureau of Public Assistance. Typical of state administered welfare schemes, this office's purpose was to administer the distribution of welfare payments (to the elderly, disabled and sick). Legislation set the rules governing whether or not applicants were entitled to assistance. The Public Assistance workers' basic task was to ensure appropriate payments went to qualified applicants and to weed out those who did not qualify. The office was supposed to distribute assistance *efficiently*, meeting the legitimate needs of applicants, and *fairly*, within the legal framework. Because applicants were often highly stressed, there was a lot of pressure on office workers to be able to justify their decisions as conforming to the legal specification of what ought to be done. So here was a work environment with abundant detailed, formal rules of procedure and demands to justify actions by reference to them. There was a strong tension between the theoretical ideal of what ought to happen, and the practical reality of what actually did.

Zimmerman concentrated on the difficulties faced by receptionists of the 'Intake Division' whose position made what they did crucial to managing the practicalities of realising the theoretical ideal laid down in the rules. This was because the receptionists did the initial screening of applicants for eligibility for assistance, and then assigned them to intake caseworkers for more detailed assessment. At the end of the intake process, eligible applicants were passed on to the 'Approved Division' for routine administration and periodic re-assessment.

The significance of focussing on the receptionists stems from the fact that, being situated between a flow of incoming applicants and a number of caseworkers, they were pressured from both sides. Both applicants and caseworkers were potential and conflicting sources of difficulty which receptionists would have to manage.

Receptionists were committed to maintaining a smooth, orderly flow of work during the day, and ending the day with no half-processed applications. Good order meant firstly, that cases were completed at a sufficient rate to prevent complaints from applicants, but with sufficient time allowed to investigate each case to ensure that appropriate assistance was given. Speeding up the flow must not be achieved by taking shortcuts and careless work. But secondly, good order meant that a 'fairness' rule be followed to ensure equality of treatment for applicants and intake case workers. The central plank of operationalising the intake procedure was the rule for allocating cases to caseworkers, 'first come, first served' (Zimmerman, 1971: 227). Each day a table was drawn up listing available caseworkers down one side and numbers for allocated cases across the top. Ideally caseworker 'A' was allocated applicant 1, caseworker 'B' applicant 2 and so on. Only when all the available caseworkers (say 'A'–'F') had cases, should caseworker 'A' be allocated a second applicant. The goal was to distribute the processing equally. If it was, it would be justifiable. Caseworkers would be unable to argue that some are given easier or harder daily caseloads. That was the theory.

In practice it was impossible to stick literally to this rule, but this did not result in chaos. Nor did it mean that the rule was irrelevant to securing orderly activity, as we shall see. Receptionists secured order in a practical context of varying pressures. Not every day was the same. The numbers of applicants of different kinds could vary as could caseworker availability. Cases varied in the difficulty they posed for processing. Some could be dealt with quickly, others not. Applicants themselves could create 'scenes', be threatening, or confused, or have special circumstances requiring exceptional consideration and so on. Caseworkers had reputations for their strengths and weaknesses when processing particular kinds of cases. Some worked faster than others. They had known preferences for certain kinds of cases, just as applicants had preferences for particular caseworkers. We can imagine the variety of considerations receptionists had to keep in mind when assigning applicants to caseworkers. Their practical skill was to do the allocating, keeping the work flowing and queues as short as possible, while preventing objections from applicants and caseworkers. Any departure from the ideal had to be justifiable. How was this done?

People must sometimes depart from routines to make the workday 'come out right' (Zimmerman, 1971: 229) as when caseworker Jones was about to be assigned a third applicant before she had finished interviewing her first applicant of the day. Keeping to the 'first come, first served' rule where an early case is taking an unusually long time, will result in a long wait for later assigned cases and create potential trouble. In this case, Jones's third assigned applicant, having waited over an hour, was reallocated to another caseworker. The rule was broken, or rather suspended, but only after discussion and on the decision of a senior receptionist. The 'unfairness' in giving Jones's third case to another caseworker who had already cleared her own cases, had to be justified by reference to the exceptional nature of Jones's first case. That some cases just do take a long time was understood as a 'fact of life'. Receptionists' interest in achieving the smooth, rapid processing of applicants could be frustrated by intake case workers' need to take their time with applicants

(Zimmerman, 1971: 231). Similarly, when faced with assigning 'difficult' applicants, it may be wiser to suspend the 'first come, first served' rule in favour of the applicant being dealt with by a particular caseworker who was known to be good at handling such cases. Zimmerman cites an example of two caseworkers, Hall and Kuhn, exchanging applicants because of such considerations (1971: 233–4). Everyone who worked in the Intake Division knew that there are such exceptional cases, that certain caseworkers handle them best, and that suspending the rule of fairness on such grounds was justifiable.

These simple examples show what is involved in the everyday enactment of bureaucratic organisations. The ideals enshrined in the formal procedures do not apply themselves. To work, bureaucracy needs workers who are competent rule users. They must be positively oriented to rule guidance, and be able to account for their actions in terms of them. But they must also be able to assess the relevance of the rules on a case-by-case basis. Formally organised activity necessarily depends on the creative interpretation of cases and the exercise of judgement about the practical wisdom of suspending rules.

This ordinary creative enactment of the organisation depends on two kinds of knowledge. First, workers must understand the general purpose, or 'spirit', of the organisation, which helps them when deciding whether or not to apply or suspend the rules. Second, they must know about the routine difficulties faced by everyone working in the organisation doing the job. This practical background knowledge includes an understanding of the typical, if not precisely predictable, 'snags', which threaten the normal flow of business. Workers must know how to maintain the 'spirit' of the organisation, by operating with ideas of 'normality' (the rules routinely apply), and 'exceptions' (treated as 'one-offs', which do not compromise the ideal of what ought to happen normally). Being able to justify cases of rule breaking as 'exceptions' allows the rules to be upheld, but not at the price of impractical, rigid literalism.

Cultural resources such as bureaucratic rules require actors to have substantial knowledge about the practical contexts and make judgements about relevance. This is what being 'reasonable' means. Failure to keep the rules can be explained by pointing to features of the practical context that everybody who knew about the job would accept as a reasonable excuse. Every organisation and culture, once it is set up, depends on this continuous, moment-by-moment, context-specific enactment of rules by its members using their capacity for practical rationality. The creative practical activity of actors energises social forms and keeps them in being. When fully automated systems of administration are infuriating to those who try to use them, it's often because they lack a human actor's ability to make adjustments for non-standard cases.

How medical specialists (haematologists) diagnose and treat blood disorders

Our next case involves the occupational world of haematologists, specialists in treating blood disorders such as leukaemias, anaemias or haemophilia. Like the Assistance Officers, they have to be practical and reasonable, but the very different nature of their work-setting affects what it means to be 'practical'. If anything, pressure to be able to justify decisions publicly is greater for medical consultants than for members of the Intake Division of the Bureau of Public Assistance. Paul Atkinson's *Medical Talk and Medical Work* (1995) gives an insight into the practical activity of supplying haematological expertise in the very complex contexts of contemporary hospital environments in the US and Britain. From our non-expert point of view, and as potential patients, we encounter consultant physicians when they deliver authoritative, confident-sounding opinions, which may have major implications for our lives. The individual doctor appears as 'the expert' who carries sole moral responsibility for the opinion. We do not see the interactional process, behind the scenes, where opinions are formed and decisions made, which Atkinson's study reveals.

These experts' work involves a lot of talking. We could say that specialist medicine would be impossible without talk. Talk is the primary communication medium of ongoing interactional situations in which it is possible for participants, drawing on their knowledge and experience, to express their sense of what is relevant. Talk is quick and responsive to context. So where one is frequently, routinely and urgently trying to solve complex, often unique, problems, such as identifying patients' blood disorders and choosing effective treatments, talk is especially important. Haematologists work by arranging and rearranging the contents of collections of complex and often imprecise data until they feel able to recognise a pattern, which allows them to suggest a diagnosis and appropriate treatment. They do this in small groups whose members talk all the time. This talk mobilises the available fund of expertise, provides a mechanism for criticism and a basis for moral support. As Atkinson insists, the talk is not *about* the work, it *is* the work.

If one studies the moment-by-moment activity of such work/talk one has to recognise the significance of the fine-grain detail of communicative interaction. It is difficult to convey in print and we do not have the space to reproduce the extended passages of talk discussed by Atkinson. But a few themes can be illustrated to reinforce the general point that without enactment by talking, the institutions of haematology could not deliver their service to the rest of us.

Simultaneous looking and talking

Take looking at slides through a microscope. Slides of a patient's blood are routinely examined during case conferences, and it is striking that the microscope in the seminar room where patients' cases are discussed, allows for simultaneous viewing by four people. This allows them to discuss one another's ideas about what they are seeing. In a context where little is obvious, suggested identifications of different kinds of cells and their conditions are criticised in the search for a consensus. This is particularly important in training students to interpret what they see in the 'right' way, and in teaching them to recognise and describe relative to conventional benchmarks or types. Simultaneous viewing allows senior experts to provide ostensive definitions, defining by pointing and saying 'There!' and supplying the technical label. The talk develops students' visual recognition and reporting skills (Atkinson, 1995: 74–89).

Managing uncertainty, authorising opinion, performing seniority

The above example introduces three of Atkinson's interrelated and central themes, *dealing with uncertainty, the several ways to authorise opinion and the performative nature of seniority.* Experts' reputations depend on providing the best knowledge there is in their field. This may sometimes tempt them to behave as though they know when they actually do not. But generally, well-founded expertise involves managing rather than denying uncertainty (Atkinson, 1995: 111). Particularly when talking to other experts, knowledge claims must be carefully qualified. Performing expertise means showing that knowledge contributes powerfully to decisions, but also acknowledging its limits.

So typically, case discussion is a formal ritual, beginning with a relatively junior doctor offering a narrative about the patient's condition and history of treatment to a critical audience of students and senior colleagues. The narrative assembles and interprets the available information, including descriptions of personal experience of the patient. These presentations are delivered rapidly, and must have sufficient detail, chronology, key events and clinical reasoning, demonstrating a sufficiently close attention to the case. It must be interpreted as a history of puzzle solving, but not overloaded with ill-digested details, supplying information on a 'need to know' basis (Atkinson, 1995: 97–104). Accounts are typically interrupted by requests for additional precision or criticised for their interpretations by senior members of the audience.

Given this, presenters have to be skilled at grading their expressions of certainty and uncertainty, and at deploying various authorities for the information in their accounts. Rhetorical skill is required to balance delicate judgements about what weight to place on different parts of the story, depending on context (Atkinson, 1995: 117). Since they are junior, presenters must give the source of their information: other doctors, other specialties, laboratory technicians, journals, textbooks, for example. These sources have to be assigned degrees of trust based on the collective experience of the occupational group. Trust is also involved when it is necessary to tell histories of inadequate investigations, mistaken treatments and treatments which are suspected of making matters worse.

A simple example is the tendency of haematologists to disparage the efforts of primary care practitioners to treat blood conditions with additional iron (Atkinson, 1995: 125). Another is the possibility of overdosing patients with drugs such as heparin. Lab reports are known to have margins of error. Data may be mislaid and have to be reconstructed from memory. The following short excerpt displays these features:

> At that point we were concerned that he [the patient] might have heparin-induced thrombocytopenia and/or thrombosis secondary to heparin. So we suggested they discontinue the heparin. I went over things in great detail with Dawson the chief surgical resident, who appeared to remember a lot of the data from the lab sheets and med sheets that were lost. What we thought might be possible is that all the way along heparin has been potentiating his syndrome. If you accept the fact that heparin is bad for him you can sort of go back through his history, and at every step of the way see where the institution of heparin appeared to make him a little bit worse .... I'm making up a flow sheet so I can show Dawson and make sure we're not talking ourselves into something that isn't actually true. I'm not completely sure. (Atkinson, 1995: 119)

Here the junior physician is telling a difficult story about incompetent record keeping and decisions that, with hindsight, may have been wrong. Her narration is also about the practical steps taken to recover the situation. She is talking to fellow professionals who all know that mistakes are made and that treatments can make matters worse. Given this understanding, the presenter justifies her actions by appealing to memory, not just anyone's memory, but that of a senior physician, and by producing a documentary record, the 'flow sheet', to provide objective substance to the subjective awareness of the problem which had emerged during their talking.

As a senior person, Dawson's memory is thought to be a sufficiently good basis for reconstructing the lost records. Seniority is an important resource for authorising opinions. Atkinson calls it the 'voice of experience' (Atkinson, 1995: 131). This draws lessons from relatively long and unique personal experience. Most obviously, the diagnostic opinions of certain key consultants are highly respected and routinely cited with confidence. In Atkinson's material the name of a particular clinical pathologist, Carol Green, was far more frequently mentioned than those of any of her colleagues. Her skill in interpreting biopsies and her careful pronouncements were taken as the best available (Atkinson, 1995: 125–6). This deference was highly functional for the less certain and less experienced. She provided a local, personal leadership.

More ordinarily, senior figures lead by supervising and advising juniors in case conferences. In fact seniority requires doctors to be able to provide relevant stories from their personal experience to help shape the interpretation of evidence and decide on treatment. As we have seen, haematology teams must arrive at decisions, and overcome interpretative uncertainty. One strong source of authoritative knowledge is the 'voice of science', represented by the research journal literature. Citing journal articles routinely supports arguments. But though this may be 'good science', its relevance for actual cases being analysed must be decided. This is where the 'voice of experience' of respected senior figures, speaking from their personal experience, comes in. Juniors support their own suggestions by referring to the published science, but this is articulated with the lessons of practical experience of their immediate seniors.

The 'voice of experience' often speaks anecdotally, or uses personal maxims, in sharp contrast to the impersonal discourse of scientific medicine generally (Atkinson, 1995: 137–47). For example, a clinical possibility may be illustrated by a personal reminiscence:

> I remember a case that I saw a couple of years ago that really bears on this point ... Maybe I told you about this girl already but let me tell it again for the benefit of the students ... she was at a party with her family on New Years' Eve and was *well*. The next day didn't feel very good. Everybody was joking ... but she didn't have too much to drink, and she became acutely ill during the day... and she had a very severe Coombs positive haemolytic anaemia with fifty per cent retics or something like that ... and for some reason we did a bone marrow, I don't know why. It was *very* megaloblastic ... this thing was building up for a few days ... but in *those* few *days* it probably exhausted the folate reserves right there in the *bone* marrow. It's a very early sign of marrow overactivity, or demands on the marrow ... That's what you have here. (Atkinson, 1995: 139–40)

Seniority is also importantly performed, by giving advice. The next excerpt follows a junior doctor's reporting that the patient has been treated with a thousand milligrams of Cytoxan, 30 milligrams of Adria and 120 milligrams of VP16 for a day:

Senior: I think we should go up on the Adria.

Junior: Right, that's what I thought – keep the Cytoxan where it is? Or do you wanna

Sen: You could probably go up on both

Jun: Twelve hundred?

Sen: Yeah

Jun: And fifty [*of Adria*]

Sen: Twelve hundred [*of Cytoxan*] and forty-five [*of Adria*]

Jun: Forty-five

Sen: Hahahh

Jun: Witchcraft. And the VP for only a day?

Sen: You could probably give him two days and see how he does. (Atkinson, 1995: 140–1)

Here, uncertainty about how to fine-tune the treatment and monitor its effects is overcome by accepting the senior doctor's advice. The junior doctor's exclamation 'Witchcraft' suggests they recognise the arbitrariness involved. The decision to go for only 45 milligrams of Adria, rather than the suggested 50, reflects perhaps the senior's habits of caution, or general disposition to see less experienced doctors as tending to push things too fast. Later in the same discussion the senior remarks, 'I wouldn't try to push it up. I think you might get into a little trouble', and, 'I'd be dubious about going faster.' This sort of consideration is expressed by another senior doctor to explain his preference for caution; 'I'd probably go with that kind of regimen. And the reason is that I'd like to get a little response before I go in with more multiple drugs, just in terms of her being intravenous' (Atkinson, 1995: 141).

Doctors with a wealth of experience of analysing actual cases, perform seniority (similar to the senior administrators in the welfare agency when authorising rule breaking). Everyone in haematology knows that the standard examples in the textbooks are insufficient as a basis for deciding what to do about actual cases, which present unique problems. Analysis and treatment has to proceed on an investigative basis, constantly checking for emerging negative or positive effects. That treatments have the potential to harm is a constant background worry. Patients having unique histories and conditions means that haematological advice has to be constructed for each on the basis of practical judgement. The whole practice depends on the process of talking to make decisions. This is a collective, interactive process, facilitated by ritualised occasions and deference to the authoritative 'voices' of science and experience. From the perspective of the younger medics it offers an opportunity for 'situated learning' (Lave, 1991).

The 'art crit' and the architectural competition

The practices of resolving doubt in medical contexts throw light on our third case, that of acts of aesthetic judgement revealed by studies of the fine art 'art crit' (Thornton, 2008; Elkins, 2012). As ethnographers of the art world show, art students across the developed world expose themselves to a judgement process rather different from that involved in deciding on medical treatments. Clearly they experience the insufficiency of their own creativity. Something more is needed which is supplied by the exercise of the creativity of others, namely senior artists. Art students' uncertainty about the quality of their work is addressed and partially resolved by resorting to the creative role-enactment by seniors of lead roles in a specific educational context, the 'art crit'. Here a student usually presents their work to more than one tutor and a group of fellow students.

As we saw in Chapter 1, the modern artist, unlike their traditional counterpart, lacks clear rules defining in advance what a satisfactory work of art should be like. In the absence of such objective knowledge and of criteria of correctness against which to assess work, the judgement process becomes self-authorising. In the doctors' deliberations about what patients are suffering from and how to treat them, they make continual reference to objective considerations such as the likely effects of quantities, frequencies and the interaction between various treatments. There is a science of blood chemistry. Patients improve or get worse and may die. There is a sense of needing to get it right and the risks of being wrong. Though judgement is necessary it isn't so arbitrary as to be unaccountable.

Unlike senior medics, senior artists in educational institutions appear to discriminate between the good and the bad on the basis of personal preference controlled only by appealing to a consensus among similar self-authorising senior colleagues. Art schools as educational bureaucracies provide formal rational-legal shells for the practice of judgements which refer to no criteria external to themselves. Rather than seeing this as some sort of academic scandal when compared to more objective assessments in other subjects, we should understand that, if you must have judgements of quality in the absence of objective criteria, there is no other way than to consult authorised persons, typically called professors of this and that, and then accept their opinion.

What we see in contemporary fine art education is a continuous stream of judgements produced to meet students' demand for them. They sign up, not just to learn technical and academic things, but to become something, namely an 'artist', which they define very much in terms of expressing a personal, uniquely creative, identity. They learn 'how to occupy that name' (Singerman, 1999). Art education is a process of self-discovery. The uncertainty this self-attention generates about their identities as artists and about the value of their role performance, results in psychological dependence on any straws of relevant judgement that may be grasped. The 'art crit' is the regular but infrequent institutionalised event taking several formats which is intended to enable students to progress with the journey to discover and develop their artistic creativity. Regimes vary in who speaks and how any guidance is generated. The ethnography is only suggestive of what happens. But one generalisation appears reliable; crits provide a social setting for the student's private self, as manifested in their art practice, to begin to make itself public. 'Crits' typically start with a student presenting their work by trying to describe what it means. Seniors sense that the student's self is implicated in issues of meaning and tend to respond by talking instead about how the work looks, its materials and technique. This is an instance of what Goffman calls tact, the deliberate avoiding of loss of face for the student (Box 7.1). Only towards the end, when sufficient confidence on both sides has been built up may attention shift to questions of meaning. The 'crit's' end product is some sort of documentary record and memories which can be referred to in the future for justifications of what will be done next. ('I did this because you said that then.')

Another conspicuous property of 'art crits', as the satirical film *Art School Confidential* shows, is that negative criticism from fellow students compromises solidarity and is considered deviant. Students need knowledgeable friends who reciprocate encouragement. Criticism is more easily accepted from seniors than equals. There is great variation in the style and effects of performances of seniority (Thornton, 2008). They range from the self-indulgent, theoretically mystifying, bullying and domineering to the careful, sympathetic and constructive. The best to be hoped for is to be taught by trusted, tactful, art seniors who understand that students' insecurities can only be contained by a sustained, consistent enactment of seniority.

Things seem easier in the more applied arts such as graphics/illustration, surface pattern, ceramics, design or architectural glass. Though originality is valued, it is not the only criterion of quality because projects have to meet objective tests of competence. These arts fall under the category of 'craft' (sometimes disparaged by enthusiasts for 'fine art'). For example, the materials for architectural glass make quite specific technical demands, whatever the design. But nonetheless meeting objective criteria may not remove the need for other kinds of judgement which have to be justified in other ways.

Architectural competitions provide further examples of how success depends on more than meeting standards of technical competence. Here, the availability of a document, the brief, defining what is wanted, does not remove the need for interpretation (Kreiner, 2009; Van Wezemael et al., 2011). Competitors continually refer to the brief (with its specific demands about site, function, costs and so on) for guidance, and submit a range of entries all of which can be justified by reference to it. Choosing the competition winner is also a creative action – one of deciding what is best in the emergent context of a field of entries with their range of specific properties. The brief is a documentary resource which can be used retrospectively to justify the eventual choice. Its availability to be used in this way allows judges to respond to what the entries show to be possibly unanticipated positive potentialities of the brief. As we saw in Chapter 1, technical rationality does not usually result in only one way of solving a problem (which requires it being supplemented by non-technical criteria).

Conclusion

The studies of the work of a welfare office, a medical specialism, fine art education and architectural competitions show the activity involved in the intense, fine-grained, moment by moment realisation of organised practices. There are four major elements, judgements of relevance, talk, justification and practical knowledge. Whatever the content of the formal rules prescribing what ought to happen, these rules have to be judged to be relevant and applicable to the cases currently under consideration. There are always times when to get the work done it is judged better not to follow the rules too literally. Central to making judgements of relevance, is talk. Talk is the principle mechanism of decision-making for welfare workers, medics, art students and teachers, architectural practices and competition juries. This is why the social theorists who specialise in analysing action are drawn to the analysis of conversation. Conversation has proved central to being practical, a fact demonstrated clearly by the haematologists. And finally, the activity of locally producing and reproducing social organisation involves deferring to certain justifying principles, or theoretical ideals, often supported by reference to authorising documents. Though they provide a moral framework, these principles and rules about what ought to happen, cannot make anything actually happen. But they do provide moral resources for representing events and actions as appropriate. However, given that in the real world, following the rules literally, is not possible, justifying stories must also appeal to practical knowledge of experienced people, to 'excuse' as 'reasonable' in the circumstances, activities which appear to deviate from organisational ideals.

It is therefore true to say that social institutions and practices are, as Garfinkel and the ethnomethodologists insist, 'skilful accomplishments'. But to explain social life we need to do more than focus on episodes when these skills are used. Crucial to this chapter's main examples is the fact that the activities described take place within what can be called *establishments*, complex organisations which provide the settings (for example the places, equipment, roles, powers of office, hierarchies of status, rewards) for the action. Establishments have histories during which they are brought into being, and are located in an environment of other institutions and practices which condition what can be done by actors. The easiest way to end this chapter and announce the topic of the next is to point out that nowhere in Zimmerman's account of his welfare office does he mention the politics of the taxation which pays for welfare provision.

Atkinson also suggests the insufficiency of analysis restricted to the local work and talk of organisations. First he notes that the activity of his American haematologists is conditioned by their working in a medical market place, where everything they do has a published price. Second, he is impressed by the fact that the cultural forms of medicine, the 'ceremonials and liturgies of the clinic', have a remarkable stability, despite rapid changes in medical science, government policies and bases of financing (Atkinson, 1995: x). The same can be said of the 'ceremonials and liturgies' of fine art education and of architectural competitions across the industrialised world. These considerations suggest other kinds of process contributing to the constitution of social regularities. After all, medics have a long-established and well-developed professional culture and are a very powerful occupational group, better able than most to dictate the conditions of work and rewards. Less powerful perhaps, but just as pervasive, is the occupational culture and reward structure of contemporary artists and art teachers. Each occupational category is differentially located in a structure of relative advantage compared to other occupations and the possibilities of using its power to maintain its position. These are matters of social structure which have made regular appearances in our discussion of the insufficiency of individuals, nature, culture and now action. In the following chapter we can, at last, give social structure our full attention.

Questions related to themes in this chapter

This chapter has provided ethnographic examples illustrating the way in which action needs to be incorporated into social explanations. It has shown how, in all sorts of situations, from the highly rule-governed to the very uncertain, actors have ways of making them practical.

1) Why didn't the receptionists described by Zimmerman, always follow the informal rule 'first come, first served' for assigning cases to case-workers?

2) Why is seniority an important organising principle in both the diagnostic medical meeting (Atkinson) and the art crit (Elkins, Thornton)? What do you think are the major similarities and differences between these two types of occasion?

3) Describe situations where, in order to uphold some social rule (for instance, conform to a dress code) you have had to improvise.

4) People sometimes contrast formally organised situations with ones where participants 'make it up as they go along'. Provide examples of each type of situation and consider whether the extremes of complete constraint or complete freedom of action ever actually exist.

5) Having read this chapter, do you think that it's possible to produce a computer programme which will offer clients, patients, customers as good a service as human actors can?

PART V

The concept of social structure

CHAPTER 9

What does social structure explain?

We now come to our final concept, social structure, which should be as fundamental a part of any social analyst's tool kit as culture and action (see Figure 9.1 in conjunction with Figures 5.1 and 7.1). Though particularly used by sociologists, anybody interested in social life requires it. We have already had to use it ourselves in earlier chapters as the explanatory insufficiency of the other, equally necessary concepts, to account for the patterns and regularities depicted, became clear.

In the Introduction, for example, we criticised those who saw patterns of educational success and failure as explicable simply in terms of the properties of individuals, ignoring the fact that they are already located in a class structure giving differential access to educational resources. Children in the educational system are not isolated individuals, but begin life located or positioned within distributional orders. They are distinguished by differences of sex, region, class, housing, health, ethnic classification, language and religion, for example. All these are factors consequential for various kinds of educational outcome and worth researching. How each child is positioned to engage with the education system affects how they relate to it and vice-versa. Children do not choose their position at the start. It is their inheritance, for good or ill.

The effects of structural location were also seen in Chapter 2 when we showed how the disadvantaged position of ghetto blacks in a racist, capitalist, labour market helped explain the economic strategies they pursued. To understand Huaorani technical choices in Chapter 4, it helped to know about their

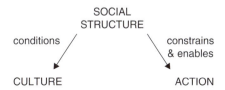

Figure 9.1 What the social sciences contribute to social explanation: social structure

historical experience/position of extreme social isolation from surrounding peoples, while differences in social power were seen to affect the outcomes of interactions between European settlers and both the Huaorani and Dunne-za. Considering patterns of consumption among British middle class professionals in Chapter 6, we found it useful to note how they were positioned in an economy structured into public and private sectors. And in Chapter 8, we have just seen that to understand the actions of welfare bureaucrats, medical professionals, fine art students and participants in architectural competitions, requires reference to the objective properties of certain practices and their institutional settings which define positions and assign powers to those who occupy them. Strong tendencies of thought and behaviour are created for those who are located in different positions of this kind.

In all these cases 'social structure' refers to particular kinds of precondition of action which exert their own sorts of constraint. Along with culture they are part of the environment of action, 'setting the scene' of conditions to which action, at any given moment, responds. For, as explained in Chapters 5 and 7, just like culture, social structures are also partly produced by action. That is, the social environment which conditions present action is the outcome of the interaction between actions, cultures, the natural environment, individuals and social structures in the past. In the same way present action will contribute to producing outcomes which will condition subsequent action. Social structures share with culture the property of being a medium of this 'historical' process. Both cultures and social structures are outcomes of past activity which have acquired the capacity to 'carry' the past into the present, making up a constraining legacy which conditions activity in the present. Figure 7.2 on 'Action', describing the historical process, applies here too.

However, though both cultures and social structures carry the past forward, they are different kinds of relatively autonomous realities which work in their own distinct ways. Thus, for example, inheritance rules (culture) define how property should be divided. However, what these rules say will have social structural implications which may or may not be understood and/or intended by those who apply them. For example, whether a rule says property must be divided equally between all the deceased's children, or that it should be passed undivided to the eldest male, will have major social structural consequences. These may include whether there is a long-term concentration of family wealth, the size and viability of agricultural landholdings over time, and the relative economic power of men and women. It may also condition who is likely to favour which kind of inheritance rules, and say, a high rate of inheritance tax.

Though culture and structure interact, they need to be kept analytically separate in order to recognise their various distinctive properties and mechanisms. Social structures such as inequality of landholding are products of social interaction which 'escape' from the control of those whose actions originally created them, to become durable material conditions of the action of subsequent agents. Thus, just as with elements of nature, when people consider social structures it is because these are entities which have specific conditioning properties, whether they like it or not, and whatever their attitudes towards them. Though peoples' ideas can have consequences for the origination and continuation of given social structures, neither the logic of the ideas nor whether they continue to be believed are sufficient to explain these structures' durability or conditioning powers.

Given the frequency and relative ease with which we have already used the concept of structure in this book, you might assume that applying it to social reality, was unproblematic. This is not the case. A long-running debate has generated a huge, contentious and often confusing literature about if and how the term should be used (López and Scott, 2000; Martin and Dennis, 2010; Elder-Vass, 2010). A persistent problem is that the term is used to refer to a *kind of object*, 'a social structure', and to a *kind of abstraction*, 'structure', which by giving access to an aspect of social reality, can be used in explanations of social objects. Also, the determinist (and 'anti-human') implications of various kinds of **'structuralism'** have provoked much greater caution about using the term 'structure', than 'culture' or 'action'.

Our approach all along has been to demonstrate that there is a kind of causation at work in social reality, (not covered by 'culture', 'action', 'individuals' or 'nature') for which the term 'structure' is appropriate. We relate to the technical debates by taking the position that there is a meaning of 'structure' which satisfies the same two criteria as do all our kinds of causes. Thus we use the term 'structure' to refer to a particular kind of causation which is necessary but insufficient in social explanation. It can therefore only be used in a non-deterministic way. The question now is, what kind of relatively autonomous causation, working in mutually conditioning relations with the other four, does structure bring to the practice of social explanation?

Social structure defined (i): relations between positions

We have already introduced the fundamental idea of social structure, saying it is a set of interrelated social positions, each one of which is defined and constituted by the relations it has with other positions. It is these relations between positions which have explanatory potential. The idea of a 'structure' can be illustrated by contrasting it with the idea of an 'aggregate'. Bricks lying on the ground where they have fallen from the back of a lorry form a random aggregate, a whole with no systematic relations between its elements. But to build them into an arch they have to be arranged such that the relations between the bricks have major mechanical consequences. The ones at the bottom bear more weight than those at the top; knock out the keystone and large sections of the curve may collapse. The important thing to keep in mind is that though an actual arch is an object (which might be called 'a structure') it is an object as a consequence of the particular way its components are arranged or related, that is structured. By being structured in a particular way, a potentiality of the bricks, to make an arch, is actualised. But without the bricks and their properties, the structuring relations would have nothing to work with. Moreover these relations have to be mobilised by builders – they cannot apply themselves to the bricks! Thus we think of structure as an effect of an active process of structuring where agents use, intentionally or not, the properties of arrangements. As we use the term, structure is a property of social products such as families, football teams, churches, class systems, institutions and organisations, not a synonym for them.

In most situations, people are more like the bricks in the arch than those scattered on the ground. They are systematically related to each other through being located in positions in varieties of social structures, positions which, by virtue of their relation with other positions, have consequential outcomes. People in high positions in social hierarchies, for example, derive relative advantages which are systematically linked to the relative disadvantages of those in lower positions.

Social structural analysis has the job of identifying the many different processes which effectively 'fix' numbers of people into different interrelated positions which have consequences for their potential for acting and relating to one another. Structural analysis is always specific to the object being explained and looks for a particular kind of legacy of past action which sets the scene for action in addition to the scene setting done by nature, culture and individuals. History shows there have been many different ways in which structuring powers have interacted with the other four in complex ways to constitute environments for action. Some structuring conditions are rather common (even universal) while others may be unique to specific circumstances. How long the consequences of structuring last to condition action is likely to be highly variable as are the ways the consequences are responded to by both those who are advantaged and disadvantaged by them. The ways in which either individuals, or cultures or actions or nature are subject to the constraints and opportunities of structuring, is emergent and depends on changes in relations among the other three kinds of causes.

We now have to begin considering some of the more important sources of differences of social position ('consequential arrangements') which have the capacity to condition action.

Examples of 'consequential arrangements': the formal properties of networks, effects of serial ordering, number and scale

We have just suggested it is helpful to think of the concept of social structure as referring to all the forms of 'consequential social arrangements' that constrain us. This definition implies that social structuring involves the relative autonomy of 'arrangements' as such. We can begin considering this sort of autonomy by providing some simple examples of unavoidable 'positioning' which affect social relations.

For example, every child has a position in a birth order which shapes their relations with their parents and any brothers and sisters. Consider the effects of being an only child, or of being born first or later in a birth order of siblings. Surely these differences of position are consequential? The predicament of only children is often discussed. There are advantages (usually a two to one parent-child ratio) and disadvantages (relative isolation, being 'spoilt', being cross-pressured to be an ally in parental conflicts). All positions give their occupants certain powers but also expose them to liabilities (Sayer, 1992: 105). Now consider being first-born. Are first-born constrained differently from their younger brother(s) and/or sister(s)? Does anybody think different positions in this serial order have no consequences? We doubt it. There is evidence suggesting first-borns do better educationally, but are less confident and adventurous than second and subsequent siblings. Sulloway found later-born children (Darwin among them) massively over-represented in the ranks of scientific innovators (Sulloway, 1996: 42–3). Serial ordering necessarily affects access to resources; in families only first-borns are ever going to experience being repositioned from having all the attention to having only some of it. This is a property of their position that is independent of the quality of the attention they receive. It is a strictly objective and structural problem which insightful parents have to deal with whether they like it or not.

Take a related example. Do you think that the numbers of members of a group such as a family, and whether they are odd or even, makes a difference? Doesn't scale affect the resources available for the well-being of each child? Does the ratio of adult carers to dependent children matter? Could the internal politics of families be affected by the impact of large or small, even or uneven numbers, on balances of power and possibilities of coalition formation (Simmel, 1964: 87–174; Caplow, 1968)?

Georg Simmel (1858–1918, German)

(1892) *The Problems of the Philosophy of History*, New York, Free Press (1977).
(1907) *The Philosophy of Money*, London, Routledge (2011).

(1903) *The Metropolis and Mental Life (in Wolff below).*

(1916) *Rembrandt: An Essay in the Philosophy of Art*, London, Routledge (2005).

Simmel on Culture: Selected Writings, ed. Featherstone, M. and Frisby, D., London, Sage (2000).

(1902–1917) *The Sociology of Georg Simmel*, collection edited by Wolff, K.H. New York, Free Press (1964).

We can extend the discussion of numbers to consider scale effects for examples of much larger organisations such as **nation-states**. Why are there relatively few very small nation-states, in terms of population and territory? Is there something about being small which restricts the likelihood of the emergence and/or persistence of political independence? Does the ability to sustain relations of 'independence' from other states involve questions of access to sufficient resources – raw materials, labour, food supply, trading partners, defensible borders, military alliances, a sufficient degree of internal coordination, transport and so on? Are these things likely to require that the state has a minimum size? Gellner's discussion of the development of nationalism, which we look at in Chapter 10, is relevant here (Gellner, 1973).

Conversely, can political and other kinds of organisations become too big for their own good? There are few very large nation-states and generally no more than two superpowers. Maybe there are certain advantages to being small(er). What disadvantages are there to being very large, geographically, organisationally, economically, militarily and in terms of population? We do not need to discuss the question of scale effects at length – it is a technically interesting topic – but only to insist that it is an example of a kind of structural constraint. It sets the scene for actors, who have to work around it whether they like it or not.

Finally, consider the properties of social networks – assemblies of connected individuals, linked by many forms of 'networking' (McLean, 2007). Like physical networks such as electricity grids, rail or air transport systems, social networks have objective properties. There is a considerable literature analysing, for example, the implications for cost, time-saving and resilience of different ways of connecting up power stations and consumers, and configuring links between railway stations or airports – shortest routes via a central hub are not always the most reliable or quickest (Vromans et al., 2006; Ip and Wang, 2009; Miller-Hooks et al., 2012). In analysing social networks, Granovetter (1983) concentrates on two variables: firstly, variations in the number and configuration of connections in a network, and secondly, the character, particularly the strength, of relations between the connected.

Relations vary in what they may be used to carry: mutual identification, trust, information, partial or inclusive sharing of concerns. A single individual may have a set of friends who all know each other, interact frequently to form a densely knit network of strong ties, sharing identities, multiple concerns and risks. Here relations are difficult to make or break. This individual may also be simultaneously the centre of a set of acquaintances who are relatively easy to add to or drop, because they do not share special concerns or a strong common identity and are only weakly tied to one another (if at all), even though each may have their own, densely knit network of strong ties. Granovetter suggests that heavy dependence on what a densely knit network provides can be a trap because the 'closure' of strong ties risks weakening access to opportunities and information from outside. Conversely, the 'openness' of weak ties, offers useful possibilities for 'bridging' clusters of strong ties and drawing on sources of information which can be activated when needed, with low investment. Weak ties are likely to connect dissimilar people who cannot make automatic assumptions about one another, encouraging social imagination.

Weak ties are functional in many contexts. For example, Giuffre (1999) suggests that artists who continually maintain weak ties to many loosely knit networks receive more critical attention than those who are either only linked sporadically, or whose long-term connections are to densely knit networks alone. This is consistent with Granovettor's claim that opportunities for jobs and occupational variety tend to widen for job seekers, if information flows through weak ties. And with ethnographies documenting the difficulty experienced by those reliant on strong local ties to find work in areas of major economic decline (Morris, 1992, 1995). Though the advantaged will tend to gain greater benefits from their weak ties than the disadvantaged, limiting information about job opportunities to what dense local networks provide is likely to narrow opportunities, whatever the substantive character of the networks.

As we saw in our discussion of 'The Flats' in Chapter 2, whether employed or not, the poor and insecure may concentrate on maintaining strong local ties to cope with economic pressure, rather than built weak ones which might allow a few to escape. However, there are exceptions, for example the strong networks of the poor aren't always entirely local. Stack's later work depicts the significant non-local, though still kin-based ties of some Northern blacks to those remaining in the South. These were connections which could be mobilised to help their return to the region when this seemed to offer preferable opportunities (Stack, 1996). And earlier, during the Civil Rights period in the South, the weak ties linking the individual densely knit black church congregations to each other and to the black colleges were central to the rapid mobilisation of large numbers in protests such as the Montgomery bus boycott in 1956–7 (McAdam, 1999).

Social structure defined (ii) distributions of power and resources

We have been emphasising the way positions are related is a powerful conditioning force in human life. Children are obviously caught up in conditions of life which they do not control and do not choose. But so are we all; the positioning effects of the past constrain us at every turn as we move through life, far beyond the point when we have got over our education. The central implication of social structure, we have seen, is that we inhabit a social world, not just of culture, but of relations between positions that is already set up for us. The social world is already arranged and these arrangements are potentially consequential.

We now move from considering the consequences of different *forms* of structuring and begin to consider what makes *differences of position within any given structure* so consequential. This involves examining the substantive implications of structuring. The first consideration is that, as all this book's examples show, with positions go resources, whether these be the attention parents can give their children, having a room of one's own, opportunities to earn income, having defensible frontiers, or the authority conferred on seniority. So this conditioning of the distribution of powers to actors is a major reason why the concept of social structure is so important for social explanation.

To appreciate the force of the structuring of social interaction and the part it can play in social explanation first think of all the important resources one needs in order to act. The list might include money, health, education, housing, information, legal rights, transport, credit, jobs and political representation. Now think how one is constrained by the way access to resources is distributed, and the social arrangements one has to participate in to access any of them. One has to fulfil expectations associated with specific roles (positions) such as employee (to gain wages), student (for access to grants, loans, discounts, cheap fares), next of kin (for possibilities of inheritance), tenant (if you want rented accommodation) and citizen (for rights to education, health care and police protection).

Some resources are more abundant and easier to get at than others for someone in a given position. There are, analytically speaking, two interrelated variables here. Improving your resources is not just a matter of increasing their amount, but of altering your relations with some relevant other people. This is because positions in structures are relationally defined (for example, teacher to pupil, creditor to borrower, employer to manager and manager to worker). Thus how a given position is occupied has implications for how others are occupied – an increase in pupils' autonomy normally entails a decrease in teachers' disciplinary powers for instance. Differences of positions in systems of social relations imply access to different kinds and levels of resources and opportunities which constrain and enable action. Those with similar access will tend to share identities and interests though the fact that actors are evaluating and self-committing animals means there can be no automatic connection between structured position, identities or what people understand to be their interests.

Social structure defined (iii): kinds of social power and the organisation of practices

In the examples just given, powers were associated with the roles people play as participants in different kinds of practices. Bearing in mind what we said in Chapter 3, about human nature being intrinsically social (since individuals are unable to survive as isolates), location in some sort of organisation of positions is unavoidable. The production of the necessities of existence as well as biological reproduction are only done by engaging in collective practices which involve relations between more or less specialised **roles**. Collective practices have to be organised and that involves defining the various contributions participants should make to the collective enterprise. These definitions of roles define how those playing them ('incumbents') ought to relate to one another, and what their respective powers are. Collective practices therefore generate organisations of sets of interacting role positions using certain structuring relations.

Collective practices, for example producing food, bringing up children, or providing health care or justice, involve people in discovering how to do things together, making the best use of the powers that are available to them in the circumstances. This is not just a process of technical development and it has not generally been done in a spirit of equality. Rather, it has involved those with power to dominate trying to force on others forms of practice which they think will be in their, the powerful's, interests. (When considering the destruction of traditional hunting grounds, Chapter 4 asked whose interests were served by the change to industrialism.) The organisation of practices is the result of a combination of constraints. Some are technical, arising from the material nature of what is being done. Others arise from the use of social power. The practices that emerge from this process have to be sufficient to get the job done, but how they are organised will reflect the distribution of power.

The general point is that the social structuring of practices reflects the use of power and has consequences for the distribution of power. Organisations of roles emerge as the consequence of learning and struggles and may be institutionalised, that is, subjected to a process of formal regularisation; jobs are specified, rules are written, expectations are made prescriptive, and sanctions are put in place. However, whatever the degree of institutional rationalisation, role performance is never exactly limited by the formal rules, for two different sorts of reasons. First, there are those discussed in the previous chapters on action; performing formal roles demands exercising practical judgement. But second, institutional settings of roles provide an environment which role players can work to their own advantage, allowing them scope to create their own structure of positions and relationships which operates 'informally'. We saw, for example, in Chapter 8, how informal exchanges of clients between case workers were arranged. This is the realm of discretion, informal privileges, cliques and networks.

Structural problems of organisations

Even though one may be very powerful, to build an organisation to undertake some practice or other means having to confront basic objective issues of organisational technique and design. And often it is the case that moves designed to facilitate achieving some aspect of an organisation's purpose will pose another set of problems which then need dealing with. Suppose, for example, you want to increase the productivity of an organisation – perhaps a factory. One method is to analyse what it does and break this down into separate parts, assigning each of them to different categories of worker. Because they now have to be proficient in only part of the total process, workers can become more skilled and efficient at their particular tasks. However, specialisation can only yield its benefits if attention is paid to a new problem it creates – ensuring each of the specialised parts of the production process remain coordinated and work together smoothly. This may involve ensuring both that the now separated *activities* and the *people* who perform them are appropriately connected up (Lockwood, 1976). In more social theoretical language, *differentiation* creates problems of system **integration** and social *integration*. It is unavoidable and something has to be done to solve it, or the benefits of specialisation will be difficult to achieve. Famously, Durkheim made it his life's work to identify the forces which could maintain social integration in the face of the disintegrating effects of an increasingly specialised **division of labour** in modern times (Boxes 5.3 and 9.1).

Another recurring problem, at least from the perspective of those running organisations, is that of control. This is particularly evident where it cannot be assumed that those in charge of an organisation and those being organised within it define their interests identically. Just consider the problem of control faced by the monarch of an absolutist state, the head of a large school, or the boss of a large company. They cannot be everywhere at once, directly

Box 9.1   The division of labour, social cohesion, solidarity and integration

Durkheim defined sociology as 'the science of moral life'. He sought to understand the positive and negative implications of changing from a way of life conforming to the authority of the past (traditionalism), to one devoted to change, in order to realise a different and better future (modernism).

He thought individuals in traditional societies are tied together by having a common experience of life and an emotionally-strong attachment to their social identity. Here common identity is regularly reinforced by collective ritual performances, which programme emotional response to collective symbols. This 'mechanical solidarity', of accepting the obligations of belonging to a group, is based in the shared density of immediate concrete embodied experience.

For Durkheim the central problem of modernity was to identify the conditions for being able to lead a moral life despite the combined divisive effects of highly valuing the individual, scientific rationalism, a highly developed division of labour, constant technical and occupational change and the loss of traditional forms of community and religion. The multiplying and destabilising of social identities and of skills and knowledge, means that individuals tend to experience their differences rather than commonalities, making sustaining meaningfulness, shared identities and obligations, problematic.

But Durkheim felt leaving the past behind need not (as many critics believed) mean abandoning morality. He searches for a source of emotionally-compelling experience in modern societies to provide the foundation for moral commitment of individuals to one another and to society. Disengagement from society can cause 'anomie', (where normative values fail to regulate wants, making satisfaction impossible) and can lead to suicide. Durkheim finds what he wants in mechanisms of 'organic solidarity', a form of commonality based in difference rather than sameness. Though the division of labour makes individuals' occupational experience different, solidarity is encouraged by (a) recognising individuals' continuing interdependence in the production process, (b) the shared experiences and common identity of occupational groups or 'associations' and (c) participation in a labour market where the allocation of individuals to roles and differential rewards is 'meritocratic'. That is, on the basis of aptitude, educational qualifications and relative scarcity. Durkheim thought that differences of reward need not undermine social cohesion provided they were felt to be just.

Thus individualism could be a primary shared social value and basis of moral life. Durkheim favoured limiting the role of inheritance in modern societies, feeling its rewarding of membership of families rather than individual talent and effort, produced social disintegration.

supervising those they depend on. They will have to use some methods for indirect control. The rulers of the historically early forms of large organisation (e.g. states and empires), tended to use the threat of force (made credible by intermittent and dramatically staged violence – Ivan the Terrible earned his name this way), networks of informers, and religious sanctions.

A range of techniques has also evolved in modern organisations, each tending to have their own advantages and limitations. For example, where work tasks are highly routinised and the division of labour so fine-grained that workers only require minimum skill to perform their small, repetitive tasks, they may be easy to supervise and control. Typically, global fast food chains, such as McDonald's, in order to make certain of profitability try to remove uncertainty by simplifying and standardising production methods and products, and limiting the risk of conflict with workers by preferring to hire young people and substituting workers with machinery wherever possible (Ritzer, 2010). Reducing risk by continually rationalising work processes contributes to work becoming increasingly insecure, decreasing workers' bargaining power, and making it impossible for them to take time to become skilled, and committed to 'quality-driven work' (Sennett, 1998, 2008).

One reason why employers often try to organise the workplace in ways which deskill the workforce, is to reduce the power that accrues to specialists (Braverman, 1974). Managers find it easier to know if unskilled workers are up to scratch than workers dealing with unpredictable situations using highly specialised skills the managers themselves lack. A recent study discussing the historically problematic status of the technical experts dubbed 'computer boys', however, provides an illustration of why it's not always possible to do without such experts (Ensmenger, 2010: 225–8). Since the wide-spread introduction of computers, organisations have become increasingly dependent on highly skilled programmers to design, maintain, modify and expand the software being used in live systems embedded in complex networks of social, organisational and technological systems. Ensmenger describes recurring fears about the shortage of programmers and also about their difficult personalities, and documents assorted schemes to routinise, deskill and partially automate their work. These however have met with limited success because rather than starting from scratch, what many programmers actually do is 'continuity engineering', or 'adaptive maintenance', exploiting the adaptability of existing applications by improvising solutions. Because the problems tend to be unique, there is little potential to automate or develop standard procedures for non-specialists. So organisations remain dependent on, and vulnerable to, programmers who continue to hold a strong hand and are routinely vilified as untrustworthy outsiders ('artistic', 'cowboys', 'hackers'), demonstrating poor social integration.

Advantages and limits of bureaucracy

One way of considering bureaucratic organisation is as a particular set of techniques for the substantially indirect controlling of labour, in pursuit of organisational goals. It involves specialisation of roles, but not inevitably their deskilling. Bureaucracies appoint people on the basis of their expertise, to make sure that they are competent to perform their roles. There is regular but not continuous monitoring of their work. Formal job-definitions ensure there is no doubt about what is expected, while a payment system which combines providing economic security for workers to inhibit corruption (such as favouring their own kin or demanding bribes), with rewarding exceptional performance, encourages internal competition and inhibits work-place alliances. Bureaucracy is an organisational method playing on the internal motivation, self-interest and capacity for self-direction of employees. It is a brilliant political technique of domination which gets bureaucratic workers to discipline themselves, following rules, even emotionally identifying with them, in the absence of close supervision.

However, as we might now expect, though sophisticated, the bureaucratic method of organisation has its own structural problems. Here are some. First, bureaucracies try to anticipate all the kinds of situations which concern them, and to specify rules and regulations for their handling. But as the discussion of the welfare bureaucracy in Chapter 8 pointed out, there are always cases which do not fit the rules, or require employees to exercise judgement about which rule to apply. So rules are not enough and the effort to stick too closely to them may result in inefficiency despite satisfying the psychological needs of 'bureaucratic personalities' (Merton, 1957). Indeed there may be situations (such as the perpetual software crises serviced by the 'computer boys') where risk-taking and innovation, rather than rule following, are needed to solve the problems. Thus encouraging conformity to prevent corruption by making employees sufficiently economically secure, needs to be counterbalanced by rewarding risk-taking innovation where it furthers the interests of the organisation. Bureaucracy may not be the best, easiest or even possible form to go for in some kinds of situation.

There are further examples of the way in which even generally beneficial features of bureaucratic organisation can have potential downsides. Bureaucracies are hierarchies, controlled from the top. Those above need to know what is going on below them. But maybe it is in the interests of those at lower levels to control the flow of information upwards so that it does not harm their own career prospects and so on. In any case, usually only those filling a position can really know all the details of what is involved in actually doing it. So those at the top of bureaucratic organisations will always be making decisions based on incomplete information. Bureaucracies are vulnerable to internal differences of interest and shortfalls of knowledge which may get in the way of their effective functioning. Hence the uneasy relations between skilled specialists such as programmers, and those with authority, but not programming expertise, who try to manage them.

Structural contradictions

A **structural contradiction** involves a situation where structural factors make strategies favourable to the achievement of one goal simultaneously disadvantageous for the achievement of another desired outcome. There are two main types of structural contradiction. The first is caused by the *internal* characteristics of a structure. The tensions we have just been discussing between the potential to increase efficiency by fragmenting work tasks but to simultaneously decrease it because of the time and effort spent on reintegration, provide an example of an internal contradiction. As do circumstances where the advantages of rules clearly specifying what should be done, are counteracted by their inhibiting useful innovation.

The second type of contradiction is caused by *external* relations between structures, for example between feudal and capitalist agricultural relations of production. Or it is an outcome of people's simultaneous location in different structures. For example, individuals' positioning within both class and national structures can cause contradictions. You are both working-class and British so which way do you jump? Do you support your class interest or your national interest? Will you volunteer to fight the German working-class in the First World War trenches? ('Yes' in 1914, but conscription had to be introduced in 1916.)

Capitalism and its contradictions

Probably the best-known examples of 'internal' structural contradictions are entailed by capitalism (Box 9.2). Capitalism is a form of organisation to produce. It is a way of coordinating labour, materials, technology, decision-making and rewards. Capitalists attempt to secure profits by competing against other producers, firstly by seeking to drive down the costs of production, keeping wages as low as possible, and mechanising the production process and, secondly, by trying to maximise demand. However this form of economic organisation creates several problems for itself.

One is the tension between workers' roles as producers and as consumers. If workers' wages rise this may threaten profits. But so do wages that are too small to motivate workers and/or to allow them to buy the products the

Box 9.2 The distinctiveness of capitalist class structuring

In pre-capitalist feudal and caste societies, people are typically unable to move out of the estate or caste they are born into. These are life-time positions and there may be legally or religiously enforced prescriptions and proscriptions, rights and duties linked to them. By contrast, class boundaries are not enshrined in law, may be more or less sharp or fuzzy and more or less, though never completely, impermeable. This, together with the fact that there are no legal prescriptions connecting particular class positions with particular life styles, helps explain why people can fail to recognise class structuring. There is always some inter and intra-generational class mobility. State policies, in particular with regard to education and the inheritance of assets, affect patterns of mobility as can changes in the character of the economy. For example, upward mobility from lower class positions is likely to increase if the number of jobs requiring skilled labour grows rapidly. Personal mobility is a major reason why an individual's cultural preferences may be 'misaligned' with those typical of other occupants of their present class location. People can therefore subjectively continue to feel a member of a class position they in fact no longer objectively occupy.

What groups people together into classes, is an economic system which systematically links life chances to mode of participation in the economic order. Classes are categories of people who share similarities in their opportunities for economic reward by virtue of their location or positioning in the economic structure. Theorists debate how clear-cut the boundaries are between different classes in contemporary capitalist society, where the main boundaries lie, and which particular aspects of economic participation are key for determining life chances and structuring people into classes. However, ownership or non-ownership of different kinds of economic asset (particularly productive and non-productive property and skilled or non-skilled labour power) is usually held to be central. Possession or lack of organisational assets which derive from the capacity to control the labour of others in the workplace is also often seen as significant. Note that the distribution of assets is *relational*. With the exception of the self-employed who both own and use their means of production, a category of non-owning producers and of non-producing owners are dependent on each other for the possibility of their existence. Similarly, some have the capacity to control others in the workplace only because others lack this and are subject to control. The distribution of assets significantly affects the differing levels of reward people derive from their economic participation, because it is a major determiner of people's market power. For example, those with skills are generally in shorter supply than those who lack them and so the former are typically in a stronger market position than the latter. Those who would be unable to survive unless they can continually sell their labour are in a weaker bargaining position than those who possess assets which enable them to survive without immediately participating in the market. Those who possess organisational assets in the workplace often have skills and may sometimes be in a position to directly set their own levels of remuneration, or to claim that maintaining their authority over those they control requires they earn more than the latter. Because life chances can be affected not only by an individual's own assets but those of other household members, some commentators suggest that the household rather than the individual should be the unit of class analysis.

Wright, E. O. (1997) *Classes*, London, Verso.
Wright, E. O. (2005) *Approaches to Class Analysis*, Cambridge, Cambridge University Press.
Savage, M. et al. (1995) *Property, Bureaucracy and Culture: Middle Class Formation in Contemporary Britain*, London, Routledge.

capitalist is selling. So wages must not be too low, in order to allow profitable consumption.

Workers' changing capacity to consume is one reason why demand and thus production fluctuates. The ideal labour force is one that can be easily expanded (to minimise lost production) or contracted (to minimise labour costs). A flexible labour force often has a core, and a sector (a 'reserve army of labour') which is only intermittently employed (for example as casual labour or on short term, even zero hours contracts), but able to survive and maintain its potential availability for work when not employed. Capitalism needs solutions to this problem of the unemployeds' survival, variously drawing on the individual and collective (including kin-based) resources of the out-of-work themselves or of the state. So, for example, in China rural migrant workers used in the new 'sunbelt' industrial cities, personally absorb the costs of their unemployment by returning to subsist in the countryside where they retain household land rights allocated in the 1970s (Lee, 2007: 206–10). In some other societies, state funded welfare maintains those not currently needed in the workforce, though at levels designed to make employment, when available, the more attractive option.

Support for the non-employed to retain their future capacity for work is one example of a social cost. Others are meeting workers' health, education and housing needs. Employers would rather not pay for these through raising wages. So they favour their being met by someone else – usually the state. Capitalists can therefore have an interest in the welfare state, but the welfare state has to be paid for out of taxation and capitalists do not want to pay high

taxes! However, where the threat to the labour supply seems sufficiently serious, and the state, for various reasons is unable or unwilling to act effectively,
capitalists may fund these costs, as demonstrated by South African mining
companies agreeing in 2002 to pay for the anti-AIDS health education of their
workers and fund medicine for workers – but not their families.

A further contradiction of capitalism, Marx suggested, is that mobilised
by their competition with each other, capitalists invest in technical developments which increase productivity, opening up the possibility of producing
sufficient to meet general human needs. But this potential cannot be realised,
since output can only be produced for those who can pay. The poor with the
greatest needs will obtain the least, while the wealthy create an unnecessary
market for luxury goods. That profits depend on a sufficiency of consumers,
frequently leads to attempts to replace satisfied demands with new, unsatis-
fied ones. The result is the continuous cycle of replacement of old products
by new, typical of contemporary consumer societies – something we can now
recognise as embodying one final contradiction. That is between an infinite
demand for new resources and their finite availability. This sets the scene
of contemporary environmental politics which concentrates on renewing
resources and sustainably meeting needs rather than demands.

Coping with structural contradictions

Structural contradictions can be thought of as setting problems for actors to
solve. Sometimes the only complete solution to contradictions is to abandon
the structuring relations all together. Total structural change is the strategy
of revolutionaries. But it is seldom practical, simply because the past casts
too long a shadow and cannot simply be denied. Though some have tried,
for example, in the killing fields of Cambodia. Utopian social thought tries
the experiment of conceptualising perfectly integrated structures without
contradictions. But practical social theories tend to acknowledge that perfect
functioning is not generally possible – rather there are instances of more or
less smoothly operating organisations. Where firms or government departments swing back and forth between apparently opposing policies, pursuing
each in turn until its downsides become too great to ignore, this is often due
to poorly handled attempts to deal with intrinsically incompatible structural
requirements. But it may be possible to specify the points of contradiction
and structural tension as issues around which some sort of containment,
limitation, careful management, and compromise or balance can be struck.
Contradictions can often be coped with fairly successfully. The impression
of a smooth running organisation is usually the result of skilful management, a long period of learning about the structural problems, acceptance of

necessary compromises, a relatively stable environment of action, and good fortune in avoiding accidents.

Thus when governments make economic policy in an environment where companies are international and able to move, they have to cope with a tension between making their country as attractive as possible (by for example offering low tax rates, low social costs) and getting what they can from those companies when they do locate there (in the way of taxation and low unemployment). Given capitalist companies have to locate somewhere and have an interest in keeping social costs down, they may try to achieve enough profit (rather than maximise it), and agree to pay some tax while working to keep the state's demands down to a 'reasonable' level. This structurally derived difference of interests produces routine struggles between governments and companies. An example, from 2000–01, is UK car makers threatening to shift their car component orders outside Britain, thereby putting 750,000 jobs at risk, if the government imposed a new energy tax. The Chancellor had already cut the National Insurance contributions the employers had to pay for each worker, but the car makers felt this was insufficient, given their industry is energy rather than labour intensive. They used their ability to create job-losses, which would cost the welfare state in unemployment benefit, to try to force a change of policy. The Government response involved judging the seriousness of the threat, and considering whether to reduce the energy tax a bit, and/or increase the N.I. exemption, a bit. In the event they judged that the threat of job losses because of energy tax levels was small and that car makers were influenced primarily by wage levels and labour quality. Motor manufacturers routinely shift their orders for components to get them as cheaply as possible and the energy tax was not likely to be a major factor in making British suppliers uncompetitive.

But this sort of situation is generic to social life. Everyone finds themselves having to balance the demands of contradictory structural locations and practices. It is often difficult and generally stressful – as the working parent facing their boss's demand that they attend a meeting while their child is sick, knows all too well. Another classic case is that of people whose roles in the middle of hierarchies mean they need to satisfy demands from above and below. Should the foreman side with the workers or the management? Does the waitress satisfy the demands of her customers or of people in the kitchen? Is the sergeant one of the men or one of the officers? Is the petit-bourgeois shopkeeper a worker or a capitalist? They are structurally required to acknowledge the interests of both positions, and are poorly placed to succeed unless they can cultivate special negotiating skills and privileges, for example, places (the sergeants' mess, the Rotary Club) where they can unwind away from the constant friction of their public lives.

Structural positions and interests

These examples show that there is a systematic connection between positions in distributional orders, the logic of the kinds of distributional order that they are, and the *interests* of the people in the different positions (Swedberg, 2005). Interests are collectively formed by the logic of position, and people often act on them (as we have been suggesting throughout this book). Thus we inhabit a social world characterised by typicality and strong tendencies (Kemp, 2012).

Take a very simple example. It is a logical truism, that those at the top of any given stratification order cannot go any higher. If they change their position it can only be for the worse. But though this is a truism, in the logical sense, it is nevertheless interesting; it tells us something about the implications of stratification orders – in particular that those at the top are likely to be defensive. They will tend to resist changes which widen the opportunities for upward mobility of those lower down, unless they can be persuaded that they will not lose when those below them gain. This generally involves policies of expansion so that everyone can improve their lot, without threatening the differential advantage of those at the top (Rueschemeyer, Stephens and Stephens, 1992). Those in middle positions may similarly want to prevent challenge from below, but along with those at the bottom, may also seek upward mobility. This may require learning the ways of those above them and dealing with differences between their culture of origin and that associated with the position they aspire to. (We saw in Chapter 6 how moving from a lower to a higher position can involve changing one's sense of humour.)

Typically supporters of conservative parties do so to conserve their privileges and the status quo, while it is the disadvantaged who attempt to change the existing state of things by supporting 'progressive' movements and legislation, voting for left-wing parties and so on. 'Floating voters', shifting between left and right, tend to be those in the middle who want to improve their situation but also guard against loosing what they already have. This has been a very strong pattern and the focus of a major empirical research tradition which tries to track changes in how classes define their positional interests and shape the policies and parties they support (Achterberg, 2006; Achterberg and Houtman, 2006; Dorling, 2006). Generally voting continues to be aligned with class despite a widening of interests beyond the economic to encompass cultural and environmental concerns.

But notice we have only suggested from which ranks in a stratification order support for political positions is likely to come, not that everybody in a given rank supports the same position. That would be an example of structural determinism. The nature of social structuring is to condition, not determine, action. This means support for political positions is an outcome of an interaction of the conditioning forces of social structure, culture and action, as well as the distinctiveness of individuals and that, despite strong tendencies creating patterns in behaviour, acting against type is normal and allowed for. Thus we should expect a given political position to be supported by individuals from a variety of ranks and that individuals may change what they support during their lives.

Working-class conservatives and socialist aristocrats are the exceptions to the rule. But they are not uncommon, unintelligible or random. They are explained as the outcome of various responses to the interaction of contradictory structural pressures, or kinds of experience, strongly held cultural commitments, and strength of moral personality which may work against each other.

Thus, though disadvantaged in class terms, some workers feel advantaged by their membership of a national community and a 'British way of life', and want to conserve this 'privilege', (perhaps in the face of (mis)perceived threats from immigrants), more than they want to reduce their class disadvantage. Others may see conservative parties as representing a higher class and vote for them out of deference – believing they know best. Conversely, ambitious workers may vote this way from a desire to join or usurp, rather than defer to those above them. In the case of a socialist aristocrat, the strength of personal commitment to the political and moral ideals of socialism and democracy, based on universal values expressed in, say, religious beliefs or political theory, implies that they must pay a price, by giving up aristocratic privileges. Though few achieve complete consistency between their equalitarian commitments and their privileged life-style, some are sufficiently committed to make considerable sacrifices to ensure their behaviour is consistent with their beliefs. They go against the grain of their structural conditioning. That interests are collectively formed by positions in social structures, that these interests may contradict one another and cross-pressure groups and individuals, and that as a result, there is a measure of indeterminacy in how people respond to their structural positions, is a fundamental insight of Marx, Weber and Bourdieu.

We can sum up the discussion so far by saying that action takes place in an environment of already existing institutions and practices. These have their relatively autonomous properties which condition action. We cannot just do as we like but have to work within the framework of an already arranged social world. What there is to do, and what there is to do it with, are to a large extent predetermined. These institutions and practices position actors thereby conditioning their interests, particularly their attitude to change. But positions also create dilemmas for actors. Firstly, being positioned in several different orders distributing different resources creates conflicts of interest, and secondly, the expectations linked to any given role may be contradictory. There may also be contradictions between the expectations of different roles in an actor's **role set**, and there may be contradictions within and between whole institutions, and within and between whole institutional spheres. These are the sorts of relations which figure in the analysis of the integration of social systems and the nature of structural conditioning or constraint.

What affects the relative durability of the products of social structuring

We can now turn to the question of how action, interaction and culture are implicated in the production, reproduction and transformation of social structures. Various hints of what is involved have already been given. One factor contributing to stability is that practices which work well enough, tend to acquire a certain inertia as people try to extract value from their past investments and avoid the costs of change (this is sometimes referred to as 'path dependence'). However, it's always possible that an incremental build up of more negative consequences will reach a 'tipping point' where the advantages to be derived from efforts to change outweigh those of carrying on as before. Or a shift in external factors can generate a crisis, forcing a change in practice, as we saw when considering technical choice in Chapter 3.

How actors use their structural positions, the legacy of their own and others' actions, is the most important conditioner of whether social structures persist or not. But unless we subscribe to individualism, we know that structures themselves condition the interests of individual and collective actors, and their capacities to further them. Whatever the interests of actors, they have to have the power to influence outcomes if they are to get what they want. And the sad fact is that the power to influence outcomes is unequally distributed. So, if those with the greatest power want to conserve their advantage they are in the best position to do so. They can use their power to defend their hold on it. They will have sufficient surplus resources to expand them by investing, diversifying, experimenting and consolidating. Typically the powerful try to control the future by securing legal protections for property, regularising inheritance rights, supervising marriage, investing abroad, securing tax exemptions, cultivating reputations as social benefactors, encouraging deference, influencing political culture and so on. They try to reduce the desire of those below them to oppose them, whether by making this seem too dangerous, by presenting their superior position as in the general interest, or by concealing that they are exercising power at all (Bachrach and Baratz, 1962). They take out 'insurance policies' against some future time when their privileges may be successfully attacked. Dictators often open Swiss bank accounts! These are all techniques for transmitting positional advantage, the outcomes of structuring, into the future. They are important mechanisms which carry the past, transmitting it into the present to constrain action, equivalent to the transmittable, learnable symbolisation of the mechanisms of culture. Central to the mechanisms of social structure are the 'media' of transmitting differences of power across generations.

This brief discussion of the strategies and mechanisms used by the powerful to defend and increase their advantage, provides a simple example of how ways of structuring feed back into their reproduction, reinforcing the hold of a set of conditions of action. Such cycles of reproduction of stratified orders can be very durable. Marx spoke of what he called Asiatic societies as 'vegetating in the teeth of time' – and we can wonder at the slowness of democratising the British House of Lords or allowing women to vote. The general point is that where we are faced with explaining the long-term persistence of a distributional and institutional order we must look at the socially reproductive methods, particularly of the powerful. They are the long-term winners of an extended period of social competition. From an initial episode of securing dominance, the winners, let us say the Norman nobility following the invasion of Britain in 1066, set about dividing up the spoils and consolidating their advantage. We can see the latter's castles all around us here where we are in South Wales. Some of their descendants are only now losing their formal political power, as their residual techniques for defending their position, particularly deference, fail.

Possibilities of change: multipliers, thresholds and emergence

The other side of the picture is the strategies and mechanisms used by those interested in reducing their disadvantages. From a position of relative weakness, the crucial issue is how to assemble sufficient power to counteract the reproductive forces they are up against. The organising of collective actors is an important *multiplier* of power. All strata organise, but it is particularly important in the repertoire of those who, as individuals, are weak. Trade unions, cooperative societies, credit unions, housing associations, 'new' social movements, 'people power', are examples. In each case, the transformation of a structure of disadvantage, depends on using techniques to increase power (be it political or economic) sufficient firstly, to bring about change, and secondly, to institutionalise the new order, that is place the gains on a reproducible footing. However, though combination can increase the capacities of the individual, even collectively they may still be disadvantaged in relation to the individually strong, because it is generally more difficult to sustain a large organisation of individually weak people than a small organisation of individually powerful ones. Small elites of well-coordinated powerful members are intrinsically better placed to keep themselves ready for action (Piven and Cloward, 1979).

The problem the disadvantaged face, of putting together sufficient power not only to produce change, but also to sustain any gains and avoid falling back into the previous condition of disadvantage, shows the importance of rising above a '*threshold*' of power sufficient to permit the emergence of a new configuration of advantage and disadvantage (Granovetter, 1978, 1983). Remember in Chapter 2, how Stack's friend, Ruby, failed to accumulate enough resources to cross the threshold required to make her escape from her dependence on kin? Work on black and white access to mortgages, and thus home ownership, in the United States provides us with further examples of how lack of capital, low income and discrimination can interrelate in complex ways that make it difficult to escape disadvantaged structural positions intra- or inter-generationally.

In their original study *Black Wealth: White Wealth*, Oliver and Shapiro (1997) documented how blacks found it more difficult than whites to obtain mortgages and thus the potential to make capital gains from housing. This was a consequence of their lower income levels and lesser employment security, but also of direct discrimination by mortgage providers, who saw the areas where (because of their low income and discrimination) blacks sought housing, as being risky. Oliver and Shapiro further showed how those who did borrow often had to do so on less favourable terms than whites for several reasons. Low incomes and lack of financial help from parents, for example, meant that they could not pay large deposits which reduce the interest rates for the loan. They could also only afford smaller loans, which attract proportionately higher administrative charges. Thus, those who did buy immediately paid more for less than their white counterparts, which variously reduced their capacity to improve their situation. Paying $4–8,000 more than their white counterparts for a $35,000, 25-year loan, they lost the opportunity of investing this sum profitably, or of using it to finance their children's education or to help them with house purchase in their turn. Also, the cheap housing in poor neighbourhoods, which was all they could afford, promised less capital appreciation than the residences of wealthier whites. Thus the disadvantaged and discriminated against, paid proportionately more for a less worthwhile investment, often failing to acquire the resources which could propel their children out of the disadvantaged situation (Oliver and Shapiro, 1997: 136–70).

But the reasons why relatively few blacks were able to use housing to change their economic situation in the 1980s, don't account for Shapiro's more recent claim that the wealth gap between black and white families has nearly tripled between 1984 and 2009 (Shapiro et al., 2013). The causes of this 'catastrophe' are too complex to unravel fully here, but they relate firstly to an increase in the number of blacks able to enter the housing market – but on highly problematic terms. And secondly to the very high percentage of such wealth as blacks have, being concentrated in housing (they don't have enough to diversify their capital holding). This made them especially vulnerable to the 2007 onwards property price slump which was partly triggered by increased black ownership.

During the 1990s it became easier for blacks to borrow, not because discrimination weakened, or their risk rating improved. It linked to a restructuring of credit finance which led it to seek new markets for expansion. This was encouraged by the innovation of supposedly risk-reducing secondary investment products which by bundling together collections of high and low risk primary loans actually made risk assessment problematic. Euphemistically dubbed 'sub-prime', high-risk blacks, easily accessible within their concentrated neighbourhoods, became an expanding market for aggressive selling of mortgages with very unfavourable borrowing terms. The result was the temporary, rapid expansion of black wealth, primarily in home equity, followed by a foreclosure crisis as harsh borrowing terms, and increasingly insecure employment, for those who lacked substantial savings, prevented many from keeping up payments. As the situation spiralled downwards many could not even pay off debts through sale of their properties whose falling values, because of oversupply and emptying neighbourhoods, no longer covered them. Tempted by lenders who perhaps misunderstood the risks involved, many blacks had got a foot on the property ladder but lacked resources to keep it there. Shapiro claims that between 2007–09 blacks lost 21 per cent of their wealth compared to whites, 12 per cent (Oliver, 2008; Rugh and Massey, 2010; Shapiro et al., 2013). The circumstances of the housing crash may be particular, but they provide one example of how having only limited resources often makes their retention difficult.

The capacity to accumulate sufficient resources to make it possible to retain and then inter-generationally transmit them, is often a precondition for reconfiguring the long-term distribution of power. In fact humans lived for most of their history in small hunter-gatherer bands which were egalitarian and stateless, because of the difficulty of solving this problem. Although the original hunter-gatherer societies must have been led by dominant individuals on the basis of their physical and intellectual powers, these powers were relatively temporary and could not be stored and transmitted to others – say their children. There was no way of developing a surplus and getting power above the threshold required to make it inheritable. Power could not be passed down the generations and thus no durable stratification system could develop. This did eventually emerge but under very special environmental conditions such as those encouraging the development of agriculture described in Chapter 3 (Box 3.2).

Conclusion

The concept of social structure (summarised in Figure 9.2) implies five funda-mental claims:

1) A major feature of social reality is that it consists of interrelated social positions.
2) These relations between positions have their own properties.
3) These must be distinguished from the properties of the particular indi-viduals who occupy the positions.
4) Social-structural properties include mechanisms which distribute power to actors and make for durable power structures.
5) The cultures and actions of actors are conditioned, rather than entirely determined, by the relational properties of the positions they occupy.

SOME PROPERTIES OF SOCIAL STRUCTURING
Generally SOCIAL STRUCTURES distribute resources and interests for action.

Social Relations between Positions
(e.g. stratification systems)
have potential for long-lasting systematic effects.
+
Distributes resources and interests
(e.g. material inequalities, typical cross-pressure dilemmas for given positions).
+
Media and techniques of social power
(e.g. money, property, inheritance laws etc.)
transmit advantages and disadvantages.
+
Formal and logical structuring
(e.g. serial ordering, number effects, scale effects, network effects).
+
Organisational structuring
(e.g. bureaucracy)
hierarchies of formal statuses and roles
+
Emergence of informal structuring
+
Structural contradictions
(e.g. differentiation and integration).
+
Relatively durable & extensive social systems
(e.g. capitalist class system, criminal justice system, family system, nation-state system).
+
Relations between systems
(e.g. between economic, family, education, legal, and state-welfare systems).

RELATIVELY AUTONOMOUS
POWERS CONDITIONING
and mediated by
ACTION & CULTURE

SOCIAL STRUCTURE
is necessary
for social explanation

Figure 9.2 *Summary – the relative autonomy of social structuring: how it works*

Social structure is therefore an important source of the predictability of behaviour and contributes to the explanation of typicality in social experience. However this must be qualified by saying that how the differences arising from positioning (such as resource inequalities) constrain individuals is a complex matter. It depends on what they are trying to do, on how they work with what they've got, and what price they are prepared to pay to act, possibly motivated by virtuous intentions, against the logic of their positional interests. The rich often lose their fortunes out of bad luck or incompetence but also, sometimes, voluntarily give up privileges for moral reasons. Similarly the poor may get rich by luck and/or effort and talent, and equally make choices about the price they are prepared to pay to get what they want and do what they think is right. There is room in social theory for unselfish, morally motivated actors who put the good of others above their own, positionally conditioned, self-interest. But the fact that virtuous individuals can make a difference in no way undermines the claim that being positioned in a structure of inequality has major constraining effects of a specific kind on all the occupants of a given position.

Questions related to themes in this chapter

This chapter has examined the concept of social structure, showing it involves (i) relations between positions and (ii) distributions of interests, power and resources.

1) What does Granovetter think is the 'strength' of 'weak' ties? In what kinds of circumstance might they be particularly useful to those seeking work?

2) Imagine two countries. In the first, 60 per cent of the population is under 25 and 10 per cent over 65. In the second, 20 per cent are under 25 and 35 per cent over 65. What effect might these differences in age structure have on (a) economic growth rates, (b) social stability and (c) crime rates in the countries involved?

3) Your child is just old enough to begin school. There is a choice between one with a small total intake and small classes each containing children from a wide age band, and a large school with bigger classes of children of the same age. What kind of factors do you think about when making your choice between these differently structured schools?

4) Think of two different social structures in which you are located. How well does the role you have in the first structure fit with your role in the second? What do you do when a conflict of interest arises?

5) People in disadvantaged positions within a social structure can potentially improve their situation by changing their position within the structure, or by changing the character of structure or by moving out of it. Why are these changes often difficult to make?

CHAPTER 10

Testing the explanatory value of social structure

We will now do for social structure what we have already done for the other four concepts we are claiming are necessary, but insufficient, for social explanation. In this instance, our examples are ones where, initially, concepts other than social structure might seem to do all the explaining. But while we recognise that they play a role, we show how powerfully social structure is in fact operating in these cases.

'Supremely individual' acts as effects of social structure

Our first cases follow Durkheim's famous precedent when he demonstrated the significance of social structure by discussing the limits of individualist and environmentalist explanations of an apparently utterly individual act – suicide. He showed that the tendency to kill oneself varied with the kinds of social structure available to participate in, and with the location of people within these structures (Durkheim, 1897). His chief target was psychological explanation, which he felt was insufficient to explain differences between the suicidal tendencies of whole collectivities (such as religious groups) recorded in the statistics of comparative suicide rates (see Box 9.1).

There are many other examples of behaviour, belief and feeling which seem to flow spontaneously from each individual, but which are patterned by the person's location in social structures. A famous example is romantic love. We may like to think that love strikes because of some unpredictable, maybe mysterious, attraction evoked in one individual by the entirely personal properties of another. But that the vast majority of us are smitten by individuals in similar positions in class or 'racial' hierarchies, with the same ethnic identities as ourselves, requires we modify this view. There is cultural and social structural clustering of mate selection. Indeed, the idea of romantic love itself, and especially belief in its validity for selecting one's future spouse, is neither universal nor natural, but is particularly characteristic of modern societies where the power of the senior generation to control their children's mate selection is weakened (Parsons, 1954: 187–9; Frankfurt, 2004; Badiou, 2009).

Tony Ashworth's First World War study provides a further example of social structure's impact on emotions (Ashworth, 1980). His work (which parallels Durkheim's *Suicide*) shows that aggression and bravery, were not simply individual dispositions, but varied systematically between elite and non-elite battalions, weapon specialist units (e.g. snipers, machine-gunners, hand bombers) and non-specialist ones, and between the first phase of local, personal control of violence (before the winter of 1915–16) and the following period of more thoroughly bureaucratised, impersonal command (Ashworth, 1980: 45–6, 77, 82–4). Individuals' behaviour varied with their positions relative to technologies, organisations and command structures (Ashworth, 1980: 48–53). Though there might be some variations between the valour of individual soldiers in the same unit in the same situation, the overall differences between units were not to be explained by distinctions in the personal qualities of those who composed them.

However, explanations in terms of any of the key concepts dealt with so far, and not just individualism, are likely to need supplementing by reference to the causal effects of social structure. We continue to illustrate the importance, but then also the insufficiency of social structural explanations, below, with reference to two case studies. In the first, the claims of nature, and in the second those of culture have been argued to be particularly compelling, but can be shown to be insufficient. Both examples deal with phenomena which are effects of the long-term, global, social structural transformation called '**modernisation**', which the social sciences were invented to understand. But though our examples show very powerful structural causation, even here we insist that social structural*ism* is inappropriate.

The origins of modern nationalism and the nation-state

Historical sociology (sometimes called '**macro-sociology**') tries to explain very long-term, wide-spread, change in the patterning of people's behaviour and beliefs. One such development is the emergence and diffusion of the doctrine of nationalism. Nationalism stipulates that the social world should be conceptualised as naturally divided into groups or 'nations' (usually associated with a specific territory) whose members, by virtue of some common origin, share the same culture and usually, language, constituting an ethnic group. It then argues that each such group has an inbuilt (i.e. natural) desire to be self-governing and enjoy national self-determination. Each nation should have its own 'nation-state' with congruent political and cultural boundaries. Nation-states promise inclusion (though not necessarily equality) to those who adequately conform to their culture. So the problem is, 'Why should this doctrine and principle of state formation have emerged and become so popular around the world, over the last two hundred years or so?'

Nationalist ideologists themselves have offered one answer by arguing that the human species is naturally divided into the different national groups which they recognise, and that it is natural for people to reject rule by those culturally different from themselves (Gellner, 1997: 8–9). Deriving culture from nature, nationalists typically see their nations as having great historical depth. However, since nationalist demands for nation-states are comparatively recent, they have to explain why the supposedly primordial desire to avoid rule by cultural outsiders has not always been manifest. Their typical resort to mysterious processes and metaphors, such as 'national awakening' by charismatic leaders, is less than satisfactory. The 'nations are natural and eternal' argument does not explain why national*ism* was 'switched on' and remained 'on' for the last two centuries. We need some other, non-naturalistic factors to explain why the ideas, leadership, emotion and commitment typical of nationalist movements, occurred when they did.

Cultural implications of modernity

One of the most influential approaches to this question, Ernest Gellner's *Nations and Nationalism* (1983) and *Nationalism* (1997), suggests that nationalism was produced by macroscopic changes associated with modernisation. This social structural development changed the way people were positioned to pursue their interests during the period in which nationalism emerged. By 1700, Western Europe was organised into intensely competitive states. Extended struggle between fairly evenly matched major states meant for a long time there was constant pressure to upgrade the techniques of power to gain a competitive advantage. 'Each major geopolitical state was itself a virtual network of production, distribution, exchange and consumption (....) in a wider regulated interstate space' (Mann, 1986: 514). Production, the organisation of labour, state administration, commerce, transport, agriculture and law among others, started to break free from traditional techniques. This is the period when industrialisation, bureaucratisation, urbanisation and rationalisation intensified to form, by about 1850, the complex referred to as 'modernisation'. Tried and tested practices and ways of legitimating social arrangements typical of traditional, agrarian societies, were challenged by the competitive advantages provided by the new, rationalised, relatively impersonal methods.

Ernest Gellner (1925–1995, Czech)

(1959) *Words and Things: An Examination of, and an Attack on, Linguistic Philosophy,* London, Routledge (2005).
(1964) *Thought and Change,* Chicago, University of Chicago Press (1978).

(1983) *Nations and Nationalism,* Oxford, Blackwell.

(1988) *Plough, Sword and Book: the Structure of Human History,* Chicago, University of Chicago Press (1990).

(1997) *Nationalism,* London, Weidenfeld and Nicholson.

Modernisation radically changed the field of action for people conditioned and positioned by thousands of years of experience of agrarian society where they were organised into a multitude of small communities, identifying with their own local, oral, context-dependent, 'low' cultures. Most people, in societies of this type, interacted within a small area and were spatially and socially, relatively immobile. The local division of labour and status hierarchy was seen as natural and unchangeable. The small ruling elites, whose interaction was not spatially restricted, dominated primarily by military and religious intimidation. They had access to literacy, a basic 'high' cultural technique, permitting symbolic representation and analytical distancing from reality, but used it primarily for intra-elite communication. Such societies did not need the rulers to share the culture of the ruled, so political, cultural and linguistic boundaries often diverged. Most people did not need the literate 'high' culture of their rulers, to participate in the local social relations that mattered to them.

The modernisation of power techniques meant adopting the generalising analytical approach to all problems encouraged by literacy; attacking ignorance, inconsistency and inefficiency. As we noted when discussing this rationalisation process in Chapter 6, no privileged spheres of meaning were exempt from analysis. In a world understood as universally subject to the laws of science, modernisation broke reality down into bits which might be profitably rearranged into new combinations. Education had to be developed to teach, not the multiplicity of different eternal truths held dear by the many local 'low' cultures, but generic techniques for analysing and manipulating reality. This was the new, highly valued knowledge for producing, and participating in, a world of ceaseless change.

Education became standardised, universalised and less specialised, allowing for occupational flexibility during an individual's lifetime. In agrarian societies specialisation could be very intense; think of the technical brilliance of craft production in agrarian empires. But such specialist achievement was the outcome of generations of workers perfecting their traditions. Modern life, by contrast, requires people be mobile, spatially, socially and in their imaginations. They must relax their attachments to the tried and tested and search for new improvements. Those well positioned to pursue their interests in modern society are educated into the type of culture which escapes confined local horizons. This culture is 'high' because it overarches the multitude of local cultures. Typical of the cultural response to post-traditional structuring are tendencies towards omnivorous and reflexive cultural consumption (discussed in Chapter 6), and increased interest in establishing the weak ties of low density networks (discussed in Chapter 9).

Modernisation and state education systems

Modernising states promote the dissemination of 'high' culture in order to make their populations competent in the latest power techniques. They need literate, numerate workers, engineers, scientists, officials, military, teachers, health specialists and so on, to be competitive with other states. But this interest of states coincides with the desire of many in their populations to tap into the benefits of participating in the non-local spheres of interaction modernisation opens up. Locality and kin are no longer sufficient to provide the generic knowledge needed for effective use of opportunities in the non-local world. Thus many seek formal education and to live in political units big enough to sustain educational establishments which can supply it. Modern states all invest in education systems and are under constant pressure to expand provision (Archer, 1979; Collins, 1979). Access to education is a universal demand of people caught up in modernisation.

Egalitarianism and cultural competition

What are the connections between the modernisation process and the growth of nationalism? There are two: egalitarianism and cultural competition. Because modernisation and industrialism constantly change the division of labour in the search for improvement, modern societies are comparatively egalitarian, with people trying to increase their power by using their generic education to keep up with the latest techniques. Although as we showed in Chapter 9, the privileged typically seek and have resources to retain advantages, where technologies continually change, rewards from particular specialisms may be relatively quickly displaced by those accruing from later, better techniques. This tendency for investments in specialisms to be undermined means that people experience a social world of upward and downward mobility as their fortunes rise and fall. Modern societies have, compared to agrarian societies, relatively 'open' social structures, because mechanisms for accumulating and transmitting social advantages across time are comparatively weak.

This is reflected in their stratification systems and terms for legitimating inequalities. Differences of reward can be great in industrial, class structured, societies but, in relation to pre-industrial social orders, they tend to be graduated and not easily used as impermeable barriers to interaction (Box 9.2). As suggested in earlier chapters, discontinuities tend to be most likely in the lower reaches, where unqualified labour finds it hard to assemble and transmit resources to lift its children off the bottom. But even such sharp breaks are unintended and not formally prescribed, unlike many of the stratifying divisions in traditional, agrarian societies, where status divides are often strong and interaction between those of different ranks ritually formalised. Industrial societies tend to encourage flexibility and complexity so that the social properties of individuals become more randomised, difficult to predict and provisional. The working assumptions for full participants in modern social orders is that, though they may have different cultures of origin, and be located in classes, they are strangers who are in the same modern industrial 'boat' as each other, can operate modern 'high' culture, and are all included in the competition for success.

Here is the core of Gellner's theory. He argues that inequalities generated by informal stratification mechanisms of industrial social structures are tolerable for the relatively disadvantaged, firstly, to the extent that the advantaged are felt to have earned their rewards by their own individual talent and effort, and secondly, that there are opportunities for the disadvantaged to improve their lot by the same means. Being disadvantaged should not exclude one being considered a legitimate competitor; winners and losers stay in the game. But where the advantaged and the disadvantaged are culturally distinguished, and the persistent disadvantaging of ethnic groups undergoing modernisation supports the suspicion that they are being excluded from the game on cultural grounds, then nationalism will flourish. Gellner describes the experience of the culturally disadvantaged, well:

> People really become nationalists because they find that in their daily social intercourse, at work and at leisure, their 'ethnic' classification largely determines how they are treated, whether they encounter sympathy and respect, or contempt, derision or hostility. The root of nationalism is not ideology, but concrete daily experience. (1996: 123)

We can now turn to the second key connection between modernisation and nationalism, that is, cultural competition. Given the expectation that the business of modern life be conducted in terms of a unified 'high' culture, a central problem for modernisers is how to transform existing culture(s), the legacy of the agrarian era, into an effective medium of the said 'high' culture.

Early modernising states (e.g. England and France) had already established high levels of cultural and linguistic unity and thus a de facto coincidence of cultural and political boundaries. Their pre-existing cultures could provide the idiom and language of their new education systems. Only at their peripheries did the introduction of a state education system involve overriding local cultures (e.g. Welsh, Gaelic, Breton, Basque). 'Big' cultures became the carriers of the passport to modernity, and little cultures declined because they were marginal to modernisation. Their members had to learn the alien tongue or forego the benefits of participating in modernity.

However, in regions modernising later, and in the context of culturally and linguistically divided states, competition ensued between culturally distinct groups to become the (high) cultures of states big enough to sustain education systems. Where a large political unit, like the central European Hapsburg Empire, overarched a number of relatively large, culturally distinct populations, suppression (though sometimes tried) was impractical. Here, modernisation involved the state developing an education system which somehow cultivated 'high' cultural homogeneity while giving substantial recognition to some of its (more similar) cultures, and simultaneously provoking its more distinctive ethnic groups to try to establish their own states with their own educational uniformity. To be left as a culture without a state or 'political roof', as Gellner calls it, was avoidable only if the population and potential territory was sufficiently large to resource a sustainable independent state. Generally, cultures big enough to encourage their intellectuals to imagine forming their own state, have tried to create one. Little cultures have tended to be squeezed out, or lingered on, suffering the humiliations of cultural exclusion. Gellner suggests, at best, only about 10 per cent of the world's cultures/languages are supported by a nationalist movement, and far fewer actually achieve statehood (Gellner, 1983: 44–5).

Central to Gellner's theory is the compulsory effect of industrial or modern society whose techniques offer growth and the promise of material improvements. Once this promise is recognised, and the attractions of mobility felt, access to its generic culture matters. The language and idiom of formal education is the gate to this precious 'high' culture. If one already has that language one is lucky. If one does not, access is more costly. If exclusion from the chance of mobility (because one's culture is not recognised as a medium of 'high' culture by the state's education system) is unacceptable, one has two options. Either learn the educational establishment's language, and assimilate the dominant form of high culture, or take the nationalist route to try to create a state, so that one's own language can be that of an education system. This route has two aims: to create a state offering mobility chances to its members, and to make the agrarian era's cultural legacy into one capable of carrying the burdens of high culture. Successful nationalist movements do not simply revive folk cultures; they remake them into versions of modern culture. Where neither assimilation nor independence is possible, prolonged trouble is very likely.

This is Gellner's explanation of nationalism in terms of the social structural development of modernity and industrialism. Basically the cultural and social structural legacies of the agrarian world must be transformed. Past investments have to be re-evaluated for their usefulness in new conditions. Put simply, does what worked for millennia in the countryside of say, the agrarian empires of Asia or feudal Europe, still work in the industrial cities of modern industrial states? Social structural developments force cultural competition and re-evaluation. So the story nationalists tell about themselves, that nationalist sentiments and the politics of making culture and state coincide are universal and natural, is rejected. As Gellner puts it: 'Nationalism is not what it seems and above all not what it seems to itself' (Gellner, 1983: 56).

Gellner's is a macroscopic structural analysis placing heavy emphasis on social structure. However it is not overwhelmingly structural*ist*, because structures are thought of as only conditions of action. Social structures, cultures and action interact. The coming of modernity alters the environment of practices, roles and kinds of power; it alters the potentialities and available opportunities. It forces re-evaluation of past investments and reconfigures interests. But it is actors who move out of the agrarian world, making their choices about how much of the old they want to keep and what sort of investment in the future they want to make. Not everyone sees the nationalists' political solution as the best bet for social justice. Others, for example, have backed internationalism or socialism. They have chosen to play down the significance of cultural differences, seeking to develop new, modern, cultural continuities and political forms which overarch the boundaries of nations. Or they have decided that the unacceptable inequalities are actually produced by class structuring rather than cultural exclusion. Those who are advantaged by class structuring would generally prefer the disadvantaged not to make this interpretation and often use nationalism to deflect criticism of their advantage. Moreover, as modern societies continue their development, new needs may undercut nationalism and political units' ethnic homogeneity. As with the European Union, states can be linked into larger political structures in order to increase their competitive capacity. Or their internal cultures can be diversified by in-migration. This can lead to new struggles if migrants seek more, or less, assimilation than the host society favours, but the acceptance, even valuing, of some new, intra-state multi-culturalism is also a possibility.

Modernisation and the maintenance of moral reputation: Bangladeshi women in London and Dhaka, from the 1980s to 2010s

We can now turn to our second and different kind of example of what happens when traditional agrarian cultures encounter modernity. Here we will draw principally on research by Naila Kabeer, beginning with *The Power to Choose* (2000), a study of Bangladeshi women garment workers in Dhaka and London. This provides insight into the concrete interactional and experiential realities of the processes Gellner talks about in a more abstract way when accounting for nationalism. Kabeer investigates a case where modernity has arrived recently and rapidly. It enables us to see that structural causation has a certain complexity arising from several features. First, people are simultaneously positioned within many social structures, and conditioned by interaction between effects of these positions. Second, these social structures are themselves interacting, (sometimes systematically), and changing, so their positioning effects on individuals and groups may vary. Third, the impact of these combined and changing structural forces is mediated by the action of those caught up in them. Thus, though modernisation in Bangladesh radically transforms the opportunity structures open to some women, these structures may change, and whether their lives are actually transformed depends on the different strategies used to respond to them. Kabeer shows how the impact of Bangladesh's modernisation on everyday working and domestic life and the intimacies of personal and family relations, depends on choices.

The paradoxical weakening of purdah in Dhaka and its reinforcement in London

Kabeer's study records an emerging contrast between the behaviour of Bangladeshi women in Dhaka, and those living in London as participants in the first phase of migration to Britain in the 1970s and '80s. Both groups share a religion, Islam, and an agrarian cultural heritage placing strong emphasis on male authority and female subordination, including purdah, the practice of excluding women from the public, non-domestic realm. It is this cultural commitment that many had assumed would hinder Bangladesh's economic development. However, when Kabeer returned to the country in 1984 after a three-year absence, she saw large numbers of young women going to and from work on the streets of Dhaka. In the time she had been away something radical had happened; as a matter of everyday routine, women were now working in the newly expanding factories, earning their own wages, and appearing in public spaces unsupervised by male kin, just as Western women do in modern European cities. This contradicted expectations and the traditional norms still in force when she had left in 1980. Some women at least, seemed to have rapidly made their escape from the local, agrarian world. How was such a transformation possible so quickly? The problem was compounded by the fact that in a modern city, London, Bangladeshi women, far from participating in public life, were virtually invisible. Just where one might expect them to be easily stepping onto the stage of modernity, they behaved as though the traditional norms of purdah constrained them as strongly as ever. They lived more like agrarian village women than modern citizens. What maintained the strength of their traditional culture in London?

So here is the contrast in 1984; in Dhaka, where conformity with patriarchy and purdah ought to have been strong it had weakened: and, in London, where it ought to have been weak, it was strong. Given that both sets of women operated in terms of a common original culture, this culture cannot account for the differences in behaviour. It must be interacting with other causal forces to shape two different decision-making environments. Cultural norms and institutionalised gender hierarchies operate in the context of other structural mechanisms which distribute resources to actors playing the roles assigned to them. Patriarchy, male domination, is not merely a principle of political legitimation. It is a system of rule where the cultural norms affirm male dominance, and where the mechanisms for distributing material resources favour men as a category. Thus, where we see patriarchy rapidly weakening, it is likely to be the result of changes in the material resourcing of men, rather than of a sudden loss of belief in the principles of legitimation. Similarly, where patriarchy is reinforced, we should look at changes in the distribution of resources to find out what is renewing its vigour.

To explain the differences between decision-making environments we must consider the interaction of all the relevant resource-distributing, interest-forming structures, which can produce the tendencies and typicality we want to understand. These vary in their length of operation, their spatial extension and capacity to influence the lives of large numbers of individuals, cultures and organisations. For convenience we can think of such structures as ranging from the macroscopic, involving large numbers of people, possibly very extended in time and/or space, to the microscopic, where positional differences hold for relatively few people for the period that they occupy the positions involved.

How social structures shape decision-making environments:
the case of Dhaka

We will focus initially on Dhaka. What factors positioned women to challenge, to 'take on culture' as Kabeer puts it (Kabeer, 2000: 136)? At the most macroscopic level they are post-imperial participants in a rapidly globalising, capitalist economy and the Islamic world, located in one of the poorest country on Earth. How these macro factors link to the relevant decision-making environments of a particular generation of women, experiencing rapid change, becomes apparent at a more immediate level of structuring. The 1970s was a decade of political and economic crisis in Bangladesh. The 1970 cyclone was followed by a bloody war of independence from Pakistan (1971), a ruined economy, rising prices, the international oil crisis (1972), massive crop failure (1974–5), the army coup and assassination of Bangladesh's first leader, the secular socialist Mujib (1976), growing government corruption, unemployment and poverty (estimated to have doubled between the 1960s and the 1980s). All this intensified the long-term crisis in the countryside where population growth reduced landholding size and increased landlessness (which stood at 41 per cent in 1971), making many more people dependent on unreliable wage earning in a stagnating rural economy. This unique combination of factors created a situation favourable to beginning a shift from a traditional economy of peasant landholding, localised labour markets, kinship patronage and communal social control to one of commercialised agriculture, monetarisation and impersonal relations typical of modernity. The eventual result was reduced participation in agriculture and diversification into trade, services, crafts, transport, construction and last but not least, migration, to less populated regions, abroad, or to cities like Dhaka. In the 1980s, 81 per cent of Dhaka household heads were migrants from the countryside, only 19 per cent were born in the city (Kabeer, 2000: 58).

By 1981 real agricultural wages had fallen to 64 per cent of their 1964 level. Better-off farmers economised on labour, invested in mechanisation and commercial gain rather than maintaining their traditional patronage of local labour – women's traditional post-harvest agricultural work greatly reduced. The better placed could sponsor their sons' education and migration abroad and seek government employments (which grew after independence). Those without land, money, education or elite contacts lacked these options; they remained dependent on the declining agricultural labour market (Kabeer, 2000: 59). In these circumstances traditional moral certainties gave way to chronic uncertainty.

This gives only the broadest sketch of the major destabilisation of traditional agrarian society in Bangladesh, which radically reduced many men's power to maintain their households from their own efforts as agricultural wage-earners. Without land, and with only poorly rewarded, irregular, labour-market opportunities, they found it increasingly difficult to meet their patriarchal responsibilities (Kabeer, 2000: 136–41). Patriarchy required female obedience in return for male provision. Men were supposed to protect and feed their women (Kabeer, 2000: 130–1, 187). But when men's economic power declines so does the value of women, and men's normative commitment to them. Women become more of an economic liability – as shown by the growth from the 1960s of 'demand' dowry, which increased what women (and their families) had to pay to get married. Parents with several daughters could be quite impoverished by the effort to marry them. Concurrently, the incidence of divorce, separation and abandonment rose, along with female-headed households (Kabeer, 2000: 60–2), and women started to improve their 'fall-back' position, by earning and saving (Kabeer, 2000: 161–87).

Strategies for reducing patriarchal risk

Women, particularly poor women, became exposed to 'high patriarchal risk'. That is, accepting purdah, as the price for male support, became increasingly unreliable. Nonetheless, the female share of employment only rose from 5 per cent to 7 per cent between 1967 and 1987. Most women accepted only home-based work, (crop processing, cleaning or crafts) or were prepared to go no more than a few hundred metres to work in neighbouring households. Though deeply internalised, purdah's resilience derived from the strength of *shamaj*, the **moral economy** of the local village, where everyone knows everybody else's business, making **deviance** difficult to hide. And, as we saw in Chapter 2, maintaining ones' moral reputation is particularly important for people reliant on locally-based reciprocal exchanges of resources. Religious authorities used sacred texts to reinforce conformity to traditional norms of gender behaviour. Together with the village elites who exercised patronage in these spheres of reciprocity, they had an interest in maintaining labourers' traditional dependency and deference (Kabeer, 2000: 64).

Poor women's cultural, social and geographical positioning meant that most had to depend on unreliable men, or work and risk their own reputations (their purdah) and those of the men nominally responsible for them. The most discrediting work was public, manual labour. One woman forced into such labouring 'worked in the fields at night, by moonlight, or at times when there was the least likelihood of being seen' (Kabeer, 2000: 65). Before substantial numbers of women could reduce patriarchal risk they therefore needed not only access to reliable employment, but also means of entering a public realm of work in a way they felt was not morally discrediting – which allowed them some way of keeping purdah – preserving their gender identity, and acceptability to their families. Even those economically desperate and lacking effective male support wanted to maintain their purdah.

The rapidly multiplying garment factories provided the potentially transformative economic opportunities. They were the outcome of a global restructuring of manufacturing motivated by uncompetitive labour costs in the developed world. Encouraged by the neo-liberal, free-market favouring World Bank and International Monetary Fund, the Bangladesh government had, via its 1982 New Economic Policy, changed its development strategy from one of import substitution to export-led growth. It now offered incentives to both foreign and local investors to produce export goods, creating around 250,000 new jobs (85 per cent female) in large factories by 1985 (Kabeer, 2000: 69).

This expansion has continued so that by 2010 there were more than 3 million garment workers in Bangladesh (Rahman, 2010). The sudden initial transformation of the **opportunity structure** for women was the basis for the changes Kabeer noticed on her return in 1984. Not only did employers prefer to employ women, women preferred to work with other women in a well-organised interior space (Kabeer, 2000: 95). The gendered division of labour (cutting, packing and ironing for men, and machining largely for women), spatially segregating the sexes at work, and the use of kinship terminology to describe cooperation between the sexes as that of 'brothers and sisters', contributed to framing capitalist employment in terms of traditional domestic morality (Kabeer, 2000: 96–7). This went some way towards satisfying the desire for respectability. Wages, which though low, were seen as generally reliable, reduced patriarchal risk, and factory routines and spaces provided a setting which could be interpreted as not compromising purdah (Kabeer, 2000: 70–6). Patriarchy's subordination of women was not created by capitalism but was functionally compatible with it in this context.

However, even women whose male kin accepted the possibility of their working, had first to overcome the morally compromising obstacles of actually migrating to, and living in, the city. Migrants, coming from many different regions, were largely detached from their villages and freed from the close observation of critical neighbours. They could be relatively anonymous, free from the discipline of *shamaj* (Kabeer, 2000: 138). However, though the increase in the number of women factory workers in the 1980s had been dramatic, the vast majority of Bangladeshi women still remained subject to traditional patriarchal controls in their villages.

Kabeer reveals the ways women entering the factory economy reinterpreted the conditions of maintaining their moral reputations. Rather than simply abandon patriarchal terms of self-justification, they elaborated traditional beliefs to allow them to take advantage of the new urban opportunities.

One major move was to take responsibility for keeping their purdah. Purdah was 'interiorised' so that appearing in public spaces travelling to work every day was no longer seen as discrediting. As one put it: 'Even if I am wearing a burkah and have to get on a crowded bus, I have to push past men. Wearing a burkah won't change that. The best purdah is the burkah within oneself, the burkah of the mind' (Kabeer, 2000: 91). Men no longer had to guard it.

Another move was to reject the moral authority of religious officials and the discipline of the community *shamaj*, while insisting on winning the approval of their close male kin and acknowledging their patriarchal status. But only men who might have material patriarchal responsibilities were recognised. As Afifa put it: 'Instead of starving, if a person is working for her living, why should *shamaj* criticise her?' (Kabeer, 2000: 90) Fathers and husbands experiencing their own difficulty in fulfilling their patriarchal obligations, and who had personal knowledge of their daughters and wives, joined in this redefinition of the conditions of purdah (Kabeer, 2000: 87– 92). Together they learned about what went on inside the factories (despite traditionalist rumours), what was involved in public travel, and possible morally acceptable urban living arrangements (Kabeer, 2000: 110–13). Women's moral status rose as their men decided to trust them. As time went by, working in the garment factories became sufficiently accepted as a new form of 'women's work' that, although the stigma had not disappeared, new recruits and their families found it morally easier to participate.

Elaboration of the terms and practices of a traditional patriarchal culture so that they may be upheld in the early phase of modernisation was motivated by a coincidence of environmental, political and economic crises. One can imagine that, to begin with, choices would be made by various individuals more or less desperate, hesitant, courageous, and possibly discouraged by their families, as a risk worth taking, given the immediate alternatives. However the six-fold increase in garment factory jobs over the following three decades shows a new durable way of life has emerged with major implications for gender relations.

With garment production now contributing 76 per cent of Bangladesh's export earnings, women's labour has become a major asset for government economic policy, and women's interests have found a political voice. The 2004 constitution recognised gender equality; various policies encourage girls' education and seats are reserved for representatives in national and local government. Women have become politically active in public, demonstrating, campaigning, voting and standing for election. Some factory workers have begun to support trade unions (such as BIGU- Bangladesh Independent Garment Workers Union Federation), and try to improve pay and conditions which are often unhealthy and dangerous, as shown by the 2013 Rana Plaza building collapse in which over 1000 workers died and 2500 were injured (Rock, 2001; Ahmed, 2004; Karim, 2014).

It is now normal to see women in public spaces, using their own money for themselves and their families. Within households, working women participate in deciding economic priorities, and their earning potential has changed the expectations of parents, particularly fathers, and husbands. This registers in delaying marriage, and the birth of their first child, and reducing overall family size. The potential for a time of adolescence has opened up between, on the one hand leaving school and becoming a young wage-earner, and on the other, becoming a mother. Marriage no longer automatically entails immediate motherhood and relations with husbands have changed.

Earlier she used to depend on me for everything … now everything has changed. She earns for the family. I think her income has made her feel more secure. The job has increased her courage so she can argue now. (Husband of 25 year-old worker) (Rahman, 2010: 189)

Factory work has made women independent. They go to office alone. It has made them brave. So they now can go anywhere without help. The scenario of the streets has been changed in recent years … Lots of girls move around the streets during holiday afternoons. They are shopping for themselves. They go to cinemas. They do everything for themselves. They do not need any help from their male family members … Earlier my wife did not go anywhere without me. But now she does not require anybody. Sometimes she takes money from me and goes alone for shopping … It is okay. I do not mind. But I think she should ask me before going … I think women should behave properly. They should go with other women. They should not stay outside (the home) in the evening. (Husband of a 24 year old worker) (Rahman, 2010: 194)

Garment factory jobs involve travelling, basic numeracy and literacy, and using money. Once learned, these activities, using public impersonal media of cities, markets and formal education can be extended beyond their original applications, re-positioning those women involved, as autonomous individuals able to choose where they might go, who they encounter, and what they might read or buy. Garment jobs empower women by encouraging non-fatalistic future orientations, aspirational self-identities, and the formation of extra-familial networks of friends and acquaintances.

The fact that a de-stabilised, modified, patriarchy continues to exist in the face of 30 years expansion in female employment suggests that various normalising practical accommodations have been achieved between the experience of women earning, and patriarchal rules. There are three important conditions for this patriarchal acceptance of depending on women's earning power.

First, as we discussed with the welfare bureaucrats in Chapter 8, context-specific exceptions, excused by practical necessity, allow rules to be honoured in the breach. Exceptions do not necessarily mean the rules change, only that more interpretive work has to be done to determine what now counts as sufficiently conforming to them. This eases traditionalist encounters with crises and the rapid changes of modernisation. Second, though men are no longer the sole providers, their family dependents tend to benefit from women's income. Men's moral role, as patriarchs, is to ensure family interests have priority in the spending of women's earnings. In this way men retain their status as ultimate providers. The third condition of the normalisation of a modified patriarchy is a long period of expansion of job opportunities for women, but which nevertheless carries the risk of unemployment. Expansion is vulnerable to policy changes in importing countries. This was demonstrated when the US, which imported 46 per cent of its clothing from Bangladesh, passed the 2000 Trade Development Act, giving trade preferences to Africa and the Caribbean (Bhattacharya and Rahman, 2000). The Bangladesh industry shrank, many women lost their jobs, falling back on their supporting families (Karim, 2001). This experience showed garment jobs could not be taken for granted. Changes in the global economy, and employers' preference for young, malleable, workers, means the garment factories may not always offer a job for life. It is therefore rational for women to continue to accept (a modified) patriarchy – and its risks – as the price of a fall-back position should they lose their jobs. (Compare this with Ruby's dilemmas in Chapter 2.)

*How social structures shape decision-making environments:
the case of London's East End*

We can now briefly consider the positioning of Bangladeshi women in London, in terms of the structural variables used to explain the Dhaka situation (Figure 10.1 summarises the differences). In the 1980s when Kabeer began her research, if they participated in the British garment industry it was only as home-workers, dependent on being given work by male intermediaries. Their employment was irregular, unregulated, and poorly rewarded. It was not strongly distinguished from their other domestic tasks and their earnings tended to be absorbed into the domestic economy. Why did this relatively weak employment position exist?

First, the majority (95%) of these Bangladeshi migrants to Britain came from Sylhet, a particularly religious and culturally conservative region (Kabeer, 2000: 195), and from the class of independent, landholding peasants with the resources to pay the fare (Kabeer, 2000: 194–6). Migration abroad was an option for better-off men. The traditional community system of social control was continuous between the two counties, marriages and families were spread between them and men regularly returned to Bangladesh. Second, women migrated as the wives of men who had already gained residence rights following the increasingly restrictive Commonwealth Immigration Acts of 1962 and 1968. Men decided relatively late to move their families to Britain rather than maintain the hope of some day being reunited in Bangladesh (Kabeer, 2000: 197–8). These factors enabled *Shamaj* to continue, facilitated by the migrants' concentration in London's East End, centred on Tower Hamlets, where the face-to-face community had personal networks linking directly back to Sylhet (Kabeer, 2000: 267, 270). Third, as wives, the London women tended to be older and to have more dependent children and heavier child care responsibilities than the Dhaka garment workers, whose marital status was more varied. Fourth, during the 1960s and 70s Bangladeshi men had already established themselves in the British garment industry so (factory-based) garment work was not defined as female, as was the case in Dhaka (Kabeer, 2000: 279–80). Fifth, the British industry, supplying a volatile domestic market wanted to maximise employee flexibility – thus expanding home-working and sub-contracting (Kabeer, 2000: 207–15). Home-working was practical for immigrant women lacking education and English. It did not require they venture into the morally discrediting public space, where they might also experience racial harassment and abuse (Kabeer, 2000: 270–1). Sixth, men had employment opportunities in a variety of occupations other than garments, whilst state unemployment benefits meant even unemployment did not result in economic desperation (quite different to the position of men in the black ghetto discussed in Chapter 2, where state benefits went only to mothers). This financial safety net meant that men's ability to meet their patriarchal obligations and insist on the traditional form of purdah was stronger than in Bangladesh. Patriarchal risk was therefore relatively low so the pressure on women to earn was correspondingly reduced. Finally, the welfare state also provided free education, thus removing a major motive for female employment in Bangladesh, where women worked to pay for their children's schooling. Taken together these factors enabled men to maintain dominance over dependent women performing traditional female roles, confining them to the home. The relative economic reliability of their men buttressed by the British welfare state, together with child care responsibilities, the absence of female outside employment opportunities, language deficit, and British racism all worked to limit women's opportunities to the home (Kabeer, 2000: 278).

Discussing Kabeer's original study in the first edition of this book, we wondered how the situation she described would develop, hypothesising that as British-educated girls left school they might be better prepared and more keen to enter the world of work in Britain than their mothers. This is true to some extent. But subsequent research by Kabeer depicts a complicated situation and a stronger ability of patriarchy to retain its hold in the East End than was expected (Kabeer and Ainsworth, 2011). A key factor has been continued in-migration from Bangladesh, reinforcing traditional values. In particular, rather than marry British-born and educated daughters as they became eligible from the mid 1990s, many men prefer, or are encouraged by their parents, to bring in Bangladeshi-born women to marry. These are generally young, speak little English, have few qualifications (although benefitting from improved access to education in Bangladesh) and are isolated from their natal families. These brides are therefore poorly placed to resist pressures to fill traditional, family-oriented roles. And entering the local labour market is even more difficult for them than their predecessors given the decline in the availability of home-working, as the British garment industry has succumbed to competition from producers in Bangladesh and other developing states. The community has thus developed a structure for reproducing traditional culture by effectively insulating much of its traditional patriarchal marriage system from the undermining effects of the compulsory education of girls in Britain. The traditional, ideal female role sequence of obedient daughter, then wife, mother preferably of sons, subordinate to husband's mother, eventually becoming mother-in-law of her sons' Bangladeshi-born wives, still has considerable normative force in Tower Hamlets.

Over time, British resident Bangladeshi women have become differentiated by where they are born. But continued conformity to traditional patriarchy by Bangladeshi-born women, including recent arrivals in the same age range as British-born school leavers, means that the latter are still subject to traditionalist community norms. They may well have higher labour market aspirations and participation than the Bangladeshi-born, but generally still have to accommodate to the older generation's values when required. Kabeer and Ainsworth record one well paid, university-educated employee of a big financial company giving in to her in-laws' pressure to stop working, saying, 'I didn't want to be selfish and it was drummed into me that I was being selfish'(2011: 27). She was conforming to the norm described by a Bangladeshi-born interviewee: 'In Bengali culture the daughter–in-law looks after everyone, it is her responsibility. I do it because

Common Legacy: Islam, Patriarchy and Purdah (the norm of female seclusion) and British Imperialism.

Contemporary Macro-Economy: Global capitalist market for labour to supply cheap commodities to consumers in the 'First world'.

Dhaka		London

Macro-scopic social structures conditioning opportunities for women

Traditional agrarian. Very poor. Destabilised; chronic crisis (1970s/80s).	*Type of society*	Modern, urban, industrial. Very rich. Relatively stable.
Newly independent. No welfare system, unemployment benefit or free education. State subsidies for girls' schooling in rural areas after 1994.	*Type of state*	Old welfare state. Economic 'safety net'. Unemployment benefit for families and free education.
New, rapidly and continuously expanding. Export market. Factory machining defined as women's work.	*Garment industry*	Old and declining. Factory work limited and taken by Bangladeshi men. Home-working opportunities for women in the 1980s, but subsequently declining

High but declining	*Patriarchal risk*	Low
No	*Racism*	Yes

Meso-scopic social structures conditioning the form of local social control and freedom for women as a category

Diverse. Includes the poorest.	*Class origin of first generation migrants*	Relatively well off. Land holders.
Diverse.	*Region of origin*	One region: Sylhet.
Independent movement to Dhaka.	*Women's migration type*	Wives sponsored by earlier male migrants.
Dispersed. Not clustered by region of origin. Daily travel to work. Visible.	*City residence & women's movement in public space*	Concentrated in ethnic neighbourhoods. For first generation migrants, little movement outside the home. Invisible.

Micro-scopic social structures affecting the fates of individuals

Diverse. Tendency to delay marriage.	*Marital status & access to male support*	Most first generation migrants married: access to support. British born/educated often disfavoured as brides.
Some. Tendency to delay childbearing.	*Dependent children*	Nearly all – for first generation migrants.
Possessed by many. Garment workers' literacy low but higher than average.	*Education & language for employment.*	Possessed by very few first generation migrants although education level of later arrivals higher than of earlier. British born/educated have better education level.

Cultural elaboration

Negotiated and interiorised to permit appearance in public. Contested stigmatisation.	*Traditional Norm of Female Seclusion;* Purdah	**Bangladeshi born**: Conformity to traditional domestic confinement. Declining employment opportunities for more recent arrivals; increase in patriarchal risk. **British born**: Higher economic activity, lower patriarchal risk, but cultural conditioning still strong.

Figure 10.1 Multiple social structuring of the different decision-making environments for Bangladeshi women in Dhaka and London

it is my obligation. You get a lot of reward for it in the afterlife. This is my job so I do it' (Kabeer and Ainsworth, 2011: 32).

Examining these studies depicting the situation of Bangladeshi women in Bangladesh and the East End over time, we see that it is the interaction between the various positioning structures which accounts for what might seem at first sight to be the paradoxical differences in the behavioural tendencies of the two groups of women. To show the effect of a particular structure, imagine it was not operating. Imagine the employment opportunities for women in Dhaka without the effects of a global labour market, or the state subsidising girls' education. Imagine the patterns of residence and the economic activity of East End Bangladeshi women in the 1980s, if racism was not present and there were no home-working opportunities. Consider the opportunities for British-born Bangladeshi women today if men could not continue to import brides from Bangladesh. In both periods imagine the difference made to the power of men if unemployment benefit were not available, as was the case in the black ghetto studied by Stack (where patriarchal risk was very high, creating strong pressure for women to be economically self-reliant). In fact the combination of racism, the welfare state, and continuing immigration, has worked powerfully in London to retain community boundaries and constrain women, including those British-born and educated, to conform to traditional roles, limiting the extent to which they take up the opportunities of the modern city (Figure 10.1).

Conclusion: the necessity of social structure and the interaction of all five concepts

Gellner and Kabeer develop their analyses of the interaction of social structures and cultures in response to naturalist and culturalist arguments which fail to recognise the causal force of social structure. Nationalists claim nationalism is natural and some development theorists suggested the prospects for change in Bangladesh were poor because of the power of traditional Islamic culture. We saw that both the political ideology of nationalism, and conformity to the rules of traditional culture depend on the social structural circumstances. We also learn that though a very general structural concept like 'modernity', as used by Gellner, is useful, it is important to conduct analysis at a level which reveals the decision-making environments of actors. We can then analyse the complex, uneven, localised, patchy character of the real-life process, which often gets obscured by concepts designed to capture the broad sweep of change.

Gellner and Kabeer describe the positioning forces of social structure as distributing powers and liabilities, and creating strong tendencies in behaviour and the perception of interests. But these tendencies are only statistical frequencies which measure what large numbers of people do when put in a certain structural position. So if, as a Bangladeshi woman exposed to increased patriarchal risk because of war, environmental devastation, and rural unemployment, a friend tells you and/or your family about the new factories opening in Dhaka, you are presented with an opportunity. But because you value your relations with your Islamic family and acknowledge the norm of purdah, you are faced with a structural tension between the position you are in and the one you might want to be in - paid employee in the city. You cannot be domestic/private and economic/public simultaneously. This is a typical structurally induced dilemma. The modern power techniques, such as are assembled in garment factories in Bangladesh, create a potentiality for social structural change. But actualising it depends on the way actors, such as poor women, respond to such dilemmas. Kabeer shows how some women modified their beliefs and behaviour, and set about persuading their families that the apparent contradiction could be removed.

When we consider dilemmas faced by these women, or the British-born school leavers who wanted careers but also to please their more traditionally-oriented parents, the interaction of social structure, culture and action is revealed (Figure 10.1). Actors always face contradictory demands entailed by their existing social relations and beliefs. They are cross-pressured by their commitments. Because there are contradictions, choices usually carry costs and involve taking risks. The early garment factory workers risked their moral reputations and marriage prospects. In fact they tended to lose only the approval of distant kin. But that was a price worth paying in circumstances of severe economic hardship. They managed to trade off the slight loss of moral status, for reduced patriarchal risk. The interviews of Kabeer, Rahman, Kibria, and others, show that though social structures and cultures locate actors and define the problems they must deal with, how they do so varies enormously with their determination, knowledge, skill, idealism, courage and ability to strike compromises. The impact of the conditioning forces of social structural location depends on their strength, on what people are prepared to tolerate or risk losing, the prices they are prepared to pay (Kibria, 1998; Kabeer, 2000; Kabeer and Ainsworth, 2011; Rahman, 2010).

Once enough women were working in the garment factories, access to the opportunity to become an independent wage earner became routine. Women in Bangladesh became more powerful in a way it could be difficult to reverse. In Britain, the destabilising effects of daughters' education in British schools, predicted by Kabeer in 2000, have been limited by the continuing arrival of young women from Bangladesh who are weakly placed to challenge patriarchy. As things stand, recent data suggests that the majority of women see 'marriage and motherhood as the proper destiny for women' (Kabeer and Ainsworth, 2011). The difference between individual women and, to some degree, between those who were or were not born in Britain, is the extent to which they believe this is the only destiny. It is reasonable to hypothesise that discussions about this issue are central in relations between Bangladeshi-born mothers-in-law and their British-born and tertiary educated daughters-in-law and are likely to be critical for advances in gender equality among Bangladeshi families living in London.

Questions related to themes in this chapter

This chapter presents examples of the structural changes that produce and are produced by the experience of modernisation. It shows how these structural changes condition and are affected by the responses of people to them.

1) Why does the coincidence of political and cultural boundaries matter in modern societies but less so in traditional ones?
2) Why might size be an important condition of forming a viable national state?
3) Imagine you are an agricultural labourer in Bangladesh. What factors might have affected your attitude to your daughter going to work in a garment factory in the early 1980s and what might influence it today?
4) How does Kabeer show the way access to the resources of a welfare state can affect gender relations?
5) Using your understanding of social structural conditioning, assess the claim that in modern society you can achieve anything you want, if you desire it enough and try hard enough.

PART VI

Conclusion

CHAPTER 11

Get real: a perspective on social science

This chapter recaps and builds on discussion in the Introduction, to make more explicit our understanding of what constitutes science in general, and social science in particular. Through doing this it further elaborates and justifies our claim that the five concepts – 'individuals', 'nature', 'culture', 'action', 'structure', we have been considering in the previous chapters, have not just been chosen on a whim, but are fundamental for social science. Deciding on basic concepts for science (including basic concepts for social science) depends on what we think science itself is.

Our basic understanding of science

For us, science is the practice of finding out how and why things are the way they are – what has caused them. As we discussed in the Introduction, we are realists in the sense of holding there is an objective reality 'out there' independent of human perception of it, for science to study. We don't agree with the empiricists' claim that we can only know that which is directly available to our senses. Nor do we follow idealists who suggest there is no access to reality other than through the ideas we may have about it in our head. We do recognise that both experience and language play a vital role in the construction of knowledge and explanations, but also argue that knowledge and explanation must be governed by the way that reality actually is (Figure 0.1). Understanding of the real, external world is gained by using relevant concepts to facilitate empirical investigation and develop theories (Box 11.1).

Before we begin investigation of any specific aspect of reality – including social reality, there are some further very general, ontological, claims we want to make, that is, claims about the fundamental character of reality. These claims affect the way we would treat any aspect of reality as an object of study. We start from the premise that the 'objects' which sciences study are always complex 'wholes' resulting from relations among parts. Although these parts have causal powers, they can be identified independently of any role they may play in causing a 'whole'. The relations between parts must be conceptualised

Box 11.1   What is the appropriate form of explanation in social science? Realism versus empiricism and idealism

The philosophy of social science (e.g. Benton and Craib, 2001) often distinguishes between three views about explanation, each of which gives primacy to one of: reality, experience or language. Realists prioritise **ontology**, insisting that knowledge and explanation must be about what exists, independently of how it is experienced or explained (see Figure 0.1). Realists distinguish the *empirical* (what can be experienced), from the *real* (the mechanisms which have the potential to produce things) and from the *actual* (instances of what is produced by the productive potential of reality). That is they make what really exists the test of explanation, but fully acknowledge that knowledge involves bringing the powers of experience, observation and evidence, as well as logic, theory, reason and language, to bear on existence. In the terms of this book, reality, experience and language are all necessary for knowledge, but none alone is sufficient.

The alternatives, **empiricism** and **idealism**, give primacy to **epistemology**, that is the conditions of human knowing. For them, because there is no unmediated access to reality, the mediating elements of either experience or of language, assume overwhelming importance. Empiricists try to confine themselves to what can be directly experienced and reliably described. For them only what can be observed can be said to exist. Their explanations involve describing regular patterns of sequences and co-occurrence which have statistical reliability and provide the basis for confident predictions about future observations. From a realist point of view, empiricists disconnect experience from the reality which generates it on the one hand, and from the language of theory and the contribution of rationality on the other. Experience alone is not, as empiricists claim, sufficient. For idealists the fact that knowledge depends on the use of linguistic concepts means that it must be entirely governed by those concepts. They reject the empiricist's tactic by denying that there is any linguistically unmediated experience of the world which could provide an objective basis for description. Explanation amounts to no more than being able to offer any number of 'interpretations' in terms of the logic of various conceptual schemes. Any hope of accounting objectively for the way the world is, is given up. The test of explanatory adequacy is merely consistency with a conceptual scheme.

Thus idealism gives up on objectivity (collapsing truth into language), and empiricism on reality (collapsing truth into experience). They directly contradict one another, and both stand opposed to realism, which makes epistemological considerations secondary to ontological ones. For realists, truth depends on maintaining functional relations between ontology and epistemology, and between reality, experience and language.

Benton, T. and Craib, I. (2001) *Philosophies of Social Science*, Basingstoke, Palgrave.
Bhaskar, R. (1975) *A Realist Theory of Science*, Brighton, Harvester.
Bhaskar, R. (1989) *The Possibility of Naturalism*, Brighton, Harvester.
DeLanda, M. (2002) *Intensive Science and Virtual Philosophy*, London, Continuum.
DeLanda, M. (2006) *A New Philosophy of Society*, London, Continuum.
DeLanda, M. (2011) *Philosophy and Simulation: The Emergence of Synthetic Reason*, London, Continuum.

as 'external' to what might be related by them. These **'external' relations** between the parts which comprise wholes, are the outcomes of the parts being brought into a condition of relatedness during contingent historical processes. Being 'contingent' means that the bringing together need not necessarily have happened and therefore also the wholes which resulted – or 'emerged' – from this bringing together or synthesis, also need not have been produced. Once formed, however, these historical, contingent outcomes constitute more or less unique ensembles of effects of interrelated causal processes. For as long as these causal processes operate, subject to self-generated thresholds and feedback effects, unique wholes are contingently synthesised. This synthetic, emergentist, understanding is anti-essentialist. That is it avoids the attributing of essences (necessary, non-contingent, internal relations) to 'wholes' or 'parts' (Box 3.3). 'Essences' are timeless, whereas the emergence of wholes from the relations between parts, and of these parts in turn from the parts which compose them, takes time. A synthetic, emergentist ontology thus also avoids reification, that is the abstraction of the products of processes from the processes which caused them.

To avoid essentialising and reifying, the scientist cannot just presume in advance (by some kind of fiat, without investigation or any knowledge that might have been derived from previous research) what are the causes of the phenomenon they are investigating, how these causes interrelate and how they might have come about. To show how something emerged in a synthetic process, we cannot make any assumptions about what we might discover, although we can make use of any available scientific knowledge about the particular types of relations between the parts and wholes of the various forces contributing to the synthesising of the particular phenomenon we are investigating. Thus for example, attempting to explain an emergent pattern of collective behaviour might involve hypothesising about say cultural norms, but also, using biological science, hypothesising about the effects on behaviour of the vulnerability of human beings to certain diseases or toxins.

Wholes are comprised of parts and the relations between them, but parts are simultaneously wholes with their own constituent components. Thus all causes are caused and a job of science is to discover how earlier causal processes, when subject to contingent conditions, could have generated additional kinds of causal processes. The history of existence is one of the contingent emergence of additions to the array of causes. Just as there was a time when there were no human beings, languages, cultures or social structures such as nation-states, so there was a time when DNA was only a possibility of the earlier pre-biotic chemistry. When the Earth first formed, none of these were guaranteed to come into existence and things are not all moving towards some already predestined end. There is no teleology, but once formed, each new whole, becomes in its distinct way a condition for what is possible next. There are interrelating chains of causation stretching backwards in time, and points where qualitatively different types of reality can be seen to have emerged – as when the first living organisms emerged on Earth, or when not just living organisms but sentient life forms first appeared. Similarly, if we 'decompose' wholes into their constituent parts and subparts at any particular point in time, we will find emergent levels which have their own distinct properties which are not reducible to the properties of the parts of which they are composed. Water has different properties from those of the hydrogen and oxygen atoms it is built from, and the bits of material matter which comprise the human brain, individually lack the capacity to reason (DeLanda, 2002, 2006, 2011).

Manuel DeLanda (1952–, Mexican-American)

(2000) *A Thousand Years of Non-linear History,* New York, Swerve.
(2002) *Intensive Science and Virtual Philosophy,* London, Continuum.
(2006) *A New Philosophy of Society: Assemblage Theory and Social Complexity,* London, Continuum.
(2011) *Philosophy and Simulation: The Emergence of Synthetic Reason,* London, Continuum.

Different scientific disciplines: social reality as an object of investigation for social science

So far we have been talking about science in general but we can also speak of different scientific disciplines. These relate to particular emergent levels, (such as the chemical, the biological) distinguished by their particular objects of study with their distinctive kinds of causes. Particular disciplines focus on the particular kinds of objects with their particular kinds of causes which generate the emergent level with which they are concerned. For many purposes they may thus take for granted 'earlier' and 'lower level' forms of causation which have generated the distinctive kinds of causes with which their particular discipline is concerned. Thus social science emerged to deal with a particular kind or emergent level of reality – the social – which is constituted by its own particular types of causes. It may sometimes refer to historically earlier or 'lower level' forms of causation (such as evolutionary biochemistry or human cell biology) in its explanations, but it does not directly contribute to investigating the origins of these kinds of cause.

Ontologically-grounded social science of the kind we advocate, depends on accepting the idea that there is a class of objects – social forms – which are the products of a set of relatively autonomous causes or generative processes. This means that the most fundamental arguments of social theorists concern what these kinds of existence-producing constituents and processes are and how they operate to 'make social reality work'. What are the relatively autonomous processes that generate the empirical variety of actual, observable, social phenomena, the variety of collectivities or social forms, from the fleeting two person interaction, to the most enduring cultural traditions and organisations of power?

Basic components of social reality

We have chosen the five concepts in our basic tool kit for social theorising, not at random, but because we believe they relate to the fundamental and relatively autonomous causal powers which *together* generate the emergent level of the social. We do not think any are adequate on their own to generate the social. This is why, as we first noted in the Introduction, we reject indi-vidual*ism*, natural*ism*, cultural*ism*, action*ism and* structural*ism* (Figure 0.2). But we argue that, used together as a set, the five concepts are sufficient to enable the synthesising mechanisms responsible for the emergence of the social to be described. We also believe that, in conjunction with other, less general concepts derivable (as we showed in the Introduction) from them, they are adequate for explaining the great range of social forms. In the preceding chapters we have already illustrated the concepts' explanatory power in a wide variety of social contexts, but now we will underline why we think we need them all and why we suggest that in combination they are sufficient for social explanation. (But should it turn out that we are mistaken about the basic necessity and sufficiency of these concepts we would have to revise our list. Though it is unlikely, it is in principle possible that in the future, as a result of scientific advances, some of what we now take to contribute to causing social life may have to be rejected, replaced or added to by other causal mechanisms.)

Our choice of fundamental social theoretical concepts derives from what we think social reality is, and how, at the most basic level, we think social reality works. Our fundamental principle is insistence on the sui generis, objective character of social reality itself and the rejection of individualism. Though social phenomena are populated by individuals, individuals are not in any sense prior to, nor the most fundamental constituents of, social reality. Just as having a body, so also being socially related is a necessary and unavoidable condition of human existence. There are no unrelated human individuals. Every individual, from birth, participates in ongoing cultures and social structures, which pre-exist them. This being so, social reality at any given point in time must always consist of more than the presently existing and embodied individuals, and these non-individual elements of social reality are just as important as the individuals. These elements consist of the relatively durable materials and practices, carrying cultures and social structures over time, which must be independent of the lives of any particular individuals (Archer, 1995, 2000a).

As illustrated in the preceding chapters, and suggested in our Introduction, culture and social structure each have their own kinds of causal powers and hence relative autonomy. Though distinguishable from each another, both share a common form of time, historical time. Though everything is the product of historical process, in this context 'historical time' is that time in which the mechanisms of culture and social structure operate, resulting in the emergence, and having emerged, persistence and durability, of social phenomena. Historical time, in this context, is distinct from both the biographical time of the lives of individuals and the time of the change of nature and natural entities. The conditions for the existence of individuals include their biology, as well as the prior existence of culture and social structure. But though individuals must organically exist for there to be any social phenomena, their importance is as actors constrained to work with the resources of culture and social structure (and external nature). These are *types* of resources which pre-exist them and outlast them in historical time (even if *particular* examples of them may not always do so). The conditions of the existence of individuals interact with those for the existence of (the emergent level of) social phenomena. But to investigate that interaction they must first be distinguished from each other.

The fundamental synthesising morphogenetic mechanism generating variety and change of social forms

Social reality can be thought of as composed, on the one hand of the organic material of human individuals, with their emergent capacities for thinking, feeling, acting, and, on the other, the inorganic material of relatively autonomous cultures and social structures. Social theory concerns itself with the interaction of these two kinds of material. It is this interaction which is necessary for actualising the potential of each to contribute to the continuity and change of forms of collectivisation. In simpler language, social theory shows how the causal mechanisms of social reality have the capability to generate the multitude of human social histories.

Because human social forms are conditioned by human biology and the natural environment, we are able to draw on the natural sciences when trying to explain them. However, neither biology nor natural environment is sufficient to explain the sheer range of social forms, nor why they change in the way they do. To explain this extraordinary variety and mutability, our theory of social reality must include some further very powerful generative mechanisms to play a fundamental role in social explanation. Our main focus must be on the productive interaction between culture, action and social structure over time.

We can think of this interaction as a special kind of feedback process. If we firstly define the human, material, component of social reality as capable of action, that is as actors, secondly define the cultural and social structural components as supplying (along with nature) the resources upon which action depends, and then define action as producing culture and social structure (and mediating the impact of nature which it may also change), we have the basis for such a process. The human and non-human components making up social reality, interact over time. As we said earlier, everyone is born into a pre-constituted social world that they did not create. The cultures and social structures which we inherit provide us with some, more or less advantageous, access to resources such as language, meaning systems, values, techniques, raw materials, occupations, roles, statuses, alliances, money, power, dispositions, vested interests and so on. This sort of inheritance gives social reality its objective, constraining force over actors.

However on this view, social reality is not completely comprised of objective elements which lack subjectivity. Human beings (unlike say rocks or clouds) are not only objects caught in the coils of determining processes they can do nothing about. Rather persons are subjects, having self-consciousness, desires, intentionality, imagination and unique personalities. As individuals and as members of collective organisations they are end-seeking beings, constantly trying to realise their ideals in the face of resistant circumstances. The causal force of cultures and social structures works by distributing resources to actors and would not exist unless there were these actors making use of them in their attempts to realise their desired ends. Cultural and social structural conditioning is not only constraining, it is also enabling (Giddens, 1984; Archer, 1995; Parker, 2000).

Human beings live in open systems

Action is conditioned by the resources available to actors, but outcomes are the product of the action which determines how resources are actually used in contingent situations. This means that actors contribute to changing circumstances – but not always in the ways that they intended. Action involves actors interpreting action situations, determining the usefulness of their resources (resources which will include the cultural and social structural outcomes of previous action) and often in the process, innovating, elaborating and changing the conditions of future action. Generally actors will try to use their resources to perpetuate rewarding situations and to eradicate frustrating ones, and given inequality and differences of values and interests, action will entail conflict and attempts to strengthen positions by allying with others who share common aims. The natural, cultural, social-structural (including the economic and political), and psychological conditions of action are liable to be changed as a consequence of action. Cultural systems are changed. Distributions of resources are changed. People themselves are changed. This is the fundamentally historical 'feedback' process of human social existence resulting in ever-varying forms of collectivisation.

But though changed circumstances are partly the result of actors trying to get what they want, they are seldom exactly what they intended. The *consequences* of action for culture and social structure are largely *unintended*. The creative initiative of agents trying to get what they want can sometimes, particularly for the powerful, and in the short term, produces intended outcomes. But more generally and longer term, unintended outcomes are produced. These may be welcomed and exploited opportunistically as happy accidents, or alternatively may become a source of frustration. For example medical practices may produce unexpected side effects which may lead either to fruitful new lines of research, or to poor patient outcomes. Or action, to pursue religious salvation, may cause totally unanticipated outcomes in some other sphere of life, such as the economy, as Weber suggested in *The Protestant Ethic and the Spirit of Capitalism*. Unintended consequences are effects of combinations of **contingency**, the logic of particular beliefs and practices, actors' misunderstandings and the fact that there are many interests in conflict. All can contribute to eventual outcomes but none are determining by themselves. Thus, intentional action is a necessary part of the process of social production, but that production cannot be entirely explained as the outcome of actors' intentions.

The products of action may acquire emergent autonomous properties which give them independence from the creative control of the actors who initiated their existence. These properties of what actors produce, which they may not even realise exist, have to be investigated using theoretical ideas about cultural and social structural systems. So humans are subject to the force of cultural and social systems, but these are not automatically self-reproducing; they are not closed systems. Though they can acquire some degree of durability and become strong conditioners of action which cannot be easily changed, they always remain available for transformation by human action, and what is involved in changing them will depend on their objective properties. So social and cultural systems can be said to be 'open', but nevertheless offering differing degrees of resistance to actors who must take these objective characteristics into account, if they want to act effectively.

'Retrodictive' explanation rather than determinist prediction

Given that what goes on in the present is indeterminate – that is, outcomes depend on what people actually do with their resources, subject to contingencies, we cannot know in advance what, in fact, will happen. We cannot be sure in advance if specific arrangements and practices will change, or stay the same. We can be fairly certain that, given time, there will be some sort of change, in general, but not the specific form it will take. Prediction, on the basis of general laws of change is not possible in the social sciences. But we can identify strong tendencies at work in the present and make plausible estimates about the configuration of forces which seem most likely to shape outcomes in the immediate or mid-term future. Once we understand the cultural forms people subscribe to and the structures in which they are located, we can have grounds for suggesting that they are more likely to act in some ways than others. These estimates are inexact, but they are all that can ever be available and are well worth having. Not everything is equally changeable at every moment. The products of past action have durability, or a certain momentum to carry on conditioning action. The social condition of humans is one of conditional freedom.

Everything we have said about social ontology so far implies that the basic form of explanation in the social sciences must be historical. We have three fundamental components, historical time, the objectivity of all the different kinds of action conditions, and the powers of actors. Social phenomena are emergent outcomes of real processes which take time to occur. We cannot precisely predict them in advance, but we can hope to explain them 'retrodictively', by referring backwards in time to the processes of their emergence. Once they have come into being, we can explain social phenomena by means of historical accounts of configurations of the natural, cultural and social structural conditions of the actions of individuals and collectivities which actually occurred. Explanations show how the various causal forces interact over a period of time. This was exactly what we did, for example, when discussing the emergence of nation-states and change in Bangladeshi gender relations since the 1980s in Chapter 10. This is quite different from the view that to explain something we must be able to predict its occurrence.

Non-determinist, non-voluntaristic and objectivist social science

Our preferred kind of social explanation is scientific because it is causal and identifies generative mechanisms which have observable effects. But it is not determinist because, as we have shown, humans live in open systems and these objective forces only condition action. Because action always contributes to why states of social affairs are the way they are, we must reject determinism as a criterion of science for the social sciences. But by the same token, although action is not *determined*, it is always *conditioned*, so this type of social explanation is not voluntarist (actors are not free to do just as they like and do not produce only what they intend).

Our non-deterministic, non-voluntaristic social science recognises that actors' own understandings of what they are doing must play a part in explanation. But it is not interpretivist. That is, it does not seek to explain phenomena only in terms of the actors' own understanding of them and of their actions. Because actors' understandings are conditioned by, and interact with, the other conditions of social life, they are generally insufficient to explain reality. Explanation requires social scientists to use their own concepts.

Use of the scientist's own theoretical concepts however, does not idealise, subjectivise, or relativise, social explanation. Concepts are certainly necessary for explanation, but dependence on concepts is not determination by concepts. As we stated earlier, explanation is not governed solely by the internal logic of a particular conceptual 'discourse' but must relate to the objective world which exists independently of the concepts used to describe it. Given this, it cannot be the case that all discourses are equally valuable as instruments for understanding objective social realities. Thus we must also reject **relativism**, the belief that there are no 'external', 'independent' standards in terms of which the different concepts can be judged against each other.

Our general theory of social reality helps us look in the right places, but does not substitute for looking. Often what we discover by looking has implications for the general guidance offered by the theory of social reality. There is constant development of knowledge which results from following the guidance of social ontology, including potentially revising the basic ontological theory of social reality itself, in the light of what one discovers.

Questions related to themes in this chapter

This chapter has discussed the function of basic concepts for science in general and social science in particular.

1)   What are the functions of basic concepts in the social sciences?
2)   Discuss implications for explaining social phenomena scientifically, of the fact that humans engage in subjectively meaningful action.
3)   Discuss the possibilities for making successful predictions in social life.
4)   How might a social scientific explanation of a pattern of behaviour contribute to altering that pattern?
5)   Think of some examples of historical events which support the suggestion that humans live in open systems.

CHAPTER 12

Being practical: the uses and payoffs of social explanation

In this book we have approached social theory from the view-point of explanatory methodology. Rather than treat it as an end in itself, we have presented it as a set of conceptual tools for making (particular examples of) social phenomena intelligible as outcomes of causal processes. We have argued firstly, that some kind of social theory is necessary to produce causal explanations of social phenomena, and secondly that it is possible to move beyond the limitations of 'everyday', 'common sense' theorising by exploring, understanding and systematically applying the small set of five interrelated concepts we present in this book. We hope that, through observing how they have been applied in a wide variety of cases, readers have now gained a firm sense of the practical value of the concepts and how they function when producing explanations.

But why might we be interested in explanations? We can approach this question reflexively, applying social theory to account for its uses – for social explanation is itself socially caused. One principle type of reason for our interest might be a desire to increase our understanding because a phenomenon intrigues or puzzles and perhaps for this reason, disturbs us (we will leave aside asking why this might be the case for later – see the Coda). A second and related reason can be because there is a perceived dissonance between our ideals about what ought to happen, (themselves culturally and structurally conditioned) and our experience of what actually does happen, which motivates resort to systematic social explanation in order to account for, and help bridge the gap between the two. We may (rightly) feel that the more we understand about how and why things are, the better placed we will be to act as effectively as possible to change them to become nearer to our ideal.

Social explanation contributes to solving what we identify as problems arising in our social experience, by revealing their social causes and how these interact with other kinds of causation. Rather than rely on common sense and various everyday sources of ideas about why things are as they are, such as the media, rumour, opinion leaders and politicians, scientific social explanation attempts to provide complex causal narratives which are subject to rigorous logical and empirical scrutiny. Such narratives enable our relation with troubling social experiences to become more objective and reflective. We no longer simply react in a confused and emotional way, but have taken the first step to solving the problem, which is to understand what created it.

Explanatory social science identifies the objective and subjective components of historical mechanisms which generate the social situations we experience as problems. Its causal narratives explain how the consequences of past action continue to condition certain kinds of action in the present, which may be the source of our problematic experience. The conditions of action in the present are shown to have particular kinds of relative autonomy and to have a certain degree of durability, or resistance to change. Once we understand what is constraining the action we find problematic in these terms, we are equipped to take the next step towards solving the problem, which is to decide what to do about it.

Understanding does not guarantee that anything can be done about the problem. Sometimes what we learn from the explanation is that the forces shaping action are so strong that it is virtually impossible to alter their impact. In such cases social scientific explanation can provide only the consolation of understanding. This may free us from being dominated by the reactive emotions the problem generated in the first place, freeing up energies for more productive activity. Or it can prevent us from investing in trying to change something where the chances of success are very slim. Neither of these practical implications of understanding is trivial. They can limit suffering and wasted energy and resources. However, whether one chooses to be content with the consolations of understanding depends on the risks one is prepared to take and the intensity of desire to change what is causing the problem. Some people, knowing that they are unlikely to succeed, nevertheless foolishly and/or heroically, go ahead. But generally, by showing us what we are up against, social explanation puts us in a better position to evaluate what we need to do to change things and what the costs are likely to be.

Social explanation, levers of power and strategies for change

Sometimes the understanding provided by social explanation offers only 'consolation'. But often it provides us with powerful resources for changing conditions which frustrate, or enhancing those which advantage, us.

In the social, as in the natural world, the better we understand how things work, the better our chances are of maintaining them or changing them to be as we want. Social explanations make their contribution to choosing the best means to producing the change that is sought, by identifying the relevant levers of power. Deliberate change strategy is a matter of finding ways to have positive or negative effects on the various on-going processes. Explanatory narratives of the interaction of the various causes of the circumstances we may want to change can be read for what they tell us about opportunities to exert pressure for change in one direction or another. Such opportunities are indicated by, for example (i) the character and distribution of vested interests arising from culture and social structural positioning (ii) the functional strengths and weaknesses of the various forms of organisation, such as the mode of constructing networks (discussed in Chapter 9) being used by the interested parties, and (iii) various contradictions between interests which cross-pressure interested parties. Knowledge of these, respectively allow us to estimate who and what is likely to support or oppose the change in question (facilitating efficient coalition formation), to anticipate structural vulnerability (allowing us to predict moments of weakness in the opposition) and to exploit our opponents' dilemmas of having to choose between their interests.

Knowledge derived from social explanation can also help us decide how our aims at any given point, might best be met. Will it be better to have a small, tightly structured and controlled set of activists, or go for a broader, looser network of supporters? Will it be useful to build on existing institutional structures, or try to create new ones from scratch (Rooney, 1995)? When will reasoned argument be most effective in winning others to one's cause (Flyvbjerg, 1998)?

Strategies must relate available resources to the nature of the resistance being overcome. For example, the ineffectiveness of the London police investigation of the black teenager Stephen Lawrence's murder in 1993, motivated an effort to end racist policing practices. But how is justice for all to be achieved? Ignatieff (1999) asks if it is better to try to eliminate the racist feelings of some police officers, as suggested by the Macpherson Report (1999), or simply to insist that they concentrate on treating black people as citizens. Is the psychological purification of police personnel a possible, reliable and preferable method of securing fair policing? Would changing the ethnic composition of the force be a more realistic long-term solution? The structural and cultural conditions of police recruiting and internal institutional disciplinary practices, suggest that the quickest and most reliable results might come from rigorous, non-discriminatory application of the law, rather than attempting the psychological conversion of individual police. Racially-neutral policing is a desirable and technically possible goal, but we would be wise to choose the quickest and cheapest method for bringing it about. When we deliberately set out to change the social world we had better know what realistic goals are and how to avoid paying unnecessarily high prices for winning them.

However, though social theory is a practical tool for choosing the best means to get what we want, just as is the case with natural science, it cannot provide us with ultimate moral grounds for action. It is value neutral. Despite this, within the framework of the ultimate values people adopt – be they self-serving or altruistic or some combination of the two, theoretically-informed understanding can help them specify realistic, achievable goals. Where they do have power to act to implement their preferences, the understanding provided by social scientific explanation can steer them to make better choices.

A practical test for social theory: the challenges of climate change

All of the above is relevant for understanding what sorts of problems are posed by climate change. And for providing some strategic guidance, using the particular, multi-causal, emergentist type of social theory we have been advocating in this book. What follows is not meant to be a comprehensive analysis, only a beginning; but it should demonstrate how using the theory, non-experts in climate change are enabled to take a strategic approach to this major problem.

What kind of problem is it?

First of all it is a problem originally defined by climate scientists who discovered long-term changes in the range of normal variation of global temperatures. They found evidence of steadily increasing warming coinciding with the massive increase in burning fossil fuels which began about 1700. The consensus is that this warming is a legacy of the last three centuries of human activity. It largely results from the competition and invention motivating and enabling an increase of productive capacity by using machinery fuelled by coal, oil and gas. During the 20th century, initially in the United States, the use of cheap fossil fuels became a routine presupposition in every domain of life. Probably the single most telling consequence is that vehicular movement between dispersed specialist places (dormitory suburbs, shopping centres, office and industrial parks) has become normal and compulsory (Dennis and Urry, 2009; Urry, 2011). Trumping the many polluting effects of oil-based production, most notably plastics, is an increase in green house gases (GHGs), prominent among them C02. GHGs are thought to be raising average global temperatures, increasing evaporation, aridity, polar melting and raising sea-levels. These changes in basic parameters, interacting with complex regional climate sub-systems in ways only beginning to be understood, are likely to produce highly variable impacts on ecologies, water supplies and agricultural systems. Most climate scientists now believe that speedy action is necessary to limit GHG emissions sufficiently to keep temperature rise below a disaster threshold. So the components are clear. Humanly produced GHGs are a sufficient cause of threat to the sustainability of acceptable conditions for human life, among which are an adequate diversity of environments and species. Solutions must protect against temperature rise. These may involve various 'technical fixes' such as renewable and/or nuclear carbon-neutral energy generation, capturing the carbon from fossil-fuelled generators, and technologies for reflecting away the Sun's rays. But substantial decreases in GHGs can probably be more immediately achieved by reducing energy consumption.

Given the technical difficulty, likely time and cost of implementing many of the potential technical fixes, a flat-out commitment to technical solutions may have to await motivation by experience of the negativities resulting from having failed to limit warming earlier. In what follows, we assume that the climate scientists are right, and also that attempting to reduce energy consumption to reduce GHGs relatively quickly is unavoidable. On this basis we take the challenge for social theory to be to provide a characterisation of the problem or problems presented by trying to prevent and deal with the consequences of climate change, to understand the variety of responses to the changing understanding of the threat (discussed briefly in Chapter 6), and to provide strategic guidance for relevant agents of change.

Climate change as an emergent problem

From whatever points of view the problems of climate change are understood, they are a changing emergent product. This historical dimension is crucial; as time goes on we learn from earlier responses about what may still be possible. Ongoing research into changes in production of GHGs, including research into the effects of attempts to reduce them, alter the significance of the problem. For example, Hansen (2008) thinks the Intergovernmental Panel on Climate Change's proposed limit of 450 particles per million of CO2 by 2020 should now be a maximum of 350ppm and believes the current level of 385 has already passed the safety level.

The significance of all these sorts of figures always has to be considered in some context of ongoing activity. Most agree the situation is worsening as the GHGs of huge developing countries begin to overwhelm the very limited attempts to reduce the emissions of the existing big producers in the developed world. Factors to be assessed include the effectiveness of attempts at coordinating international action (Kyoto and Copenhagen disappointed) and of assigning responsibilities and targets (these tend to be played off against one and other, such as GHG reduction versus renewable energy investments). The potential of investments in low carbon technologies need considering (for example the effectiveness of tidal is contested, on-shore wind can provoke local resistance, solar is expensive). So too do such factors as the accumulative effects of exposure to various ways of talking about the problem, the changing status of experts and the normalisation of the problem in public discourse. These sorts of consideration impinge on estimates of what change might be possible in a given period of time. For example, Blühdorn (2013) suggests that climate change discourse, as an extension of ecological debates going back to the 1960s, may be now too old to convey a sense of urgency. It presently tends to support a politics of 'sustaining the unsustainable', advocating only what people are willing to do and what is 'practical and manageable' rather than what is necessary.

The understanding of climate change is collectively mediated

How climate change is understood to be a problem is both collectively mediated and emergent. For the human species which caused what climate change scientists define as the problem, there are as many problems as there are collectively conditioned points of view from which to interpret it. In a sense the threat of climate change makes the whole of humanity a collectivity. But it also collectivises people, in terms of their different relations to the risks, 'all the way down' through all the various scales of groupings. For example, broadly speaking, it is likely that the agriculture of the tropical and subtropical regions of the relatively poor 'south' will be substantially damaged, whereas that of the rich temperate 'north' may possibly benefit (Cline, 2007). The rich are less threatened with catastrophe but are presently the major source of the problem. They are also the major source of resources to invest in limiting GHGs as well as to protect those who are or will be threatened. Whether they do so will depend on how they interpret their social relations with the maximally endangered poor. Will they defensively prioritise a narrow conception of self-interest, or equally share responsibility for limiting the threat? Dealing with threats of climate change is done from positions in socially structured distributions of exposure to risks and of relevant powers to respond. By 2030, it is likely that most at risk will be the 2 billion poor slum dwellers living in the southern cities.

At various points in this book we have considered how relations with natural environments are conditioned by interaction between cultural frameworks, social structural positioning (by class, nation-state systems and so on), and the specific choices of individuals (Chapters 4, 6 and 10). This interaction is where interests are formed, values committed to, and risks assessed guided by situational logics. Throughout we have suggested that contradictions between interests create cross-pressures between different priorities, cross-pressures which are intrinsic to human action. Deciding how to order priorities is the ground of strategy.

Situational logics: taking positions and designing strategies

Following Archer, we suggest there are four 'situational logics': protection, opportunism, elimination and compromise, which define different kinds of situationally derived strategies for GHG and carbon-derived CO2 reduction (Archer, 1995: 213–46). Thus, where the practices we already pursue are consistent with reducing GHGs, we must protect them while also taking advantage of any contingent opportunities to reduce such gases as they arise. Where a practice seems unavoidably to produce GHGs we have to assess the potential for eliminating the practice altogether. But where that is not possible we have to strike a compromise between reducing GHGs and doing what has to be done. Just like the Nigerian complicity in everyday corruption (discussed in Chapter 6), the everyday complicity in high carbon practices (e.g. driving or flying) produces a rhetoric of excuses. Examples include simple justifications of bad practice on the grounds that 'I'm only doing what everyone else does', and the citing of short-term obligations which cannot be met without using the bad means – 'I'm flying half way round the world because I must see my new grandchild'. But volunteering excuses can be evidence for taking obligations to be honest and lower carbon-use seriously, despite it not being the highest priority in all circumstances. The transition from a high to a low carbon mode of life will be happening when there is increased recognition that compromise is happening, followed by a progressive reduction of the need for it.

Responding to climate change is necessarily a politically contested process and in retrospect the outcome, whatever it turns out to be, will be the result of a messy history of interaction between contingent forces and various more or less well informed intentions. Given the scale of the problem and the changes required, strategies will have to be many and appropriate for squeezing out the mitigation potential of all the different energy-using contexts. The initial move has to be indentifying agents with some potential powers to make choices which might mitigate climate change. These are the targets for support, recruitment or pressure to change. The means of support or exerting pressure vary with circumstances. In general these include providing information, critiques of ordering of priorities and proposals for alliances in which reciprocation between agents with differing priorities can enable compromises with positive implications for mitigating climate change. It is also possible to actualise the potential power of the weak with skilful leadership, networks, rhetoric and tactics creating new environmentalist 'agents', such as 'green' parties, environmentalist activist organisations, public transport users groups, cycling associations and local food producers. The political field has been restructured to differing degrees in different countries, so that climate change interests at least have the potential to become serious 'players' able to influence government legislative programmes.

Climate change has moved from being exclusively a concern of scientists, as it was in the early 1990s, to being a routine issue of everyday life and political discourse in the developed world. Here nearly everyone is aware of the possibility of climate change and has some opportunity to take a position with respect to it, if only to deny or ignore it. The goals of the climate change strategies of individuals and of collective agents such as environmental movements, nation-states, cities, energy companies and corporate energy consumers vary widely. Some prioritise limiting temperature rise to two degrees. Others rank limiting the increase in global warming as a high priority among others. Remember the fate of the Yasuní National Park ITT project discussed in Chapter 4, which ended up giving reducing global warming a lower priority relative to the higher priority of ending poverty? Still others seek to take instrumental advantage of opportunities to earn money and/or social status by supplying new patterns of demand motivated by genuine climate change concerns ('greenwashing').

Strategies for preventing, or more realistically, limiting climate change should therefore involve increasing the powers of those giving it the highest priority, raising it up the order of priorities of those for whom it isn't the top, and influencing the powerful, whatever their orders of priority, to use their power to produce the objective consequence of mitigating climate change. This might involve giving them reasons other than mitigating climate change, for doing the right thing. This is the particular significance of the Stern Report, which argued that investing in a low carbon economy was in the interest of the economically powerful whatever their views about the moral requirements to tackle climate change – it spoke to them in a language they could understand (Stern, 2007).

Cultural biases, multiplying subjective support and identifying
the potential for coalitions

When trying to multiply subjective support, we need to consider distinctions in fundamental aspects of how people orientate towards the world so that we can identify those most susceptible to particular kinds of appeals to move climate change mitigation up their order of priorities. What we might call their epistemological stance is one important factor. 'Realists' may grasp the reality and significance of underlying processes which they can't directly observe themselves. They may be happy, for example, to accept scientists' talk of the significance of changes in deep ocean currents a hemisphere away, or the implications for global warming of any thinning of the ozone layer. On the other hand, 'empiricists' may only be trusting of their own direct experiences and may doubt or be unconcerned about what they can't directly see or feel. Highlighting any present unequivocal effects of climate change which they can observe in their immediate environment may be the most we can do for them – unless we can manage to change their underlying orientation (Box 11.1).

Following the tactic of working with already existing orientations, we could also use cultural theory (Chapter 6) to ensure our choice of rhetoric is the most appropriate for convincing people depending on their particular cultural biases when assessing the risks associated with change. We can try to increase the confidence of the fatalistic (having acknowledged their sense of desperation about the situation), show the self-interested individualists the payoffs of making low carbon choices (having acknowledged their worries about cost), persuade the egalitarians of the benefits of trusting experts and exploiting the capacities of state institutions (having acknowledged their worries about inequality and profligacy), and work on hierarchists to take personal responsibility for contributing to change (having acknowledged their worries about macro causes such as population growth) (Douglas and Wildavski, 1982; Douglas, 1996; Hulme, 2009; Adger et al., 2009). For the resistant, cultural theory can help identify values and interests which can be used as positive framing of what would otherwise be unacceptable climate change mitigation projects.

This sort of understanding of people's cultural and social structural conditioning also facilitates identifying potential for coalitions between partners with differently conditioned biases in order to secure climate change mitigation actions by collective agencies at all levels – families, friends, community groups, schools, local government and business associations, medical practices, universities, regulatory bodies, sports organisations, charities, transport systems, tourism and leisure companies, energy producers and so on, all the way up to national governments and international organisations.

Agents, powers and time for climate-change mitigation

So far we have mainly been considering the way social theory can guide strategy by helping us understand agents' subjective relation to the problem; their knowledge and biases. This is a very important condition of climate change mitigation but is not sufficient because even where agents know what to do, they have to have the powers to do it. Being prepared to act and support policy in the name of climate change mitigation is an important resource but has to be related to distributions of power and the opportunity-costs of an emergent menu of policy options.

If, for the sake of argument, the highest priority is to ensure that by 2030 temperature has not risen more than 2 degrees, then policy choices and the relevance of various agencies must reflect the shortage of time. Can a strategy of aggressive GHG reduction be a practical possibility given the available constraining and enabling technical, cultural, political, economic and social structural mechanisms? Given the shortage of time, macro mechanisms such as stabilising human population growth and then reducing its size, a process which may already be under way, will take too long, though will be critical for limiting any rise above 2 degrees after 2030. Moreover moves to limit temperature rise to 2 degrees before 2030 will have to be made within the hitherto high carbon power environment of nation-states and global capitalism. Aggressive mitigation will involve taking a risk that there are still mechanisms objectively capable of delivering within the available time.

It is possible to place one's hope in the value of mitigation that can be achieved across the full range of agents, cultures, technologies and practices emerging as a consequence of learning by doing. This mitigation model pluralises investments with emergent potential which can receive increased investment as their respective capacities begin to show themselves. The model allows for establishing momentum and the progressive favouring of climate change mitigation so that, given time, the messy, uncertain and difficult becomes clearer and easier to do. Just as we want to inhibit hitting negative thresholds or tipping points for climate degeneration, so we can hope to generate positive ones for mitigation. Rather than merely pretending to be dealing with climate change as in the politics of 'sustaining the unsustainable', this approach seeks to put social life on a sustainable footing by the compounding of mitigation effects in a complex elaboration of the relations among current technologies, cultures and social structures. Transitions necessarily present ever changing hybrid combinations of elements of legacies and the part-formed yet to emerge. It is important to allow for the possibility and creativity of emerging hybrids even if it may be difficult always to distinguish these from the merely reassuring simulations sustaining the unsustainable.

This is not a naive, excessively ambitious approach but takes its cue from observing what is going on now and the facts of change over the last two decades. It is consistent with a 'transition management' approach exemplified by the Dutch National Environmental Policy Plan (Shove, 2010). Obviously we can only discuss a few examples to demonstrate the potential. Governments have been accumulating experience of energy conservation policies; examples are the Japanese 'Cool Biz' campaign setting the permitted temperature of air conditioners in summer in government ministries, and advising workers on what would count as socially acceptable forms of cool clothing (Tan et al., 2008), Britain's current 'Green Deal' subsidising insulation of private housing, domestic and community solar electricity generation and clean(er) vehicles (Gov.UK, 2014), and China's investment in renewable electricity generation (Davidson, 2013). States have great potential to shape energy production and consumption by altering people's parameters of choice by means of taxation, energy specifications for state contracts, urban development, public transport investment, and so on. They can also legislate to directly prohibit or require certain kinds of action. In Britain we can no longer fit non-condensing boilers, for example, and our cars must satisfy E.U. emissions standards. As competition for fossil fuels increases, stimulated by the industrialisation of the developing world, the state's raison d'être, the defence of its sovereignty, can rhetorically justify mobilising the investment in transition to sustainable energy as a contribution to self sufficiency. Thus, in Britain the choices to be considered include the opportunities provided by the extensive coast to make long-term, expensive, investment in off-shore wind and tidal generation, the opportunities offered by the geology to invest in recently developed 'fracking' techniques to extract natural gas (Zuckerman, 2013), and new nuclear generation. Short to medium-term interests in containing expenditure (popular with politicians appealing to an individualised electorate interested in the 'cost of living' and 'competitiveness'), and maintaining continuity of supply, may be set against avoiding environmental damage from wastes and GHGs and achieving renewable energy security. The structural point is that nation-states have a dominant interest in defending their sovereignty which can be used to commit themselves to huge, open ended, long-term investments. Given Britain is currently proposing to spend an estimated £6.2 billion to build two aircraft carriers (aircraft extra) and has been considering putting vast sums behind nuclear power stations, it should be equally capable, for example, of delivering a commitment to developing tidal electricity generation in the Bristol Channel.

The agentic powers of states, and of supra and intra-state organisations (for example the EU and city administrations), are complex outcomes of routinised ways of using administrative, technical and logistical capacities as well as the resources of social capital. The latter comprise reputations, good will and trust, conducive to cooperation and compliance. The particular potential of 'intermediate' levels of collective agency like municipal governments, derives from the capacity to deploy huge resources to a detailed understanding of proximate contexts to yield, for example, complex, locally responsive, adaptable, public transport systems. The concentrations of economic, political and social capital typical of cities make them potentially effective change agents as is demonstrated by congestion charging (for example in London and Stockholm), cycling schemes (e.g. Bogota, Copenhagen, Groningen, London, Hamburg, Paris) and electric vehicle infrastructure (e.g. Seattle) (Siemiatycki, 2004; Ho, 2007; Despacio, 2008; Pucher and Buehler, 2008; Gutierrez, 2009; The City of Copenhagen Technical and Environmental Administration, 2011; Börjesson et al., 2012; Eckerson, 2013; Quirk, 2014). Cycling schemes are becoming increasingly popular as commitments of elected mayors which they can deliver (ITDP New York n.d.). Intermediate level institutions all have cultural and social structural properties (e.g. departments, divisions of labour, hierarchies, roles, accounting practices, schedules and traditions) which are embodied in personnel who may have scope for pushing policies and exercising discretion according to their own biases, experience and interests. The room for manoeuvre can be quite trivial, but cumulatively can be significant. For example, cycle-friendly local authority highways designers may be able to discreetly and unofficially sequester defensible space for cyclists by where they mark the side of the carriageway. In Swansea, necessary resurfacing following the renewal of a sewer, became an opportunity to create a now very popular cycle path.

Transition has to make innovative use of the potential of the existing practices and discourses to overcome the powerful vested interests within governments, business, media and to challenge everyday cultural practices which give climate change only low or no importance. However, given the shortage of time, rather than attempt to revolutionise the framing of interests (likely to provoke strong resistance), it will be important to take advantage of the whole range of interests defined within existing frames which can be used to motivate changing to low carbon means. Existing frames are biased towards privileging the short-term, local, proximate, personal and concrete. They discount the long-term, distant, theoretical and abstract which is how climate change predictions may be viewed. Despite this, interests such as saving money, thinking of the long-term future of children, becoming self-sufficient, decongesting cities to make them safer and more enjoyable, maintaining physical fitness, supporting the local economy especially in food production are all conventional motives in a high carbon world which can be pursued by low carbon means. An example is the strategy of fostering 'alternative hedonism' (Soper, 2008). 'Hedonism', a dominant orientation of high carbon consumerism, might offer a motivational bridge to low carbon life-styles, if people could learn how to find the satisfactions of desire in post-consumer, post-extensive, practices. Soper talks of 'aesthetic re-visioning'. This might mean, helped by the efforts of cultural specialists such as artists, musicians, philosophers, comedians and so on, learning how to recognise the pleasures of the small, intensive, slow, sufficient, flexible, smart, recycled and long-lasting products of precise and limited applications of energy. Most importantly 'aesthetic revisioning' can be a medium for re-ordering priorities in favour of sharing energy-efficient public goods, spaces and services available primarily through cities (Davis, 2010). Private self-provision of space, leisure facilities and transport leads to proliferation, dispersal and suburbanisation. Alternative hedonism will not be tainted with sustaining the unsustainable if it forms a bridge to radically transformed identities and practices of urban living. It already provides a basis for coding ecological virtue and developing new symbols of social status among 'alternative' cultural groupings and arguably is increasingly influencing mainstream culture. It could be of great importance shaping urban development in the poor cities of the south, away from individualised privatised sprawl with its huge energy implications.

The susceptibility of people to this sort of cultural elaboration is based on the fact that life under high carbon conditions and systems, is itself an emergent which people have had to accommodate to, making the best of a far from ideal complex of conditions. The fact that people are routinised and compliant does not mean they are committed. Ambivalence is a safer assumption. Readiness to change incrementally may exist to be activated by opportunities to learn ways and means of relatively low risk shifting to low carbon practices.

Willingness to change cultural practices is facilitated by changes in assessments of the material risks of doing so. A common concern is the possible threat to jobs of reducing demand for the consumer goods of a high carbon-producing system. We are not qualified to make a specialist assessment of the potential. However, reducing the use of inanimate power sources could lead to an increased use of human energy. And a more local division of labour would relocate, rather than simply replace jobs. Instead of requiring a 'decrease' in consumption we could be faced with limiting growth and a restructuring of the energy required to produce what is consumed. Low carbon systems tend towards people working, whereas high energy systems discourage high labour activity both in employment and during 'leisure'. But whatever the eventual restructuring of everyday life and economy may turn out to be, the main reassurance about jobs in the period of transition is that directing investment to, for example, build wind and tidal lagoon generators, does not imply unemployment. Major change in routines can be quite fast given some 'bridge' between the old and the new, as demonstrated by the early 1980s Bangladeshi garment workers in Chapter 10. Here economic crisis forced an immediate reordering of priorities which meant adopting new practices, whose moral risks were limited by framing the new practices as conforming to traditional values.

Recent changes in retailing practices illustrate the hybrid and often contradictory character of transition. The internet facilitates avoiding travelling to shops and the sometimes 'hellish' experience they offer. But this is at the price of using high carbon, extensive delivery systems from the centralised warehouses of Amazon and the like. The long-term spatial centrifuging of retailing to out-of-town supermarkets has been recently counteracted by a centripetal development of local minimarkets, where the higher prices and reduced choice are traded for the saving of customers' time, effort and fuel. This re-localising of services is recent, pervasive and strengthening, and as far as it goes is exactly what 'hedonistic' transition to low carbon living requires. However the carbon footprint of the supply chains of the goods sold locally remains an issue until more use is made of local suppliers.

Individuals, critical self-reflection, norms and practices

The relevance of the agentic powers of individuals to facilitate transition to low carbon life styles is considerable. As beings with typical life-expectancies, having a particular relationship with time, they can experience the effects of change, anticipate benefitting from medium-term investments and acquire an interest in long-term developments which may only happen after they have died. Temporal framing is culturally and social-structurally conditioned and elaborated during life. Humans can anticipate their legacies and are agents of 'learning by doing'. They can elaborate their capabilities to become knowledgeable and self-critical about their choices of ends and means. Given that they can revise orders of priority and commit themselves to paying certain prices for what is most important to them, there is scope for voluntary 'transition heroism'. Individuals can be open to ethical arguments about not discounting their responsibilities to future others across time and space who will have to confront whatever the bad effects of climate change turn out to be (Adam, 2008).

Agency is an effect of being positioned, interrelated and resourced by cultures and structures. These provide the conditions which enable and constrain engaging with a whole range of practices with GHG and CO_2-reducing potential. Position, say as head of an oil company, can confer powers to make historically significant decisions. However, this does not mean that the cumulative effects of the actions of far less powerful individuals are unimportant. If it's the case that 35–45 per cent of global CO_2 is produced just by heating and cooling buildings (Davis, 2010) then it is important to get at the mechanisms which might offer leverage to reduce this – which will include mechanisms affecting private householders' willingness to turn down their central heating. Heating reduction is not just a technical matter. Commonly, high domestic CO_2 production is the outcome of the habitual un-reflexive routines of everyday practices such as heating, eating, washing, dressing, furnishing, child care, education, entertaining. And they are often simultaneously the outcome of the production and consumption of material symbols which code for privacy, respectability, gender and so on. What actors do when, and in what ways, is often conditioned by the pressures to conform to norms, rather than by reflecting and choosing. So who turns the heating down and to what level, may depend on negotiating the expectations of others in specific social relations. Whatever the details, such as what is felt necessary to care properly for temperature-sensitive dependents, the individual's interest in maintaining their acceptability to others is the emotional fuel for social mechanisms reproducing practices (Shove, 2003). Membership of collectivities is defined by participation in a suite of practices with symbolic value. (Remember the brief discussion in Chapter 5 about the requirements for having a party?)

To take a possibly trivial example to make an important point, British breakfasts commonly involve toast. Millions of pieces of bread are burned every day. A *'within* frame' technical fix might be a low carbon toaster (although supplying such things is not carbon neutral). The radical change *'of* frame', low carbon alternative would be to redesign the norms for breakfast, questioning the need for toast at all. Given the potential carbon-saving of such configurations, the political struggle is between conformists and those willing to take small risks of social criticism by challenging the need for breakfast toast. Risks are likely to be much bigger when it comes to questioning the norms of practices of 'cleanliness' (Shove, 2003).

'Washing' applies to how spaces and objects (kitchens, bathrooms, windows, cars and so on) are kept and to how we care for the body so that it is functional for our efforts at self-presentation ('washing' here extends into the use of cosmetics). Rules defining dirt, 'matter out of place', often go beyond the objective requirements of hygiene and, can carry a very powerful emotional charge (Douglas, 1970). Thus challenging them on grounds of their contribution to climate change becomes difficult. Similarly the discussion of Goffman (Boxes 7.1 and 7.4) suggests that changing to low washing, low cosmetic modes of self presentation carries high risks of embarrassment at least during the transition phase. The proposal to wash less for the sake of reducing GHGs and increasing environmental sustainability, may be experienced as a challenge to a deeply embedded, emotional conditioning of a sense of social order and of ideals for the self. Social rejection is a likely cost of innovation in well regarded routines. Questioning toast is one thing and may be dismissed as just silly; but questioning washing is more serious and likely to generate strong resistance.

Innovation is a process of elaboration, dissemination and routinisation through the medium of socially structured agents; leaders: followers, parents: children, teachers: students, politicians: voters, scientists: popularisers, employers: workers. Innovating low carbon strategies which can successfully challenge routinised practices will be an exercise in redefining what counts as satisfying norms under new low carbon conditions. It will be analogous to the redrawing of patriarchy in Bangladesh.

We can end this sketch of the application of social theory to strategic thinking about climate change by imagining how the first quarter of the 21st century will be described by future historians. Lacking the benefit of hindsight, strategic guidance offered by social theory consists only in identifying the 'openings' of open systems, not in providing guarantees about outcomes. It is for historians to analyse the way the openness was used in actual responses to the threat of climate change, assessed in the light of the climate change that subsequently occurs during the rest of the century. They will be in a position to suggest what turned out to be the most important agents, decisions, events and strategies of change as well as the objective effectiveness of such change. They will be able to characterise the situation as it emerged and encountered some of the consequences of agents' choices. But although they will argue about which agents and events were critical, almost certainly they will see in the record, that by 2010 a new climate-aware culture, politics and economy had evolved quite distinct from anything in say 1990. And that, despite a justifiable pessimism at the prospect of rising GHGs coinciding with a probable peaking of population by 2050, they will allow that in 2014 it was still realistic to invest in achieving low-carbon sustainability.

A word of caution

Our final position is a firm but modest one. Although we value the power and relevance of social theory we should not over-estimate its powers. Like any other disciplines, social sciences have intrinsic limitations due to the character of their subject matter as discussed earlier in this and the previous chapter. There are also always limitations flowing from the shortcomings of its present practitioners' and disciplines' own states of development. At any given point in time there will always be areas open to dispute. This should suggest a certain caution. We might be wise generally to avoid imagining that we have final explanations of why things are the way they are or guaranteed strategies for how to change things. There are two very general safeguards against over-confidence. One is, where possible, always to consult those in whose interests we may be trying to act. We cannot presume in advance to know what people want or what is acceptable to them, though research and theory may enable us to make useful predictions. The other is to be as well-informed as possible, but also not to be too ambitious in each step we take. We should ensure the possibility of feedback and monitoring the effects of changes we make, and should be willing to change our line of attack in the light of events and new knowledge. Given this modesty, what social theory has to offer is powerful, and useful. If we understand what social theory does and does not promise, we can make the most of it in a clear-eyed way, and without too much disappointment.

Questions related to themes in this chapter

This chapter has focused on ways in which social theory might be used to guide strategic thinking in general and to confront the issue of climate change mitigation in particular.

1) Assess the potential for reducing the carbon produced by the production, distribution and consumption of the food or the cleaning products and cosmetics sold in a local supermarket.
2) Consider differences in attitude among people in your locality towards transition from high to low carbon life-styles. How would you explain them?
3) Describe in general terms, examples of individuals and groups who tend to be enthusiastic about climate change mitigation and those who tend to be hostile to it.
4) Give some examples of excuses offered for high carbon activities like flying, driving, maintaining your home at a high temperature and commuting by car. How might the social acceptability of these excuses be reduced?
5) Design a strategy for your local cycling pressure group, or your local government authority, to increase everyday cycling. Use the ideas in this chapter. Also use web sources to draw on the experience of existing schemes.

Coda: the quest for explanation

In the last chapter we tried to convince you that mobilising the explanatory power of social theory could be a major contributor to understanding how far and by what means it might be possible to bring about social changes one desired. But we began by suggesting that there could be other reasons for an interest in explanation besides a desire to foster change.

A quest for explanation is often motivated by a sense that we can't understand a situation. Interest can be motivated by curiosity as to 'what' or 'how' things are, as well as 'why' they take the form they do. We have seen Savage and co seeking to establish whether it really is the case that the British middle class have become more culturally omnivorous, before looking for causes as to why, in fact, some sections of it had. Stiglitz (2012) and Wilkinson and Pickett (2010) are among researchers investigating first *whether* income inequality in the west has recently increased, and then *how* their findings could be explained and what further consequences they might have. But 'why' questions are also often motivated when *what* has happened appears clear but not the reasons for it. 'Why' questions may be evoked when we note that a particular phenomenon occurs in some contexts but not in others. Barrington Moore asked why democracy was the outcome of modernisation for some states, but dictatorship for others (1967), and McAdam is one of many who have tried to work out why some protest movements succeed when many others fail (1996). We have already seen that 'why?' questions also often arise when routine interpretations fail to satisfy because of changes in the world or actors' ways of experiencing it.

A simple example from Chapter 10: Kabeer's problem was to explain the mismatch between her expectations and her surprising experience of Bangladeshi women being freer in Dhaka than London, having anticipated the reverse. Abbing who is both an artist and an economist found himself wanting to explain not only why artists are poor but why, given their poverty, they didn't change their occupations (as both 'common sense' and economic theory perhaps led him to expect). In his preface he writes:

> As an *artist*.... when I look around me there is much that puzzles me .... Most of my colleagues.... are poor. They hardly sell, have lousy second jobs, and yet they carry on. I don't understand why they just don't quit the profession. As an *economist* and social scientist I cannot ignore this confused state of affairs.... I can't comprehend .... the abundance of artists willing to work for low pay. (Abbing, 2002: 11–12)

Experiences of dissonance between what we expect and what appears to be the case may be disturbing, sometimes producing strong emotional responses. We do not know what positions to adopt, do not know 'where people are coming from', and may feel frustrated, frightened, depressed or angry.

When we sense these strong emotions in ourselves and others it is tempting to see them as simply psychological, but in fact they are often a sign that we are experiencing the change of powerful social forces, cultural and social structural. Such change challenges our ability to anticipate others' responses, making interaction seem uncertain and risky. Unsurprisingly, the invention of social science was stimulated by experience of the confusions of **modernisation**. And a strong appetite for social explanation is still fostered by upward or downward mobility, migration, recovery from wars, education, technological change, exposure to media, transformations of generational, class, gender and sexual relations, and looming threats such as those posed by climate change. All of these challenge the social imagination and the ease with which we can take positions and relate effectively to others. If we sense that our dilemmas are effects of positioning forces we will find social explanation relevant. Consumption of social theory has increased as the massive and continual transformations of life involved in modernisation have made knowing how to relate to others, chronically uncertain.

All of the above suggests that everyone has a need for social explanation. And as we indicated in the Introduction, this book hopes not just to indicate the value of social theory – and why people might engage in it, but also to get you too to use it for social explanation. We have, for example, encouraged you to begin hypothesising about the causes of various phenomena through the questions at the end of each chapter. As you have proceeded through the text you will have encountered a wide range of examples of social explanations showing the importance of our five key concepts. Following these examples through, should have provided some powerful models to help you to construct explanations yourself. But they have some limits as 'how to do it' guides – not least because they are 'finished products', the outcomes of a creative process which is not necessarily revealed (though hints of how difficult it may have been are often found in the Prefaces and Acknowledgements of the works that we have drawn on). Indeed the idea of 'finish' suggests making some distinction between what is required to communicate the arguments and information of an investigation on the one hand, and on the other, the many elements which were implicated and experienced during the process of arriving at this point. Seeing the outcomes of others' analysis doesn't fully reveal how to get started and how to do it oneself. A bit like learning to ride a bike, there's a lot you can only get to grips with by actually having a go. But we will nonetheless end by trying to supplement what you can learn from 'finished products' with some general observations on using the five concepts for explanation, and by providing one more 'worked example'.

Using the five concepts: general observations and (one last) 'worked example'

Once one has a problem, framed it as involving social reality (already a creative interpretation) and therefore requiring social theory, the five clusters of causes may be applied more or less playfully and tentatively to begin inventing hypotheses and alternative explanatory stories. The five concepts alert us to look in the appropriate places for relevant information which might explain the emergence of the social patterns or events being analysed.

Put simply, we can consider how culture, social structure and the natural environment set a scene with potential for emergence, differentially distributing resources and commitments to certain interests. We then interpret how differentially-positioned actors, in the immediate contexts of their own circumstances, subject to the constraints of their personalities and biologically conditioned capacities, individually or collectively might strategically and creatively use resources in pursuit of various interests and commitments. All the analysis is provisional and experimental at this stage.

Getting going involves a process of interpreting available information as evidence of the workings of causal processes, mixed with more informal efforts to imagine how the scene might look from the points of view of the various actors involved. We have to refine our sense of who the significant actors might be, as well as of their interpretations of their circumstances, and of how these might have changed during the emergence of what we want to explain. We will also be starting to sense the possibility of objective systematic relations between the typical actions and meanings of differentially positioned actors. Looking at other situations which are in some respects analogous to the one in hand, may be helpful. One moves back and forth between interpreting the causal significance of existing information, and using causal stories to identify if any additional information has implications for the plausibility of particular stories and can be obtained.

Generally there is a substantial process of developing interpretations in terms of the relative contributions of each kind of causation, and deciding an appropriate time-frame for assembling the causal story of the emergence of the object being explained. During this phase of thought-experimentation, judgements will be made about how far back into the past to begin one's causal story. Given the continuous flow of interaction among the mechanisms of social reality, practical analysis demands we start the story at some relevant point, an *analytically defined* beginning. This point is not arbitrarily chosen but has to be justified as a moment when some important change(s) in conditions for action stopped and/or started. Analysis must use a time frame to define a configuration of existing conditions for interaction from which the object of explanation can be interpreted as being an emergent outcome.

A basic technique for initial thought experiments is to follow the implications for causal stories of hypothetically changing particular variables or removing them altogether (something which comparative analysis facilitates). At various points in this book our discussions of explanations have invited readers to imagine what would have been the case if things had been different. Further examples from earlier chapters could have been, 'suppose there was no legacy of slavery in the US' (Chapter 2); 'suppose there was no natural gas in British Columbia' (Chapter 4); or 'suppose there was no welfare state in London' (Chapter 10). Asking 'what if?' questions (counterfactually), as well as varying how far back in time one goes, helps develop a sense of the relative importance of contributing causes and how they might interact.

Now, let us quickly return to one of Abbing's puzzles – 'Why do artists put up with being poor?' How could you *begin* to 'play around' with the five concepts to come up with some explanatory possibilities? You might like to have a go yourself before you look at our initial ruminations – and you could always read Abbing (2002) to discover the explanation he eventually arrives at!

An obvious possibility is that artists put up with poverty because they are a special kind of *individuals* with a particular kind of *natural characteristics*. What might these be? Two thoughts come to mind which link natural characteristics to economic decision-making on the one hand, and affinity with an artistic career on the other.

Firstly, artists might be less rational than most people. If so this might account for their apparent failure to pursue an economically rational line of action. But having learned about Stack's ghetto dwellers we know it's unwise to deem people economically irrational before fully understanding the *structure* of the situation in which they find themselves. Ghetto dwellers' propensity to give away or loan what they needed themselves, appeared rational once we saw that this facilitated the long-term strategies of mutual cooperation and support, necessitated by their lack of job opportunities.

How might the structural position of artists alter the way we see their apparent irrationality? For example is an art career all that's available to them as individuals? Maybe not, but it would not be irrational to pursue one if (i) it was the best or only opportunity available, (ii) they did not believe that they were likely to face poverty, and (iii) they expected to become one of the few and famous practitioners who do get rich. In the light of these possibilities it would be interesting to find out just what they knew about the economic prospects before they set out on this path.

Then there is the structural possibility of path-dependency – once they had chosen the art route, how far might it limit subsequent choices? If, for example, you've already got debts to pay back for your art education will you want to increase them by retraining for something else? It may be a close call as to whether it's more rational to keep going and try to capitalise on past investment of time or money or cut one's losses and hope a different strategy will pay off better.

The second possibility to play with, relating to individuals, is whether opting for an artistic career is conditioned by a person's innate artistic talent or need for artistic expression – and if so what significance this might have? Perhaps most artists are poor because they lack talent and nobody wants to buy their work! But if they lack talent, why do they do it and why do they keep going? Perhaps they have *natural* drives to express themselves creatively whether they are any good at this or not. Talk to artists and they will often say they feel internally compelled to produce their work – they feel art is compulsory for them. However, though we cannot rule out the influence of innate differences between individuals these will always be manifested in forms provided by *cultural* environments. Doesn't culture strongly affect what, in any particular place or time, counts as art, and as good art? If so, innate artistic talent (or its lack) can't explain everything. And, while the fact that artists 'feel they can do no other', may help explain why they keep going without good pay, how far is this feeling 'natural' and how far a consequence of the culturally derived romanticism mentioned in Chapter 1 (whose own historical roots could be investigated if desired)?

How else might culture play a role? Does it assign high status to art in our society or some sections of it – and if so, might choosing to be a practitioner in the art world be motivated by a desire for status rather than money? Could culture affect the meaning 'poverty' has for people and thus their attitudes towards it? Perhaps artists are nearer in their outlook to the middle class egalitarians than to the postmodern managers discussed in Chapter 6. They may be willing to forgo expensive habits and possessions if they can feel 'authentic' and self-directed.

We could next turn attention from what artists are as individuals, their beliefs and tastes, to focus instead on how they *act*. Perhaps one reason they may keep going despite poor economic reward is that they value *successfully being* an artist rather than 'being successful'. If they see playing the role of artist as more than just a means to other ends, then we might want to consider in what ways they act to maintain this sense of being. Creating actual art works is the obvious candidate here, and we might try to understand possible intrinsic satisfactions of this practice. But are there other actions which are part of 'living an art life' that artists engage in that give them pleasure and help confirm that this is what they are? What about exhibiting, attending openings with other artists, perhaps establishing mutually supportive collectives and so on?

This leads us to thinking about how the art world itself is *structured* – both internally and in its relations with the non-art world. Is it tightly bounded, do insiders mainly mix with themselves? Is the art world so arranged that making art opens up other earning possibilities – teaching art perhaps? And is it so structured that the successful usually only become so late in their careers? Should our investigations suggest that our answers here be 'yes', the implications for Abbing's question about why artists keep going might be first, that concentrating one's interaction among fellow artists makes poverty easier to bear if it restricts contact with the better off; second, that even low supplementary income opportunities could remove the *necessity* to change life-course, and third, that artists need not give up on grounds of 'failure' until fairly late in the day.

Finally, in our initial speculations it might occur to us that the only poor artists are those who *are* artists. It could be worth investigating if early drop-out rates are high in the art world – and whether most who start out, in fact do what Abbing would expect and move on to something more remunerative. Investigating the characteristics of those who left and comparing them to those who stayed the course, might help us evaluate the usefulness of some of our earlier hypotheses – and maybe throw up some further possibilities to check out.

Glossary

Action, Actors, Intention, Intentionality Action is the behaviour of an actor made meaningful by the actor's intentions. Actors initiate and steer what they do in relation to the intentions ('purposes', 'goals' or 'ends') they want to achieve by their actions. Because actors can initiate and direct their own behaviour relative to their intentions, they are subjects not just objects (see Social Action; Subjectivity and Boxes 3.7 and 7.2).

Agency Agency is the capacity to make a difference to outcomes, intentionally or unintentionally. Individuals, collectivities and non-human animals can be agents. Actors may be morally-responsible agents of their actions when they understand their likely consequences, and could have done other than they did (see Action; Practice, Practices; Realist Social Theory; Structure; Structuration Theory).

Assembly, Assemblage Theory Social theory gives its own specialised meanings to everyday words such as 'assembly' and 'assemblage'. Ordinary usage might refer to a political institution (e.g. The Welsh Assembly) or a mechanical entity (a bicycle's derailleur gear mechanism perhaps) as an assembly or an assemblage. Both terms suggest processes whereby components are related in such a way as to have certain potentials (e.g. to make laws or enable gears to be changed). What they actually do depends on how they were assembled and once assembled, the conditions under which they operate. The existence and functioning of assemblies is therefore provisional and contingent. The concept of 'assemblage' helps us understand objects whose properties are contingent effects or products of unique emergent processes. The stories of these emergents have to be told by examining the period of the events during which the constituents which resulted in the product were brought together. What eventuated was not inevitable but is a contingent realisation of the potentiality of the array of contributing elements and their specific encounters during the process. Assemblage theory can be relatively structural when focused on the outcome/product. Or it can be relatively processual and historical when focused on the emergence process (Marcus and Saka, 2006). DeLanda (inspired by Deleuze) provides the most complete technical formalisation of assemblage theory. Archer's morphogenetic approach to practical social analysis is also important, because it insists on the analytical requirement for adopting a time frame for articulating processes of emergence and their outcomes.

Autocatalytic Processes A technical term referring to a feedback process, where the outcomes of a system are conditions for its transformation. For example, agricultural processes are autocatalytic where they lead to soil exhaustion which threatens agricultural viability.

Capitalism Capitalism is a way of organising economic activity. Marx emphasised the relations of production, that is the way labour and decision making is organised, separating workers from ownership of the means of production, by moving them off the land into towns and making them dependent on earning wages from capitalist employers who owned the largely industrial means of production. He saw this relation between the two classes of labour and capital as one of conflicting economic and political interests. Capitalists' profits derived from the exploitation of workers' labour power. Weber agreed with much of Marx's analysis but emphasised the importance of capitalism's universalising of market relations and the rationalising of all spheres of action by monetary calculation. Both thought capitalism had dire effects for morality and the meaningfulness of human life (see Class and Box 9.2).

Causation, Generative Mechanism, Causal Process Causation is the general process which results in states of affairs in the world. Everything that exists has been subject to causation. Causes are mechanisms capable of producing (generating) individuals, events etc. These mechanisms produce their effects over time in complex combinations. Causal analysis tries to identify the relevant mechanisms and how they interact over time (see Realism; Reasons as Causes).

Class Class systems are one type of stratification system. In class systems people are collectivised into classes, that is, objective positions of relative economic and political advantage constituted by mechanisms which distribute important material and cultural resources for action. Classes differ according to their relative material advantages and the opportunities and methods open to them to maintain or improve their access to resources. Class positions of individuals tend to be shaped by what can be inherited, as wealth (often kinds of property) and by income-earning occupations and education. Positioning is heavily influenced by the state's legal protection of private property, inheritance and tax law, and educational policies. A defining characteristic of class systems is that those empirical differences between classes which can be expressed as statistical regularities, are symptomatic of objective structuring processes. Boundaries are not formally marked or legally or culturally compulsory. Thus mobility ('openness') is permitted and even encouraged, but nevertheless, the regularities of inherited advantage and disadvantage endure over generations ensuring a predominance of immobility across generations. However, class societies vary in the relative extent of their 'openness' or 'closure' (see Stratification and Box 9.2).

Collectivity, Collectivised, Collectivism A collectivity is a collectivised population with some shared characteristics. These may affect the way the members of the collectivity relate to themselves and others, as for example, when members of a social collectivity share a language or structural position. Collectivism is the position in social and political theory which gives most value to the interests of social wholes such as groups. It is opposed to individualism, which gives priority to individuals (see Individuals, Individualism; Persons).

Conditioning, Determination Things are conditioned when they are *partially* shaped by their conditions of existence. So persons are conditioned by their upbringing. But being conditioned does not mean being determined, that is, *entirely* shaped by conditions. For example, the way a person turns out will be the result of their response to their upbringing (see Relative Autonomy).

Constraint and Enablement Giddens's 'structuration' theory popularised these terms when examining how culture and social structure condition action. He said that this conditioning involves a negative element, constraint, and a positive element, enablement. To act, actors must use enabling resources, but they are also constrained by the limits the resources impose on what they can do (see Conditioning; Structuration Theory and Box 3.1).

Context To interpret the subjective meaning actors give their action and immediate situations, we must locate both within a wider social and historical context. This requires a skilful widening and deepening of the immediate context which may reveal highly influential factors which help us make better sense of what is happening. But context has no fixed boundary; there are no rules for getting it right in some final sense.

Contingency This refers to the unpredictable and unsystematic conditions of existence we must allow for but cannot define in advance. For example, when sailing, the wind may suddenly and unexpectedly alter, forcing a rapid change of sail and direction. Social life always involves coping with contingencies equivalent to the sudden change in the wind. The contingent character of everything is a central theme of Manuel DeLanda's social ontology (see Chapter 11; Assembly, Assemblage Theory; Structural contradiction).

Creative Individualism A way of accounting for innovation, particularly in the arts, which explains it as the product of the powers of unique creative individuals. It distinguishes between 'creative' and 'uncreative' individuals and treats the creative, such as 'artists', as somehow more autonomous than the un-creative. The non-individualist alternative is to recognise the existence of relatively autonomous varieties of creative practices (arts, sciences, cooking, politics etc.) and of potentials for individuals to participate in them, subject to natural, cultural and social structural conditioning forces as well as contingent circumstances.

Cross-pressures The actions of an actor are motivated by many different interests which generally arise from their positions in various social structures. These interests often conflict and require the actor to give priority to one or some over others, and take the consequences (see Role(s), Role sets; Interests).

Culture, Symbols, Signs, Meaning(s), Language Culture is the humanly invented realm of producing artifacts and symbolic representations of meaningful interpretations of experience. Central to this invention is complex symbolic manipulation embodied in natural language. Language consists of complex signs which perform the symbolic function of standing for meanings other than themselves. This capacity is fundamental to the human imagination and ability to anticipate experience by thinking about representations of it. This is a source of enormous power, enabling humans to tap the experience of past generations, denied to other animals.

Decision-making Environment Actors make decisions in environments comprising various kinds of constraints and enablements, natural, cultural and social structural. To the extent that these environments are relatively stable, it becomes possible to predict what the typical issues are, about which choices have to be made, and which choices are likely to be made by which kinds of actors. We illustrate how this worked for Bangladeshi women in Chapter 10 (see Opportunity Costs).

Determination (See Conditioning, Determination)

Deviance, Moral Economy, Moral Reputation Social life depends to some degree on a 'moral economy' of definitions of ideals of appropriate behaviour in specific contexts. These specify what ought to happen. Positive and negative sanctions respectively, reward conformity and discipline non-conformity or deviance. Conformity results in high moral reputation and trustworthiness. Deviance is defined relative to the ideals of behaviour and belief of particular people. It is always felt by them as a threat to predictability and good order. Deviant actors quickly acquire reputations for being unreliable, morally suspicious and untrustworthy. They have careers during which their early transgressions start to 'spoil' their moral reputation. Eventually deviants learn to think of themselves as deviant, and may adopt the positive self-identities offered by 'alternative' subcultures and lifestyles.

Dialectics (Aristotle, Hegel, Marx) Dialectical thought construes the world as comprising natural kinds of existents, all in a continuous process of 'becoming' as they move towards realising their potential. It draws on Aristotle's belief that human beings have the potential during their lives, to achieve higher and higher levels of wisdom and virtue. The dialectical tradition emphasises the potentialities of different kinds of existence, and the temporality of becoming. It sees potentials as intrinsic to the essential natures of 'natural kinds'. Natural kinds have natural necessity, that is 'the necessity implicit in the concept of the thing's real essence, i.e. those properties or powers, which are most basic in an explanatory sense, without which it would not be the kind of thing it is, i.e. which constitute its identity or fix it in its kind' (Bhaskar, in Archer et al., 2001: 68). A natural kind acts in the way it must because of its intrinsic nature – it follows or is driven by its 'natural tendencies'. Knowledge of natural kinds is formulated in real definitions which are 'fallible attempts to capture in words the real essence of things which have already been identified' (ibid: 86). Though 'naturalistic', this frame of reference does not acknowledge the complete contingency of existence as recognised by modern natural science which has no room for essences. Although Marx is a transitional figure (for example admiring Darwin) he is probably Aristotle's most important representative in modern times. Standing Hegel's idealistic dialectical analysis 'on its head', he analyses the material and social conditions for realising the potentiality of the human species to become self-determining, or fully subjective, beings (see Boxes 3.3 and 5.2).

Differentiation Differentiation refers to the process and result of division of an entity into subsidiary parts, each with its own qualities. The most famous social example of differentiation is the development of the division of labour whereby production is broken down into a large number of specialised roles. Institutions internally differentiate a range of offices and functions. Another example is when status systems become increasingly differentiated by introducing finer and finer distinctions between status positions. Differentiation need not entail structural contradiction (see Division of Labour; Integration; Structural Contradiction, and Box 9.1).

Dispositions, Personality Dispositions are general tendencies of persons and collectivities to relate and behave towards social experience in patterned, predictable ways. Dispositions are partly generated through location in particular historically produced structural positions and cultures which transmit ways of relating to life on the basis of specific historical experience. This historical conditioning of persons makes their personalities similar, but does not override the fact that, as distinct persons, each has a unique personality. Personality embodies collectively influenced dispositions, but each person is a unique source of elaboration on their social and cultural conditioning (see Personal Identity and Box 7.1).

Division of Labour The division of labour refers to the organisation of complementary production roles. The complexity and contingencies of production suggest some element of specialisation will be helpful and throughout human history there has been some sort of division of labour. However industrialisation involves intensifying the division of labour into more and more specialised functions, to reap benefits of speed, consistency and quality, though often at the cost of what Marx called 'alienation'. Work is alienated where the labourer is controlled by, rather than controlling, the production process (see Differentiation; Industrialism and Box 9.1).

Elites Elites are relatively small numbers of people at the top of hierarchies, usually organised to some degree to promote their common interests. Where membership of elites overlaps, this creates opportunities to reinforce and multiply privileges and advantages. Elites often try to monopolise resources and restrict entry to their ranks (for example by imposing difficult educational, cultural or monetary tests), thereby maintaining the scarcity of their valued services and privileges (see Class; Social Status).

Emergence (See History)

Empiricism Empiricism is an epistemology which claims knowledge is possible because humans are sensory beings in direct physical contact with the world which provides 'sense data' which can be faithfully recorded. For empiricism, knowledge is essentially descriptive and non theoretical. The problem with this theory of knowledge is that it cannot say how we should choose the language used for descriptions. For example, what terms should we use to describe colours of objects? Description is not automatic; cultural and socially-relative judgements of appropriateness are involved (see Idealism; Realism; and Box 11.1).

Enablement (See Constraint)

Epistemology Epistemology is the theory of knowledge, that is of, how we know things. What are the general conditions of knowledge? How is knowledge of the various kinds of reality possible? These are epistemological questions (see Empiricism; Idealism; Realism; Ontology and see Box 11.1).

Ethnography   Ethnography is the practice of describing cultures. It is the basic practice of Social Anthropology, a social science developed by people who wanted to understand societies other than their own (Davies, 2007). Ethnographies are vitally important for the social sciences in general, and sociologists also produce them for their own societies. Ethnographic descriptions often precede social explanation. They provide information about the interaction of environment, culture and social structure which facilitates comparison of different ways of life.

Ethnomethodology   Harold Garfinkel invented the term 'ethnomethodology' to refer to the analysis of the methods actors use to interpret their experience and establish meaning and truth sufficiently plausible, for the time being, to provide a basis for continuing to act. (He was influenced by Wittgenstein's theory of meaning as being dependent on actors' judgments.) Ethnomethodology emphasises the provisionality of meaning and its dependence on immediate concrete contexts of interaction. It sees 'ethnomethods' for inhibiting doubt and uncertainty as central to the rationality of common sense. Meaning is a 'practical accomplishment' dependent on actors' intepretive skill and shared background understandings of what the practical demands of types of situation are. That social phenomena involve the continuous use of these skills, strongly influenced Giddens' 'structuration' theory (see Structuration theory and Boxes 3.1 and 7.3).

Explanation and Understanding   We explain something by showing why it had, necessarily, to be the way it is. This requires an account of the interaction of all the causes contributing to producing the thing being explained. Science aims for explanation. In a general sense, understanding is enhanced by explanations. However, 'understanding' is also used in a more restricted way to refer to using appropriate cultural rules to interpret symbolic expressions, cultural objects, texts and uses of language, so that they can be understood, relative to some points of view, usually those of the originator and of the interpreter. Because human action is informed by symbolic expressions, particularly of intentions, the social scientist must achieve an understanding of what actors are doing in the actors' own terms, as a necessary step towards explaining what they are doing.

External Relations   (See Internal Relations)

Functionalist Theories   Functional explanations explain why any social phenomenon is the way it is, by showing what its functions, or effects, are. In some cases, once in existence, the effects of something (e.g. an education system) can feed back to ensure its continued existence (e.g. those who have personally benefited from it or can see advantages in having an educated population, support it). But functional explanations cannot explain how that something comes into existence in the first place. Functionalism has difficulty explaining historically produced phenomena. Parsons' abstract functionalist systems theory implies that the functional needs of social systems produce the institutions and practices required to meet those needs.

Generative Mechanism/Process   (See Causation)

Hierarchy   A dimension of social structure, hierarchy is the ranked social positions within some sphere of action. Most institutions are organised into hierarchies. Positions are defined in terms of kinds and amounts of social power, privilege, and discretion (see Social Status; Social Power; Elite(s)).

History, Emergence, Time   History is the product of the social process involving the interaction of the conditions of action with the creative input from action itself, producing largely unintended outcomes. Emergence refers to the way that, in this process, outcomes qualitatively different from their causes, 'emerge' over time, sometimes rapidly, sometimes more slowly. Social causation takes time to work itself out (see Morphogenetic approach).

Idealism   Idealism, as an *epistemological* position holds that knowledge depends on the logical and meaningful relations between ideas. The world, existing independently of what is thought, is regarded as inaccessible. Idealism is the opposite of empiricism. Idealism in *social theory* holds that social phenomena are explained by reference to subjective meanings, that is, the ideas actors hold and refer to, organise their action and social arrangements. Idealist social theory tends to place all the explanatory weight on culture and systems of meaning (see Epistemology; Empiricism; Realism; and Box 11.1).

Individuals, Individualism   'Individual' is a logical term referring to one of a class of entities. All such classes, say, cats, volcanoes or bicycles, are composed of individuals. The class, 'humanity', is made up of individual humans. This kind of individual has the species characteristics of humanity including the potential to become a person, which almost all born as humans thankfully do become. In *social theory*, individualism treats human individuals as the necessary and sufficient condition for explaining social phenomena. In *political* and *moral* theory, individualism defines the individual as the source of the good, and the well-being of individuals as the highest value against which to test political arrangements and moral principles (see Rational Choice Theory and Box 1.2).

Industrialism Industrialism uses inanimate sources of power (e.g. water, steam, hydrocarbons, nuclear, 'renewables') to extend the speed and volume of production. Mechanisation, urbanisation, rationalisation and modernisation are all entailed by the shift from traditional ways of production to industrial ones (see Division of Labour; Integration).

Institution An institution is an organised way of doing certain things, the outcome of a process of institutionalisation, whereby certain ways of doing things are progressively reinforced, making them relatively reliable. This process often involves conflict and the exercise of social power (as in the institutionalisation of parliamentary government in the UK which involved a civil war). Institutions may be defined formally by constitutional rules, hierarchies, career paths, job descriptions etc., but they may be entirely informal, such as the conventions of good manners (e.g. forming an orderly queue).

Integration Integration refers to the modes of relation between differentiated elements of structures. Being 'well integrated' implies relations of compatibility and absence of contradictions. In social theory '*social* integration' refers to the qualities of relation between interacting individuals and groups, and '*system* integration' to relations between the non-human components of social systems (Lockwood, 1976) (see Differentiation; Division of Labour; Structural Contradiction).

Intentionality (See Action)

Interests In social theory, interests do not refer to just anything which particular individuals might be interested in (say fishing or football). They refer to relatively enduring orientations to social relations conditioned by structural positioning and cultural commitments. They form a background against which individuals make their own choices about the relative importance they give to their own interests as opposed to those of particular collectivities, and who they support in competition between interests (see Cross-pressures).

Internal and External Relations between Parts and Wholes There are two ways in which this distinction is used. First, objects can be analysed as wholes made up of relations between parts. Relations are 'internal' where the identity of each part depends on the function it performs in constituting the whole. Thus the identity of each part is 'whole dependent'. For example, the parts making up cultural practices, e.g. works of art such as painting or poetry, are 'internally related'. Winch promoted this meaning of 'internal relations' to insist that the logical relations 'internal' to the use of language were immune to the influence of 'external', non-logical, causal relations with non-linguistic reality. On the other hand, scientists approach wholes as being made up of 'externally' related parts which have an identity independent of the whole they are a part of. Such relations are the result of contingent processes bringing together pre-existing elements to function as parts of some emergent whole. Scientists use 'synthetic reason' to study these contingent processes of emergence of 'wholes' out of pre-existing forms of existence (See Chapter 11). Second, in a simpler everyday sense, any whole (say, a family) may be thought of as having a boundary between its inside and its exterior. The interior is a matter of 'internal relations' between its parts (say between parents and children), whereas relations between the whole and its exterior are 'external' (say between family and school system).

Macro and Micro Sociology   A useful, if imprecise, distinction between the study of large-scale and possibly long-lasting social phenomena and the study of small-scale, possibly relatively short-lived ones. The central social theoretical issue is the relation between what takes place in interaction between persons and groups, and the material, cultural, institutional and social structural contexts of their activities. Once uncoupled from differences of scale most social analysts are happy to describe what they do as working out how these two 'levels' interrelate. It becomes possible to recognise (a) in some situations what might seem 'small', such as personal interaction (for example that between powerful heads of state) can have major consequences for long-lasting phenomena, and (b) that what might seem 'large' and long-lasting, such as language and law, are important conditions of small scale and momentary phenomena.

Mediation   The power of actors to modify or shape the way natural, cultural and social structural conditions impinge on them (see Conditioning, Determination; Relative Autonomy; Constraint and Enablement).

Methodological Individualism   An approach to social explanation holding that human individuals are the only kind of reality with the necessary and sufficient causal powers to generate social phenomena. There is plenty of scope for theorising and argument about what individuals' socially productive causal powers are, and which are necessary or sufficient for explanation. However all variants of MI accept that explanation refers to individuals living contemporaneously with the social phenomenon being explained. A key question is 'Do the socially important causal powers of specific individuals cease when they die?' If you answer 'no' then you have to accept that once dead, an individual's causal powers must use some non-individual forms or mechanisms to carry them into the time after death. Opponents of MI hold that social phenomena, especially the long-lasting ones, cannot be explained without reference to such non-individual mechanisms.

Modernisation, Modernity, Modernism   Modern*isation*, which some see as universal and inevitable, is the historical process of displacing pre-modernity with modernity. In pre-modernity life is lived according to examples from the past, the wisdom of the old, and traditional cultural authorities. Modernisation usually involves a confrontation with traditional forms of religion.

Modern*ity* is the general condition of social life where change and improvement is actively sought.

Modern*ism* refers to a cultural attitude of preferring 'the modern' in any sphere of activity. A self-conscious aesthetic modernism did not appear until the late 19th century, long after modernisation began (see Postmodernity and Postmodernism; Universalism and Box 9.1).

Moral Economy   (See Deviance)

Morphogenetic Approach   This approach to social analysis gives priority to describing how the cultural and social structural conditions of action are transformed by action over time. The central idea is that particular social phenomena can be abstracted from the flow of continuous eventful interaction by framing them as participating in a 'morphogenetic cycle'. This is a three phase sequence in which *the past* sets conditions (cultural and structural) for *present actors* whose interaction with the conditions in action situations has intended and unintended outcomes for *the future*. This approach allows that both the *subjectivity* of actors and the *objectivity* of cultures and structures are distinguishable, balanced and interdependent contributors to the origination, reproduction and transformation ('morphogenesis') of the forms of social life (see Figure 7.2; Assembly, Assemblage Theory and Box 3.1).

Nation-State and Nationalism   The nation-state is a type of political organisation where the state monopolises the use of force and law-making within a territory in which the population is imagined to subscribe to a common cultural identity, usually involving speaking a common language and sometimes sharing important cultural commitments such as religion. These presumed shared cultural identities are used as a basis for constructing the political identity of citizens. Nationalism is the doctrine that each culture should be self-governing and have its own state. This has been a popular idea during the course of modernisation, which tended to uproot traditional forms of political organisation (see Chapter 10; Modernisation, Modernity, Modernism).

Naturalism and Positivism   Naturalism in social science is committed to the idea that all kinds of nature must be explained in terms which are compatible with one another. 'Positivism' was an early movement committed to naturalism by modelling social science on an empiricist understanding of the methods of the natural sciences. 'Positivism' is the doctrine that the only worthwhile knowledge is scientific knowledge and that this knowledge can guide value choices. This idea was promoted by Comte in his *Course in Positive Philosophy* (1830–42) and supported by J.S. Mill (see Empiricism and Box 1.2).

Necessary and Sufficient conditions Conditions are necessary where they *must* obtain if the conditioned entity is to exist. Oxygen is a necessary condition of human life. But it is not sufficient because human life requires a lot more than just oxygen! Only where all the conditions for the existence of an entity are operating, are they sufficient (see Relative Autonomy).

Objectivism In social theory, objectivism directly contradicts subjectivism, holding that only properties of, and relations between, objects are relevant for explaining social phenomena (see Subject/subjectivity, Subjectivism and Box 3.1).

Ontology Ontology is a branch of philosophy which theorises the basic conditions of existence and what can possibly exist. It is a precondition for theorising about the possibility of knowledge which is the province of epistemology. Knowledge depends in part, on the properties of knowers and of the objects of knowledge, which are ontological questions (see Epistemology; Chapter 11; Box 3.3 and Figure 0.1).

Opportunity Costs and Opportunity Structure Economics refers to 'opportunity costs' when considering what is involved in making rational choices between alternatives. Each option is an opportunity to make some gain but has some cost attached to it. Rational choice theory uses this concept and it is useful when analysing choice-making in situations where we know about the field of alternatives actors are considering when choosing. Opportunity structures are configurations of opportunities (with their associated costs and benefits) open to given actors in given positions and situations (see Chapter 10; Chapter 12; Decision-making Environment; Rational Choice Theory).

Personal Identity and Social Identity Personal identity is the way a person understands the meaning of their own positions in the world. It involves a constantly developing narrative, reflecting about their past and their intentions for their future. It is a private construction and interpretation of their experience. It makes reference to, but is not defined by, that person's social identities. A social identity is a definition of a person by others, for purpose of social interaction. These definitions are primarily positional, referring to roles, statuses and social types. Social identities, unlike personal identities, are not private and unique to each person (see Individuals, Individualism and Boxes 7.1 and 7.4).

Persons   (See Dispositions, Personality; Individuals, Individualism; Personal Identity and Social Identity.)

Post-modernity and Postmodernism   Post-mode*rnity* is the general social condition of, having become modern to a significant degree, experiencing some of its typical problems. Symptoms of post-modernity are the developing structural contradictions of industrialism and nation-state politics, and the emergence of postmodern*ism*. Postmodernism is the cultural reflection on the situation of post-modernity, which favours abandoning modernity and modernism. Because modernism is universalist, criticising it is often thought to imply abandoning universalism in favour of relativism. However the most coherent, and thus compelling, postmodernism is not relativist in its claims for the importance of maintaining interaction among, rather than reduction of, a diversity of futures, social identities, and cultural traditions subject to certain limit conditions for communication and justice. Modernism often proposes one standard or form (the 'best'). Postmodernism is happy to maintain diversity and a range of criteria of 'the good' (see Modernisation, Modernity, Modernism; Universalism).

Practice, Practices   Practice (in general) is what all humans do when they individually and collectively apply their imaginations, equipped with their cultural and structural legacies, to trying to realise their various interests. Practices are particular distinct ways of doing things which have their own relative autonomy. Thus what is involved in making pots, meals, wine or motorcycles, doing the laundry or holding a meeting, are distinct practices. Practices of making are distinct from practices of selling. Practices are done with varying degrees of reflexivity and attention, often more or less automatically (see Chapter 12).

Primary and Secondary Socialisation   Primary socialisation is the initial process whereby a neonate is first inducted into a specific human world of relationships, language and culture. This first specific experience is the basis of general social competences and makes secondary socialisation possible. At any age, new recruits to nearly all collective activities have to learn how to perform as trustworthy participants (i.e. committed and competent) in existing arrangements of roles and practices. This learning constitutes secondary socialisation.

Production, Means and Relations of   (See Capitalism)

Rational Choice Theory   RCT tries to explain the actions of individuals and the emergence of collective phenomena as the outcome of the rational calculation of opportunity costs by individuals equipped only with natural self-interest and rationality. Social phenomena are seen as depending on the pre-social properties of individuals. RCT proposes that individuals are the only agents, rationality the only mode of evaluating the choice of means, and psychology the sole natural cause of wants. Gary Becker (1976, 1996) and Jon Elster (1986) are leading representatives of this approach (see Chapter 1; Individuals, Individualism; Opportunity Costs; Rationalisation, Rationality, Reason).

Rationalisation, Rationality, Reason Rationalisation is the general process of using reason to criticise practices and theories objectively, to make them more efficient at achieving desired goals.

Rationality is humans' capacity to use powers of reasoning. Reason concerns itself with the objective, empirical and logical properties of the world and the truth of theoretical representations of it. Reason is concerned with defining what has to be accepted about the world and our situations, whether we like it or not. In this sense it is dispassionate. But reason is not disconnected from the emotions: feelings can be criticised as too weak when reason suggests they ought to be strong ('unfeeling') and too strong when reason suggests the experience being responded to does not merit them (e.g. 'sentimental'). Rationality helps maintain the general value of emotional response against being over- or under-used, and helps determine which feelings are appropriate as response to different kinds of experiences.

Realism As an **ontology**, Realism holds that objective realities exist independently of the experiences they offer us and what we can say about them. Because experience only gives us surface evidence of the workings of reality, it is necessary to theorise what reality consists of. So, as an **epistemology**, Realism holds that knowledge depends on theoretical discovery of the properties of reality, by asking what would have to exist to produce what we experience. Theoretical reasoning and empirical evidence interact in the knowledge process (see, Empiricism; Idealism and Box 11.1).

Realist Social Theory Realist social theory tries to specify the complex objective and subjective properties of social reality which are responsible for social experience and are therefore necessary to explain it. Realism does not equate social reality with social phenomena which can be experienced, nor with what participants say about their experience. It holds that social reality is a complex interaction between the relative autonomies of individuals, nature, culture, action and social structure. This is what gives it the necessary causal powers to produce the variety of empirical social phenomena we experience (see Dialectics, Aristotle, Hegel, Marx; Empiricism; Idealism;

Individuals, Individualism; Morphogenetic Approach; Persons; Realism; Relative Autonomy; Structuralism).

Reasons as Causes   Winch's *The Idea of a Social Science* used an interpretation of Wittgenstein's recognition that meaning depends on 'agreement in judgements', to argue that causal explanation was completely inappropriate for understanding social reality. However he only argued against the empiricist concept of cause represented by what David Hume called 'constant conjunction'. Since relations between social meanings were logical and thus internal relations, they could not be causal relations which were necessarily 'external' and contingent. This is true, but it is possible to argue that though reasons are logically related to what they describe, they nonetheless contribute to the complex causality resulting in social phenomena, since they are as externally and contingently related to everything else in the causal mix as is any other kind of cause. The giving of reasons is a necessary but not sufficient element in the mechanisms which produce what we are interested in (see Explanation and Understanding).

Reference Group Theory   Developed by Merton to exploit the insight that people's attitudes to their social experience vary depending on who they compare themselves with. It is an example of 'middle range' theorising, building on the theoretical stimulus of the data in *The American Soldier* (Stouffer et al., 1949) (see Introduction).

Relative Autonomy   Realist social theory suggests that the different kinds of causes are autonomous to the extent that they have their own distinct causal powers and must therefore always be reckoned with; but the autonomy of each is relative to (limited by) the autonomy of the others. Each relatively autonomous kind of cause only contributes by conditioning outcomes, and is therefore necessary but not sufficient to explain outcomes. Determination of specific outcomes is the synthetic product of a combination of relatively autonomous causes. Each kind of causation 'mediates' the force of the others (see Conditioning, Determination).

Relativism   (See Postmodernism; Universalism)

Role(s), Role Sets   Social Roles are positions entailing prescriptive expectations and rules defining how incumbents should behave. These ideals are backed by various positive and negative sanctions. A person occupies a set of roles and must cope with the pressures to satisfy possibly conflicting role expectations. Role incumbents must make choices about which negative sanctions they can avoid or tolerate and which sanctions they positively desire.

Rules   (See Reasons as Causes; Ethnomethodology)

Signs, Symbols   (See Culture)

Situational Logic   Actors try to achieve their goals in specific circumstances. These 'action situations' may favour or disfavour the attaining of particular goals and present actors with more or less costly options. Situational logic defines four modes of relating the goals being sought to the properties of the circumstances in which they are being sought. These four are defined by two variables; first, the extent to which situations make goal attainment either easy or difficult, and second, the extent to which actors insist on ideal outcomes. Thus situations can be analysed for how they require actors to be *opportunists* when presented with favourable circumstances, to *eliminate* unfavourable ones, *make compromises* to get a measure of what they want against oppositions, and *defend* what cannot be compromised (see Chapter 12).

Social Action   Action is social when the actor intentionally takes account of the consequences of their action for other people. Weber provided the most important analysis of the concepts necessary to think about social action (see Box 7.2).

Social Identity   (See Personal Identity and Social Identity)

Social Power, its Media and Techniques   Social power is the capacity to get others to act as you want them to. It involves controlling other people which requires appropriate resources and techniques. These include actual and threatened violence and other forms of intimidation, bargaining, bribery, credit, rewarding by offering symbols of social status, etc. Such techniques use resources such as physical force, money, legal rights and cultural authority. These provide the wherewithal of domination. There are three interrelated bases of social power: cultural (the capacity to define the meaning and value of situations), economic (the capacity to control the production and distribution of material resources) and political (the capacity to determine decision making and have available effective use of physical force) (see Box 3.6).

Social Status   Social status attaches to persons and collectivities on the basis of some principle of evaluation by others. High social status can be used to dominate others, secure privileges for children and accumulate material resources. For example the high social status of some religious orders idealising poverty, such as the Franciscans in the 13th century, enabled them to accumulate vast wealth and Papal patronage. Although wealth often contributes to high social status this isn't always the case – for example if the source of wealth is deemed discrediting (see Stratification; Roles, Role Sets; Hierarchy and Box 5.1).

Strategies, Strategic Action   Strategies are preferred methods for orchestrating action and situations to achieve goals at acceptable costs. They involve interpreting the opportunity costs entailed by situational logics (See Action; Opportunity Costs; Rational Choice Theory; Situational Logic).

Stratification   The process generating inequalities of various kinds. The results are structures of 'strata' or 'rungs' on ladders of relative advantage and disadvantage. Stratification happens at micro and macro levels of structuring and may be short-lived or endure over generations. Once inequalities appear, differences of interests are created and become a focus for social competition (see Class; Elites; Social Status; Hierarchy; Social Power; Industrialism and Box 9.2).

Structural Contradiction, Logical Contradiction   Marx introduced the notion of structural contradiction to help understand how major social change happened. He suggested that over time, systems for producing tended to feedback negatively, undermining the conditions necessary for the system's continuity. This idea that human social arrangements, which start out functioning well, can come to undermine, or contradict themselves, is of fundamental importance for social explanation. A logical contradiction is where propositions or arguments use incompatible elements; formally they assert 'a' and 'not a'. Both cannot be true (see Chapter 9; Auto-catalytic Processes; Internal and External Relations).

Structuration Theory   Giddens adopted the term 'structuration' to refer to the process of structurally-conditioned action feeding back to reproduce and modify those structural conditions. He argued that the relation between structure and action was one of 'duality'. That is, they were not analytically separable, because structures only existed when they were 'instantiated' i.e. when used by actors. His favoured example is language. When not being used, structures have only a 'virtual' existence. This position is opposed by realist social theory, which argues that structures have a real existence, and a relatively autonomous causal force. On the other hand Stones (2005) attempts a constructive revision of Giddens's theory (see Constraint and Enablement; Realist Social Theory and Box 3.1).

Structure, Social Structure, Structuralism   Any arrangement of components making up a whole can be called a structure. A social structure is an organisation of relations between social positions with consequences for social interaction. There are many ways in which interaction is socially structured. A given person is located in a number of social structures which condition their interests and actions, sometimes in contradictory ways. Structuralism is the doctrine that the properties of structures are the most important in explanation. Structures are given this priority if thought to be able to account for historical change and novelty. Thus 'systems functionalism' sees change as the creative maintenance of 'equilibrium' within the system and adaptation to environmental pressures arising outside it. French structuralism, associated with Levi-Strauss, holds that structure is 'generative' in the way that a grammar organises language enabling it to be used to talk about more or less anything in novel ways. This idea is extended to all social and cultural practices (see Structural Contradiction; Interests; Realist Social Theory; Relative Autonomy; Structuration Theory).

Subject/Subjectivity, Subjectivism Subjectivity involves having a unique point of view, a self-identity, from which it is possible (though not inevitable) to be self-reflective about the meaning and consequences of one's own life and actions. A subject is a being which can, in Mead's words 'be an object to itself'. While the behaviour of objects is non-intentional, subjects' actions can be guided by their intentions. Subjectivism in social theory holds that the subjectivity of actors is the key to explaining social life (see Action, Actors, Intentions, Intentionality; Objectivism and see Box 3.5).

Sufficient Conditions   (See Necessary Conditions)

Symbolic Interactionism A school of sociology concentrating on the immediacy of interpersonal interaction and the negotiation of meaning. It celebrates the creativity of actors in the ongoing work of performing their roles and social identities. It contributes to micro sociology, but has difficulty linking this to social phenomena and processes which endure for long periods of time. Its social theoretical focus is on individuals, action and culture, at the expense of social structure (see Ethnomethodology and Box 7.1).

Tendencies, Typical(ity), Statistical Probabilities or Likelihood The evidence for the existence of the mechanisms of social reality may take the form of descriptions of the general properties shared by populations of individuals. Properties of populations, some of which may be effects of their social relations and interaction, may be open to statistical measurement. Measurements of probabilities or likelihoods, give a degree of precision to what can be said to be typical of populations. Because individuals are unique and mediate the influence of social causes conditioning them, not every member of a population will exhibit all its typical characteristics. There will be exceptions. The social conditioning of relatively autonomous individuals allows for both shared social characteristics (social facts) and individual exceptions who exist and act against type (see Class).

Understanding   (See Explanation)

Universalism This holds that there are both truths about the world and moral principles and virtues, to guide social conduct and administration of justice, which are valid for everyone, irrespective of their personal feelings, cultural differences or historical context. Universalism opposes relativism, which argues that truths are relative to and dependent on such differences, and that therefore there are as many truths as there are points of view. Universalism holds open the possibility of deliberately transcending what it regards as the contingencies and restrictions of cultures, by the use of reason to assess evidence and the logic of arguments. Universalism is implicit in rationalisation and the realist approach to social science (see Modernisation, Modernity, Modernism; Postmodernity and Postmodernism).

Universalistic, Particularisic These are two opposed orientations to making choices about how to behave in social interaction. Universalism prioritises applying values equally to everyone with regard to education, law, health care, access to housing etc. For example exams should be marked anonymously to ensure that all candidates are treated the same. Particularism gives priority to privileging people who matter most to you. Typically most people are particularistic to some degree about their own children and parents, giving them priority. Particularistic prioritising can be given on the basis of membership of family, sex, occupation, friendship, religion, language, ethnic group etc. Thus police who are more lenient with traffic offences of kin than non-kin, or doctors who advantage the health care of their own parents, are being particularistic and might be criticised from a universalistic point of view.

Bibliography

Abbing, H. (2002) *Why Are Artists Poor? The Exceptional Economy of the Arts*, Amsterdam, Amsterdam University Press

Achterberg, P. (2006) 'Class voting in the new political culture: economic, cultural and environmental voting in 20 Western countries', *International Sociology, 21, 2*

Achterberg, P. and Houtman, D. (2006) 'Why do so many people vote "unnaturally"? A cultural explanation for voting behaviour', *European Journal of Political Research, 45, 1*

Adam, B. (2008) Sustainable Futures: Past and Present Challenges and Opportunities, *BRASS Seminar: Changing the way people act and relate*. Cardiff, Sept.

Adger, W. N. et al. (2009) 'Are there social limits to adaptation to climate change?', *Climate Change*, 93, 335–54

Adorno, T. W. (2002) *The Stars Down to Earth: And Other Essays on the Irrational in Culture*, London, Routledge Classic

Agrawal, A. (1999) *Greener Pastures: Politics, Markets, and Community Among a Migrant Pastoral People*, Durham, N.C., Duke University Press

Ahmed, F. E. (2004) 'The Rise of the Bangladesh Garment Industry: Globalization, Women Workers and Voice', *National Women's Study Association*, 16, 2

Alia-Klein, N. et al, (2008) 'Brain Monamine Oxidase A Activity Predicts Trait Aggression', *Journal of Neuroscience, 28, 19*

Althusser, L. (1971) *Lenin and Philosophy*, London, Verso

Althusser, L. (2001) *Lenin and Philosophy and Other Essays*, New York, Monthly Review Press

Anderson, E. (1990) *Street Wise: Race, Class and Change in an Urban Community*, Chicago, Chicago University Press

Anderson, E. (1999) *Code of the Street: Decency, Violence and the Moral Life of the Inner City*, New York, W. W. Norton & Co.

Archer, M. (1979) *The Social Origins of Educational Systems*, London, Sage

Archer, M. (1988) *Culture and Agency*, Cambridge, Cambridge University Press

Archer, M. (1995) *Realist Social Theory: The Morphogenetic Approach*, Cambridge, Cambridge University Press

Archer, M. (2000a) *Being Human*, Cambridge, Cambridge University Press

Archer, M. (2000b) 'For structure: its reality, properties and powers: A reply to Anthony King', *The Sociological Review*, 48, 3

Archer, M. (2003) *Structure, Agency and the Internal Conversation*, Cambridge, Cambridge University Press

Archer, M. (2012) *The Reflexive Imperative in Late Modernity,* Cambridge, Cambridge University Press

Archer, M. and Tritter, J. Q. (eds.) (2000) *Rational Choice Theory,* London, Routledge

Archer, M., Bhaskar, R., Collier, A., Lawson, T. and Norrie, A. (eds.) (1998) *Critical Realism: Essential Readings,* London, Routledge

Ariès, P. (trans. 1962, 1996) *Centuries of Childhood: A Social History of Family Life,* London, Pimlico

Ashworth, T. (1980) *Trench Warfare 1914–18: The Live and Let Live System,* Basingstoke, Macmillan

Atkinson, J. M. and Drew, P. (1979) *Order in Court: The Organisation of Verbal Interaction in Judicial Settings,* London, Macmillan

Atkinson, P. (1985) *Language, Structure and Reproduction,* London, Methuen

Atkinson, P. (1995) *Medical Talk and Medical Work,* London, Sage

Bachrach, P. and Baratz, M. (1962) 'Two Faces of Power', *American Political Science Review,* 56, 4

Badiou, A. (2009) *In Praise of Love,* Paris, Flammarion

Baert, P. (1998) *Social Theory in the Twentieth Century,* Cambridge, Polity Press

Bagguley, P., Mark-Lawson, J., Shapiro, D., Urry, J., Walby, S. and Warde, A. (1990) *Restructuring: Place, Class and Gender,* London, Sage

Barnes, B. (1995) *The Elements of Social Theory,* London, UCL Press

Barnes, B. (2000) *Understanding Agency,* London, Sage

Baron, N. S. and Segerstad, Y. H. (2010) 'Cross cultural patterns of mobile phone use: public space and reachability in Sweden, the US and Japan', *New Media and Society,* 12, 1

Barth, F. (1959) *Political Leadership among Swat Pathans,* London, Athlone

Baszanger, I. (1997) 'Deciphering Chronic Pain', in Strauss, A. and Corbin, J. (eds.), *Grounded Theory in Practice,* Thousand Oaks, CA, Sage

Becker, G. (1976) *The Economic Approach to Human Behaviour,* Chicago, Chicago University Press

Becker, G. (1996) *Accounting for Tastes,* Cambridge, MA, Harvard University Press

Becker, H. (1982) *Art Worlds,* Berkeley, University of California Press

Bennett, T. et al., (2009) *Culture, Class, Distinction,* London, Routledge

Benton, T. and Craib, I. (2001, 2nd ed. 2010) *Philosophies of Social Science,* Basingstoke, Palgrave Macmillan

Bernstein, B. (1971) *Class, Codes and Control,* London, RKP

Bhaskar, R. (1975) *A Realist Theory of Science,* Brighton, Harvester

Bhaskar, R. (1989) *The Possibility of Naturalism,* Brighton, Harvester

Bhattacharya, D. and Rahman, M. (2000) 'USA Trade and Development Act 2000: A Response from Bangladesh Perspective', *Centre for Policy Dialogue (Bangladesh) Occasional Paper Series, Paper 6*

Bloor, D. (1976) *Knowledge and Social Imagery,* London, RKP

Blühdorn, I. (2013) 'The governance of unsustainability: ecology and democracy after the post-democratic turn', *Environmental Politics,* 22, 1, 16–36

Boden, D. (1994) *The Business of Talk: Organisations in Action,* Cambridge, Polity

Börjesson, M. et al. (2012) 'The Stockholm congestion charges 5 years on: effects, acceptability and lessons learnt', *Transport Policy,* 20

Bourdieu, P. (1981) 'Men and Machines' in Knorr-Cetina and Cicourel (eds.), *Advances in Social Theory and Methodology*, London, RKP

Bourdieu, P. (1984) *Distinction: A Social Critique of the Judgement of Taste*, Oxford, Routledge Kegan Paul

Bourdieu, P. (1985) 'The Genesis of the Concepts of Habitus and Field', *Sociocriticism*, 2: 11–24

Bourdieu, P. (1986) 'From Rules to Strategies', *Cultural Anthropology, 1*

Bourdieu, P. (1990a) *In Other Words: Essays towards a Reflexive Sociology*, Cambridge, Polity

Bourdieu, P. (1990b) *The Logic of Practice*, Cambridge, Polity

Bourgois, P. (1995) *In Search of Respect: Selling Crack in El Barrio*, Cambridge, CUP

Braverman, H. (1974) *Labor and Monopoly Capital: the Degradation of Work in the Twentieth Century*, New York, Monthly Review Press

Brody, H. (1986) *Maps and Dreams*, London, Faber

Brody, H. (1987) *Living Arctic*, London, Douglas and MacIntyre

Brody, H. (2001) *The Other Side of Eden*, London, Faber

Bruce, S. (2000) *Fundamentalism*, Cambridge, Polity

Button, G. (1987) 'Answers as interactional products: two sequential practices used in interviews', *Social Psychological Quarterly*, 50

Calhoun, C. (1997) *Nationalism*, Buckingham, Open University Press

Caplow, T. (1968) *Two against One: Coalitions in the Triad*, Englewood Cliffs, NJ, Prentice Hall

Carrithers, M. (1992) *Why Humans Have Cultures*, Oxford, Oxford University Press

Cicourel, A. (1968) *The Social Organisation of Juvenile Justice*, New York, J. Wiley

Cline, W. (2007) *Global Warming and Agriculture: Impact Estimates by Country*, Peterson Institute for International Economics, Washington DC.

Cohen, S. (2001) *States of Denial*, Cambridge, Polity

Collins, R. (1979) *The Credential Society: An Historical Sociology of Education and Stratification*, New York, Academic Press

Collins, R. (1992) *Sociological Insight: An Introduction to Non-obvious Sociology*, New York, Oxford University Press

Collins, R. (2000) 'Situational stratification: a micro-macro theory of inequality', *Sociological Theory*, 18, 1

Cowley, R. ed. (2000) *What If?* London, Macmillan

Craib, I. (1997) *Classical Social Theory*, Oxford, Oxford University Press

Crosthwaite, P. (2010) 'Blood on the Trading Floor: Waste, Sacrifice and Death in Financial Crisis', *Angelaki*, 15, 2

Crosthwaite, P. (2011) 'Phantasmagoric finance: crisis and the supernatural in contemporary finance culture' in, Crosthwaite, P. (ed.), *Criticism, Crisis and Contemporary Narrative: Textual Horizons in an Age of Global Risk*, London, Routledge

Cunningham, P. G. and Parker, J. (1978) 'Two selves, two sexes: deference and the interpretation of a homosexual presence', *Sociology and Social Research*, 63, 1

Davidson, M. (2013) 'Transforming China's grid: sustaining the renewable energy push', *The Energy Collective*, 24/9 http://theenergycollective.com/michael-davidson/279091/transforming-china-s-grid-sustaining-renewable-energy-push

Davies, C. A. (2007) *Reflexive Ethnography: A Guide to Researching Selves and Others*, London, Routledge

Davis, D. B. (1966) *The Problem of Slavery in Western Culture*, Ithaca, NY, Cornell University Press

Davis, M. (2000) *Late Victorian Holocausts: El Nino Famines and the Making of the Third World*, London, Verso

Davis, M. (2010) 'Who will build the Ark?', *New Left Review*, No. 61, Jan–Feb

Degler, C. N. (1971) *Neither Black nor White*, NY, Macmillan

DeLanda, M. (2002) *Intensive Science and Virtual Philosophy*, London, Continuum

DeLanda, M. (2006) *A New Philosophy of Society*, London, Continuum

DeLanda, M. (2011) *Philosophy and Simulation: The Emergence of Synthetic Reason*, London, Continuum

Deleuze, G. and Guattari, F. (orig. 1980, 1987) *A Thousand Plateaus*, Minneapolis, University of Minnesota Press

Dennis, K. and Urry, J. (2009) *After the Car*, Cambridge, Polity

Descola, P. (1997) *The Spears of Twilight: Life and Death in the Amazon Jungle*, London, Flamingo

Descola, P. (2005) 'Ecology as cosmological analysis' in Surallés, A. and Hierro, P. D. (eds), *The Land Within: Indigenous Territory and the Perception of the Environment*, Skive, Denmark, Centraltrykkeriet

Despacio, A. (2008) 'Bogotá: edging back from the brink', *Sustainable Transport*, 20

Diamond, J. (1997) *Guns, Germs and Steel: A Short History of Everybody for the Last 13000 Years*, London, J. Cape

Diggs, I. (1953) 'Color in colonial Spanish America,' *Journal of Negro History*, 38

Donner, J. (2007) 'The rules of beeping: exchanging messages via intentional "missed calls" on mobile phones', *Journal of Computer-mediated Communication*

Dorling, D. (2006) 'Class alignment', *Renewal: The Journal of Labour Politics*, 14, 1

Douglas, M. (1970) *Purity and Danger*, Harmondsworth, Pelikan

Douglas, M. (1975) *Implicit Meanings*, London, RKP

Douglas, M. (1982) *In the Active Voice*, London, RKP

Douglas, M. (1986) *Risk Acceptability According to the Social Sciences*, London, RKP

Douglas, M. (1996) *Thought Styles*, London, Sage

Douglas, M. (1996) *Natural Symbols*, London, Routledge

Douglas, M. and Wildavski, A. (1982) *Risk and Culture: An Essay on the Selection of Technological and Environmental Dangers*, Berkeley, University of California Press

Duneier, M. (2007) 'On the legacy of Elliot Liebow and Carol Stack: context-driven fieldwork and the need for continuous ethnography', *Focus*, 25, 1

Durkheim, E. (orig. 1897, 1952) *Suicide*, London, RKP

Durkheim, E. (orig. 1895, 2014) *The Rules of Sociological Method*, New York, Free Press

Durkheim, E. (orig. 1912, 1995) *The Elementary Forms of Religious Life*, New York, Free Press

Eagleton, T. (2000) *The Idea of Culture*, Oxford, Blackwell

Eckerson, C. (2013) 'Groningen, The Netherlands: The Bicycling World of Your Dreams' http://www.streetfilms.org/groningen-the-netherlands-the-bicycling-world-of-your-dreams/

Elder-Vass, D. (2010) *The Causal Power of Social Structures,* Cambridge, Cambridge University Press

Elias, N. (orig. 1939; revised trans. 2000) *The Civilization Process,* Oxford, Blackwell

Elkins, J. (2012) *Art Critiques: A Guide,* Washington DC, New Academia Publishing

Elkins, S. (1976) *Slavery: A Problem in American Institutional and Intellectual Life,* (3rd revised edition), Chicago, University of Chicago Press

Ellis, L. (2008) The Housing Meltdown: why did it happen in the United States?, *Bank for International Settlements, Working Paper,* 259

Elster, J. (ed.) (1986) *Rational Choice,* Oxford, Blackwell

Ensmenger, N. L. (2010) *The Computer Boys Take Over: Computers, Programmers, and the Politics of Technical Expertise,* Mass., MIT Press

Evans-Pritchard, E. (orig.1940, 1987) *The Nuer: A Description of the Modes of Livelihood and Political Institutions of a Nilotic People,* Oxford, Oxford University Press

Flyvbjerg, B. (1998) *Rationality and Power: Democracy in Practice,* Chicago, University of Chicago Press

Flyvbjerg, B. (2001) *Making Social Science Matter,* Cambridge, Cambridge University Press

Foucault, M. (orig. 1963, 2003) *Birth of the Clinic: An Archaeology of Medical Perception,* London, Routledge

Foucault, M. (orig. 1966, 2001) *The Order of Things: An Archaeology of the Human Sciences,* London, Routledge

Foucault, M. (orig. 1976–84, 1989–1998) *The History of Sexuality,* Vols. 1–3 Harmondsworth, Penguin

Fournier, M. (2007, 2013), *Emile Durkheim: A Biography,* Cambridge, Polity

Frankfurt, H. G. (2004) *The Reasons of Love,* New Jersey, Princeton University Press

Friedman, S. (2011) 'The cultural currency of a "good" sense of humour: British comedy and new forms of distinction', *British Journal of Sociology,* 62, 2

Friedman, S. (2012) 'Cultural omnivores or culturally homeless? Exploring the shifting cultural identities of the upwardly mobile', *Poetics,* 40, 5

Garfinkel, H. (1967) *Studies in Ethnomethodology,* Engelwood Cliffs, Prentice-Hall

Gellner, E. (1973) 'Scale and nation', *Philosophy of the Social Sciences,* 3

Gellner, E. (1983) *Nations and Nationalism,* Oxford, Blackwell

Gellner, E. (1996) 'The coming of nationalism and its interpretation: the myths of nations and class', in G. Balakrishnan (ed.), *Mapping the Nation,* London, Verso

Gellner, E. (1997) *Nationalism,* London, Weidenfeld and Nicholson

Gerth, H. and Mills, C. W. (eds.) (1948) *From Max Weber,* London, RKP

Giddens, A. (1984) *The Constitution of Society,* Cambridge, Polity

Giuffre, K. (1999) 'Sandpiles of opportunity: success in the art world', *Social Forces,* 77

Gladwell, M. (2000) *The Tipping Point,* London, Little, Brown and Co.

Goff, T. (1980) *Marx and Mead,* London, Routlege

Goffman, E. (orig. 1959, 1990) *The Presentation of Self in Everyday Life,* Harmondsworth, Penguin

Goffman, E. (orig. 1961, 1991) *Asylums,* Harmondsworth, Penguin

Goffman, E. (orig. 1963, 1990) *Stigma,* Harmondsworth, Penguin

Goffman, E. (1969) *Where the Action Is,* Harmondsworth, Allen Lane

Goffman, E. (1971) *Relations in Public,* New York, Allen Lane

Goffman, E. (orig.1974, 1986) *Frame Analysis: An Essay on the Organisation of Experience,* Boston, North Eastern University Press

Goffman, E. (1983) 'The Interaction Order,' *American Sociological Review*, Vol. 48

Goodwin, C. (1984) 'Notes on Story Structure and the Organisation of Participation' in J. M. Atkinson and J. Heritage (eds.), *Structures of Social Action: Studies in Conversation Analysis,* Cambridge, Cambridge University Press

Gov.UK (2014) 'Green Deal: energy saving for your home or business', https://www.gov.uk/green-deal-energy-saving-measures (accessed 29/1/2014)

Granovetter, M. (1978) 'Threshold models of collective behaviour', *American Journal of Sociology*, 83

Granovetter, M. (1983) 'The strength of weak ties revisited', *Sociological Theory,* 1

Gremillion, T. M. (2011) 'Reducing carbon emissions from the developing world through compensated moratoria: Ecuador's Yasuní initiative and beyond', http://works.bepress.com/thomas_gremillion/1

Gutierrez, S., (2009) 'Seattle getting 2,500 electric car charging stations', Seattle pi http://www.seattlepi.com/local/transportation/article/Seattle-getting-2-500-electric-car-charging-883743.php

Haberle, S. G. and Lusty, A. C. (2000) 'Can climate influence cultural development? A view through time', *Environment and History*, 6

Hall. J. A. (ed.) (1998) *State of the Nation: Ernest Gellner and the Theory of Nationalism,* Cambridge, Cambridge University Press

Hansen, J. (2008) 'Global Warming Twenty Years Later: Tipping Point Near', *Testimony before Congress, 23/6/2008*

Harris, M. (1970) 'Referential ambiguity in the calculus of Brazilian racial identity' in N. E. Whitten and J. F. Szwed (eds.), *Afro-American Anthropology,* NY, Free Press

Hegel, G. W. F. (orig.1824, 1956) *The Philosophy of History,* New York, Dover

Henderson, M. (2008) *50 Genetic Ideas You Really Need to Know,* London, Quercus

Herdt, G. H. (ed.) (1996) *Third Sex Third Gender: Beyond Sexual Dimorphism in Culture and History,* New York, Zone Books

Heritage, J. (1984) *Garfinkel and Ethnomethodology,* Cambridge, Polity

Ho, S. (2007) 'Bogota's Bikeways: A Network Supported by Policies and the TransMilenio', *Green Design and the City, Transportation Paper, 9, 25 http://www.greendesignetc.net/transportation_07(pdf)/Ho_Susan_Bogotas_Bikeways(paper).pdf*

Hughes, J. A., Martin, P. J. and Sharrock, W. W. (1995) *Understanding Classical Social Theory,* London, Sage

Hulme, M. (2009) *Why We Disagree about Climate Change,* Cambridge, Cambridge University Press

Husserl, E. (orig. 1913, 1982) *Ideas Pertaining to a Pure Phenomenology and to a Phenomenological Philosophy,* Dordrecht, Kluwer Academic Publishers

Hutchinson, S. E. (1996) *Nuer Dilemmas: Coping with Money, War and the State,* Berkeley, University of California Press

Hyde, K. L. et al. (2009) 'Musical training shapes structural brain development', *The Journal of Neuroscience*, 29, 10

Ignatieff, M. (1999) 'Less Race Please', *Prospect, 40, April 10*

Ip, W. H. and Wang, D. (2009) 'Resilience Evaluation Approach of Transportation Networks', *International Joint Conference on Computational Sciences and Optimization*

Jackson, B. and Marsden, D. (1962) *Education and the Working Class,* London, RKP

Joas, H. (1992, trans.1996) *The Creativity of Action,* Cambridge, Polity

Johnson, M. H. (2001) 'Functional brain development in humans', *Nature Reviews Neuroscience, 2*

Jordan, W. D. (1969) 'American Chiaroscuro: the status and definition of Mulattos in the British Colonies', Foner, L. and Genovese, E. (eds.), *Slavery in the New World,* Englewood Cliffs, NJ, Prentice Hall

Kabeer, N. (2000) *The Power to Choose: Bangladeshi Women and Labour Market Decisions in London and Dhaka,* London, Verso

Kabeer, N. and Ainsworth, P. (2011) *Life Chances, Life Choices: Exploring Patterns of Work and Worklessness among Bangladeshi and Somali Women in Tower Hamlets,* Tower Hamlets Council

Karim, L. (2014) 'Disposable bodies: garment factory catastrophy and feminist practices in Bangladesh', *Anthropology, 6, 1*

Karim, S. (2001) 'Attacks in US dash Bangladesh's hopes for export recovery', *The Daily Star;* at www.dailystarnews.com/200109/200117/n1091705.htm#BODY1091701

Kays, J. L. et al. (2012) 'The dynamic brain: neuroplasticity and mental health', *The Journal of Neuropsychiatry and Clinical Neurosciences, 24*

Kemp, S. (2012) 'Interests and structure in dualist social theory: a critical appraisal of Archer's theoretical and empirical arguments', *Philosophy of the Social Sciences, 42, 4*

Kibria, N. (1998) 'Becoming a garments worker: the mobilization of women into the garments factories of Bangladesh', *United Nations Research Institute for Social Development, Occasional Paper, 9*

King, A. (1999) 'Against structure: a critique of morphogenetic social theory', *The Sociological Review, 47, 2*

King, A. (2007) 'Why I am not an individualist', *Journal for the Theory of Social Behaviour, 37, 2*

Knoop, D. and Jones, G. (1933) *The Medieval Mason,* Manchester, Manchester University Press

Koyré. A. (1957) *From the Closed World to the Infinite Universe,* Baltimore, John Hopkins University Press

Kreiner, K. (2009) 'Architectural competitions: empirical observations and strategic implications for architectural firms', *Nordic Journal of Architectural Research, 21, 2/3*

Lash, S and Urry, J. (1987) *The End of Organised Capitalism,* Cambridge, Polity

Lave, J. (1991) 'Situating learning in communities of practice', in L. Resnick, J. Levine, and S. Teasley (eds), *Perspectives on Socially Shared Cognition,* American Psychological Association, Washington

Lee, C. K. (2007) *Against the Law: Labor Protests in China's Rustbelt and Sunbelt,* Berkeley, University of California Press

Le Roy Ladurie, E. (1972) *Times of Feast, Times of Famine,* London, Allen and Unwin

Levi-Strauss, C. (1974) *Structural Anthropology*, New York, Basic Books

Lewis, B. (1990) *Race and Slavery in the Middle East,* New York, Oxford University Press

Lewis, P. (2000) 'Realism, causality and the problem of social structure,' *Journal for the Theory of Social Behaviour,* 30, 3

Lewontin, R., Rose, S. and Kamin, L. (1990) *Not in Our Genes,* Harmondsworth, Penguin

Littlewood, R. (2002) 'Three into two: the third sex in Northern Albania', *Anthropology and Medicine,* 9, 1

Lizardo, O. and Skiles, S. (2012) 'Reconceptualizing and theorizing "omnivorousness", genetic and relational mechanisms', *Sociological Theory,* 30, 4

Lockwood, D. (1966) 'Some sources of variation in working class images of society', *Sociological Review,* 14, 3

Lockwood, D. (1976) 'Social integration and system integration' in Zollschan, G. K. and Hirsch, W. (eds.), *Social Change: Explorations, Diagnoses and Conjectures,* Hoboken, John Wiley

López, J. and Scott, J. (2000) *Social Structure,* Buckingham, Open University Press

López, J. and Potter, G. (2001) *After Postmodernism,* London, Athlone

Lorusso, L. (2011) 'The justification of race in biological explanation', *Journal of Medical Ethics,* 37

MacIntyre, A. (1999) *Dependent Rational Animals,* London, Duckworth

Mackinnon, C. (2006) 'Difference and dominance' in Hackett E. and Haslanger S. (eds.), *Theorising Feminisms,* Oxford, Oxford University Press

Mair, W. (1980) *Forgotten Land, Forgotten People: A Report on the Alaska Gas Pipeline Headings in British Columbia,* Ottawa, Northern Pipe Line Agency

Malinowski, B. (orig. 1922, 2014) *Argonauts of the Western Pacific,* London, Routledge

Mann, M. (1986) *The Sources of Social Power: A History of Power from the Beginning to 1760,* Cambridge, Cambridge University Press

Marcus, G. E. and Saka, E. (2006) 'Assemblage', *Theory, Culture and Society,* 23, 2–3.

Markle, D. T. (2010) 'The magic that binds us: magical thinking and inclusive fitness', *Journal of Social, Evolutionary and Cultural Psychology,* 4, 1

Martin, B. (1981) *A Sociology of Contemporary Cultural Change,* Oxford, Blackwell

Martin, P. and Dennis, A. (eds.) (2010) *Human Agents and Social Structures,* Manchester, Manchester University Press

Marx, K. (orig. 1844, 1959) *The Economic and Philosophic Manuscripts of 1844,* Moscow, Progress Publishers

Marx, K. and Engels, F. (orig. 1845, 1974) *The German Ideology: Introduction to a Critique of Political Economy* (includes the *Eleven Theses on Feuerbach*), London, Lawrence and Wishart

Marx, K. (orig. 1852, 2008) *The 18th Brumaire of Louis Napoleon,* Rockville, Serenity

May, T. and Williams, M. (eds.) (1998) *Knowing the Social World,* Buckingham, Open University Press

McAdam, D. (1999) *Political Process and the Development of Black Insurgency, 1930–1970,* Chicago, University of Chicago Press

McAdam, D. et al. (1996) *Comparative Perspectives on Social Movements: Political Opportunities, Mobilising Structures and Cultural Framings,* Cambridge, Cambridge University Press

McCrone, D. (1998) *The Sociology of Nationalism*, London, Routledge

McLean, P. D. (2007) *The Art of the Network: Strategic Interaction and Patronage in Renaissance Florence*, Durham NC, Duke University Press

McNeill, W. H. (1983) *The Pursuit of Power*, Oxford, Blackwell

Mead, G. H. (orig. 1934, 1967) *Mind, Self and Society*, Chicago, University of Chicago Press

Merton, R. (1957) *Social Theory and Social Structure*, New York, Free Press

Mikkola, M. (2012) 'Feminist Perspectives on Sex and Gender', *Stanford Encyclopedia of Philosophy* (Fall 2012 edition)

Mill, J. S. (orig. 1861, 2013) *Utilitarianism*, Create Space Independent Publishing Platform

Miller-Hooks, E. et al. (2012) 'Measuring and maximizing resilience of freight transportation networks', *Computers and Operations Research*, 39, 7

Mills, C. W. (1951) *White Collar*, New York, Oxford University Press

Moore, B. (1967) *Social Origins of Dictatorship and Democracy*, London, Allen Lane

Morgan, E. S. (1972) 'Slavery and freedom: the American paradox,' *The Journal of American History*, 59

Morris, L. (1992) 'The social segregation of the long term unemployed in Hartlepool', *Sociological Review*, 40

Morris, L. (1995) *Social Divisions: Economic Decline and Social Structural Change*, London, UCL Press

Mouzelis, N. (1995) *Sociological Theory: What Went Wrong?* London, Routledge

Nisbet, R. (1962) 'Sociology as an art form', *The Pacific Sociological Review*, 5, 2

Nuffield Council on Bioethics (2002) *Genetics and Human Behaviour: The Ethical Context*, Nuffield Council on Bioethics, http://www.nuffieldbioethics.org/sites/default/files/Genetics%20and%20human%20behaviour.pdf

Oliver, M. L. (2008) 'Sub-prime as black catastrophe', *The American Prospect*, 20, Sept.

Oliver, M. L. and Shapiro, T. M. (1997, 2nd ed. 2006) *Black Wealth, White Wealth: A New Perspective on Racial Inequality*, Oxford, Routledge

Ozkirimli, U. (2000) *Theories of Nationalism*, Basingstoke, Macmillan

Paine, R. (1971) 'Animals as capital: comparisons among northern nomadic herders and hunters', *Anthropological Quarterly*, 44

Parker, J. (2000) *Structuration*, Buckingham, Open University Press

Parker, J. (2006) 'Structuration's future: from "all and every" to "who did what, where when, how and why?"', *Journal of Critical Realism*, 5, 1

Parry, S. and Dupré, J. (2010) *Nature after the Genome*, Oxford, Wiley-Blackwell

Parsons, T. (1937) *The Structure of Social Action*, New York, Free Press

Parsons, T. (1951) *The Social System*, New York, Free Press

Parsons, T. (1954) *Essays in Sociological Theory*, (Revised edition) New York, The Free Press

Parsons, T, (1971) *The System of Modern Societies*, Englewood Cliffs, Prentice Hall

Patterson, O. (1982) *Slavery and Social Death: A Comparative Study*, Cambridge, MA, Harvard University Press

Peterson, R. A. (1992) 'Understanding audience segmentation: from elite and mass to omnivore and univore', *Poetics*, 21

Peterson, R. A. and Kern, R. (1996) 'Changing Highbrow Taste: from snob to omnivore', *American Sociological Review*, 61

Pipes, D. (1981) *Slave Soldiers and Islam: The Genesis of a Military System*, New Haven, Yale University Press

Piven, F. F. and Cloward, R. A. (1979) *Poor People's Movements: Why They Succeed and How They Fail*, New York, Vintage

Porpora, D. V. (1989) 'Four concepts of social structure', *Journal for the Theory of Social Behaviour*, 19, 2

Pucher, J. and Buehler, R. (2008) 'Making cycling irresistible: lessons from the Netherlands, Denmark and Germany', *Transport Reviews*, 28, 4

Quirk, V. (2014) 'Hamburg's plan to eliminate cars in twenty years', *Arch Daily, 07/1/2014 http://www.archdaily.com/464394/hamburg-s-plan-to-eliminate-cars-in-20-years/*

Rahman, M. A. (2010) *Women's Employment in Garment Factories in Bangladesh: Emancipation or Exploitation?* M.A. in Gender and International Development, University of Hull

Ray, L. (1999) *Theorising Classical Sociology*, Buckingham, Open University Press

Renzeti, C. and Curran, D. (1992) 'Sex-role socialization', in Kourany, J. Sterba, J. and Tong, R. (eds.), *Feminist Philosophies*, Essex, Prentice-Hall

Ritzer, G. (2010) *The McDonaldization of Society 6*, London, Sage

Rival, L. (1996) 'Blowpipes and spears: the social significance of Huaorani technological choices', in Descola P. and Palsson G. (eds.), *Nature and Society: Anthropological Perspectives*, London, Routledge

Rival, L. (2002) *Trekking through History: The Huaorani of Amazonian Ecuador*, New York, Columbia University Press

Rival, L. (2010) 'Ecuador's Yasuní-ITT initiative: the old and new values of petroleum', *Ecological Economics*, 70

Roberts, J. (2007) *The Intangibilities of Form: Skill and Deskilling in Art after the Readymade*, London, Verso

Rock, M. (2001) 'Rise of the Bangladesh independent garment workers' Union [BIGU]', in Brown, A. et al. (eds.), *Organising Labour in Globalising Asia*, London, Routledge

Rooney, J. (1995) *Organizing the South Bronx*, Albany, State University of New York Press

Rose, S. (1997) *Lifelines: Biology, Freedom, Determinism*, Harmondsworth, Penguin

Rueschemeyer, D., Stephens, E. H. and Stephens, J. D. (1992) *Capitalist Development and Democracy*, Cambridge, Polity

Rugh, J. S. and Massey, D. S. (2010) 'Racial segregation and the American foreclosure crisis', *American Sociological Review*, 75

Runciman, W. G. (1966) *Relative Deprivation and Social Justice*, London, Routledge

Runciman, W. G. (1983, 1989) *A Treatise on Social Theory*, Vols 1 & 2, Cambridge, Cambridge University Press

Runciman, W. G. (1998) *The Social Animal*, London, HarperCollins

Russell, R. (1972) *Bird Lives!* London, Quartet Books

Sahlins, M. (1968) 'Notes on the original affluent society', in Lee R. B. and DeVore, I. (eds.), *Man the Hunter*, Chicago, Aldine

Sahlins, M. (1999) 'Two or three things I know about culture', *J. Royal Anthropological Institute* (NS), 5

Savage, M., Barlow, J., Dickens, P. and Fielding, T. (1992) *Property, Bureaucracy and Culture,* London, Routledge

Sayer, A. (1992 2nd edition) *Method in Social Science: a Realist Approach,* London, Routledge

Sayer, A. (2000) *Realism and Social Science,* London, Sage

Schutz, A. (1962–66) *Collected Papers, Vols 1–3,* Dordrecht, Martinus Nijhoff

Schutz, A. (1937 (trans. Walsh, G. and Lehneert, F. 1967)) *The Phenomenology of the Social World,* Evanston, Northwestern University Press

Sennett, R. (1986) *The Fall of Public Man,* London, Faber

Sennett, R. (1990) *The Conscience of the Eye,* London, Faber

Sennett, R. (1998) *The Corrosion of Character,* New York, Norton

Sennett, R. (2008) *The Craftsman,* Harmondsworth, Allen lane

Shapiro, T. et al. (2013) 'The roots of the widening racial wealth gap: explaining the black-white economic divide', *Institute of Assets and Social Policy Research and Policy Brief*

Shove, E. (2003) *Comfort, Cleanliness and Convenience,* Oxford, Berg

Shove, E. (2010) 'Beyond the ABC: climate change and theories of social change', *Environment and Planning, A,* 42, 6

Shuter, R. and Chattopadhyay, C. (2010) 'Emerging norms of text messaging in India and the United States', *Journal of Intercultural Research,* 39, 2

Siemiatycki, M. (2004) 'The international diffusion of radical transportation policy: the case of congestion charging', *Planning Theory and Practice,* 5, 4

Simmel, G. (trans. Wolff, K. H.) (1964) *The Sociology of Georg Simmel,* New York, Free Press

Simmel, G. (ed. Frisby and Featherstone) (1997), *Simmel on Culture,* London, Sage

Singerman, H. (1999) *Art Subjects,* Berkeley, University of California Press

Skierkowski, D. and Wood, M. (2012) 'To text or not to text: the importance of text messaging among college-aged youth', *Computers in Human Behaviour,* 28, 2

Skocpol, T. (1979) *States and Social Revolutions,* Cambridge, Cambridge University Press

Smith, A. D. (1998) *Nations and Modernism,* London, Routledge

Smith, D. (1991) *The Rise of Historical Sociology,* Cambridge, Polity

Smith, D. J. (2008) *A Culture of Corruption: Everyday Deception and Popular Discontent in Nigeria,* Princeton, Princeton University Press

Soper, K. (2008) 'Alternative Hedonism: cultural theory and the role of aesthetic revisioning', *Cultural Studies,* 22, 5

Stack, C. (1997 (first ed. 1974)) *All Our Kin,* New York, Basic Books

Stack, C. (1996) *Call to Home: African-Americans Reclaim the Rural South,* New York, Basic Books

Stanworth, H. (2006) 'Protestantism, anxiety and orientations to the environment: Sweden as a test case for the ideas of Richard Sennett', *Worldviews: Global Religions, Culture and Ecology,* 31

Stern, N. (2007) *Economics of Climate Change: The Stern Review,* Cambridge, Cambridge University Press

Stiglitz, J. (2012) *The Price of Inequality,* London, Penguin

Stones, R. (2005) *Structuration Theory,* Basingstoke, Palgrave Macmillan

Sudnow, D. (1978) *Ways of the Hand,* Cambridge, MA, Harvard University Press

Sulloway, F. J. (1996) *Born to Rebel,* London, Little, Brown and Co

Swedberg, R. (2005) *Interest,* Buckingham, Open University Press

Tan, C. K. et al. (2008) 'Innovative climate change communication: team minus 6%', *Global Environmental Information Centre Working Paper Series, 2008–001*

Tannenbaum, F. (1946) *Slave and Citizen: The Negro in the Americas,* New York, Vintage

The City of Copenhagen Technical and Environmental Administration (2011) *Good, Better, Best: The City of Copenhagen's Bicycle Policy, 2011–2025, http://kk.sites.itera.dk/ apps/kk_pub2/pdf/823_Bg65v7UH2t.pdf*

Theusch, E. et al. (2009) 'Genome-wide study of families with absolute pitch reveals linkage to 8q24.21 and locus heterogencity', *American Journal of Human Genetics,* 85, 1

Thompson, M., Ellis, R. and Wildavski, A., (1990) *Cultural Theory,* Boulder, Westview Press

Thornton, S. (2008) *Seven Days in the Art World,* London, Granta

Toman, W. (1996) *Family Constellation,* Northvale, NJ, Jason Aronson

Treaty 8 First Nations (T8FNs) Community Assessment Team (2012) *Telling a Story of Change the Dane-zaa Way,* http://www.ceaa.gc.ca/050/documents_staticpost/63919/ 85328/Vol3_Appendix_B-Treaty_8.pdf

Trexler, R. C. (2002) 'Making the American Berdache: choice or constraint?' *Journal of Social History,* 35, 3

Turner, B. S. (1999) *Classical Sociology,* London, Sage

United Nations (1991) *Contemporary Forms of Slavery: World Campaign for Human Rights, Fact sheet 14,* New York, U.N. Centre for Human Rights

Urry, J. (1990) *The Tourist Gaze,* London, Sage

Urry, J. (2011) *Climate Change and Society,* Cambridge, Polity

Van Wezemael, J. et al. (2011) 'Assessing "quality": the unfolding of the "good": collective decision making in juries of urban design competitions', *Scandinavian Journal of Management,* 27

Vromans, J. et al. (2006) 'Reliability and heterogeneity of railway services', *European Journal of Operational Research,* 2, 16

Waldinger, R. D. (1996) *Still the Promised City? African-Americans and the New Immigrants in Post-industrial New York,* Cambridge, MA, Harvard University Press

Warde, A. et al. (2007), 'Understanding Cultural Omnivorousness: Or, the Myth of the Cultural Omnivore', *Cultural Sociology,* 1, 2

Watson, J. L. (ed.) (1980) *Asian and African Systems of Slavery,* Oxford, Blackwell

Weber, M. (orig.1917–19, 1952) *Ancient Judaism,* New York, Free Press

Weber, M. (orig. 1905, trans. Kalberg, S., 2002) *The Protestant Ethic and the Spirit of Capitalism,* Oxford, Blackwell

Weber, M. (ed. Roth, G. and Wittich, C.) (1968) *Economy and Society,* New York, Bedminster Press

Weber, M. (ed. Kalberg, S.) (2005), *Max Weber: Readings and Commentary on Modernity,* Oxford, Blackwell

Weisman, A. (2007) *The World without Us,* New York, St. Martin's Press

Westermann, W. L. (1955) *The Slave Systems of Greek and Roman Antiquity,* Philadelphia, American Philosophical Society

Whyte, W. S. (1957) *The Organisation Man,* New York, Touchstone

Wilkinson, R. and Pickett, K. (2010) (2nd ed.) *The Spirit Level,* London, Penguin

Williams, R. 1983 (revised and updated edition) *Keywords,* London, Fontana

Winch, P. (1958 (2nd ed. 1990) *The Idea of a Social Science,* London, Routledge

Wittgenstein, L. (Anscombe trans.1963) *Philosophical Investigations,* Basil Blackwell

Wright, E. O. (1997) *Classes,* London, Verso

Wright, E. O. (2005) *Approaches to Class Analysis,* Cambridge, Cambridge University Press

Wright, G. and Kunreuther, H. (1975) 'Cotton, corn and risk in the nineteenth century', *Journal of Economic History*, vol. 35, Sept.

Young, A. and Twigg, L. (2009) '"Sworn Virgins" as enhancers of Albanian Patriarchal Society in contrast to emerging roles for Albanian Women', *Etnološka Tribina*, 32, 39

Zimmerman, D. H. (1971) 'The practicalities of rule use' in Douglas J. D. (ed.), *Understanding Everyday Life,* London, RKP

Zuckerman, G. (2013) *The Frackers: the Outrageous Inside Story of the New Energy Revolution,* London, Portfolio Penguin

Index